'It all began with an improbable wager: ask 35 scholars to each write something intelligible about every single paragraph in one of the texts included in Jacques Lacan's magnum opus, *Écrits*, so as to generate a commentary on the entire 800-page volume. And yet, after years of preparation, the wager has paid off: we have here some useful and at times brilliant examples of textual explication! Cryptic formulations are lucidly unpacked, and mysterious references are provided, giving the serious reader myriad keys to fascinating texts'.

    Bruce Fink, *Translator of* Écrits: The First Complete Edition in English (2006)

'Let's face it: Lacan's *Écrits*, one of the classical texts of modern thought is unreadable – it remains impenetrable if we just pick the thick volume up and start to read it. Hook, Neill and Vanheule provide what we were all waiting for: a detailed commentary which does not aim to replace reading *Écrits*, but to render it possible. The three volumes do wonder, their effect is no less than magic: when, after getting stuck at a particularly dense page of *Écrits*, we turn to the corresponding pages in the commentary and then return to the page of *Écrits* which pushed us to madness, the same lines appear in all the clarity of their line of thought. It is thus a safe prediction that Hook, Neill and Vanheule's commentary will become a kind of permanent companion of the English translation of *Écrits*, indispensable for everyone who wants to find her or his way in its complex texture'.

    Slavoj Žižek, *International Director of the Birkbeck Institute for the Humanities, Global Distinguished Professor of German at New York University, Professor of Philosophy at the European Graduate School and Senior Researcher at the Institute for Sociology and Philosophy at the University of Ljubljana*

'These essays will be an invaluable resource not only for those approaching the *Écrits* for the first time but also for seasoned readers. Broad in scope yet following the detail of the text, they help guide us through Lacan's difficult prose, elucidating, contextualising and clarifying, and reminding us time and again of the precision, power and originality of his rethinking of psychoanalysis'.

    Darian Leader, *Psychoanalyst working in London and member of the Centre for Freudian Analysis and Research*

READING LACAN'S ÉCRITS

Reading Lacan's Écrits is the first extensive set of commentaries on the complete edition of Lacan's *Écrits* to be published in English, providing an indispensable companion piece to some of Lacan's best-known but notoriously challenging writings.

With the contributions of some of the world's most renowned Lacanian scholars and analysts, *Reading Lacan's Écrits* encompasses a series of systematic, paragraph-by-paragraph commentaries that not only contextualize, explain and interrogate Lacan's arguments but also afford the reader multiple interpretive routes through the complete edition of Lacan's most labyrinthine of texts. Considering the significance of *Écrits* as a landmark in the history of psychoanalysis, this far-reaching and accessible guide will sustain and continue to animate critical engagement with one of the most challenging intellectual works of the twentieth century.

These volumes act as an essential and incisive reference-text for psychoanalysts and psychoanalytic psychotherapists in training and in practice, as well as philosophers, cultural theorists and literary, social science and humanities researchers. This volume covers the first two sections of the *Écrits,* providing close readings of the first eight essays.

Calum Neill is Professor of Psychoanalysis and Continental Philosophy at Edinburgh Napier University in Edinburgh, Scotland. He is the author of *Jacques Lacan: The Basics* (2023), *Ethics and Psychology* (2016) and *Without Ground: Lacanian Ethics and the Assumptions of Subjectivity* and editor of *Lacanian Perspectives on Blade Runner 2049*. With Derek Hook, he edits the Palgrave Lacan Series.

Derek Hook is Professor of Psychology at Duquesne University in Pittsburgh, USA, and Professor of Psychology at the University of Pretoria in South Africa. He is the author of *Six Moments in Lacan* (2017) and *A Critical Psychology of the Postcolonial* (2012) and editor of *Lacan on Depression and Melancholia* (with Stijn Vanheule) (2022) and *Lacan and Race* (with Sheldon George) (2022). With Calum Neill, he edits the Palgrave Lacan Series.

Stijn Vanheule is Professor of Psychoanalysis and Clinical Psychology at Ghent University in Belgium, a practising psychoanalyst and a member of the New Lacanian School of Psychoanalysis. He is author of *Psychiatric Diagnosis Revisited* (2017) and *The Subject of Psychosis* (2011) and editor of *Lacan on Depression and Melancholia* (with Derek Hook) (2022).

READING LACAN'S ÉCRITS

From 'Overture to this Collection' to 'Presentation on Psychical Causality'

Edited by Calum Neill, Derek Hook and Stijn Vanheule

Routledge
Taylor & Francis Group

LONDON AND NEW YORK

Designed cover image: Dmitriy Moroz / Alamy Stock Photo

First published 2024
by Routledge
4 Park Square, Milton Park, Abingdon, Oxon OX14 4RN

and by Routledge
605 Third Avenue, New York, NY 10158

Routledge is an imprint of the Taylor & Francis Group, an informa business

British Library Cataloguing-in-Publication Data
A catalogue record for this book is available from the British Library

Library of Congress Cataloging-in-Publication Data
Names: Neill, Calum, 1968- editor. | Hook, Derek, editor. | Vanheule, Stijn, 1974- editor.
Title: Reading Lacan's Écrits : from 'Overture to this collection' to 'Presentation on psychical causality' / edited by Calum Neill, Derek Hook and Stijn Vanheule.
Description: Abingdon, Oxon ; New York, NY : Routledge, 2024. | Includes bibliographical references and index. |
Identifiers: LCCN 2023038384 (print) | LCCN 2023038385 (ebook) | ISBN 9781032437378 (paperback) | ISBN 9781032437361 (hardback) | ISBN 9781003368649 (ebook)
Subjects: LCSH: Lacan, Jacques, 1901-1981. Écrits. | Psychoanalysis.
Classification: LCC BF173.L1423 R435 2024 (print) | LCC BF173.L1423 (ebook) | DDC 150.19/5–dc23/eng/20231206
LC record available at https://lccn.loc.gov/2023038384
LC ebook record available at https://lccn.loc.gov/2023038385

ISBN: 9781032437361 (hbk)
ISBN: 9781032437378 (pbk)
ISBN: 9781003368649 (ebk)

DOI: 10.4324/9781003368649

Typeset in Bembo
by Deanta Global Publishing Services, Chennai, India

For all our students: past, present and future.

CONTENTS

CONTENTS

EDITOR AND CONTRIBUTOR BIOGRAPHIES

John Dall'Aglio is a Clinical Psychology PhD student at Duquesne University. His clinical and scholarly research interests are in Lacanian neuropsychoanalysis. He was awarded the 2021 New Author Prize from the *Journal of the American Psychoanalytic Association* for his work in this area.

Mattias Desmet is a Professor of Clinical Psychology at the Department of Psychology and Educational Sciences of Ghent University (Belgium), and he works as a psychoanalyst in private practice. Desmet is the author of the books *The Pursuit of Objectivity in Psychology and Lacan's Logic of Subjectivity: A Walk on the Graph of Desire*. Furthermore, he is one of the founders of the Single Case Archive. In 2018, he received the Evidence-based Psychoanalytic Case Study Prize of the Association for Psychoanalytic Psychotherapy, and in 2019, he received the Wim Trijsburg Prize of the Dutch Association of Psychotherapy.

Derek Hook is a Professor and Clinical Supervisor in Psychology at Duquesne University and an Extraordinary Professor of Psychology at the University of Pretoria. He is the author of *A Critical Psychology of the Colonial* (2011) and *Six Moments in Lacan* (2017). Along with Calum Neill, he co-edits the *Palgrave Lacan Series*. He is also the co-editor of *Lacan and Race* (with Sheldon George). He maintains a YouTube channel including many lectures on Lacanian psychoanalysis.

Kareen Malone is an Analysand in Formation with the Après Coup Psychoanalytic Association (New York), Professor Emerita of Psychology (University of West Georgia) and Fellow of the American Psychological Association. Author of numerous chapters and articles, she co-edited three books on Lacanian psychoanalysis and co-authored *Science as Psychology*, and is a recipient of the American Psychological Association's William James Award. She is in clinical practice in Atlanta and corresponding faculty at the Emory University Institute of Psychoanalysis.

Calum Neill is Professor of Psychoanalysis and Continental Philosophy at Edinburgh Napier University and the Director of Lacan in Scotland. He is co-editor, with Derek Hook, of the *Palgrave Lacan Series* and author of *Jacques Lacan: The Basics* (2023*), Ethics and Psychology: Beyond Codes of Practice* (2016) and *Without Ground: Lacanian Ethics and the Assumption of Subjectivity* (2011).

Carol Owens is a psychoanalyst and Lacanian scholar in Dublin, Ireland. A member of the APCS, APPI and affiliate member of CPUK, she is also the founder and convenor of the Dublin Lacan study group. She is series editor for *Studying Lacan's Seminars* at Routledge and book review editor at *Psychoanalysis, Culture and Society*. Her most recent publication is *Precarities of 21st Century Childhoods: Critical Explorations of Time(s), Place(s), and Identities* with Michael O'Loughlin and Louis Rothschild (Lexington Books, 2023).

David Pavón-Cuéllar is a Mexican Marxist Philosopher and Critical Psychologist. He is Professor of Psychology and Philosophy at the Universidad Michoacana de San Nicolás de Hidalgo in Morelia, Mexico. His last books include *Psychoanalysis and Revolution: Critical Psychology for Liberation Movements* (with Ian Parker, 1968 Press, 2021), *Marxism and Psychoanalysis: In or Against Psychology?* (Routledge, 2017), *Lacan, Discourse, Event: New Psychoanalytic Approaches to Textual Indeterminacy* (with Ian Parker, Routledge, 2013) and *From the Conscious Interior to an Exterior Unconscious: Lacan, Discourse Analysis and Social Psychology* (Karnac, 2010).

Christopher Reed Johnson holds a postgraduate degree in Psychology from the University of West Georgia, where he first became interested in Lacanian psychoanalysis under the tutelage of Kareen R. Malone. He is currently working on a forthcoming book wherein he further investigates the ideas presented in his thesis – *Space-time, Non-being, & the Void in the Field of Psychoanalysis*. In doing so, he seeks to trace the theoretical developments of Space and the Subject throughout the entirety of Jacques Lacan's published and unpublished seminars.

Sinan Richards is both a British Academy Research Fellow based at King's College London and an Ordinary Member of the Centre de recherches interdisciplinaires sur le politique (CRIPOLIS) based at Université Paris Cité. His book *Dialectics of Love: Sartre and Lacan* is forthcoming with Palgrave Macmillan's *Lacan Series*. He is currently finishing off another monograph entitled *Homo Alienatus: Freedom and Psychosis in Lacan and Fanon*.

Benjamin B. Strosberg is a Doctoral Candidate in the Department of Psychology at Duquesne University and a Psychological Associate based in Santa Barbara, California. His research interests lie at the intersections of psychoanalysis, phenomenology, and Frankfurt School Critical Theory, and he has published on topics including psychosis, perversion, education, teletherapy and anti-Semitism.

Stijn Vanheule is Professor of Psychoanalysis and Clinical Psychology at Ghent University, Belgium. He is also a privately practising psychoanalyst and member of the New Lacanian School for Psychoanalysis. He is the author of *The Subject of Psychosis: A Lacanian Perspective, Psychiatric Diagnosis Revisited – From DSM to Clinical Case Formulation* and *Why Psychosis Is Not So Crazy*.

ACKNOWLEDGEMENTS

As scholars working on Lacan in the early 21st century, who wouldn't have wished for a guide to his notoriously impenetrable *Écrits*? The three of us were each working to address this struggle in our own ways; through teaching, through writing, through organising reading groups. A chance encounter at a conference in China brought our individual efforts together and gave rise to the conversations that eventually resulted in the four volume set, *Reading Lacan's Écrits*, the final instalment of which you have before you. It is through working together that we made this possible. Working together, not just the three of us, but working together with some of the best writers in the Lacanian field – scholars, academics and clinicians – who have taken up our challenge to grapple with Lacan's prose and turn it into something accessible. While we asked people to adhere closely to the text, and to follow a fairly firm format, the resulting commentaries are far from bland, homogenous readings. Each interlocutor brings their own voice to the work and brings fresh insights into the text. We want to thank all those who have contributed to the project over the last decade. Without your patience, time, knowledge, curiosity and care, this mad project simply would never have reached fruition. Thank you.

Of course, this whole project would have been much more challenging without the excellent and complete translation of the *Écrits* produced by Bruce Fink. We are grateful to Bruce both for his work of translation and for his unfailing support of the project as a whole.

We would also like to thank WW Norton for permission to reproduce the original figures from the *Écrits* and the Department of Psychoanalysis and Clinical Consulting at Ghent University for their generous financial support.

Calum, Derek and Stijn

REFERENCES TO THE *ÉCRITS*

Given that our aim in this project has been to offer extensive commentaries on all of Lacan's papers collected in his *Écrits*, we have adopted a referencing convention whereby we include the page number followed by the paragraph number of the phrase or section being quoted, referring to *Écrits: The Complete Edition* by Jacques Lacan, translated by Bruce Fink. Copyright © 1996, 1970, 1971, 1999 by Editions du Seuil; English translation copyright 2006, 2002, by W.W. Norton, Inc. Used by permission of W.W. Norton & Company.

JACQUES LACAN'S SEMINARS

Throughout this book the following abbreviations are used when referring to Lacan's seminars:

S1: Seminar 1 (1953–1954): Lacan, J. (1975/1988) *The Seminar. Book I: Freud's Papers on Technique*, trans. J. Forrester, ed. J.-A. Miller, Cambridge: Cambridge University Press.

S2: Seminar 2 (1954–1955): Lacan, J. (1978/1988) *The Seminar. Book II: The Ego in Freud's Theory and in the Technique of Psychoanalysis*, trans. S. Tomaselli, ed. J.-A. Miller, Cambridge: Cambridge University Press.

S3: Seminar 3 (1955–1956): Lacan, J. (1981/1993) *The Seminar. Book III: The Psychoses*, trans. R. Grigg, ed. J.-A. Miller, New York NY: W. W. Norton & Company.

S4: Seminar 4 (1956–1957): Lacan, J. (2021) *The Object Relation: The Seminar of Jacques Lacan, Book IV:*. Trans. Adrian Price. Cambridge. Polity.

S5: Seminar 5 (1957–1958): Lacan, J. (1998) *The Formations of the Unconscious: The Seminar of Jacques Lacan, Book V*. Trans. Russell Grigg. Cambridge. Polity.

S6: Seminar 6 (1958–1959): Lacan J. (2019), *Desire and its Interpretation: The Seminar of Jacques Lacan, Book VI*. Trans. Bruce Fink. Cambridge. Polity.

S7: Seminar 7 (1959–1960): Lacan, J. (1986/1992) *The Seminar. Book VII: The Ethics of Psychoanalysis*, trans. D. Porter, ed. J.-A. Miller, New York and London: W.W. Norton & Company.

S8: Seminar 8 (1960–1961): Lacan, J. (2001/2015) *The Seminar. Book VIII: Transference*, trans. B. Fink, ed. J.-A. Miller, Cambridge: Polity.

S9: Seminar 9 (1961–1962): *Le Séminaire IX, L'Identification*, unpublished.

S10: Seminar 10 (1962–1963): Lacan, J. (2004/2014) *The Seminar. Book X: Anxiety*, trans. A. R. Price, ed. J.-A. Miller, Cambridge: Polity.

S11: Seminar 11 (1964): Lacan, J. (1973/1994) *The Seminar. Book XI: The Four Fundamental Concepts of Psycho-Analysis*, trans. A. Sheridan, ed. J.-A. Miller, New York and London: W.W. Norton & Company.

S12: Seminar 12 (1964–1965): *Le Séminaire XII, Problèmes cruciaux pour la psychanalyse*, unpublished.

S13: Seminar 13 (1965–1966): *Le Séminaire XIII, L'objet de la psychanalyse*, unpublished.

S14: Seminar 14 (1966–1967): *Le Séminaire XIV, La logique du fantasme*, unpublished.

S15: Seminar 15 (1967–1968): *Le Séminaire XV*, l'acte psychanalytique, unpublished.

S16: Seminar 16 (1968–1969): Lacan, J. (2023) *The Seminar Book XVI: From An Other to the other*. Trans. Bruce Fink. Cambridge. Polity.

S17: Seminar 17 (1969–1970): Lacan, J. (2007) *The Seminar. Book XVII: The Other Side of Psychoanalysis*, trans. R. Grigg, ed. J.-A. Miller, New York and London: W.W. Norton & Company.

S18: Seminar 18 (1970–1971): Lacan J. (2006), *Le Séminaire. Livre XVIII. D'un discours qui ne serait pas du semblant*, Paris: Éditions du Seuil.

S19: Seminar 19 (1971–1972): Lacan, J. (2019) *...or Worse: The Seminar of Jacques Lacan, Book XIX*. Cambridge. Polity.

S20: Seminar 20 (1972–1973): Lacan, J. (1998) *The Seminar, Book XX, Encore: On Feminine Sexuality, the Limits of Love and Knowledge*, trans. B. Fink, ed. J.-A. Miller, New York and London: W.W. Norton & Company.

S21: Seminar 21 (1973–1974): *Le Séminaire XXI, Les non-dupes errent*, unpublished.

S22: Seminar 22 (1974–1975): *Le Séminaire XXII, R.S.I.*, unpublished.

S23: Seminar 23 (1975–1976): Lacan, J. (2005/2016) *The Seminar. Book XXIII: The Sinthome*, trans. A. R. Price, ed. J.-A. Miller, Cambridge: Polity.

S24: Seminar 24 (1976–1977): *Le Séminaire XXIV, L'insu que sait de l'une-bévue s'aile à mourre*, unpublished.

S25: Seminar 25 (1977–1978): *Le Séminaire XXV, Le moment de conclure*, unpublished.

S26: Seminar 26 (1978–1979): *Le Séminaire XXVI, La topologie et le temps*, unpublished.

INTRODUCTION

La trahison de l'écriture

Derek Hook, Calum Neill and Stijn Vanheule

What kind of book is Lacan's *Écrits*? This is a more pressing question than it may appear. Knowing what type of book the *Écrits* is would provide us with a strategy for how one might go about reading – if "reading" is even the most appropriate imperative in this context – this baroque, intimidating, ever-elusive text.

An unwieldy, conglomerate "urtext", the *Écrits* might appear to have no clear precedent. There is, so it would seem, no collection of writings quite like it. For Élisabeth Roudinsco (2014), however, certain other equivalents can be cited:

> *Écrits* is a summa that resembles both Saussure's *Course in General Linguistics* and Hegel's *Phenomenology of Spirit*...it functions as the founding Book of an intellectual system, which, depending on the era can be read, criticized, glossed or interpreted in many ways. (p. 99)

While there is certainly truth to this characterization, there are nonetheless a series of qualifications that should be made here in respect of Lacan's relation both to his own *Écrits* and to writing more generally.

In comparison with Freud's oeuvre that of course exists in the collected form of the Standard Edition, Lacan's written work exists in a far more scattered and diffuse state. Formally, this work occupies a place in the interstices between the performative and the textual, between an oral teaching and the written word. Lacan's oeuvre, we might say, resists collection, and encapsulation, just as it appears to resist writing itself.

One initial response to the above question would simply be to say that the *Écrits* is not a "book" at all, at least not in the sense of being something an author produces with the express wish of being published, understood or even read. If we are to follow Roudinsco's (2014) account, it appears that François Wahl – former analysand of Lacan's and editor at Éditions du Seuil – played a more important role in motivating and conceiving the text than Lacan did himself. Prior to the eventual 15 November 1966 publication date of the *Écrits*,

1 DOI: 10.4324/9781003368649-1

Lacan's writings were in a fragmentary state, appearing in select psychoanalytic journals that few could access. And, as Roudinesco intimates, Lacan preferred it that way: "Lacan feared plagiarism...he allowed the written trace of his spoken word to appear solely so as to have it circulate in the restricted milieu of Freudian institutions and journals" (p. 94). Staggered across various periods of his teaching and juxtaposed against the oral performance of his weekly seminar, the *Écrits* thus represented the slow and apparently unwilling accretion of Lacan's writings. As Bruce Fink (2004) speculates:

> Lacan may have only reluctantly agreed to publish his *Écrits* after Paul Ricoeur published his thick volume *De I' interpretation* translated as *Freud and Philosophy: An Essay on Interpretation*...Lacan certainly did not want Ricoeur to take credit for the return to Freud that Lacan himself had been championing. Lacan claims [in Seminar XVIII] that the texts in his *Écrits* had to be pried away from him. (p. 178)

Écrits then was a reluctant text – or such is the myth that has grown around it – a much delayed "book", published, largely, it would seem, at the urging of others, late in Lacan's life (he was 65). The factor of circumvention and delay seems telling. This consideration of deferred arrival – which contrasts so strongly with Lacan's frequent stress on anticipatory/pre-emptive modes of temporality in the *Écrits* – is, in retrospect, indicative less of Lacan's reticence than – perhaps – of his *desire*.

Lacan had a famously low opinion of published writing as a means of disseminating psychoanalytic knowledge – hence his dismissive reference to "*poubellication*" (a contraction combining both garbage can and publication). In Seminar XX, during a session entitled "The function of the written", Lacan offers a pronouncement on the *Écrits*:

> There is an anecdote to be related here, namely, that one day, on the cover of a collection I brought out – *poubellication*, as I called it – I found nothing better to write than the word *Écrits*.
>
> It is rather well known that those *Écrits* cannot be read easily. I can make a little autobiographical admission – that is exactly what I thought. I thought, perhaps it goes that far, I thought they were not meant be read. That's a good start. (Lacan, 1988, p. 26)

Commenting on this passage, Fink (2004) notes that Lacan never characterizes his seminars as *poubellication*, adding furthermore that while Lacan claimed to find no major errors in the published version of the seminars, such errors were to be found in the *Écrits*. Not only then is the *Écrits* (as *poubellication*) apparently fit for the dustbin, but it is also effectively untitled: "*Écrits*" ("writings") is, one might argue, more a *description* than name, more the avoidance of a title than a title. Lacan's gesture here calls to mind Magritte's (1929) famous *La trahison des images,* proclaiming instead: *This is Not a Book.*

The medium of the spoken word, with all its lyricism, enunciative ambiguity and prospective revelation, was, for Lacan, a far more suitable medium than the published word for the transmission of psychoanalysis. In the opening of *The Instance of the Letter,* Lacan professes concern that what he presents "might stray too far from speech, whose different measures are essential to the training I seek to effect" (412, 1). He goes on to announce that what we are about to read will be "situated between writing and speech…halfway between the two" (412, 1). So whereas speech is associated with what is generative and valuable, writing, by contrast, "allows for…[a] kind of tightening up", which "leave[s] the reader no way out than the way in, which I prefer to be difficult" (412, 2).

Elsewhere, Lacan similarly refers to the written text as something that "can only be woven by forming knots" (Seminar XIX, May 10, 1972). Writing here is presented not merely as challenging – puzzling, enigmatic – but also as wilfully obstructive. These comments connote as much a celebration of the spoken word as an aversion to what is written, a suspicious relation thus – to paraphrase Magritte – to *La trahison de l'écriture.* One is left with an image of the text as an intricately and deceptively designed labyrinth. This may in fact be one particularly apt way of describing "writing in my [Lacan's] sense of the term" (412, 2), that is, as precisely *labyrinthine.* The *Écrits* then, following this thinking, are more maze than book.

In this context, Jacques-Alain Miller (2010) states that Lacan's *Écrits* actually have a provocative function in relation to his seminar. The texts within the *Écrits* don't provide us with some synthesis of his oral teaching but contain "the waste" of his teaching: elements that he didn't discuss in public because of time restraints; and, more importantly, sensitive points to which his audience would have reacted with reluctance. Significant elements Lacan's audience could not easily accept, and which they would be treated as the waste of his discourse, were condensed, and sent back to them in a written form. Thus considered, the *Écrits* constitute the symptom of the seminars.

This yields an interesting strategy for reading the *Écrits.* The *Écrits,* we might argue, is pivotal to Lacan's oeuvre, but provides us with a non-"Standard Edition" of his ideas. Through Lacan's kaleidoscopic text, ideas get compressed, distorted, disguised and subjected to the multiple dream-work operations that separate latent from manifest contents of Lacan's theoretical desire. Whereas the Freudian text is a prime instance of the secondary process – contradictions are avoided wherever possible, rational clarity is attained throughout – the Lacan text is more akin to the primary process, "structured like a language", making use of all and every rhetorical or linguistic device possible.

Lacan's description of his own style as "between writing and speech" provides us with a suggestion regarding how we might go about commenting on his texts. Rather than attempting to fix the significations put in play by his style of "spoken writing", we might seek to stress the multiple significations apparent therein, to invoke multiple voices speaking in – or through - what is presented on the page. Rather than the Rosetta Stone that enables the unlocking of other obscure writings, Lacan's *Écrits* is far more akin to a literary Babel. A text "not meant to be read" could, after all, mean a text that *should be made to speak*, and speak in multiple voices.

Alternatively, a text "not made to be read" might simply mean: not to be understood. Following this logic, the *Écrits* surely works less within the pragmatic goals of comprehension or rational intelligibility than as a means of inducing in us the perplexity and the suspension of knowledge that the analysand experiences in respect of the analyst and the analytic process itself. We might conclude that Lacan's assemblage of lectures-turned-writing is possibly less book than psychoanalytic tool – a desire- or transference-engendering device. "[W]hen all is said and done", opined Anthony Wilden:

> even if the curious mixture of penetration, poetry, and willful obscurity in the *Écrits* seems designed to force the reader into a perpetual struggle of his own...perhaps there is a method [in this] madness. Lacan has always told his readers that they must, "*y mettre du sien*". (1968, p. 311)

The *Écrits*, in this further sense, is *not* a book: it is a type of infinite text; it does not end, it cannot be finished; it continues to escape the "imaginarization" of our attempts at assimilation. We might then agree – at least in part – with Roudinesco's idea that

> the *Écrits* should be viewed less as a book than as the collection of a whole lifetime devoted to oral teaching. Hence the title Écrits, to signify trace, archive, something that does not come undone, does not vanish, cannot be stolen: a letter arriving at its destination (2014, p. 96).

If it is not a book, then what is the *Écrits*? How to view this dense, obscure assemblage of signifiers? As a doctrinal text, perhaps the "Talmud" of Lacan's return to Freud? A manual of Freudian-Lacanian clinical practice. As the constitution (or more likely in Lacan's case a "de-constitution") of his own emerging Freudian school of psychoanalysis? A hystericizing object of desire and interpretative scrutiny? An extended manifesto against the ossified norms of the ego psychologists and the International Psychoanalytic Association, indeed, a diatribe against a degraded form of psychoanalysis? Lacan's *magnum opus*? Perhaps a (love) letter to psychoanalysis and those allegiant to Freud's own inaugural psychoanalytic desire? The Lacanian answer to this extended line of questioning must surely be: Yes.

References

Fink, B. (2004). *Lacan to the Letter: Reading Écrits Closely*. Minneapolis/London: University of Minnesota Press.

Lacan, J. (1998). *The Seminar of Jacques Lacan, Book XX, Encore: On Feminine Sexuality, the Limits of Love and Knowledge, 1972–1973* (edited by Jacques-Alain Miller, translated by Bruce Fink). New York and London: W.W. Norton.

Lacan, J. (2018). *...or Worse: The Seminar of Jacques Lacan, Book XIX*.

Miller, J.-A. (2010). *L'orientation Lacanienne – La vie de Lacan*. Unpublished Seminar. https://viedelacan.wordpress.com/2012/11/19/iv-lacan-contre-tous-et-contre-lacan/.

Ricouer, P. (1965). *De l' interpretation*. Paris: Seuil. (Translated as *Freud and Philosophy: An Essay on Interpretation*, trans. D. Savage (New Haven: Yale University Press, 1970)).

Roudinesco, É. (2014). *Lacan: In Spite of Everything*. London: Verso.

Wilden, A. (1968). *Speech and Language in Psychoanalysis: Jacques Lacan*. Baltimore & London: The Johns Hopkins University.

1

OVERTURE TO THIS COLLECTION

Derek Hook, Calum Neill and Stijn Vanheule

"The style is the man himself"

"Overture to this collection" opens with a quotation from the celebrated naturalist and author, Georges-Louis Leclerc, the Comte de Buffon: "The style is the man himself" (3, 1). Along with Diderot, Voltaire and Rousseau, Buffon was once considered one of the "Big Four" of French Enlightenment literature. His once exalted status – he was once, as Miller (2014) tells us, fêted by a series of French kings who "admired him without limit" (p. 150) – has declined to the point where today he is considered a relatively minor intellectual figure. This memorable line was drawn from a text, *"Le Discours sur le Style"*, delivered by Buffon on the occasion of his formal reception into the auspicious *Académie Française* on 25 August 1753. Buffon advanced there that "Writing well consists of thinking, feeling and expressing well, of clarity of mind, soul and taste ... The style is the man himself" (*"Le style c'est l'homme même"*) (Buffon, 1894, p. 18).

This aphorism has, subsequently, come to be interpreted in a variety of ways. One might in fact advance that misinterpretation has proved the rule here. As Fellows and Milliken (1972) argue, Buffon's pronouncement has frequently been "cited in justification of excessive eccentricities of style, in defence of the right of the individual to develop to the full his most bizarre idiosyncrasies" when in fact the fuller context of Buffon's text "effectively blocks any such interpretation" (p. 153). In what follows, it will be necessary to spend some time further contextualizing and (re)interpreting this phrase. This being said, the proliferation of differing interpretations of Buffon's words – indeed, the varying echoes, the frequent misreadings, banalizations and reversals of his meaning – are of just as much interest to Lacan at the outset of his *Écrits*, inasmuch as they speak to an issue of considerable importance to the French analyst: the transmission of psychoanalysis and how the public will engage and assimilate his own contribution to the Freudian field.

It is worth pausing here, at the outset, to stress the irony of Lacan's reference to Buffon's *Le Discours sur le Style*. Within this famous essay, Buffon considered

DOI: 10.4324/9781003368649-2

6

all purely verbal ingenuity to be suspect; he pitied authors who resorted to gratuitous ornamentation; prose, he maintained, should be "paraphrasable", clear, lucid and without a trace of ambiguity; a style appropriate to addressing a cultivated reader should, furthermore, be concerned primarily with clearly expressed ideas (Fellows & Milliken, 1972). Bearing all of this in mind, we are forced to ask: Is it possible to find a better literary description of what Lacan's own infamously opaque and baroque writing style *is not*? While Buffon's thoughts on style are more paradoxical than they may at first appear, the question nonetheless emerges: Why would Lacan wish to begin the much-anticipated collection of his most significant written work by citing someone whose thoughts on literary styling were seemingly diametrically opposed to his own? Surely Voltaire, Buffon's adversary, a writer whose eccentricities and preference for a polemical and irreverent style seems much more suited to Lacan's own approach, would have been a more apt literary figure to cite in this context? This appeal to Buffon seems thus to enact Lacan's own theorization of the split between the content of a statement and the act of its enunciation; Lacan's opening might be read as the equivalent of the liar's paradox enunciated by Epimenides (which Lacan himself cites in Seminar VII (1986/1992, p. 82): "I am lying to you". This gesture seems to say: "Don't believe what I say; there is truth in what I say", a sentiment which itself calls to mind Freud's borrowing from Shakespeare's Polonius, more specifically yet, the hope – key to the dialectics of truth and interpretation within psychoanalytic practice – that "the bait of falsehood" might take "a carp of truth" (Freud, 1937, p. 262).

An intention is thus announced within the first lines of the "Overture". Lacan wants us to enter into a game, be it one of sophistry, something akin to the guessing "game of even or odds" (43, 7) described in Lacan's engagement with Poe's *The Purloined Letter*, or, more challengingly yet, the anxious "game" of deduction and deliberation of the prisoner's dilemma outlined as in *Logical Time and the Assertion of Anticipated Certainty*. Whatever type of game Lacan has in mind, it is – needless to say – a game of the signifier, a game to be played within the auspices of the symbolic, and, as importantly, with reference to the Other and the elusive *object a*. Lacan, accordingly, positions the reader before a puzzle in much the same way as he does in the first full essay in the *Écrits*, the *Seminar on "The Purloined Letter"*, which, as he tells us in justifying why he picked it "out of chronological order" to open the volume, presents an "entryway into my style" (4, 3). We will need to work on the text – indeed, on *all* the texts within the *Écrits* – and "pay the price with elbow grease" (5, 1) if these writings are to yield to us something of consequence. It is true, the "Overture", like much of Lacan's work, can be approached like a riddle needing to be solved (hence no doubt his praise for Edgar Allan Poe's fiction, which, he says, "is so powerful in the mathematical sense" (4, 10)). And yet we can go further: the "Overture" itself exemplifies the notion of *object petit a*, or, as we might put it in today's parlance, it contains a number of "easter eggs". It consists of a densely interwoven series of literary allusions and self-references containing oblique and hidden meanings. For all of these reasons – the performative enactment of the split between statement and enunciation, the text's role as puzzle, as *object a*, the citation of a well-known phrase whose meaning remains elusive – the "Overture" remains an instructive piece of writing with which to begin Lacan's *Écrits*.

Let us return to Buffon. In quoting Buffon, Lacan is, in effect, invoking the multitude of voices who have cited the famous literary figure, drawing our attention to the fact that the quotation has slipped into common usage and has, consequently, come to be intoned without thought to its sense. Through this echo-chamber effect, Buffon's phrase has taken on a life of its own. Added to this is the apparently self-evident quality of the pronouncement: the idea, in short, that the particularities of an author's individual expression – particularly once aligned to the idiosyncrasies of form – might underlie the substance of the speaker, of "the man himself". We thus run the risk, due to the Babel-like proliferation of differing interpretations and the apparent obviousness of Buffon's declaration, of it eluding us altogether. There is, in fact, considerable nuance to Buffon's pronouncement. Buffon is concerned with how the progressively developed vehicle of an author's style represents both the irreducible singularity of that author's voice and, simultaneously – and here comes the paradox – a timeless universality, which is itself reflected in the ideals of unambiguous communicative clarity. For Buffon, say Fellows and Milliken (1972), citing Buffon's own words within their own account:

> The creative writer ... must imitate nature, whose productions achieve perfection "because she works according to an eternal plan, from which she never departs." The human mind, though it can create nothing, can "lift itself by contemplation to the level of the most sublime truths." The writer's value is to be measured by the extent of his insight into the essential form of things. It is in this context that the most famous aphorism ["Style is the man himself"] must be understood ... *One man's vision, perfectly articulated, assures immortality. ... A mastery of style ...* assures the personal fame of a particular author precisely because it *is one of those universal intellectual qualities that make one man's effective communication with others*; it is a guarantee that his vision of things, his insights will not be lost. (Fellows & Milliken, 1972, pp. 152–153, *emphasis added*)

There is an apparent contradiction here. All that is distinctive about the author, the very facet of their singular style, can result in that which is eternal, essential, "the most sublime of truths". Personal style seems thus both a paramount concern, even though at the very moment of its apotheosis it is subsumed by the universal. An intriguing paradox.

Before developing this line of speculation, we should pause a moment to note the ways in which Buffon's ideas on style and articulation start to seem applicable to the Freudian practice of psychoanalysis. Worth noting here is Buffon's insistence that form is the most important aspect of content, that, ultimately, there can be no dichotomy between form and content. Such assertions, on behalf of a man considered to be a master of the art of rhetoric, resonate with Lacan's attention to the enunciative dimension of speech and the materiality of the signifier. They also chime with the emphasis that Lacan places, in *The Instance of the Letter*, on the many rhetorical tropes that analysts should attend to when listening to discourse as "aligned along the several staves of a musical score" (419, 7). And so, having highlighted the apparent incongruity of Lacan's opening citation of Buffon's dictum, we now find a modicum of common ground between the two men. (This is one example of how the maze of a Lacanian text can turn us around, cause us to consider retracing our steps, even to retract an earlier interpretation). Various historical criticisms of Buffon are worth noting here. Buffon was considered, for example, incapable of simplicity; he wrote in an overly opulent fashion; he always preferred making an extravagant impression to the selection of an exact term of description (Fellows & Milliken, 1972). Such allegations suggest that the two stylists may have more in common than we had previously thought.

And yet Buffon's paradoxical concordance of singularity and the universal remains puzzling. We have in Buffon, as Freeman (2020) observes, the idea that style must be cultivated – for it cannot simply be imitated – and yet, there is also the declaration that style is the very essence of humanness, that since good style "manifests the full flowering of human nature, it bears no distinguishing characteristics of the particular writer" (p. 266). The individual author, we might say, dissolves by means of their mastery of their own distinctive style. As "the exemplar of the form of the species, the good writer is no one in particular" (Freeman, 2020, p. 266). This paradox pertains of course to Lacan himself. While clearly possessing a highly distinctive, indeed, a properly inimitable and "non-paraphrasable" prose style, Lacan remained concerned with the effective transmission of psychoanalysis via various formalized and scientific means (algorithms, schemas, formulas, mathemes, typology, etc.), which, via the universality of their form, hopefully avoid the simplifications and assimilations that had so debased the findings and breakthroughs of Freud's psychoanalysis. Unexpectedly then, the interpretative labour required to unlock facets of Lacan's gratuitously ornamented and impenetrable prose style results, perhaps, in a more effective – and polyvalent – transmission of psychoanalysis.

"So powerful in the mathematical sense"

Rather than being satisfied here with a glib attempt to resolve this (proto-Hegelian) paradox between singularity and the universal, we might note that it foregrounds an inherent quality of the signifier as such. That is to say, language, particularly in its enunciative/spoken dimension, permits for an infinite variety of singular articulations, even while its broader dimensions (most significantly, the processes of metonymy and metaphor) are structural and, indeed, universal, certainly inasmuch as they underlie the very possibility of language as such. We find a possible variation of this idea (the coincidence of the singular and universal enabled via the signifier) in Lacan's above-cited description of Poe's fiction as being "so powerful in the mathematical sense of the term" (4, 10). This is a reference to the role of exponents in mathematics, that is, to the power to which a given number is to be raised (the number of times a number is to be multiplied by itself). Interestingly, given that exponents in mathematics *simplify* multiplication problems and also refer to an (exponential) increase, we have, embodied in the same principle, the functions of *reduction* and *proliferation* (or, simplification and increase). This seemingly contrary pairing could be said to apply to Buffon's thinking on style, which is both something that is highly cultivated and distinctive (advanced, we might say, increased, via multiplications of itself) and yet that attains, via careful refinement, the quality of "those universal intellectual qualities that makes possible one man's effective communication with others" (Fellows & Milliken, 1972, p. 153). This simultaneity of multiplication and refinement, of proliferation and reduction (especially with respect to meaning), is – as already remarked – one of the primary functions of the signifier, and Lacan's texts often work in an exemplary manner to dramatizes these two symbolic operations.

Lacan's daughter, Judith Miller, in her own (2014) commentary on the "Overture", adds something significant here, helping us better understand what mediates the relationship between the highly personal and the universal in Buffon's thoughts on style:

> Buffon maintains a parallel between style and nature, correlating their processes and production. Just as nature works on an eternal outline from which she never separates, and prepares in silence the seeds of her productions, so style consists first of patiently developing concepts and organizing ideas that are productive. From there the foundations of the "immortal monuments" on which style is able to build are assured… The main task of style, then, is to reach a point of view that allows one to obtain ideas that are productive and gather the main threads of the subject at hand. All else follows from this position, the point of view that [as Buffon states] "ideas will follow and the style will be natural and easy." The author will then be blocked by nothing, he will have no more hesitation, will not face any embarrassment, and will only experience pleasure … Through style, the author knows a *jouissance* that Buffon defines in terms proper to describing the relief of a woman when she gives birth, or *jouissance* as such. (2014, pp. 144–145)

There is much that is of significance here, perhaps primarily the idea that the mediating factor between the highly personal and universal truth is nature itself (likewise interesting is the link Miller establishes between style and *jouissance*, something to which we will soon return). While Lacan would, of course, reject any direct explanatory appeal to nature, the idea that the subjective particulari-ties of an individual might give voice to the universal (and vice versa, that the universal might give form to certain particularities of subjective experience) has an established history in psychoanalysis. Freud's frequent recourse to the myths of antiquity, and Lacan's own Lévi-Straussian study of myths in terms of their structural organization – see, for example, his discussions of Freud's Oedipus Complex – are relevant in this regard.

Further theoretical complexities also come to light here which suggest addi-tional reasons why Lacan might have been drawn to Buffon's ideas and to the naturalist's thoughts on the relation between language and nature in particular. A case in point being the notion that there may be a two-way relationship between language and nature: language, in its ideal usage, coming to resemble the natural world and the idea of language nevertheless possessing the capacity to re-shape – or stand in the place of – that natural world.[1] The idea of a two-way relation between language and nature might seem rather non-Lacanian, unless one accepts the fundamental point, as already asserted by Lacan in his paper on the mirror stage, that the relation of human being to nature is never harmonious and is inherently marked by division and discontent: "In man this relationship to nature is altered by a certain dehiscence at the very heart of the organism, a primordial Discord" (78, 2). This discord cannot but find expression in how we use language. Buffon dreamt of unambiguous linguistic expression. Lacan, on the other hand, articulates, through his papers collected in the *Écrits,* the notion that language use is never transparent. It always bears witness to the dimension of the Other that makes up the unconscious. This Other is expressed via linguistic tropes that destabilize the straightforwardness of all communication.

"Man is no longer ... a reference point"

Let us return though to how Buffon's aphorism might be re-interpreted and/ or adapted. Where Buffon might somewhat simplistically be understood as arguing that the manner in which one writes reflects, in an unproblematic way, the person of the writer, Lacan would want to question any such relationship, not simply because the reflection may not be so direct or transparent but, more problematically still, because the solid starting point upon which Buffon's claim rests, "man", is, for Lacan, "no longer so sure a reference point" (9,1). Lacan appears here to be offering an oblique tip of the hat to the anti-humanist thesis of Foucault's formidable *Les Mots les Choses* (*The Order of Things*), which was published the same year that Lacan penned the "Overture". For Lacan, however, "man" is not just "an invention of a recent date" that was destined soon to be erased, in Foucault's famous words, "like a face drawn in sand at the edge of the sea" (1973, p. 387). The historical figure of man is also an

11

imaginary figure, an imaginization – hence the derisory tone Lacan adopts towards Sartre's existential humanism, a philosophy which, as Lacan puts it in his theorization of the mirror stage, "ties the illusion of autonomy in which it puts its faith to the ego's constitutive misrecognitions" (80, 1). It is thus crucial that Lacan follows his tacit endorsement of anti-humanism with a reference to the imaginary register. The highlighting of the latter theme is continued in the lines that follow. In referring to a literal instantiation of style, that is, to how "the image of the cloth that adorned Buffon" might "keep us inattentive" (9, 1), Lacan is alluding to the lure of the imaginary which both familiarizes and keeps at bay anything that might be too disruptive to the identity-making faculties of the ego. Lacan is also – more directly yet – referring to the Prince of Monaco's famous rebuff directed at Buffon, the allegation that Buffon "could write only with his hand floating in lace cuffs", an idea which became very much a part of Buffon's public image (Fellows & Milliken, 1972).[2]

We should exercise caution however. There is more afoot here than a routine warning against the fixating qualities of the image. By the same token, we should not be content to equate style with adornment or vainglorious forms of artifice. While it is tempting to read into Lacan's words a series of his own foregoing concepts and refrains, that would close down the game of signification he is spinning around us. (We might paraphrase Lacan's warning in "On My Antecedents": "My students occasionally delude themselves into thinking that they have found "already there" in my writings [something they wish to find]" (53, 3). We should, as such, beware of flatfooted readings of Lacan). To be sure then, Lacan certainly is alerting us to the trappings of the imaginary – to the splendour of being "dressed up" in an image. He seems to mock such pretensions precisely by referring to an image of a man known for his extreme vanity. And yet, crucially, Lacan is just as dismissive of the idea that behind the *méconnaissance* of the image there might be an authentic "identity" of sorts existing beyond the jurisdiction of the signifier, which is to say, beyond the various symbolic processes that make it – and, not incidentally, *style* itself – possible. Style cannot as such be reduced to embellishment; it is not to be relegated to the category of that which is artificial or merely decorative. It is more than imaginization. This is worth stressing given the prospect of a short circuit between style and substance – or between form and content – to which both Buffon's aphorism and the everyday practice of Freudian psychoanalysis alert us. Style and substance, for Buffon and Lacan alike (albeit in somewhat different ways), can be said to represent two sides of the continuous surface of a Mobius strip. Adrian Johnston makes an aligned point in stressing how for Lacan that which is artificial, fictional, "non-substantial" can nonetheless be of fundamental structuring importance:

> the subject's identifications at the level of Imaginary-Symbolic reality (i.e., the world of images and words) are fictional, virtual constructs, insubstantial ideals that are nonetheless much more than mere

epiphenomena insofar as these ideals entail structuring effects that reverberate throughout the entirety of the individual's multi-layered being. (2007, p. 282)

Johnston's reference to the "subject's identifications" is crucial, because in Lacan's various comments on Buffon and style, he is also, implicitly, speaking of the dimensions of identification pertaining to the subject. This leads us to consider the implications of Lacan's calling upon Buffon not only as an imaginary persona but also as an effect of the symbolic order.

"in a context of impertinence"

Buffon was, of course, a celebrity in 18th-century France – a celebrated personage, an acknowledged genius of the first rank (in addition to being considered a pompous egotist!). He was the subject of a literary portrait by a young 24-year-old lawyer, Marie-Jean Hérault de Séchelles. Séchelles visited the ageing Buffon (by then in his late 70s) at his home in Montbard and published an account of the visit as *Voyage à Montbard* (1785). Lacan proves attentive here to the symbolic functions of a proper name, to Buffon's name more specifically, slyly noting that the original title of *Voyage à Montbard* was *Visite à Buffon*. The intimation here is that Buffon had been slighted by virtue of (the removal of) his name in the retitling of Séchelles' book, a sleight seemingly redoubled by Lacan's reference to the "buffoonish reporting" (9, 2), which has resituated Buffon's saying, "in a context of impertinence" (9, 2). (We might observe here, parenthetically, that to speak of an act that "resituates the saying … in a context of impertinence" (9, 2), is also to speak of the psychoanalytic situation and "resituating" of the signifier that such a context enables).

Again the spectre of the imaginary is to be detected: an ego-to-image rivalry appears to underlie not only the resituating impertinence of Séchelles' portrait but also the possibility that "the host" might have been "outdone by his guest" (9, 1). Séchelles' own style is noteworthy in this respect inasmuch as he appears to adopt a somewhat exaggerated tone of obsequiousness, drawing the reader's attention to, not so much Buffon's fame, but Buffon's *desire for fame*. The reference to "a fantasy of the great man" is interesting in this respect. Fink (2006) points out that "*Un fantasme du grande homme*" could be rendered as "one of the great man's fantasies" (p. 766), observing also that it is not entirely clear to whom the fantasy belongs. Séchelles himself may thus have become entangled in the fantasies of Buffon even as he mocks him via a tone of exaggerated reverence. In respect of "*Un fantasme du grande homme*", we are simultaneously presented with:

1) a general fantasy of the great man
2) the great man's own fantasy of himself
3) Séchelles' fantasy of Buffon

4) the possibility – an interesting prospect highlighted by Fink – that "the fantasy organizes him [Buffon] in a scenario" (Fink, 2006, 766).

Given the myriad possibilities implied by Lacan's famous pronouncement "desire is the Other's desire" (690, 2), we would have to conclude that all of the above possibilities might well be concurrently true.

"the man ... in the adage"

We have then – as anticipated – an additional layer to the questions of identification raised above. Style might well be "the man himself" (in the sense of engendering an impression, a persona, image, etc.), but the man might himself be *a function of a name*, a name which can just as easily be lampooned as it can be celebrated via various nominations, titles and honours (such as Buffon's election to the illustrious company of the *Académie Française*, which was thought by Buffon to have elevated him to the rank of Immortals, and which occurred, incidentally, because a place had been left empty by the death of the Archbishop of Sens). In respect of Buffon, we have then both "a fantasy of the ... man" conveyed via a portrait and "the man discussed in the adage" (9, 3), that is, the subject as represented by the signifier (to which we might add: for another signifier).

"There is nothing natural here"

Lacan's following note, "There is nothing natural here" (9, 3) could be said to apply as much to Lacan's own view of language – here to be sharply differentiated from any ideas (Buffon's included) of how nature and language might be harmonized – as to Voltaire's many barbed retorts to Buffon's massive, multi-volumed *Histoire naturelle*. (Actually, the dismissive quip has been ascribed to the Patriarch of Ferney, who referred to the *Histoire* as "*pas si naturel*"). A few words of contextualization will help us better grasp the significance of the putdown Lacan is citing here. Voltaire subscribed to a Newtonian view of the universe which he believed to have been arranged in an orderly manner from the outset. Such a "pre-set" universe was decidedly *not* subject to processes of natural change and evolution. Voltaire's perspective was thus completely at odds with Buffon's development of ever more complicated concepts pertaining to a world of living organisms undergoing continuous natural change. As Fellows (1955) tells it: "Privately and in his correspondence [Voltaire] condemned Buffon as a quack and a madman", largely because Buffon "held to epigenesis, a theory that maintained that in each individual animal the organs are always formed anew" (pp. 232–233). Suffice it to say that this one-liner thus condensed a long and complicated history or rivalry between the two men. The dispute between Voltaire and Buffon is curious in the context of this particular phrase, as it might now be more conventionally levelled against Voltaire, thus emphasising the discursive over the immediately natural.

"Our message comes to us from the Other"

We have, however, digressed from our discussion of Séchelles' style. This style was both affected, and affected *by* the one Séchelles assumes to address, which is to say both Buffon, as the interlocutor of the interview, and the reader, to whom Séchelles would wish to present a certain version of Buffon. This reader furthermore, would expect to recognize the characterization he, Séchelles, is presenting. The two recipients of Séchelles' writing – his reader and Buffon himself – can thus be said to exert a determining influence on Séchelles' style, perhaps obviously so, inasmuch as he takes these recipients into account in the very process of writing. Séchelles's style then, Lacan tells us, reflects less the man himself than *the one who is addressed*. This, Lacan tells us, complies with a principle he proposed in his earliest seminars: "Our message comes to us from the Other ... in an inverted form" (3, 5 – 4, 1). This is an assertion Lacan has made many times before (in *Seminar on "The Purloined Letter"*, Lacan states that the "sender ... receives from the receiver his own message in an inverted form" (30, 2)). Wittily, and self-reflexively, Lacan observes that this point is supported even in the case of his own utterance insofar as it was reflected back to him by "an eminent interlocuter" (4, 1). The history of this Lacanian formula and the various ways it can be applied deserves a sustained study all of its own (see Zafiropoulos (2010) for a helpful overview). Suffice it to say, after hinting for many years that the formula was not his own, that it had indeed itself come from the Other, Lacan, in a 1974 talk *"La troisième"*, finally relented and revealed the identity of this "eminent interlocutor" that he had withheld for the 21 years that has passed since he first invoked it in Seminar I: Claude Lévi-Strauss.[3] Interestingly, this axiom of communication can also be said to apply to Buffon. In his speech to the *Académie Française*, Miller remarks:

> He says it clearly: he only returns to them what they have given him. "Gentlemen," he says, "I can only offer to you your own good, that is a few words on style." He was able to find those ideas in reading their works. Addressed back to them, these ideas reach their destination, to be transmitted to future generations. (2014, p. 144)

If one's own message is received back from – if not largely determined by – an Other, then speaking might seem futile, at least if one is attempting, through speech, to attain the original, singular perspective of an individual speaker. The hopes of humanistic individualism seem thus dashed ("man" here being "reduced to nothing but the echoing locus of our discourse" (4, 2)). And yet Lacan's question is rhetorical. For psychoanalysis there decidedly *is* a point in "addressing our discourse to him [the Other]"; it is only in this way, via the "echoing locus of our discourse" that the unconscious — understood here precisely as the *discourse of the Other* - might speak. Psychoanalysis does not, as such, serve the ideals of (existential) humanistic individualism — invariably centred, as they are, for Lacan, around the ambitions and aspirations of an ego — although it most certainly does facilitate the expressions of the subject of the signifier, which is to say, the desiring subject of the unconscious.

"It will be up to this reader"

If we abide by the formula of communication described above ("one receives one's message from the Other in an inverted form"), then questions directed at Lacan by his prospective readers — however frustrated or irreverent — necessarily play an important role in the making of Lacan's message, and, moreover, in the forging of his style. In so far as the Other is invoked in an appeal to a future, to a possible addressee, then Lacan's prospective readers ("the reason … put forward to convince me to publish a collection of my writings" (4, 3)) clearly instantiate the Other for him. One is reminded in this respect of Lacan's own position in delivering his weekly seminars. In conducting his seminars — and by extrapolation, in assuming an authorial position — Lacan's position is arguably less that of the master (or agent in the master's discourse) than that of the subject whose unconscious might speak (the enunciative position within the discourse of the analyst).[4] Given then that Lacan's readers instantiate the Other, then it is from this point of reception that Lacan may — following his own formula — receive his own inverted message. We might add to this: it will be via the deferred action of this future reception — a sobering responsibility for Lacan's future readers — that the French analyst, via the temporality of the future anterior, "shall have been … what [he was] … in the process of becoming" (247, 7). This idea seems affirmed by Lacan's assertion that "It will be up to this reader to give the letter in question … the very thing he will find as its concluding word: its destination" (4, 5). It is perhaps surprising for those of us used to struggling with the letters Lacan has left us, for those of us who are used to locating him as the master (as the transference inducing "subject supposed to know"), that he seems here so willing to cede the agency of his texts, or, more appropriately perhaps, the "agency of the letter" that his texts constitute.

"He is no more feigned than the truth"

We've referred above to "Overture to this collection" as a puzzle, an easter egg, a riddle. Structurally, it might be more apt yet to say that the "Overture" is a kind of Russian doll. The echoing maxim ("style is the man himself") yields a first interpretation (concerning the person of Buffon himself, for example, or anti-humanism, or the rivalry of the imaginary register) only for us to discover another possible interpretative variation nestled within the first. Having begun with Buffon's proclamation about style, Lacan has by now foregrounded the question – and the function – of his own cryptic style. As already noted, Lacan states that he has chosen to open the collection with the essay "Seminar on 'The Purloined Letter'" as an "easy entryway into my style" (4, 4). Anyone who has read the essay in question may wonder at this characterization. There is clearly some irony at work here. Beyond the irony, however, Lacan's point is well made. It is not that "Seminar on 'The Purloined Letter'" is an easier read than the essays which follow. Rather, "Seminar on 'The Purloined Letter'" allows us to understand Lacan's own arguments about discourse. It is in this sense that it can be understood as something of a key to the fundament on which the *Écrits* are built.

The kernel of this point is the question of reading, of attending to the multiple spiralling signifiers set in play by Lacan's lucubration. It is only then that the reader, in reading, produces that which was to be read. Here the reader discovers, according to Lacan, not so much something of the text as something of himself; "that he is no more feigned than the truth is when it inhabits fiction" (4, 5). Fiction, as we know, comes in many forms but never is it simply opposed, structurally speaking, to truth. On the contrary, as Lacan reminds us in "The Subversion of the Subject", truth only emerges in a fictional structure (684, 2). Like truth, the subject requires a fiction in order to be articulated, in order to be spoken, which, in the case of both the truth and the subject, is to say that they require a fiction in order to be. This is not to suggest a pretence, insofar as a pretence might be understood to suggest a reality or greater Truth behind a form of semblance. In reading, the reader returns – or adds to, re-articulates – the message (which one receives in an inverted form) which entails an articulation that is the possibility of his or her own subjective emergence. This possibility of a subjective emergence (the reader realizing that he or she "is no more feigned than the truth" (4, 5)) seems thus an effective answer to the question posed above ("What is the point of addressing our discourse to him [the echoing locus of our discourse]?" (4, 2)).

"The parody of my discourse"

Continuing the theme of how a message is put to use by a reader or recipient (hence, the reference to the "purloining of a letter" (4, 6)), Lacan seems to wonder what will become of the letter of his *Écrits*. One prospective result is parody, whether we understand the act of parody here to retain a certain reverence towards the source text (implying thus "the precedence of the trajectory that is parodied" (4, 6)) or as involving the aspect of mockery, caricature, an effective lampooning of an earlier author such that "one sees the shadow of the intellectual master dispelled" (4, 6). The resulting effect of dispelling the shadow of a master is something that Lacan approves of, although he – naturally, being Lacan – fails to qualify what that particular effect is.

Presumably, Lacan has in mind the effect of transference which initially makes analytical work possible – engaging as it does the unconscious of the analysand (or reader) – despite the fact that it must ultimately be dissipated, lest it remains forever fixated on the figure of the master. Such imaginary preoccupation with the figure of the master occurs at the cost of subjective emergence, at the cost, in other words, of the emergence of the subject's desire.

Importantly, for Lacan, no matter the extent to which they are supposed to occupy a position of knowledge, the analyst should not embrace a Buffonesque position as intellectual master but rather, as he will later stress in his discussion of the four discourses, the analyst should work to occupy the position of *object a*. Such a position is – as Lacan discusses at length in his 13th seminar, which he was conducting at the point he was writing the "Overture" – that of the object cause of desire, that which sets the train of signification in motion.

In discussing Poe's "The Purloined Letter", Lacan draws our attention to the echo between the title of Poe's story and the famous 18th-century poem by Alexander Pope, "The Rape of the Lock". Poe's story is usually translated into French as "*Vol de la letter*" and Pope's poem is usually translated as "*Le vol de la boucle*". The *vol* here means theft, removing from the French the potentially confusing and mistaken reference to sexual rape we may hear in Pope's title. In fact, Pope is invoking an earlier sense of "rape", with its Latin etymology, meaning to steal or snatch away. Leaning on this echoing *vol,* Lacan is able to draw our attention to the *boucle* of the title as well. While *boucle* is the term for a lock of hair, it more specifically, in this context, means a curl. It is a loop. So from Pope's poem concerning the uninvited snipping of a piece of a woman's hair, Lacan is able to conjure the theft of a loop, linking Poe to Pope to his own deployment of topology and alluding to his concept of *objet petit a*.

"The Rape of the Lock" relates an apparently true event concerning two English families. Lord Robert Petre had enacted the titular theft, cutting off a piece of Arabella Fermor's hair without her consent. The scandal that followed this act led to a serious rift between Petre and Fermor's families. Lacan appears to be drawing our attention to the manner in which a seemingly "trivial thing" (Pope, 1717) can come to function as something like the organizing principle of reality. The lock in question is cut off, both a remainder and a reminder, but it is in its absence that its potency lies, through the significances imputed to it by the various players in the tale. Taken simply as a piece of hair, the lock is a mere component of what makes up Arabella's style. Here Lacan is making a bridge to what he has already said about style in reference to Buffon. Pope's poem is not addressing the power of the neglected signifier but uses parody to pinpoint how a seemingly insignificant stylistic element can organize reality: "Pope, thanks to parody, ravishes ... the secret feature of its derisory stakes" (4, 7). The secret feature Pope grasped so well through his parody of a serious conflict between two families is the object *a*. The piece of hair Lord Petre purloins is a stand-in for the scopic object that provokes the desire of the Other. By secretly taking away such a barely visible and seemingly trivial thing, Lord Petre destabilizes the field of desire. Pope's baroque description reveals how the theft should be read as an intrusion in the agalmatic space that is used to support Arabella's attractiveness.

18

Here, in the "Overture", Lacan states that "Our task brings back this charming lock" (4, 8), in the form of a loop. Psychoanalysis is not only concerned with the subject of the unconscious, but it also engages with the objectal dimension that causes all manifestations of subjective division. While, on the one hand, psychoanalytic practice has Poe-like characteristics, as the analyst addresses the unconscious such as it is expressed in speech, on the other hand, it consists of a Pope-like dimension too. Whether the analysand is offering beautiful associations to the analyst or demanding clever interpretations, there is only one object that is being provoked: object *a*.

Remarkably, Lacan's *Écrits* does not include a paper from the mid-1960s in which the object *a* is discussed in any detail. There are a few brief points or asides which were added during publication, such as footnote 14 from "*On a Question Prior to Any Possible Treatment of Psychosis*", or rather brief discussions, as can be found in "*The Subversion of the Subject and the Dialectic of Desire*". Beyond these, the hidden cause of desire appears to remain hidden in the *Écrits* too. In the "Overture", Lacan nonetheless warns his "new reader" (4,3), i.e., the reader who has not been attending his then-unpublished seminars, that to get in touch with his discourse, it is crucial to grasp the concept of object *a*.

To situate the object *a* conceptually, Lacan frequently, from Seminar IX on, discusses topological models such as the Moebius strip, the Klein bottle, the cross-cap and the so-called interior eight (*huit intérieur*) or inverted eight (*huit inversé*) (Greenshields, 2017). The interior eight is a loop (*boucle*), a portion of which is twisted through 180° and turned inwards to be enclosed by the larger loop. Arabella's charming lock of hair (*boucle de cheveux*) should remind us of the internal eight, which Lacan here describes as "a knot whose trajectory closes on the basis of its inverted redoubling" (4, 8). The interior eight is one of Lacan's simplest models used to discuss the relation between the subject and object *a*. The model shows how "The subject is, so to speak, in a relation of internal exclusion towards his object" (S13, session 1 December 1965).

"What emerges at the end ... goes by the name of object *a*"

We know that Lacan thought of his notion of object *a* as one of his most important contributions to psychoanalysis. The final lines of the "Overture" underline this point, situating the concept as the outcome of the succession of essays gathered in his *Écrits*: "what emerges at the end of this collection ... goes by the name of object *a*" (4, 10). This object-cause of desire is, crucially, to be read in conjunction with the constitutive division that *is* the subject. Hence the idea of "the division in which the subject is verified" (a Freudian postulate *par excellence*) is now supplemented by Lacan with the further qualification that this verification occurs in "the fact that an object traverses [the subject] without them interpenetrating in any respect" (4, 10). It helps to bear in mind here that object *a* can be read as *the convexity of the subject's lack*, as the subject's lack-in-being as it is positivized in an external attribute, as the "objectal counterpart"

19

(Žižek's (2013) phrase), that sustains the desiring subject "between truth and knowledge" (5, 1). The status of the object *a* relative to the subject is, in other words, definitively extimate; its *ex-sistence*, its apparent "subtraction", is a crucial condition of possibility of the existence of the desiring subject as such (one is reminded here of one of Lacan's inspirations for the concept, namely Freud's (1905) notion of the impossible object of primal satisfaction, the paradoxical "lost" object that the subject ceaselessly attempts to re-find, despite the fact that it was never possessed in the first place).

And now Lacan returns to Buffon's aphorism, affording the formulation a further psychoanalytic articulation (albeit one that was present, even if in a somewhat latent capacity, "right at the outset" (5, 1) of Lacan's text[5]). There is certainly much to say on this topic (style understood as object *a*) as it relates to psychoanalysis and Lacan's own writings more generally, but it is worth pausing for a moment to note a few biographical notes offered by Miller:

> Buffon was a living expression of his speech on style ... What Buffon always desired was ... glory – it comes by itself, he said, to whoever has been able to accede to style... [I]t was to defining the object of his desire that Buffon devoted his work – this object that comes in addition, but only the Other can give him ... glory. Buffon's conviction was that it is only obtained by style ... Style revealed itself to Buffon as the object of his desire. (2014, pp. 150–151)

Despite the apparent equivocation (Miller sees both glory and style as objects of Buffon's desire), this passage proves informative. Miller goes on to say that Buffon's desire defined "a proper space of writing and language" (p. 150), suggesting, furthermore, that the possibility of Buffon's discourse was based on lack. We might clarify – and add to – Miller's description by offering the following: Buffon's writings take on the impossible task of dealing with his lack, and style, precisely as Buffon's object *a* takes on the mediating role between these two domains – Buffon's lack and the overarching yearning for glory that demands a recognizing Other.[6]

There are many routes we could take in developing the implications of style as object *a*. We could say for example that "the style that is the man" (to tweak Buffon's phrase) is *that in him which is more than him*. This would be to draw on the terms that Lacan uses in Seminar 8 to describe the agalma, and more directly yet, that elusive, *je ne sais quoi* quality of the libidinal treasure – another aspect of object *a* – which underlies what is most desirable in the other. (Interestingly, in Greek, "agalma" can be understood both as an offering to the gods and an ornament, or we might add, by extrapolation, an *ornamentation*). While this prioritization of style as object does not invalidate the various foregoing interpretative forays as regards Buffon's pronouncement ("The style is the man" understood in terms of imaginary capture, as indicating the paradoxical continuity between style and substance, etc.), it certainly does bring something different to light. "In the place ... marked for Buffon", Lacan now – in the most declarative section of the article – calls for "the falling away of this object" (5, 1). While there are of course different possible interpretations of what Lacan has in mind by "falling away", the soundness of such a strategy within the clinic seems evident: accentuating the lostness of object *a* evokes desire; it thus stirs up the motor force of analytical work.

Such a reading seems justified considering that such a falling away paradoxically "isolates the object" (5, 1), an idea we might convey simply by saying that we never desire the objects of our desire so keenly as when they are lost to us. Such an accentuation of desire causes the subject to question what really underlies the everyday (alienated) desires (of the Other) by which they are so enthralled. It calls those desires – and along with them, associated imaginary identifications and aspirations – into question, freeing the neurotic subject from such alienating destinies at the same time as it enables the subject – and here follows one potential outcome of a successful analysis – to open themselves up to desire as *pure form*. This desire – perhaps a variant of the purified desire that Lacan speaks of in Seminar VII – is able both, paradoxically, to sustain the subject ("between truth and knowledge" (5, 1)) even while the subject seems to disappear. Importantly, this disappearance should not be read in a terminal sense as the end or extinction of the subject, it is instead the logical correlate of the object *a* being foregrounded. As we might put it: the temporary eclipsing of the subject via the accentuation of object *a* (the subject's "objectal counterpart") is the condition of possibility for the emergence of the desiring subject of the unconscious, that is, the subject of psychoanalysis.

"Lead the reader to a consequence in which he has to situate himself"

Reading the *Écrits* takes the reader on quite a journey. The volume consists of unique milestone papers. The path of exploring these is never smooth, not in the least because Lacan strictly adhered to his own style. He simply never gave his audiences exactly what they were asking. Demands are not simply there to be fulfilled. In Lacan's view, students and analysands alike should work and articulate their own way of dealing with lack and with the object *a* which arises in the void between truth and knowledge. Therefore, a major goal for Lacan in his *Écrits* is that each reader should situate him or herself in relation to what the papers relate and evoke.

At the close of the "Overture", Lacan tells us "*nous voulons du parcours – dont ces écrits sont les jalons et du style que leur adresse commande amener le lecteur à une conséquence où il lui faille mettre du sien*". Bruce Fink renders this sentence as:

With this itinerary, of which these writings are milestones, and this style, which the audience to whom they were addressed required, I want to lead the reader to a consequence in which he must pay the price with elbow grease.

Returning to the French original allows us to appreciate something of the density of the message Lacan is offering and a richer sense of how he wishes the *Écrits to be received*.

The first thing to note is the position Lacan accords to these writings. The *Écrits* are not the course (*parcours*) themselves but are placed in a subservient position to the greater project, the course of learning – or better yet, a type of truth-encounter – Lacan is attempting to set out. The various essays which make up the *Écrits* are but the milestones (*jalons*) along the way. There are three angles from which we might perceive a milestone. From a functional perspective, a milestone marks the distance still to be travelled. It is 243 km from Paris to Montbard. A milestone, in this sense, describes the ground not covered. This assumes a teleological position. From a certain vantage point and a certain distance, what we might call a god's eye perspective, the milestones also break up the distance covered. The original Roman *miliarium* worked this way, breaking up the journey without even indicating distance, creating a rhythm or scansion more than anything else. From a social point of view, the fact of the milestones' existence also tells us that someone else has been this way before. This perhaps links to the idiomatic French usage which could be rendered something like "to pave the way". Given the context - the fact that Lacan is writing a new opening essay for his long-awaited book – we should perhaps keep in mind that *jalon* is also a bookmark. A placeholder. Reading the *Écrits* clearly is going to require many pauses.

The second part of the sentence, "*du style que leur adresse commande amener le lecteur à une conséquence où il lui faille mettre du sien*", could be translated more straightforwardly as "the style that their address commands brings the reader to a consequence in which he has to situate himself". Although, to be fair, there is no straightforward translation that is ever going to capture all of the complex layers implied in Lacan's prose. There is necessarily work, and hard work, implied in reading the *Écrits*, and it is this that Fink conveys with "elbow grease". The phrase could also be translated as "to pull one's weight", a reading which perhaps marries Fink's emphasis on work to the more idiomatic sense of situating oneself that is also crucial here. It suggests an ethics of reading, consistent with the ethics Lacan has by this point developed in his seventh seminar, where the subject comes to assume responsibility for their own position and, crucially, in this context, for their own interpretation.

The *faille* in this final clause also itself translates as overture, referring then to the title of the short *écrit* of which it is a part. But *faille* is also fault, as in a geological fault, a crack in the ground. At the point where we are being told that the reader must situate himself, we have a fault line, a crack, an opening. So the opening of the *Écrits* – which would have been the last of the écrits to be written – marks not only a beginning, and, then, an ending, but also an incompletion and thus an invitation. Here where there is a crack, a lack, the reader must insert himself. Rather than hold the *Écrits* as a body of knowledge, Lacan is perhaps telling us, engage with it as a collection of provocations and, through so doing, seize this opportunity to place yourself in relation to the gap which is in you more than yourself.

Notes

1   As Hanna Roman (2018a) notes in the context of French 18th-century science, language was understood as comprising the building blocks of both human nature and external nature. Language, in other words, was not merely a means of communication, but was *the foundation of real and imagined worlds*. Roman goes on to stress that Buffon redefined the discipline of natural history, thinking of it in terms of the creation of relationships (indeed, *modes of rapport,* a resonant phrase to Lacanian ears(!)) between the mind and the world in the form of written expression. For Buffon, the longer the natural historian studied nature, focusing on its order and operation, the more their language would come to resemble the world. This, as Roman (2018a) qualifies, was, importantly, a two-way relationship: nature could be reproduced in words, and words soon could come to stand in the place of nature. Buffon's later work thus presents us with "a vision of a future where the art of human language and the artificiality of human landscapes would become the new natural" (Roman, 2018b). A Lacanian retort to these fascinating speculations might simply be to suggest that a non-rapport underlies the apparent prospect of a rapport between mind and nature or – more pertinently yet – language and nature. Miller (2014), for example, highlights the relationship between nature and language in Buffon, but stresses the ultimate incompatibility of the two. Whereas nature is multidimensional, language is linear, "Thus Buffon's perpetual concern was to overcome the structural inadequateness of language for rendering the density and multidimensionality of nature" (p. 149).
2   Bruce Fink's "Translator's Endnotes" (2006) likewise notes that Buffon was historically portrayed as wearing "a grey silk bonnet and red dressing gown with white stripes while writing" (p. 766).
3   It is worth citing Lacan's own account directly:
     This is the story of the message that everyone receives in an inverted form. I have been saying this for a very long time … In truth, I owe it to Claude Lévi-Strauss. He leaned over to one of my good friends – his wife, Monique … and said, about what I was expressing, that that was it: everyone received his message in an inverted form. Monique repeated it to me. I could not find a better formula for what I wanted to say at the time. He was the one who foisted it off on us. (Lacan, 1975, pp. 180–181)
4   Slavoj Žižek offers a nice formulation in this respect: "in his seminars … it is not that he [Lacan] is analysing the public; the public is his audience, his big Other … he literally improvises there" (Žižek, Aristodemou and Frosh, 2010, p. 425).
5   We see this by attending to one of Fink's translator's endnotes. In referring to the second sentence of the "Overture", Fink observes that the French lines for "the cloth that adorned Buffon while he wrote" (*"linge parant Buffon en train d'écrire"*) contain the suggestive signifier "linge":
     linge here perhaps alludes to the role of pieces of cloth as transitional objects – tickle blankets, blankies … associated by Lacan with object *a*… Here it is perhaps object *a* that obscures or replaces "man". (Fink, 2006, p. 766)
6   We would need to embark on a lengthy description of Lacan's theorization of the difference between alienation and separation in Seminar XI to fully illuminate how object *a* operates as a mediator of sorts between the subject and the Other. For present pur-

poses, it suffices to cite Fink's (1995) helpful account of how object *a* mediates between subject and Other (or child and mOther):

Object *a* can be understood … as the *remainder* produced when that hypothetical [subject-Other/child-mOther] unity breaks down, as the last trace of that unity, a last *reminder* thereof. By cleaving to this rem(a)inder, the split subject, though expulsed from the Other, can sustain the illusion of wholeness; by clinging to [object *a*], the subject is able to ignore his or her division. (Fink, 1995, p. 59)

References

Buffon, G. L. C. (1894). *Discours Sur le Style*. Paris: Libraire Ch. Delgrave.

Fellows, O. E. (1955). Voltaire and Buffon: Clash and conciliation. *Symposium*, 9 (2): 222–235.

Fellows, O. E., & Milliken, S. F. (1972). *Buffon*. New York: Twayne Publishers.

Fink, B. (1995). *The Lacanian Subject between Language and Jouissance*. Princeton: Princeton University Press.

Fink, B. (2006). Translator's endnotes. In J. Lacan (ed.), *Écrits*. London and New York: Norton.

Foucault, M. (1973). *The Order of Things*. New York: Vintage.

Freeman, E. (2020). *From Case Study as Symptom to Case Study as Sinthome*. PhD Dissertation. Pittsburgh: Duquesne University.

Freud, S. (1905). *Three essays on the theory of sexuality*. SE, 7: 123–243.

Freud, S. (1937). *Constructions in analysis*. SE, 23: 255–269.

Greenshields, W. (2017). *Writing the Structures of the Subject Lacan and Topology*. London and New York: Palgrave.

Johnston, A. (2007). *Žižek's Ontology: A Transcendental Materialist Theory of Subjectivity*. Evanston: Northwestern University Press.

Lacan, J. (1975). La troisième. *Lettres de L'Ecole freudienne*, 16: 177–203.

Miller, J. (2014). Style is the man himself. In E. Ragland-Sullivan & M. Bracher (eds.), *Lacan and the Subject of Language*. London and New York: Routledge.

Roman, H. (2018a). *The Language of Nature in Buffon's Histoire Naturelle*. Liverpool: Liverpool University Press.

Roman, H. (2018b). Language, science and human control of nature: The case of Buffon's 'Histoire naturelle'. Voltaire Foundation. Accessed at: https://www .voltaire.ox.ac.uk/news/blog/language-science-and-human-control-nature-case -buffon's-'histoire-naturelle'.

Zafiropoulos, M. (2010). *Lacan and Lévi-Strauss or The Return to Freud (1951–1957)*. London: Karnac.

Žižek, S. (2013). *Less than Nothing: Hegel and the Shadow of Dialectical Materialism*. London: Verso.

Žižek, S., Aristodemou, M., & Frosh, S. (2010). *Unbehagen* and the subject: An interview with Slavoj Žižek. *Psychoanalysis, Culture and Society*, 15: 418–428.

2

THE SEMINAR ON "THE PURLOINED LETTER"

Kareen Ror Malone and Christopher Reed Johnson

Background history and context of publication

The 'Seminar on "The Purloined Letter"' presents an analysis by Jacques Lacan of Edgar Allan Poe's story 'The Purloined Letter' (1844/2004), the third (and last) in his Dupin detective stories. The detective Monsieur C. Auguste Dupin is widely recognized as the prototypical hero of the modern detective novel, as portrayed by Sherlock Holmes (Mabbot, 1988). The following summarizes Poe's story, which will be elaborated further as needed to follow Lacan's argument in the 'Seminar on "The Purloined Letter"'.

The story of 'The Purloined Letter' is about a highly coveted letter, of which the contents are never revealed. The scene begins with the Queen of France in the royal boudoir reading a letter. When the King suddenly interrupts her, she fails in a hasty attempt to hide it, and instead casually places the letter down on the desk to avoid the King's notice. As it sits 'innocently' on the royal bureau, the nefarious and quick-witted Minister D____, having witnessed the scene, lifts the letter because he ascertains it has been nonchalantly set on the desk precisely to avoid drawing the attention of the King. Just as casually, the minister replaces the original letter with a facsimile. Simultaneously, the Queen, who must avoid arousing the King's attention, is a helpless witness to the theft. The Queen needs the letter returned to her, as it affords the unscrupulous Minister unchecked power over her. In her desperation, she employs the Parisian police to help retrieve it. After many tireless, failed efforts of the police to secure this letter, deducing that the Minister must keep it at his side, the Prefect of the police turns to detective M. Dupin. Both Dupin and his companion, the latter narrating the characters and events in the story, listen to the Prefect's account of the theft. Having experience with 'senseless crimes', Dupin brings a particular perspective to detection methods in solving a case. Although the Prefect describes the letter's contents to Dupin, the reader is only told about the outer envelope. Dupin responds by telling the Prefect to search the Minister's premises again. When the Prefect returns empty-handed, further dismayed at the letter's elusiveness, Dupin, after securing a portion of

DOI: 10.4324/9781003368649-3

the Queen's generous reward, surprises the Prefect by producing the purloined letter. After the Prefect leaves in joyous bewilderment, Dupin then describes to his companion how he obtained the letter.

In Dupin's recap, he speaks on various subjects – such as analysis, deduction, and the epistemological limits of the police – seemingly contradicting himself at times. For Lacan's purposes, there is one significant anecdote recounted by Dupin, namely, the story of a child genius playing a game called 'even and odd'. The game of even and odd centers around one's ability to guess the correct hand in which an opponent has hidden a coin. Dupin additionally expounds on various other topics. He also discloses that he has left a facsimile for the Minister in an envelope containing an unusual note, which refers to Greek mythology. Together, Dupin's discourse contains erudite philology and many paradoxes, all of which are entertaining contributions to Poe's story. Lacan's recounting and summary of the story is as fetching as any of the many articles written about 'Seminar on "The Purloined Letter"' since its initial publication.

Lacan's 'Seminar on "The Purloined Letter"' originally appeared in the journal *La Psychanalyse* (1956a) under the title '*Le séminaire sur "La Lettre volée"*', which was also its name in the French version of the *Écrits*. Both publications include an introduction preceding the main body of the text. The 'Seminar on "The Purloined Letter"' draws heavily on earlier lectures from Lacan's yearly seminar of 1954–1955 (a 'seminar' usually refers to a yearly collection of lectures denoted by the year(s) in which they were taught). He held such yearly seminars for decades. The seminar containing the lessons that focus on 'The Purloined Letter' by Poe is published in English as *The Ego in Freud's Theory and in the Technique of Psychoanalysis* (S2, 1978/1988), often referred to as *Seminar II*. Lacan alludes to these classes in this text from the *Écrits*.[1]

Much of Lacan's seminar of 1954–1955 is devoted to an explication of Freud's *Beyond the Pleasure Principle* (1920/2003).[2] Following the core concepts of Freud's text, Lacan's seminar examines the death instinct and repetition. Along similar lines, in his approach to Poe's story, Lacan points to what he calls the 'symbolic' register to understand unconscious determination and psychological inertia.

In many ways, not all of which can be addressed here, Lacan's seminar of 1954–1955 illuminates the fuller meaning of this essay's aims in the *Écrits*. For example, at the end of Chapter XV, 'Odd or Even? Beyond Intersubjectivity' (S2, 1978/1988:188–190), he has two of his class participants play the game of even or odd while a third person takes notes. Using their feedback, Lacan illustrates how players inevitably develop patterns that dictate the hand he or she uses to hide the coin. The sequence of choices, which are deliberate efforts to deceive the other player, ultimately reveals patterns connected with the 'symbolic inertia' of the unconscious subject, namely the subject's repetition patterns. Trying to figure out this pattern of repetition is a more effective technique than trying to guess where the coin is hidden through certain types of inference (i.e., "If I were him, I would do 'x'"). The latter technique is what Lacan would refer to as being caught up in the imaginary.

Lacan's idea is to highlight the patterns that determine a person's choices, ways that cannot be inferred from appearances or identification with the thoughts of the other. Instead, he emphasizes distinguishing a symbolic reading of a pattern, which he compares to playing a game with a thinking machine (where we could neither identify with the machine nor read any supposed visual cues). In other words, there would be no imaginary support from which to guess. Reflections on the thinking machine segues into Lacan's ideas about the importance of cybernetics, which he addresses explicitly in Chapter XXIII of the same seminar in the lecture 'Psychoanalysis and Cybernetics, or On the Nature of Language' (S2, 1978/1988:294–308). His explication offers an additional perspective on the rationale behind the last three sections of the *Écrits* essay on Poe's story, particularly in the section 'Parenthesis of Parentheses', which deals with formal patterns and sequences. In *Seminar II*, particularly in the class Lacan devotes to 'The Purloined Letter' (S2, 1978/1988:191–205), he speaks more about the silence of the characters and its importance to the success of Poe's plot. In psychoanalytic terms, the inability to speak about particular moments or experiences is called *repression*. Such important insights are also found in the *Écrits* essay, but Lacan does not spend as much time explaining them.

Lacan chose 'The 'Seminar on "The Purloined Letter"' to head off the French *Écrits* against his editor's advice (Roudinesco, 1993/1997:325), causing it to be chronologically out of order in terms of when it was initially written (whereas most other essays are in chronological order). The editor of the *Écrits*, François Wahl, urged Lacan to 'justify' the chapter's placement, and the remarks he makes in the 'Parenthesis of Parentheses' section aim to do exactly that – even though most readers rarely venture beyond the main portions of the text to read the final sections (Fink, 1996).[3] In the introduction to the *Écrits*, the 'Overture to the Collection' (1966b/2006),[4] Lacan points out that his analysis of 'The Purloined Letter' is prophetic of ideas that he later developed.

Neither Lacan's seminar on Poe nor a translation of the full text was included in the first English publication of the *Écrits*. First translated by Jeffrey Melman for *Yale French Studies* (Lacan, 1956b/1972), it featured only the main body of the essay, exclusive of the 'Introduction', which, by the time it appeared in the newest translation of the *Écrits* (1966a/2006), was added and moved to the end (wisely called the 'postface' by Bruce Fink (1996:173)). Despite Melman's omissions in the first translation, his version has served as the basis of many commentaries in English about Lacan, Poe, literature, and psychoanalysis. Strangely, Anglophone critics of French literature and commentators such as Jacques Derrida seldom mention the aspects of Lacan's seminar that do not appear in the initial English translation (Liu, 2010).

American literary and cultural critics have widely discussed this abridged English version of Lacan's 'Seminar on "The Purloined Letter"'. Shoshana Felman (1988) primarily uses this translation to elucidate different forms of reading inspired by Lacan's analysis of Poe's text. Felman's exposition, echoing Lacan, notes that the precarious question of 'how to read' permeates the *Écrits* and is linked to his choice of placing the 'Seminar on "The Purloined Letter"' as its opening essay (1966b/2006:4). For Felman, Lacan demonstrates a different form of reading beyond the typical application of psychoanalytic knowledge or psychobiography, for example, that Poe wrote horror tales to avoid adult sexuality (Felman, 1988). Conceptualization of the relationship between psychoanalysis and fiction implies mutual implication, where each is read through the other.

Even more literary criticism was generated in response to an essay published in *La Carte Postale* called '*Le facteur de la vérité*' (1975a/1980), a critique of Lacan's reading of Poe by famed deconstructionist philosopher Jacques Derrida. The first English translation of this critique, published in *Yale French Studies* 52 as 'The Purveyor of Truth' (1975b), also appeared in 1975. A later translation of the same essay by Alan Bass emerged five years later in *Positions* (Derrida, 1981). In this essay, Derrida suggests that the famous phrase from Lacan's text, 'a letter always arrives at its destination' (30), implies a teleological view of the letter, because Lacan already knows where the letter is going to end up. According to Derrida, the course of the letter and the letter itself resemble Lacan's idea of the phallus – the indivisible over-arching signifier that defines the aims of any text or subject. Given this imputed devotion to a privileged signifier (Lacan's idea of a 'pure signifier', which we discuss below), Derrida asserts that Lacanian psychoanalysis forces its categories on Poe's literary text, where all roads lead to the phallus. Meaning is not disseminated; it is totalized. In Derrida's eyes, the frame of Poe's tale could be set differently, particularly in terms of writing itself. Finally, Derrida is suspicious of Lacan's notion of truth. Other notions, such as the place of the narrator and the place of the body, are also of much concern to Derrida.[5]

While ceding excellent insights on Derrida's part, an essay by Barbara Johnson (1975/1988) addresses many of Derrida's concerns. Her argument is basically founded on cross-readings of the respective writings of Lacan and Derrida. She notes Lacan's ideas of the letter and the phallus are much less rigid and totalized than Derrida asserts. Derrida's 'frame' of literature has its own teleological ends and reductions. She contends Lacan's conceptualization of the letter as one that 'always arrives at its destination' (30) does not mean its destination is pre-ordained. Slavoj Žižek (1992) has also written a piece about the letter always reaching its destination, which brings in relations of contingency and the necessity to understand it.

The letter in Poe's story has many effects on the characters. Like the return of repressed material, Poe's letter determines how the narrative unfolds, the course of each character's actions, and how these actions are recounted. The repetition in Poe's story – the two scenes of theft – is determined by the effects of what is not there, by what is hidden or missing, yet right there on the surface. Like the signifier, the letter is simultaneously present and absent (35).

The 'Seminar on "The Purloined Letter"' is one of the flashpoints between Lacan and his Anglophone audiences.[6] Consequently, such audiences may run across many remnants and texts derived from arguments that literary critics assumed concerning Poe, Derrida, and Lacan (Žižek, 1992; Gallop, 1985). In a compilation that contains several accompanying essays (including an abridged edition of Derrida's critique of Lacan's seminar on Poe), the exegesis of Lacan's texts by John Muller and William Richardson (1988) reflects this bevy of interest in Lacan's reading of Poe. It also contains many carefully researched annotations of the seminar itself, as well as comments on the 'Presentation of the Suite'. For his part, Lacan alludes to a few of Derrida's critiques in an essay called '*Lituraterre*' (1971), where he speaks about the psychoanalytic meaning of the concept of the letter and the psychoanalytic notions of writing and inscription. In one of the editions of the French *Écrits*, Lacan also refers to Derrida's understanding of writing versus his own conception of the letter (Johnson, 1975/1988:220). In neither case is Derrida mentioned by name (Laurent, 2007). Lacan's theory of writing is reflected in his idea of a letter that emerges within the psychoanalytic process of reading what resides within the analysand's speech. It requires some deductive abilities, like Dupin's detective work. Still, it is not the same idea of writing found in deconstructionist philosophy.

In sum, the 'Seminar on "The Purloined Letter"' is intellectually prescient in Lacan's own estimation, a factor that may account for his strong inclination to make it the leading chapter of the *Écrits*. Bruce Fink's translation of his essay into English faithfully follows the format of the French *Écrits*, including the additions Lacan crafted for the French version, and the re-ordering of the leading essay and 'Introduction' that follows.

There are four sections of the 'Seminar on "The Purloined Letter"'. The first section is Lacan's 'seminar', which is devoted to expounding Poe's text. The next three sections situate the first part – namely the 'Presentation of the Suite', the 'Introduction', and the 'Parenthesis of Parentheses' sections. These final sections increasingly turn to how one can understand the psychoanalytic dimension of Poe's work in terms of interrelations related to chance, probability, and cybernetics 'to figure out how a formal language determines the subject' (31).

Themes in the text

Providing a summary of the themes in this wonderful essay poses some problems, given the rich background of Lacan's 'Seminar on the "Purloined Letter"'. First, one needs to present the text's ideas as they relate to psychoanalysis, not literature *per se*. One must translate ideas from the story and the paradigm of cybernetics presented in the postface into a clinical context. Lacan affirms that psychoanalysts must receive their ethical and foundational orientation as particular to psychoanalytic praxis. In this proclamation, Lacan speaks to analysts, not literary critics or those involved in computer science and mathematics

(Glynos & Stavrakakis, 2001:691–692).[7] Given this lecture is addressed to a clinical audience, the 'Seminar on "The Purloined Letter"' is about foundational ideas concerning the nature of the unconscious subject and the practice of analysis.

Second, though prescient on many fronts, Lacan's text should be read as a way of understanding his ideas as they were articulated at the time. In this case, the text's three mainsprings are 1) the many meanings of the letter, 2) the autonomy of the symbolic and repetition automatism, and 3) the question of 'reading' the 'writing' of the analysand or of a text.

Even though 'Seminar on the "Purloined Letter"' represents an earlier period of Lacan's teaching, it remained a constant reference point for him, yet foundational on its own terms. His ideas on the letter were continually evolving, and this essay prefigures many concepts found in later publications.[8] Some of his subsequent preoccupations include a different idea of the 'one', a conceptual foreshadowing of the '*petit objet a*' (or simply '*object a*'), and the significance of the letter and the 'pure signifier', all of which are fundamental and continue to develop as significant concepts in the Lacanian canon.

One important example of this foreshadowing is repetition and the singularity of the letter. Lacan did not think about the whole person as many psychologists do. Still, he did try to articulate what appears to constitute the particularity of a single subject as 'one'. In an endnote to the 'Seminar on "The Purloined Letter"' (47 n. 10), he notes the question of the one in the face of the division of subjective experience announced by the unconscious. In this slightly ironic endnote, philosophical approaches to the question of the one are contrasted with the idea of a singularity (as in the letter) that he opposes to unity (as in a gestalt) (16, 3).

Over time, Lacan refines his ideas of the letter and its relationship to both the subject and repetition. Repetition requires a doubling, even a tripling, to be such. It thus retroactively creates a sort of set equivalent to a 'one'. Lacan revisits the nature of this 'one', or 'One', concerning repetition in a much later lecture series from 1971–1972 called *The Knowledge of the Analyst* (S19a, 1972). This issue of the one and the many was initially a preoccupation of the Greek philosopher Parmenides (a philosopher who fares a little better than those Lacan dismisses in the endnote referenced above).[9]

Leaving behind what Lacan anticipates in the 'Seminar on "The Purloined Letter"', Lacan's work on Poe also demonstrates how the symbolic dimension, represented therein by the letter, operates autonomously. With its many cybernetic and probabilistic demonstrations, the postface shows how a chain of interdependent *signifiers*, as purely differential marks operating in a network of patterns, recursively repeats itself, with some inherent gaps to its pattern of repetition. Thinking machines produce a repeating series that remains constant until an intervention from 'outside' breaks in at a particular spot. This sort of autonomous recursive repetition is the inertia of the symbolic that Lacan discusses in this lecture. He starkly distinguishes the symbolic inertia of the subject from the imaginary inertia he associates with the mirror stage and the ego.[10] In Poe's story, obtaining the letter entails 'possession' by the letter (22). The letter's possession induces this inertia, manifesting as *repetition automatism* (or *repetition compulsion* as it is called in English-speaking psychoanalytic circles).

Repetition is seen in the letter's displacement in its circulation among the characters. Lacan refers to the repeating positions as intersubjective relays (21). Once Dupin 'reads' the pattern, like the child genius in the game of even and odd, he can ascertain how the Minister must have hidden the letter. Dupin is attuned to Minister D____, while the police examine the premises of the Minister's apartment. As we discuss more fully later, the Minister 'repeats' the Queen's positioning when he has the letter. As Dupin moves up to a center-stage position in the tale, Lacan talks about the movement from 'accuracy' to 'truth', the latter being a truth of the subject (15).

Lacan uses the general plot and details Poe supplies to disentangle the roles of the letter. This letter is a 'pure signifier', in that it is a letter without contents. Poe never reveals the letter's contents to the reader. Instead, its contents can only be surmised by how it affects the characters' actions. For Lacan (17,1), the letter in Poe's tale also functions as an epistle – a quality that Lacan uses to think about how this 'pure signifier' carries subjective weight for both its recipient and its sender (e.g., as with the fetish-like quality of love letters (19,3)). Throughout his reading of Poe, Lacan often uses the idea of the letter interchangeably with the unconscious as a chain of signifiers 'in so far as it wanders about' (S2, 1978/1988:209). However, like the letter, these signifiers do not refer to things or meanings in the sense of worldly referents. Instead, these signifiers are the differential elements that form part of a series propelled by its own logic. The story's characters are merely caught in its wake.

The signifier, as taken up by Lacan, should be distinguished from the sign. Ferdinand Saussure defines the signifier as a 'word image' (Lacan, 1957/2006:416–417): it is given meaning through its differential value with other signifiers. Constrained by their context, each signifier is ultimately conjoined with a concept or *signified* in Saussure's language theory (Dor, 1998). Psychoanalysis has little interest in the everyday agreed-upon meanings of conscious experience that link the signifier to a particularly given meaning (signified). As such, Lacan focuses more on how the unmoored signifier functions on its own terms, without being anchored in semantic definitions, functionality, or theories of intention.

Pausing for a moment to return to *Seminar II* (S2, 1978/1988:196–197), Lacan says in a class from that seminar that the letter in Poe is the subject's unconscious. The essential element of repetition in the story is the letter as purloined or '*en souffrance*' (20,7) as Lacan says – a 'dead letter' as postal circles in the United States say more pessimistically – meaning it is on its way but has not yet arrived. It is not delivered, yet it pervades the story to determine the inevitable transformation of the characters that reveals unconscious knowledge and identifications, as well as fantasies. Here the letter indeed functions as the unconscious.

31

One of the essential points articulated thus far is that Lacan states a concept of the letter in 'Seminar on "The Purloined Letter"' that concerns him throughout his career. The letter must be deciphered insofar as a 'letter' is purloined. The theft marks the subjective division that determines the subject's identifications, actions, and fantasies – pointing to a subject's truths, but not often known in and of itself. Instead, the letter is known in its effects. Thus, one of its essential qualities is that it is a letter *en souffrance* – a letter in waiting or waylaid (there is also an allusion to suffering). The letter is transmitted and simultaneously 'repressed'.

Fundamentally, the King, as both imbecile and ruler (28, 1), is the only one who can fully understand and judge the letter (20,3). Nevertheless, he is and will remain the most unaware. There are positions in language and culture that will always remain blind to the errant, purloined letter. In *L'insu que sait de l'une bévue, s'aile à mourre, 1976–1977*, Lacan speaks yet again about 'The Purloined Letter':

> At no moment has the Minister who has kept this letter in short as a pledge of the good will of the Queen, at no moment has the Minister even the idea of communicating this letter, to the King, for example, who is moreover the only one who would find himself in the position of understanding the consequences. The truth one might say, 'demands' to be said. It has no voice to demand to be said... Absolute knowledge, I would say does not speak at any price.
> (S24, n.d.:2.15.77)

In Poe's story, the letter cannot be spoken of; neither Dupin nor the Minister can say, 'Hand over that letter'. Its effects depend on the letter not being opened and 'used'. The Minister loses his power over the Queen if he cashes out and uses the letter against her. As in the psychoanalytic clinic's work, there is this cycle of repetition – perhaps established through the intersubjective positioning – as the analysand's speech circles around what cannot be said or brought to the 'law' of language. Nevertheless, it has been written, even if the contents are unknown. Analysis as such maintains an essential relationship with *how to read*.

Overall, this essay's first theme is that of the letter in its relation to repetition. The second theme concerns the relation of analytical work with *reading* psychoanalytically and the power of fiction in its subjective truth. Poe's original story of 'The Purloined Letter' contains multiple perspectives and positions within the plot's narration, like the numerous positions by which the analysand's speech marks its supposed author and audience. These layers are evident in the two scenes where the letter is purloined, which the narrator recounts from the other characters' renditions in the story. The reader never witnesses the scene itself, but instead is required to maintain awareness of who is speaking, as well as attention to how the narrator transcribes his or her accounts. One must attend to how Lacan treats Dupin as a reader of repetition and pattern, rather than a character out there seeking his quarry as an entity somewhere in reality.

Dupin makes his contempt for the Prefect's limitations known. What reality does the Prefect create when defining the letter as an object that can be ascribed attributes and then hidden? In Dupin's eyes, the letter functions in relation to the Queen and the Minister, particularly their respective positions vis-à-vis the moment of theft. Dupin is looking for something else, namely what Lacan talks about as the truth of the subject, rather than 'objective' truth.

Poe was fascinated with writing a compelling crime/detective novel that contained a dynamic power outside motivations, eyewitnesses, or grisly crimes (Poe, 2006). In other stories, Dupin often works from witness accounts or newspaper stories. Through the fissures and deductive leads discerned from these accounts, Dupin can reconstruct the crimes. Similarly, Lacan encourages his readers to be alert, not to become enamored by imaginary dynamics where one identifies with others as personalities, heroes, or protagonists, or as complements to oneself. For example, identifying with one's analysand to intuit his or her motives, or even becoming caught up in the analysand's story, are not effective techniques that can be used to read the analysand's unconscious repetitions.[11] One 'reads' the layers of a narrative by attending to who is speaking and how they speak. Through 'the channels of the symbol' (21, 2), one reads the repetition of the signifying chain, identifying elements that may be displaced and forming all too familiar patterns.

In how one reads, Lacan seeks to emphasize the ascendance of the symbolic over the imaginary in creating desire and the subject. As part of the logic of the symbolic, there is a pure signifier, one untamed by a signified – in other words, a signifier out of place and out of joint with the laws ruling meaning and order. Parallel to how a physicist tracks an electron, we can know the letter by its effects, which are revealed through the identifications and desires it displays in its travels (Dor, 1998).

When Dupin speaks of his escapade at the end of the tale, the narrative shows the effects the letter has had on him by revealing his desire. He clearly asks to be read as both deceptive and truthful, which is apparent given his use of contradictory statements and superfluous remarks (29,6). He uses language to play with his addressee. In an analysis, the analyst's keen ear must be able to hear similar posturing and positioning, because the subjective dimension that seemingly motivates a lie or deceptive speech equally implicates an unconscious truth. This supposed subject behind the utterance supplies literature with the subjective truth critical in giving fiction its veracity (Schneiderman, 1991). In most fiction, the supposed subject of each character becomes entangled in the intersections and interstices of the narration, creating the conditions for questions and identifications for the reader (14,5).

As in *Book II: The Ego in Freud's Theory and in the Technique of Psychoanalysis*, Lacan uses cybernetics to understand the autonomous power of the signifier in his analysis of Poe's text.

> Speech is, first and foremost, that object of exchange whereby we are recognized, and because you have said the password, we don't break each other's necks, etc. That is how the circulation of speech begins, and it swells to the point of... constituting the world of the symbol which makes algebraic calculations possible. The machine is the structure detached from the activity of the subject. The symbolic world is the world of the machine.
>
> (S2, 1978/1988:47)

For Lacan's work, the postface clearly marks an essential stage in developing the utility of formalization (Milner, 1991). Given this, it is unfortunate, as Bruce Fink (1996) notes, that most readers pay very little attention to the postface in Lacan's 'Seminar on "The Purloined Letter"'. Lydia Liu (2010) makes the same point about the reception of the last three sections of this seminar. Lacan explicitly and implicitly refers to scholars in the field of cybernetics throughout this lecture and in his contemporaneous teachings. The game of even and odd that C. Auguste Dupin elaborates, and that Lacan adopts as central, thus introduces the cybernetics project into a realm of chance relationships where the subject makes its mark through alternations of presence and absence. Here absence not only opposes presence; the signifying operation also allows signifiers to be absent and present simultaneously. Poe's purloined letter exemplifies this principle. Although the game even and odd is not a perfect analog to what the analyst needs to learn about deciphering the repetition compulsion, it does open the door to understanding how Poe's story and analytical work are 'so powerful in the mathematical sense' (Lacan, 1966b/2006:4).

Lacan's explication marks a stage in his work that eventually leads to his later interest in topology. 'Topology is part of mathematics, which formalizes places and shifts without measurement, but for psychoanalysis, it is a writing of structure' (LaFont, 2004:3). It is not surprising that Lacan mentions in an endnote (48 n. 26), as well as in the 'Overture to the Collection' (1966b/2006:4), that the 'Seminar on "The Purloined Letter"' anticipates the importance of topology. Many Lacanians also note that this lecture is indicative of his developing interest in topology.[12]

The text: Annotations and concepts

(6) The seminar opens with an epithet from *Faust* (Goethe, 1837:1.2458–60): 'And if luck lends itself / And if it sends itself, / Thus mind intends itself'. The final two lines of this verse of the stanza's last line from Faust often presents significant variations in its translation: 'Our jargon with thought

and with reason is burdened' (1837:1.2459–60). Regardless of the translation, the lines that serve as Lacan's epigraph are spoken by the witches' familiars (often presented as monkeys or apes) who are in the witch's kitchen where potions are brewed. The draught Faust will imbibe is accompanied by non-sensical incantations invoking blasphemy and irrational magic powers (Goethe, 1837/2014). The scene of the kitchen as well as the epigraph are words with-out sense, words of animals implying meaning but might be simply gibberish. Yet these liminal utterances evoke the passions of Faust and suggest that the stammering and poetic rhymes possess a different logic from rationality/con-sciousness. In both translations, the animal verses tie meaning to chance utter-ances, which, as the above suggests, is relevant to Lacan's ideas in this lecture.

Aside from the epigraph, Lacan's text on Poe's story is peppered with liter-ary and philosophical allusions, both by Lacan and those borrowed from Poe's story. In addition to tracking these allusions down, there are further complexi-ties. The translator's notes of the *Écrits* astutely bring up many ambiguities and assonances that Lacan uses as part of his teaching. Obviously, what works well rhetorically in French is sometimes harder to convey in English.[13]

The 'Seminar on the "Purloined Letter"' first establishes the signifying chain's psychoanalytic significance, which refers to the linked signifiers or material marks, words, and differential sounds drawn upon in speech. Lacan posits that the signifying chain is at the core of the *repetition compulsion*. The repetition compulsion points to a perplexing set of data gathered from psy-choanalytic experience. Even though specific experiences cause suffering, individuals repeat such experiences directly or indirectly. Such inexplicable actions defy the assumption that the human organism primarily seeks pleasure (Evans, 1998).

For Lacan, the repetition compulsion, or *repetition automatism*, is a mat-ter of the 'insistence of the signifying chain' (6,1). This insistence is not at the conscious disposal of the individual. Repetitions occur following their own rules, autonomous from the conscious agency. 'The *insistence* of the signifying chain [is]...a correlate of the *ex-istence*... in which we locate the subject of the unconscious' (6). This refers to what Lacan calls the 'eccen-tric place' of *ex-istence* as the locus of 'unconscious thought', which is other from, or outside of, the centered subject of consciousness. Lacan's use of *ex-istence* is from the work of German philosopher Martin Heidegger. The Heideggerian notion of the 'standing out' of the human being (*Dasein* or 'Being-there' in Heidegger's lexicon) involves *ex-istence*, which is human as dwelling as an openness in Being. As this opening in Being, each human is separate from all other beings (Harries, 1967). Lacan borrows the term *ex-istence* to express a sense of the human being as discordant with itself and to indicate the *ex-centric* nature of the unconscious subject generated and deciphered in the place of the Other. Here the Other refers to a location removed from the subject's conscious sensibilities and intentions (often called the *locus of the Other* by Lacan). As such, every utterance has this otherness in it, with its unintended twists and turns as heard by the speaker's interlocutor or in the ambiguities of language itself. Lacan and Heidegger differ in the intended meaning of their use of *ex-centric* (Heidegger, 1993).

Moving forward, Lacan emphasizes the distinction between the symbolic and imaginary registers. The imaginary register, based on identifications and dyadic symmetries, cannot be ignored. The insistent chain of signifiers 'appears' through identifications covering the holes and discontinuities within the signifying chain. In Poe's story, these identifications are precise. For example, there are many similarities between the detective Dupin and the Minister D____: both are mathematicians and poets, both 'steal the letter', and both have names beginning with the letter 'D'. However, such appearances, images, counterparts, and little others (the fictional characters of the drama) are not the driving force or determining factors of the story. Instead, the story's logic is the determining factor that organizes Poe's tale, where the placement of the characters is governed by how they act when they have the letter and how they look for the letter in its absence. In this context, the interrelated positions of the characters operate like elements in an interconnected chain.

Next, Lacan refers to fundamental dimensions of psychological structuration, relating them to grammatical and rhetorical effects. As one example, Lacan's notion of foreclosure, from the French *forclusion*, is foundational in his theory of psychosis. This idea of foreclosure began its psychoanalytic journey in the context of 'negative hallucinations' and debates about disavowal as a repudiation of castration. By 1956–1957, Lacan had attached the notion of foreclosure to the absolute exclusion of a fundamental signifier that establishes a psychic function, what he called the *Name-of-the-Father*. The *Name-of-the-Father* instantiates the symbolic order with its rules, regulations, limitations, and impasses that constrain the one who speaks (S3, 1981/1993). This marks a time of transition for the infant, who had previously existed as the signifier or object of the mother's desire. Foreclosure then both functionally and literally relates to the operations of language. Similarly, as Lacan indicates, foreclosure (*forclusion*) in the French language is also attached to a form of speaking that assumes that specific facts no longer form part of reality. Although it is a somewhat antiquated conception, it has a history of being a rhetorical trope (Rudinesco, 1997).[14]

Repression is, of course, 'specific to' the signifying chain, where what is repressed is removed from what is said. Yet, it still returns through various rhetorical tropes, like ellipses, catachresis, assonances, hyperboles, and other innumerable parapraxes of speaking (i.e., the famous Freudian slips of the tongue). Even the censorship of dream work operates through condensation and displacement – mechanisms of dream formation that Lacan frames as the fundamental rhetorical devices of metaphor and metonymy. Negation is obviously an element of language critical to the speaker's inclusion in the spoken. Thus, Lacan strongly affirms the importance of attending to speaking and the logic implied by speaking: the structure, sequences, and peculiarities that pervade speech, instead of the sense toward which it points (e.g., language as an adaptational tool).

(7) When Lacan says, 'it is the symbolic order which is constitutive for the subject' (7,1), he suggests that the basis of psychoanalysis itself is the structure of speech and language qua logic. He clearly relates 'the major determination the subject receives from the itinerary of the signifier' (7,1) to why fiction is possible. If we believe the fiction we read, whether in the form of propaganda or in 'real' fiction, it is because the work of the signifier links us to the actual words we read, supposing for us as readers that a subject exists behind the words that induce us through the consistencies and gaps in its signifying links. We might think the author arbitrarily cooks up a story, but Lacan insists there is a 'symbolic necessity' that drags the reader through its unfolding. Immediately following this allusion to the signifier's path, Lacan turns to a critical moment in Poe's tale, namely Dupin's exposition of the child who so expertly plays the game of even and odd. Here Lacan refers to his seminar of 1954–1955, where 'we very recently gleaned something of importance' (7,3). By examining the game in terms of finding the patterns in how one plays, and by how it shows the logic of Poe's construal of the letter in 'The Purloined Letter', we can see how the game and the story ultimately rely on the features of language that are of interest to Lacan (S2, 1978/1988:7).

In his examination of *repetition automatism*, Lacan introduces another one of his significant threads, the importance of games of chance and probability. One might think of Freud's well-known assertion in *The Psychopathology of Everyday Life* (1901/2003:265) about asking someone to generate a random set of numbers. Eventually, such numbers will prove providential, either to the subject's repressed or conscious self-knowledge. Generally, the game of even or odd introduces how a given symbolic system is constrained in terms of probable outcomes, where the 'order' of arrangements might appear to be governed by chance, but, in fact, where the order mirrors a particular organization that reflects the subject's unconscious in relation to specific outcomes, other people, and so on.

Next, Lacan turns to how Poe's drama is put into place (*mise-en scène*), where he notes the distinction between the narration of the events and the events themselves. Never does the narrator put us, as readers, at the scene without the explicit filter of a character's recounting of it. According to Lacan, this tells us a lot about what Poe may be up to in the story. It is clear from the other two Dupin tales of Poe's trilogy that Poe is intrigued by having Dupin deduce an event from the secondary accounts of the characters or other sources. In other words, never is there an omniscient narrator putting us at the scene. In Poe's 'The Mystery of Marie Roget' (1842/2006), Dupin uses newspaper stories and reports. In 'The Purloined Letter', the real scenes are invisible beyond the narration of the characters. The scenes where the letter is stolen and taken back are played out in silence. Lacan refers to the first 'crime' scene of the story, occurring in the 'royal boudoir' (7,8), as the primal scene.[15] Here, the letter's theft must be suffered in silence, without knowing the meaning of the letter for either the Minister or the Queen. The Minister determines the letter's importance to the Queen merely by espying her emotional reaction and by observing her attempt to hide it from the King.

Analogously, Freud (1918/1966) views the real primal scene as a traumatic and excessively intense witnessing of parental coitus, resulting in effects that cannot be spoken. He discusses the primal scene most extensively in a case history of a Russian aristocrat whom he names 'The Wolf Man', where it is presumably a memory from late infancy that the patient constructs within analysis. It emerges from various sources: a recurring dream of wolves, his childhood memories, his sexual attitude, and a word derived from the servant in his parent's house. It is still problematic for Freud's case whether the infantile sexuality aroused from witnessing the scene indicates the analysand *actually* saw the scene, or if he constructed it through bits and pieces of various experiences. In any case, the primal scene refers to something unspeakable that marks the subject.

(8) Returning to the story, the letter's purloining in the inaugural scene is characterized as traumatic, at least for the Queen. The arrival and theft of the letter threaten the conjugal pact. In the case of royalty, the threat is multiplied because it seemingly transgresses the authority that maintains the law of the land, that is, the fidelity to the ruling monarch. Why is it that the Queen cannot let the King see the letter she is reading? Whatever message the letter conveys, the theft happens without speech, the Minister's 'lynx eye' being a reading of another's *jouissance*.[16]

Before leaving the first scene of the theft of the Queen's letter, he brings up an essential reference to the subjective division. In using the word 'quotient', he seeks to indicate a division that leaves a remainder. The analyst keeps this remainder in his peripheral vision, even if he does not yet 'know what to do with it' (8,3). An errant letter of much interest, but with no known contents, has entered circulation, placed into a circuit of exchange where its effects will now snag others.

The letter entails specific formal properties: 1) without semantic content, the letter induces *jouissance* and 'score[s] [a] hit' (6), to use a line from the epigraph; 2) similar to the letter in the unconscious, it remains unintegrated or unrealized; 3) it is staged within a particular structure: 'three moments, ordering three glances, sustained by three subjects, incarnated in each case by different people' (9-10, 6); 4) its unconscious circuit plays out within this organization of exchange; and, 5) it only exists as such because it is an element of exchange, which bestows its importance. Once one enters the signifier's circuit as an element of exchange, one becomes a divided subject, like the radical change of the Queen, whose self-possession and possession of the letter suddenly take a detour and turn into a blackmail situation.

As emphasized in the text, Lacan wants us to notice that there is a remainder to this division, in this case, the Minister's facsimile. A subject is never wholly

38

subsumed or totally dominated by his or her reception of the letter. Like the Minister's facsimile, there is a part left over. The facsimile is left to deceive the King and hide the fact that the Queen wanted to possess this important letter but has been deprived of it. The remainder left from letters exchanged within the clinic may be enigmatic to the analyst in clinical work, but it should never be neglected. As the reader of Poe finds at the end of the story, this remainder/ facsimile is crucial. According to Lacan, although the 'real' letter is vital, the seemingly incidental replacement, which may seem like debris, should not deter the analyst from keeping said replacement in mind. As a general principle, the throwaway lines and the trash of the analysand's speech comprise the vital material for analytic work (8,2).[17] In this vein, Lacan refers to James Joyce's play on the letter as a litter (17,6).

Lacan's use of the word 'remainder' is a clue for the more seasoned reader. It evokes the *object a*, which he also refers to as a remainder (although he could hardly have meant this at the time). Philip Dravers (2004) speaks of how Lacan teases out of Poe's tale the division of the subject, which we just discussed. The division Lacan highlights produces the letter as a singular signifier, a 'pure signifier' (23), of which the effects do not refer to something in the world, but to the mark made on a subject that enters the circuit of exchange with others (a purloined subject). As Poe's letter is the object that causes the characters' desire, the letter also presages the Lacanian idea of the *object a* as both remainder and cause of desire, which Lacan notes in the 'Overture to this Collection' (1966b/2006:4).[18]

(9) Returning to the narrative, Lacan recounts the *second* scene of the letter being purloined. In this part of the story, Dupin regains the letter by taking it from its hiding place in plain sight while the Minister is distracted. Like the first scene, there is nothing spoken, and Lacan emphasizes this silence again. Dupin replaces the letter with what Lacan calls the 'remainder', an imitation that he also refers to as the *semblant*. The *semblant* has many Lacanian nuances and is associated with the imaginary. The *semblant*, as what the other or object appears to be, becomes more important in Lacan's teaching, as the relationship between appearances and the symbolic becomes critical. Here one sees how the 'fake' letter functions as an imaginary substitute for the absent yet ever-present purloined letter in its symbolic trajectory. The *semblant* hides discontinuities and 'maintain[s] the appearances of a normal exit' (9, 1). The play of the *semblant* in Poe's story functions within the game of possessing or dispossessing the other of the letter to maintain a particular position of the symbolic order (the King in the story).

In Lacan's words, Dupin 'ravishes' the letter from the Minister. Here it is important to notice that Lacan's use of the word 'ravish' anticipates his later remarks on Dupin's behavior, given its relation to violence, sexual enjoyment, plundering, and ecstatic rapture. Therefore, the exchange is not only exemplary of a repeating pattern in an abstract sense, but also deeply implicated in a radical enjoyment that has consequences for at least three characters, namely

Dupin, the Minister, and the Queen, all involved in illicit activities in their involvement with the purloined letter.

Following the chronology of Poe's story to organize his initial exposition, Lacan gives the reader a taste of what can be hidden in the *semblant* by disclosing what Dupin writes to the Minister, which is hidden inside the facsimile envelope. It contains two lines from a play by Crébillon that allude to a horrendous act of savagery brought about by betrayal in the royal court. It reads: '*Un dessein si funeste, / S'il n'est pas digne d'Atrée, est digne de Thyeste*', which translates into English as 'So fatal a scheme, / If not worthy of Atreus, is worthy of Thyestes' (Lacan, 1966a/2006:767). This is the first time any message in the letter is conveyed to the reader, even though it is only a facsimile. At the end of Lacan's exposition on this part of the story, he spends a lot of time discussing the meaning of Dupin's choice of message to the Minister and its relation to the meaning of the letter, both psychoanalytically and concerning the story.

The play that the above message is taken from is Crébillon's interpretation of Atreus and Thyestes' myth. The playwright Claude Prosper Jolyot de Crébillon was famous in his time and had a taste for horror. His rendition of the tale had little sympathy for infidel queens – or 'whores', as he called such women – and apparently presented a rather gruesome version of the infamous dinner.[19] Born into the cursed line of Tantalus, Atreus and Thyestes are twin brothers. Their father, the King, exiles them from their homeland because they have committed fratricide at their mother's request. Settling in Mycenae, Greece, both Atreus and Thyestes vie for the throne of Mycenae through endless machinations, including murder, incest, theft, and various other infidelities. In the most horrific of events of this rather sordid intergenerational tale, Atreus promises his brother reconciliation, preparing the unknowing Thyestes a dinner made from the blood of his own sons as part of a soup (an act of '*sang chaud*'). Atreus then brings the remaining body parts in on a platter (the accounts vary on which parts). Afterward, Thyestes lays yet another curse on the house of Atreus, setting in motion a trail of mishaps into the next generation, specifically to Agamemnon and Menelaus, who became key characters in the Trojan War.

Poe's love of horror may have dictated his choice for Dupin's message. Still, equally important is the content of this facsimile – motivated perhaps by Dupin's fantasies of revenge toward the Minister – itself an account of an intimate yet royal sort of family affair. Dupin's communication to the Minister is also reported at some remove, filtered through an interpretation of a play's interpretation of a myth. It is worth recalling from our earlier discussion of themes and Lacan's own assessment of the story that the question of who is narrating and from whom the words are taken makes a difference. The facsimile's contents, chosen by Dupin, are purloined by Poe from a playwright whose literary fortunes ran the gamut from distinction to utter failure, as did Poe's career and legacy. Many layers are involved; the words of Dupin's message are taken from another source, and their meaning implicates both Dupin and the overall significance of the letter, as Poe might have envisioned its relevance in the story. The Greek myth serves as a backdrop of royal intrigue for Poe, but how it is conveyed is vital as well. Here it may allude to the critical impasses in subjectivity for Lacan during this time (29). Still, the layering of discourse is essential. Psychoanalysts need to know how and to whom a message is conveyed.

(10) Following Lacan's relatively rich recounting of the tale (and after introducing many highly significant concepts), Lacan returns to the theme of repetition. After the Minister's first theft, the letter is now errant. However, it can be tracked as it moves along its seemingly chance course, dictated by the various positions structuring it and its personal meaning to the subject. Lacan describes the ordering of these positions as *moments*; the positions themselves he refers to as *glances*. These are touched on briefly as the three moments, three glances, and three subjects. The first glance refers to the King as the one who does not see, that is, 'a glance that sees nothing' (10, 1); the second glance belongs to the Queen, the one who sees that the Other does not see (i.e., the King as the representative of the law); the third glance is the Minister's, who 'sees that the first two glances leave what must be hidden uncovered to whomever would seize it' (10, 3). The last purveyor of this configuration takes advantage of the comedy of blindness at hand, being the one who, by accident or calculation, sees what the others do not see, thus gaining access to the letter. Not only does the Minister come into possession of the letter, but he also becomes possessed by its meaning (21,4). Like the implications that Lacan's use of the word 'ravish' evokes in his description of the theft, there is an almost demonic quality to the letter as it circulates around the royal court, ever threatening yet remaining in a state of suspension.

Lacan emphasizes that repetition is not only based on an identity of traits but that it is marked out by the intersubjectivity that structures it as well. It is not the case that one person acts like another person because they possess similar traits; instead, there is a path of repetition they share, a position in an interrelated chain of signifiers in relation to something – an 'x' that neither one acknowledges. The links and logic of the symbolic allow for the deciphering of a psychic space of the repetition compulsion, one that is not based on conscious apprehension or any presumed identification with the thoughts of the other – the latter form of identification, upon serious examination, an impossible and preposterous claim (Pavón-Cuéllar, 2010; Fink, 2007; Lacan, 1953/2006). The three positions within the intersubjective matrix that determine the possibility of the letter's creation and repetition correspond to three logical moments or glances. Lacan describes them in terms of temporality in 'Logical Time and the Assertion of Anticipated Certainty' (1945/2006:161–175).[20] The example of a logical puzzle he uses in the chapter on logical time clearly informs his reflections on Poe, especially since Poe's fiction was of great interest to cyberneticists at the time (Liu, 2010). The conceptual and referential points of repetition, the letter, and even Poe's fictional frame are all congruent with the cybernetic theme that follows in the postface.

Shoshana Felman (1987:145) graphs these triadic positions in the drama of 'The Purloined Letter' in a similar manner to Figure 2.1 below.

Her depictions of the characters' triadic rotations recall Lacan's thematic interest throughout this seminar. The characters' blindness or sight is determined by their relation to the 'letter', or, more generally, to a signifier whose contents are unknown. In the first scene, the Minister sees the letter that the King cannot see, whereas the Queen hopes that the Minister does not see it. In the second scene, Dupin sees the letter that the police cannot see, in part because Minister D____ assumes that Dupin will not be able to see the letter that the police have not been able to find. Additional triangles and even quadrangles of circulation could be devised to represent Lacan's formalization of Poe's story. Other schemas show how the letter functions within various contexts, such as the Oedipal triangle and Freud's topography, as well as in the relationships of the characters to the imaginary and the symbolic registers (Felman, 1988:42).[21]

After Lacan's exposition of the glances, he compares the logic of Poe's characters to that of an ostrich ('l'autruche'). Lacan uses the Queen as an example, who thinks she has succeeded in hiding the letter because the King did not catch her. Throughout the essay, Lacan drives home the ascendance of the symbolic over the imaginary from the very beginning. This is essentially what the amusing example of the ostrich seeks to convey. In repression, one attempts to hide specific perceptions and experiences. However, the chain of signifiers cannot be resolved by resorting to the imaginary alone (hidden in the visual domain), as tempting as it may be for both humans and ostriches. Against World War II's backdrop, Lacan uses the example of the ostrich to note Austria's erroneous assumption, namely, that by remaining blind to Germany's intentions, they would thereby avoid the immanent political danger that was looming on the

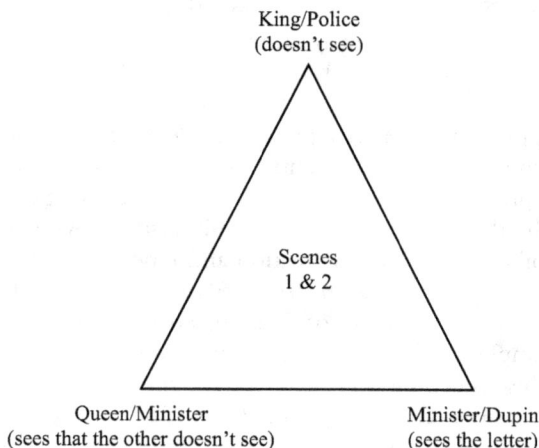

Figure 2.1 The three functional positions of the characters.

horizon. Lacan's neologism of '*l'autruiche*' contains several word plays and allusions. Whether evocative, illustrative, or both, such plays on words are critical to Lacanian clinical work, which may explain why Lacan frequently employs them in his teachings.

Following this brief digression, Lacan articulates what he calls the 'inmixing of subjects' (10,6), continuing a thread he began in *Seminar II* where he discusses scenes of one of Freud's own dreams found in *The Interpretation of Dreams* (1900/1953). The 'Dream of Irma's Injection' involves many figures from Freud's life. Freud concludes these figures are alter egos (S2, 1978/1988:161–171). These alter egos represent positions one has toward one's unconscious knowledge, generating associations in Freud's self-analysis that ultimately lead Freud to meanings associated with the oneiric image of a chemical formula in this same dream (Freud, 1900/1953:116). In an endnote to Lacan's essay on logical time, he refers to a collective subject inseparable from others in its surroundings, another form of 'inmixing'. In a later paper, published under the title 'Of Structure as the Inmixing of an Otherness Prerequisite to Any Subject Whatever' (1970), Lacan speaks of inmixing again as the issue of how the heterogeneous and contradictory nature of language induces gaps and fissures in subjectivity, evoking the division inherent to the making of the subject and in his communications with others.

Others receive and send messages in response to what we have said and attending to the fact that we are saying something to them. These interlocutors, therefore, become part of our subjective positioning, as a sort of signifier with no real referent except that of the speaker's desire. The displacement of the signifier of desire in the signifying chain reveals an interdependent network of positions for the subject, and their combinatory sequence points to the operation and placement of the letter. In the same way, we might say that the subject's unconscious desire is found in the displacements and condensations of dreams. The letter appears out of place and cannot be accessed immediately through its contents but in its effects. The real quarry is learning how to *read* displacement and structure in the interactions between subjects.

> A letter is something that is read... as a sort of extension (prolongement) of the word... But it not the same thing to read a letter as it is to read....in analytic discourse... that which is read beyond what you have incited the subject to say, which is not so much to say everything as to say anything.
>
> (S20, 1975/1998:26)

> These effects may be signifying, that is emerge in fantasies or speech. The pure signifier may be cast..., as the signifier that mediates the Other's desire.
>
> (Lacan, 1972:1.13.71; Lacan, 1957/2006)

(11) Lacan does not neglect the broader frame of culture as a proper commentary for psychoanalysis. In 'The Function and Field of Language in Psychoanalysis' (1953/2006), he comments on the modern hero, our infamous superheroes. He shows a continuing awareness of the changing place of subjectivity, not in historicist terms, but as emergent within specific parameters defined culturally, i.e., by the status of the knowledge, authority, and resources of a subject. Something is reflecting the contemporary culture in Poe's rendition of Dupin. Above the fray, Dupin is a dandy, but Lacan asks if this is really the point, although as a cultural icon we may admire the detective.

Lacan also notes that the suspense of Poe's story does not engage the reader. Almost all aspects of the crime are known after the first few pages. Added to this, when Dupin recounts the story of how he managed a successful resolution of the case, it does not ring true. So, if Dupin is not the dandy-hero and the story holds little suspense, then Lacan asks why it is that the story is so captivating. He suggests that maybe there is something else. Perhaps the letter does something to each of the characters: those who can and cannot see, those who steal the letter, and those who hold it, including the story's so-called hero, Dupin, who in his own way gets duped by the letter as well (27).[22] Dupin is equally possessed by the position in which the errant and unlawful letter puts him, to put it another way.

(12–13) In his discussion of Dupin, Lacan makes an important distinction earmarked in the themes section above. On the one hand, there is the 'silent drama' of the repetition around the theft; on the other hand, we have Dupin's (or Poe's) exploitation of the 'properties of discourse'. These two strains draw us into Poe's narrative. Initially, the theme is about the structure of repetition. Now there is an additional reflection on the intersubjective effects of how one speaks. Are we to believe the Prefect's account of the Queen's tale? Lacan suggests that Dupin's sarcastic response to the execution of the theft and the methods of the police are important to note. Moreover, the police, in being unable to hear themselves speak, are contrasted with Dupin's speech on the crime, which is full of the 'torrent of aporias, eristic enigmas, paradoxes, and even quips presented to us as an introduction to Dupin's method' (13, 7).

Such layering of the crime accounts, as crucial to detective work, is evident in all three of the Dupin series of stories (Felman, 1988; Poe, 2004; Poe, 2006). The impact of language and style aborts any kind of communication between humans, resembling the communication of bees, a source of fascination for cyberneticists, cognitive scientists, linguists, and information theorists. The bees' waggle dance, which presumably communicates to the fellow drones where the honey is, implies that bees pass along gestalts/maps of an area – thus, Lacan calls this form of communication imaginary.

Lacan puts forward that there are objects for humans as there are for bees. Humans communicate about things by giving directions and so forth, despite 'the disintegration they undergo through [their] use of symbols' (13, 1). Unlike the bees' waggle dance, human chatter is not without subjective inflections, misunderstandings, and inducements encountered to others as addressees of the letter (whether such ambiguity is intended or not). One might think of the difference between receiving directions from a GPS instead of a married couple figuring out the directions together while on a drive to an unknown location. The nuances and multiple levels of human communication underlie Lacan's remarks on the intersubjective difficulties given humans' subjection to the symbolic foundation of human communication (e.g., when discussing the best way to arrive at a new location). This same deference to the interference of symbolic mediation also founds his remark that when people think they are relating to the same object, it is through a hatred of the shared object, person, or group, which is established through a shared belief in the ideal. For example, the seemingly shared hatred of the Jews was mediated by the Nazi ideal of the Aryan through a shared refusal of certain characteristics of the hated object. This ineffable element mediates all the communication between members of such groups. Concerning hatred and ideals, there is an obvious allusion to Freud's 'Group Psychology and the Analysis of the Ego' (1921/1955) by Lacan where Freud discusses how masses of crowds bond by using ideas from significant theorists of mass psychology (e.g., Gustave LeBon), in addition to developing his own theory of group identifications.

Lacan's remarks on the nature of communication lead to the point that Lacan has been articulating throughout. He wants to demonstrate how the subject addresses another, the constraints of language that modulate his communication, and the styles of speech that all reveal a sort of subject that can inadvertently speak beyond his intentions and orient his remarks in terms of how they will be received. A subject may lie or try to lie, yet in doing so will still tell the truth. Imagine an analysand that fabricates the dreams they tell their analyst. Despite the fictional nature of these dreams, the analysand will nevertheless have to choose the material, even if these constructions originate from outside sources. When Dupin recounts his recuperation of the letter, he is obviously 'playing' his audience, with his credulous companion qua narrator serving as the foil. Nonetheless, Dupin shows his desires. The letter has positioned him so he now can be read in the same way he 'read' the Minister.

In Dupin's rather aggrandizing account of his pilfering, unlike the Prefect's factual account, one cannot read the passages or the narrator's admiring transmission of Dupin's exploits without realizing that Dupin is revealing himself as a subject. He is speaking as if he knows he is heard and/or interpreted similar to the Jewish joke that Lacan uses to explicate Dupin's rhetorical tactics. In this joke, two men meet at a train station. When the first man asks the second where he is going, he assumes the response will be a lie, so that when the second one answers, 'To Cracow', the other reproaches him: "'If you say you're going to Cracow, you want me to believe you're going to Lemberg. But I know that in fact, you're going to Cracow, so why are you lying to me?'" (Freud, 1905/1958:115; 13). In other words, the listener assumes that the speaker will lie; in a doubling back, the speaker tells the truth, knowing that it will be taken as a lie. This inescapable loop through 'how' we are heard in what we say presumes the speaker and listener's subjectivity. Language, as the Other, in its ability to allow for deception, alongside the necessary position of an interlocutor qua receiver of the message, renders the Other as Absolute (13, 6).

At this point in the story, Poe detours from treating the narrative as a matter of accuracy and enters the domain of subjective truth. Just as we believe that the fictional characters are real personages (14, 6), we also believe in the narrator's perspective of Dupin's report. Dupin's actual reasoning in scene two, as Lacan says, bears examination (13, 5). Unlike the Prefect's account, ridiculed as pompous realism, the narrator treats Dupin's account like the gold standard of 'truth' in the realist sense. However, Lacan wonders if it is not a narrative closer to the structure of the Jewish joke.

For starters, take a distinction Lacan brings up regarding the Word and Speech. Bruce Fink, the translator of the *Écrits*, notes that the poles of the Word versus Speech are probably alluding to 'The Function and Field of Speech and Language in Psychoanalysis' (Lacan, 1953/2006:230). Dupin speaks from a sophisticated position of the Word. Lacan articulates here and in the previous paper that the Word represents the covenant, bond, and intersubjectivity of speech and thus implies a relationship to subjectivity as such. The evocation of the Word by Lacan here suggests that the speech of Dupin represents the wager of a subjective position, which is found in the subject's redaction and re-emergence in the field of the Other as language. Both other and Other (of language) can be viewed as the befuddled decoders, whether in the Jewish joke or in the analyst's position in the transference. One must, therefore, attend to the style of communication (for example, even though the police Prefect, supported by the illusion that reality exists, is obliviously direct, Dupin nonetheless uses the Prefect's discourse to decode the Minister's actions). Similarly, the reader can decipher the cagey Dupin, whose retractions and obscure musings can only be approached from the Other's direction, where the listener/reader both does and does not take him at his word (so to speak).

(14) Lacan reflects on Dupin's excessive descriptions of how he figures out the letter's location and fools the Minister. Dupin fools the narrator/reader like he fools the Minister and tricks us into believing that the admission of his *modus operandi* is not itself an illusion (14). There is no getting around the Other, which is, in turn, fundamental to a new sort of logic of speaking and language that implicates the otherness in any address. The fact of 'saying to' another (the enunciation, as Lacan borrowed it from Jacobson)[23] evokes the ascendance of a pact. This covenant now stands as our guarantor.[24] Our relation to others is underlined by this pact, along with its constraints and affordances. The link between the letter and the law does not only refer to the vulnerability of the royal couple to the Minister's theft but, in Lacan's view, to the very constitution of the subject for all who enter the symbolic realm.

In Dupin's cagey monologue, he displays his erudition by showcasing the names of French philosophers, the makers of maxims, and writers (Lacan dutifully makes note of these luminaries). Dupin wryly states that the technique of the child genius, who can discern the hand of the hidden coin by reading the preferential strategies of the other child through an identification with the other's way of thinking (analysis of their physiognomy), reveals the 'spurious profundity' of such writers and luminaries (Poe, 2006:606). Whether as authors of maxims (e.g., Chamfort, La Rochefoucauld, La Bruyère) or of new epistemological views (Machiavelli or Campanella), they were merely able to pen sayings that reinforced what the public already believed or wanted to think about itself. The paradox of Chamfort's maxim, that whatever is believed by the public is foolish because it 'suits' the majority, affirms this point since obviously, most people will subscribe to this maxim, thereby rendering them part of the foolish public (14, 4). In contrast, the child genius goes beyond such appeals to human vanity by discerning the other's unknown pattern.

Dupin's subsequent lucubrations on etymology generate even more ambiguity. In Latin, *ambitus* means a going around, *religio* means exactness. *Honesti* means being respectable or becoming (Muller and Richardson, 1988:90). Still, they can also have more exalted meanings, for example, the ambition that gets us on a path relative to an ideal and a goal. In this context, Lacan mentions the Roman poet and philosopher Lucretius, who held cynical views of religion concerning the relationship between church and state. Cicero, a fan of Lucretius, was noted for his attempt to integrate philosophy with rhetoric. Cicero was an adept orator, but for him, philosophy was secondary to politics. Cicero's ambitions led to many exiles and alliances, placing in question his *modus*, which may have been either honorable or ambitious.

Lacan returns to Dupin's mocking words at the end of 'The Seminar on "The Purloined Letter"'. Lacan remarks that being ambitious is not the only way to go around in circles. Dupin and the Minister both become immobilized. When they 'hold' the letter, they are caught in its circuit and immobilized by its power. Honesty obviously is not the course of the Queen, the Minister, or Dupin. Otherwise, why not give the letter to the King? Sacred ties pull us in numerous directions. In sum, Lacan shows us what Dupin clearly indicates: that words do not appear to mean what they say. The "truth" lies elsewhere.

These asides and their (il)logical implications alert Lacan to the possibility that Dupin is 'revealing by concealing' (or vice-versa) by giving us, as readers, what we want to hear. However, the truth may reside elsewhere. Dupin's elaborate explanations and the topics he invents to convince the reader veil the subject revealed in his ramblings. For the naïve reader, as a Bohemian detective, Dupin's character plays on the same structure of belief as seeing more typical imaginary heroes as 'real personages'. It is just more nuanced as Dupin tries to throw off the reader, leveraging the readers' identification with the stalwart belief in Dupin exemplified by the narrator/companion.

(15) Thus, the deceitful aspects of Dupin's wandering narrative may also unmask a truth – a truth revealed by the interplay of disclosure and concealment. So, at this point, Lacan can easily introduce Heidegger's concept of *alethes*, which refers to the idea that the truth of a thing is revealed through its place in the opening of the world by means of human action and care.[25] Truth is not an accurate description of objects. Is Dupin obfuscating his message through his descriptions? Is the truth hiding on the surface of his words, digressions, and contradictions? Or rather, as Lacan says in 'The Subversion of the Subject and the Dialectic of Desire':

> [A]nimals show that they are capable of such behavior when they are being hunted down; they manage to throw their pursuers off the scent by briefly going in one direction as a lure and then changing direction. This can go so far as to suggest on the part of game animals the nobility of honoring the parrying found in the hunt. But an animal does not feign feigning. It does not make tracks whose deceptiveness lies in getting them to be taken as false, when in fact they are true – that is, tracks that indicate the right trail. No more than it effaces its tracks, which would already be tantamount to making itself the subject of the signifier.
>
> (Lacan, 1960/2006:683)

We are dealing with the question of Dupin's desire and thus with the sort of truth that interests Lacan – the truth as an encounter with the unconscious subjective conditions that render the individual's world, namely, the logic of one's subjectivity.

For C. Auguste Dupin, much is contained in the preliminary session, so to speak, which is the first dialogue between the Prefect, narrator, and Dupin. Dupin repeats the Prefect's exclamations about the case appearing to be so very self-evident, so simple, and yet so odd. These are clues for Dupin and tips for aspiring analysts as well (Shane, 1997). Lacan follows up on Dupin's rather derisory remarks about how the Prefect thinks criminals operate, in addition to his somewhat 'blind' and impoverished sense of where something may be concealed. Taking the blindness of the Prefect as evident, Dupin's searches of the Minister's room are compared to a parlor game involving maps, where the names of cities, provinces, and so on are read from a map. Dupin remarks that the winner of this game is the one who sees the apparent type – the large type used as an overlay on the map, rather than the tiny type that seems more obscure. All Dupin's strange ramblings about deductions, his own cagey positioning in his remarks, and his less-than-kind assessment of the police show that the search for something is not always a matter of finding it in physical space, according to Lacan. Instead, one finds what the other hides through the logic of their subjective choices. As Lacan says, 'the police have looked *everywhere*' (15, 7) in terms of physical space. However, the letter can only be found if we can see that it is not like something occupying regular space.

(16–17) Lacan relates the Prefect's ideas on searching and finding what is hidden (his blindness) to a particular conception of space. This is extremely important because the space of the police here is obviously smugly objective. It is a space that stands still as we measure it, rather than one that could be graphed otherwise through a mathematical set of coordinates, i.e., a space beyond commonsense notions. When Lacan speaks of 'space itself shed[ding] its leaves like the letter' (17, 3), the conjunction of space to a mathematical mapping – like letters, positions, and placeholders – is again evoked as a way of creating and reading topological space (Dravers, 2004; Johnson, 2013).

As far as space and place are concerned, and there is an evolving notion of space being developed here – the letter possesses the property of 'nullibiety', a quality of absence, of no-whereness (16, 1). Lacan's reference to nullibiety conveys a vibrant concept. Bishop Wilkins, the 17th-century scholar who coined the word, was a forerunner of binary information theory. He defined nullibiety as the evocation of absence relating to a combinatory, a concept now linked to Umberto Eco's semiotics (47 n. 8). This conception of absence introduces the signifier as a signifier, which 'will *and* will not be wherever it goes' (17, 2). Again, it is not a matter of space in the physical sense, but, instead, a 'psychic' space that organizes what is hidden and seen as dictated by the subject's unconscious. In 'The Seminar on "The Purloined Letter"', the unconscious is represented by the letter's movement as a chain of signifiers and intersubjective relays of repetition. Lacan's references to Bishop Wilkins, nullibiety, and his oblique allusions to coding and semiotics present how Poe's tale and Lacan's textual analyses are being pulled toward the cybernetic finish that constitutes its basis.

For psychoanalysts, Lacan establishes that the letter in Poe is not an object hidden in physical space. The letter functions as a pure signifier without content made operative through the structured repetition of three rotating positions. Lacan's letter does not refer to an object but to an intersubjective exchange that implicates the subjectivity found in the pact between speaking beings.

Ultimately, Lacan articulates the many facets of the letter as a psychoanalytic concept. He enumerates the letter, possessing many forms, as typographical, as a mere mark holding a place, and as defining a 'man of letters' versed in the arts that produce the truth of desire (Milner, 1991; Schneiderman, 1991). The letter is literal; it is to the letter, devoid of sense – a letter at the post-office awaiting delivery, *en souffrance*, and therefore tied to suffering. The letter is odd and out of place, in limbo between sender and addressee, beyond the realm of sense. In other words, it is waylaid or purloined. Lacan makes this point repeatedly, and it is the reason for his extensive etymology on Poe's choice of the term 'purloined'.

For Lacan, it is important to note that the police's visually bound space and the space of the purloined letter are joined in his conception of the symbolic

49

order. Something cannot be out of place unless there is a symbolic organization to that placement. The symbolic coordinates that indicate the letter should be there equally inform us that the letter is 'missing'. Such coordinates are part and parcel of how a letter makes its trace, which can help us locate its 'hiding' place no matter how odd or self-evident.

Thus, an analyst who listens to the analysand's letters listens as a 'man of letters'. The analyst accomplishes this by listening for a chain of signifiers, for a letter, the meaning of which is not referential but borne through the various intersubjective positions in the reality of the analysand. The letter is not manifest, but *en souffrance* (is purloined) from its original or rightful place. Regardless of its form – whether it is typographical, a matter of letters as culture, or an epistle – a letter is non-partitive; one does not receive some letter.

(18–19) One cannot seek the letter through an investigation of appearances by looking for something that fits a theory. Instead, one must (metaphorically) look for a scrap of paper, something which seems like debris. As Lacan says, echoing Joyce, 'a letter, a litter' (17, 6). Dupin's method must be that of a psychoanalyst, at least at first. In all kinds of ways, the letter in Poe's story speaks to the sorts of letters that the analyst must decipher. 'Would that it were the case that writings remain, as is true, rather, of spoken words [*paroles*]: for the indelible debt of those words at least enriches our acts with its transfers' (19, 1).

Lacan insists that speaking creates letters, which is particularly evident in his gloss of *scripta manent* (writing stays) versus *verbes volant* (words fly). Do words fly? Well, yes and no. Words stick because they incur debts. A mother says, 'I wished I never had you', and the debt is incurred or transferred. These are inscribed words. In this sense, writings scatter. As the translator's notes helpfully reveal (Lacan, 1966a/2006:769), there are many French allusions present in Lacan's comparison of writing and words (19). Lacan speaks of checks written called '*traites (ou chèques) de cavale*'. In the French idiom, 'cavalry' checks are never meant to be paid. There is also an allusion to blank checks, which can incur inestimable debt. We are swarmed with these loose, flying letters in the manner of a cavalry's mad charge (or munitions) hitting whoever is in their path. To make this concrete, Marc Vappereau (2012) conveys Lacan's observation that 'parents never hear themselves yelling'; these flying letters are incurring debts that will never be paid or that will remain infinite debts. In this light, one can see Lacan's point about love letters. Do they belong to the one to whom they are addressed or to the sender? Why do we want our love letters returned after the love loses its luster? The letter is not information but is the fact that we are in love. The letter is the material transport of that love, of a covenant.

Concerning the power of these letters, Lacan calls to mind the Knight of Eon (1728–1810), whose amorous engagements were intertwined with high-level espionage and embarrassing love letters produced by his efforts. The letter is wayward in the eyes of the law. The King is blind, and the letter escapes lawful judgment. As Lacan says, the letter situates the Queen 'in a symbolic chain foreign to the one which constitutes her loyalty' (19, 7). Further, Lacan states that 'nothing concerning the existence of the letter can fall back into place without the person whose prerogatives it infringes on having pronounced judgment on it' (20, 3), which, in this case, is the King.

(20–21) The errant letter, while out of the King's purview, rules those who hold it; simply stated, the letter possesses them. To explain this idea, Lacan elaborates further on the meaning of 'purloined', which is critical to the meaning of the letter. As a letter *en souffrance*, it is waylaid, or not yet arrived. It functions almost like an encrypted operator, its exact contents subordinate to how it alters the recipient. As the letter makes its rounds, the characters' identifications and actions are evoked and disclosed by their actions. We see that the Minister and Dupin seem to share a relationship of rivalry and similarity (in their genius). After obtaining the letter, both find themselves bound to the Queen and her secrets in ways that profoundly affect them. Poe suggests as much in the inserted message left by Dupin for the Minister, where the saga of Atreus and Thyestes is evoked. The two Greek figures, after all, were brothers in crime, banished from the Kingdom for obeying the wishes of the Queen against those of the King.

All the letter's effects are potent. The Minister sees the Queen's emotional reaction regarding the King and the letter. After taking the letter, the Minister seems strangely immobilized. Dupin, the rational detective, is unexpectedly vengeful. According to Lacan, the letter is 'the *true subject* of the tale' (21, 1). The letter, that is, our unconscious, will unfold along its interlocked chain of signifiers as an autonomous relay. Meaningless except in its relations, it will intervene and impose itself on the actors and their emotions, regardless of their traits.

(22–26) Lacan explicates these effects more specifically for the Minister and Dupin. The Minister can only ransom the letter if it is nearby and stupidly bases his plan's success on his knowledge of police methods. He has a *modus operandi* very similar to that of the Queen, hiding it in plain sight. Yet the Minister does not wager that another can espy what he has done, as he saw through the Queen's maneuvres. So again, he mistakenly repeats the Queen's maneuvers. From the reverse perspective, the Minister's possession of the letter leaves the Queen terrified that he, a man outside the law, can or will do anything. The police view him similarly.

Nonetheless, the Minister becomes ensnared in the ennui and inaction, virtually caught in the implications of possessing the letter. The Minister's stance keeps the pure signifier in holding, given that the contents remain unknown. Taking a different tack, Dupin trades one pure signifier for another, more specifically, the letter for a cash payment. In this regard, Lacan compares Dupin to an analyst.

The facsimile, or leftover, replaces the missing letter with a chosen deception. In that gesture, the letter forces a particular revelation. Lacan suggests that one attends to these seemingly useless replacements, which, in the story, are the debris of fake letters supplied by the characters. As part of the Minister's disguise, the letter is torn, chafed, and changed to a letter addressed to him by a woman. Has his adoption of a position that resembles the Queen's entailed a further feminine transformation occasioned by the letter? The reference to the diplomat, the Knight D'Eon, who disclosed embarrassing letters from royalty while disguised as a woman, intimates the question of the feminine. Is this feminization part of what happens to the Minister as well? Lacan characterizes the letter in the Minister's office as an immense female body. All Dupin needs to do is undress this woman and cast his eyes on the letter. The femininity Lacan attributes to the Minister seems more pronounced given that his position edges closer and closer to the previous position of the Queen.

While the Minister is 'possessed by the letter', Lacan attributes other feminine attributes to him. These attributions say as much about Lacan's ideas of femininity as they do about the Minister *per se*. This is not a matter of the famous Yin and Yang, where man and woman complement each other. The Yin, associated with the feminine, is characterized as shadowy, while the Yang is associated with hot light. Thus, Lacan's evocative imagery of shimmering shadows and flashing light (22) reflects these Chinese principles. Yet, with Lacan, the feminine/masculine are not complementary principles but instead femininity aligns with the liminal. In this regard, Poe's letter, as feminizing, anticipates the littoral and liminal position of the letter that Lacan elaborates later (for example, in '*Lituraterre*' (1971)).

In terms of raw affective power on the characters, the letter possesses a *noli me tangere*, an expression by Jesus to Mary Magdalene from the Bible (John 20:17) meaning 'do not touch me'. Lacan compared it with the numbing sting of a stingray in one of his allusions to Plato's symposium, *Menes* (Muller and Richardson, 1988:95). The letter does seem to numb the characters that hold it. Under its influence, the Queen is left helpless. The Minister waits (keeping the letter but unable to cash it out without losing his power). Dupin acts in odd and irrational ways.

(27–30) The effects that the letter has on Dupin are striking. He returns the letter to the Prefect once the police chief shares the Queen's reward. Beforehand, Dupin is immobile because he must maintain his so-called 'neutrality' toward the royal couple. Consequently, he acts similarly to the Queen when she occupied the same position. In transference, the analysand continuously sends the analyst purloined letters that the analyst must hold. By taking money instead of entering the game, the enjoyment or peril that comes with its possession is thereby neutralized. The analyst holds letters without allowing them to have free rein in their own unconscious fantasies, identifications, and signifying networks. Ostensibly, Dupin empties the letter of any meaning that it might have for him personally by taking the police chief's money.

Dupin adds a message to his facsimile (one to which the reader is privy). He rebuffs the Minister by inscribing some lines from a play by the French playwright, Crébillon: *Un dessein si funeste, / S'il n'est pas digne d'Atrée, est digne de*

Thyeste.[26] Momentarily ignoring the fact that Lacan changes one of the words in the first line when he presents them for the second time, we can still see the violence that pervades this inscription's meaning. The myth of the two brothers recounted earlier shows the extent of the horror contained in the context of this notation. In the 'Seminar on "The Purloined Letter"', Lacan frequently employs the word 'ravish' in the latter parts of his literary exegesis. Dupin 'ravishes' the letter from the Minister; the letter 'ravishes' its possessor. Lacan's use of 'ravish' suggests the unseemly and unlawful enjoyment that accompanies the letter's theft and possession. (Thus, not only is the letter purloined *en souffrance* because it is waiting to be read, but it is also ravished in the sense of generating an excessive and even violent enjoyment.) When Lacan changes Crébillon's lines, he substitutes *destin* (destiny) for *dessein* (design). Destiny fits in nicely with Lacan's idea of the letter as marking the subject's fate, willingly or unwillingly. Although he explores this change of the words' implications, the note is still extremely revelatory in either rendition.

After repeating and altering Crébillon's passage, Lacan speaks of the relentless rule of the signifying chain's logic and its displacements as it winds along its path in stirring us 'at the bidding of [its] bonds' (29, 4). For example, recall the horror and tragic sacrifice plaguing generation after generation in the house of Atreus. Such curses are likely to be *en souffrance* (in suffering) and are delivered to the analyst in the transference.

To account for *his* sense of vengeance against the Minister, to paraphrase Poe, Dupin asserts that the Minister had done him an evil turn in Vienna, which he had not forgotten. Like the cycle of betrayal between Thyestes and Atreus, Dupin engages the Minister in a dynamic of vengeance.

For Lacan, Dupin's nasty note suggests a feminine type of rage. The Minister breaks a social pact by intervening in the covenant between the Queen and the King. He puts a letter into circulation that needs to be cached to maintain order in the kingdom. The Minister plays the Queen, whose fantasies of the Minister's mastery and amorality are evoked. Moreover, Dupin is fond of the Queen (i.e., a partisan (29)). Therefore, he is incensed that the social ideals have been so compromised – the mystery of the signifier reduced to rubbish and the medium of blackmail. In general, Lacan notes that the feminine owes some of its charms to the law of the signifier because something is left in abeyance, and the feminine position is only partially revealed. Finally, Dupin is jealous because the Minister has the Queen at his mercy. This rage shows Dupin's love and feminine identification. These points indicate yet another axis of identification: that between Dupin and the Minister.

Altogether, these strains motivate the note to the Minister found in Dupin's facsimile. The sordid background of Dupin's chosen words, as you might recall, involves royal infidelity and a scene in which Atreus feeds Thyestes the blood of his own son.

If the letter in Poe's tale were placed on its proper course, it would go to the King. But instead of going there, it goes to the police, the not always so lawful enforcers of the law (28). It may be that some errant letters are destined to be overlooked by the King. His exalted status necessarily entails certain blindness. As the letter is kept by the Queen and exchanged for cash, it remains an empty signifier or rather a signifier deprived of any signification. What is the other face of such a signifier, one unmoored from the laws of language and its constraints? According to Lacan, this is one's question when one is in the place of one who is blind and subject to the letter in all its power.

What one always gets 'blind-sided by' are the machinations of those letters that we inadvertently bear; the letters that, like the unconscious, weave our lives within the traumas and accidental events that fuel our sense-making and speech. Referencing Aristotle, Lacan borrows the term *tyche* to capture that sense of a chance encounter, which he later develops extensively in *The Four Fundamental Concepts of Psychoanalysis* – changing the spelling to *tuché* (S11, 1973/1981). As demonstrative of the nature of our protection against this intrusion of chance and speech, Lacan recalls Scheherazade, the heroine of *The Arabian Nights* (Burton, 2004). Like her, we must construct entertaining stories for the Other to keep her death at bay.

The letter as absent signifier dictates our narratives and displacements, allowing us to mask the inevitable reality of the signifier's other side, namely of rapacious enjoyment and a ravishing loss of one's identity. At the bottom, we follow the letter's strange trajectory as we await what Lacan refers to as the stone figure of death (from Mozart's opera *Don Giovanni*). In this turn of the letter's significance, Lacan again draws upon Heidegger's idea of *Dasein*, our 'Being there', with the addendum that the concept is not so lofty. Thyestes is fed his imagined lineage, his symbolic bearing if you will. This drama, reflecting love and ambition, is set out graphically and obscenely, i.e., his temporal being is reduced to a self-destructive narrative that reveals the power, or real, behind the signifier. 'Eat your *Dasein*' (29), that is, eat your being-in-the-world in its most intimate context. Moreover, after this gruesome event, Thyestes is condemned to (symbolic/literal) exile.[27]

In facing the contingencies and desires that mark one's 'Being-there', eventually one does approach that other side of signification. Thyestes may eat his own son in the myth, but we are admonished that we shall also eventually eat our own *Dasein*. The letters that are purloined in our lives, those that we are ravished by, will continue to follow their course through the passages of our own intersubjective relays (as defined by our speech as the medium of our being). As an absolute Other and relentless chain of signifiers, the letter repeats what is yet to be realized as meaning. Our gamble with destiny intimately relates to these realizations. At this point in Lacan's thought, the intersubjective relations carry us as we offer our own subjective investments and desires to others through language. The letter operates backstage in the alternations between possible and impossible, absence and presence, under the aegis of the signifiers that carry the subject along their path, instead of the other way around. In general, the chain of signifiers crisscrosses every one of our aspirations and fantasies while at the same time remaining autonomous from our conscious designs. Indexing a repetition in the chain of signifiers, the letter fashions how the subject gets caught in his intersubjective relations and in the path of his life. Between a 'pure' signifier (no referent) and ravishment linked to death, the letter marks a destiny. Thus, as Lacan famously says, 'a letter always arrives at its destination' (30, 1).

The style here is, of course, one of a poet and a mathematician.

The 'Introduction' to the 'Seminar on "The Purloined Letter"'

Lacan's purpose in the 'Introduction' and the following sections is to illustrate how the subject is determined by formal language, by a symbolic chain that governs in the sense of chance and probability, and eternally remembers. At this time in Lacan's career, his objective is to 'teach that the unconscious is the fact that man is inhabited by the signifier' (25, 6). The autonomy of the signifier regulates the compulsion toward repetition. Even the most simplistic symbolic chains engage in the creation of rules without outside intervention.

(33–34) At the beginning of the 'Introduction' to the 'Seminar on "The Purloined Letter"' Lacan refers to a class in *Seminar II* that he gave on April 26, 1955, by the same name (S2, 1978/1988:191–205) during the year he spent tackling Freud's *Beyond the Pleasure Principle* (1920/2003).[28] Lacan indicates that psychoanalysts and other practitioners in the domain of general psychology often largely ignore Freud's explanation of *repetition automatism* (*Wiederholungszwang*)[29] instead of focusing more on the seemingly unresolvable contradictions and unthinkable speculations given in his elaboration of the *death drive* (*Todestrieb*). In short, repetition automatism is the insistence of the signifying network operating under the direction of the pleasure principle, which, as will be seen, coincides with the diminishment of pure chance (as occupying the real) and an increase in determination (as occupying the symbolic).

Lacan points out that *Beyond the Pleasure Principle* is more than just a superfluous excursion, despite serving 'as a prelude to the new topography represented by the "ego," "id," and "superego," which have become as prevalent in the work of theorists as in the popular mind' (33, 6). Lacan's assessment of Freud's new topography is that 'we are left no doubt but that the current use of these terms is bastardized and even ass-backwards; this can clearly be seen in the fact that the theorist and the man on the street use them identically' (33, 8). Lacan's meditations theoretically revise the more commonplace and anthropomorphized ego, id, and superego, which people often treat as given psychological entities. His introduction of the 'L Schema' later in this seminar serves the purpose of this revision.

Lacan's exposition focuses primarily on the concepts of *(over)determination* (*Überdeterminierung*) and a reanalysis of repetition automatism, which Freud introduces using the well-known *Fort-Da* game of his grandson. While staying with relatives, Freud observed his grandson would take a toy attached to a string and alternate between throwing it away and pulling it back. When it had disappeared, he would then vocalize what sounded to Freud like the German word *'fort'* ('gone'), and *'da'* ('there') when the object had reappeared. Freud hypothesized that the compulsion to repeat this game was performed in compensation for the mother's disappearance, thereby enabling the child to assume an active role in gaining mastery over an otherwise unpleasant situation.

In Lacan's interpretation, the child gains this mastery through the medium of speech by destroying the object, that is, 'by *bringing about* its absence and presence in advance' (Lacan, 1953/2006:262).[30] The *Fort-Da* game serves in Freud's analysis to evoke the mother's presence, even though her absence is equally produced. The word, as such, stands in for the missing object. With the initial coupling of presence and absence, a 'language's [*langue*] world of meaning is born, in which the world of things will situate itself' (Lacan, 1953/2006:228). Given the world of symbols is organized around laws of presence and absence, the question of symbolic thought ultimately returns to the formulation of *to be or not to be*. The symbolic pairing of *Fort-Da* equally designates a pivotal moment of separation for the child through negation (*Verneinung*)[31] and the moment the subject enters the structure and history of language, that is, into the determining influence of the symbolic order. It represents an inscription of the signifier that occurs on both conscious and unconscious levels.

Lacan's inclusion of Freud's *Fort-Da* game marks the mythological moment of the prelinguistic subject's insertion into the symbolic network. This insertion forces the child to submit to the symbolic conditions that simultaneously inaugurate the subject. It is a general description of the moment that marks the birth of the ephemeral subject, and the object of lack (*a*) that repetition encircles as an object cause of desire – thereby making possible the fundamental fantasy that leads to the formation of the ego. Seeking out the source for the primal and traumatic moment that initially evoked presence (+) and absence (–) is an impossibility. Reconstruction of the exact moment of one's insertion into the network of symbols is, in the end, the search for something mythological. The reason for this is the subject's inscription into a preexisting pattern (hence the tendency for repetition).

In *Beyond the Pleasure Principle,* Freud introduces repetition through the death drive or 'death instinct' (34, 5) as initially translated in *The Standard Edition* by James Strachey.[32] Concerning the death drive, Freud states:

> There are no doubt many respects in which we ourselves are going to feel dissatisfied with our conclusions thus far, which posit a sharp contrast between the 'ego drives' and the sexual drives, and argue that the former are bent on death, the latter on the continuation of life. Furthermore, it was really only the *former* that we could claim showed the conservative character of drives or – better – their regressive character, corresponding to the compulsion to repeat. For according to

our hypothesis, the ego drives arise when inanimate matter becomes animate, and set out to restore the inanimate state.

(1920/2003:119)

One of our strongest motives for believing in the existence of death drives is indeed the fact that we perceived the dominant tendency of the psyche, and perhaps of nervous life in general, to be the constant endeavor − as manifested in the pleasure principle − to reduce inner stimulative tension, to maintain it at a steady level, to resolve it completely.

(1920/2003:131–132)

Freud's theory of sexuality relies on the concept of the *drive* (*Triebe*), not *instinct* (*Instinkt*), which differs from the former in its dependence on biology. So, what is the drive? Lacan characterized it as 'a reference to some ultimate given, something archaic, primal' (S11, 1973/1981:162). He continues: 'The characteristic of the drive is to be a... constant force' (S11, 1973/1981:164) instead of a kinetic, moving force. The drive is instead energy constantly moving in a circular path. How is the drive satisfied? 'Its aim is simply [a] return into circuit' (S11, 1973/1981:179). The drive's goal is to circle the *object a* in a closed, repetitive circuit. It does not seek to obtain its object, but to circumvent it instead.[33]

For Lacan, the death drive and the pleasure principle are byproducts of the symbolic order, the same as lack, absence, and death itself. The death drive goes beyond the pleasure principle and functions on the side of the ego through repetition automatism. The symbolic order's tendency to engage in repetition automatism is the death drive; that is, it desires to return to an inanimate state itself.[34]

Lacan continues by outlining Freud's initial elaboration of unconscious memory and repetition automatism in his *Entwurf Einer Psychologie*, also known as *Project for a Scientific Psychology* (1895/1966), two crucial precursors to Freud's later conception of the unconscious. In the *Project*, Freud describes the psyche in terms of the movement of energetic quantities between electrically excitable cells called 'neurones' [*sic*], which are the basic structural units in the nervous system. Neurons transmit and receive signals through 'contact-barriers' (*synapses*) and 'cell-processes' (*dendrites*) that modify the cell's energy state, both electrically and chemically. Within the network of 'impermeable' neurons (the ψ system), a precursor of the unconscious, *facilitations* (*Bahnungen*) engender memory capacity through the synaptic alterations of these neurons, resulting in the inscriptions (*Niederschriften*) of trace associations. In other words, '*memory is represented by the differences in the facilitations between the ψ neurones*' (Freud, 1895/1966:300). Neurons that can retain an investment of energy representative of a thought or idea are *cathected* (*Gleichbesetzung*).[35] Memory is therefore a byproduct of invested energy in ψ system neurons whose synapses resist transmission and discharge of energy, causing permanent alterations in the pathways of conduction between synapses. The degree of alteration varies according to the magnitude of the formative impressions, invested energy, and repetition frequency.

Approximately a year after abandoning the *Project*, in *Letter 52 Extracts from the Fliess Papers* (1897/1966), Freud outlines a revised neurological model of memory, where inscriptions occur in stratified layers. Each layer represents different writings that are subject to rearrangement and modification as new impressions form. The concept of memory presented in Freud's ψ system sets up his later elaboration of the unconscious's inability 'to satisfy itself except by *refinding an object that has been fundamentally lost*' (34, 2).

'Unconscious memory' not only provides Freud with the opportunity to restructure his conception more rigorously but also helps locate the impact of the presence-absence binary of *Fort-Da* within the operations of language. In other words, the structure of language intervenes to suggest in infantile enjoyment that its organization arbitrates repetition as the chains of signifiers. Moreover, under the aegis of the symbolic, the letters' intersubjective effects ultimately indicate the symbolic subject, not the imaginary subject. The letter in the current seminar also shows how the symbol's play creates the *object a* in its division of the subject, which Lacan revisits later.

The conjunction between 'written' memory and the lost object becomes apparent in the pairings of *Fort-Da,* where a reconceptualization of the compulsion to repeat is an essential characteristic of the unconscious. The *Fort-Da* game is a simple example of determination inaugurated by entrance into the symbolic order, at that moment when presence and absence are 'at the moment of their essential conjunction... so to speak, at the zero point of desire that the human object comes under sway of the grip which, canceling out its natural property, submits it henceforth to the symbol's conditions' (35, 1).

Lacan reformulates Freud's neurological model presented in the *Project* and *Letter 52* in terms of the symbolic order by envisioning the traces of the neurons in the ψ system as signifiers representing structural elements. Here 'energy' refers to the quantities of energetic motion; 'facilitations of memory' refer to the signifying chain and its articulation.[36] Memory traces order themselves according to the sequences of the signifier's inscriptions. As *jouissance*, thought (or knowledge as a sort of enjoyment in suffering that both limits and determines action) operates through retention and investment (*cathexis*) to bind these traces into an 'order of writing' (S7, 1986/1997:50). The organization of these inscriptions constitutes the unconscious. It is to 'the extent that the signifying structure interposes itself between perception and consciousness that the unconscious intervenes, that the pleasure principle intervenes' (S7, 1986/1997:51). Primary processes operating on behalf of the pleasure principle are energized and animated by the flow of drives. These processes seek complete satisfaction through repetition by circling the lost object. Primary processes are unconscious, yet organized, following the laws of the signifier. In this way, the play of signifiers in signification produces the illusion of the signified. Through the unconscious intervention between perception and consciousness, *representation* (*Vorstellungen*) emerges in the appearance of substantive objects – particularly in a locale where the pleasure principle regulates the repetitive movements of the compulsion around the lost object that it keeps at a distance, which, as absent, sustains desire.

(34) Lacan proceeds by indicating that Søren Kierkegaard's idea of conscious repetition is a conceptual precursor to Freud's elaboration of the unconscious compulsion to repeat. In *Fear and Trembling: Repetition* (1843/1983), Kierkegaard's question orients itself around a comparison of recollection and repetition: 'Repetition and recollection are the same movement, except in opposite directions, for what is recollected has been, is repeated backward, whereas genuine repetition is recollected forward' (131). Whereas he equates recollection to acts of reminiscence and imaginary rememoration, Kierkegaard defines repetition in terms of intentional actions and instances of the transcendental. With this, he disassociates himself from Platonic reminiscence in favor of repetition. Albeit Kierkegaard's idea was not sufficient to capture Lacan's elaboration of repetition, especially when approached from the imaginary order, it significantly parallels it: 'the only repetition is the impossibility of repetition' (1843/1983:170). Kierkegaard's next question is worth asking from a psychoanalytic framework: 'What would life be without repetition?' (1843/1983:132). Freud takes Kierkegaard's theory of repetition – an approach that situates the dichotomy at a 'transcendental' level of Christian (repetition) versus Pagan (recollection) – to an entirely new level by 'ravishing the necessity included in this repetition from the human agent identified with consciousness' (34, 3) and situating it instead as a constitutive unconscious force. Lacan continues:

> Since this repetition is symbolic repetition, it turns out that the symbol's order can no longer be conceived of there as constituted by man but must rather be conceived of as constituting him.... It is because Freud does not compromise regarding the original quality of his experience that we see him constrained to evoke therein an element that governs it from beyond life – an element he calls the death instinct.
>
> (34, 3)

Freud's theory of repetition transforms over time, from his initial work on the *Project* in 1895 until he publicized *Beyond the Pleasure Principle* in 1920. This evolution is particularly evident in 'Remembering, Repeating, and Working Through' (1914/1958) and in a newer translation of 'The "Uncanny"' (1919/2003).

> We have learnt that the patient repeats instead of remembering and repeats under the conditions of resistance. We may now ask what

it is that he in fact repeats or acts out. The answer is that he repeats everything that has already made its way from the sources of the repressed into his manifest personality – his inhibitions and unserviceable attitudes and his pathological character-traits. He also repeats all his symptoms in the course of the treatment.

(Freud, 1914/1958:151)

In the unconscious mind we can recognize the dominance of a *compulsion to repeat*, which proceeds from instinctual impulses. This compulsion probably depends on the essential nature of the drives themselves. It is strong enough to override the pleasure principle.

(Freud, 1919/2003:145)

Whereas Freud's conception of repetition becomes associated with unconscious manifestations of drives that overpower the pleasure principle, Lacan's contribution situates the force of repetition in the unconscious signifying chain that characterizes the symbolic network.

(35) Determination in the symbolic order manifests the binary structure of presence and absence through the conjunction of the repressed signifier (marked in the unconscious) and the signified (represented in conscious experience). The signifier's (over)determination is created through temporality as intrinsic to language (diachrony/metonymy) and its simultaneous atemporal structuring (synchrony/metaphor). These two axes of language adhere to specific linguistic laws in creating signification (or 'meaning-making').

- Metonymy governs the horizontal, or diachronic, axis of language – i.e., the lateral or contextual combination of signifiers – and is roughly equivalent to Freudian *displacement (Entstellung)*.[37] It evolves through the syntactic organization and combination of signifiers over time, functioning on conscious and unconscious levels.
- Metaphor governs the vertical, or synchronic, axis – i.e., the substitution of one signifier by another signifier resulting in signification – and is comparable to Freudian *condensation (Verdichtung)*. Metaphor builds on the foundation of metonymy in producing signification, where 'a metaphor is above all sustained by a positional articulation' (S3, 1981/1993:226).

New significations occur through the connections formed between metaphor and repression. The unconscious metonymic combinations are continuously interrupted and 'redirected' by metaphoric substitutions operating in repression, which emerge as the price for new significations.[38] In other words, behind the unconscious formations that lead to conscious significations are the structural arrangements of linguistic laws of metaphor and metonymy. The signified (meaning) occupies 'the diachronic dimension of the conscious signifying chain' (Chiesa, *Subjectivity and Otherness*, 2007:203), which is the locus of language in league with the imaginary; the signifier occupies 'the synchronic dimension of unconscious signifying chains' (*Ibid*), which is the symbolic locus of language without which the imaginary would be impossible. Ultimately, language reflects the binary logic of the symbolic in that it regulates possibilities, impossibilities, and impasses by following a set of rules, exceptions, syntax, and grammar, among other conventions. As will be seen, the unconscious, as an autonomous signifying structure, is structured by these determining linguistic rules.

Many precursors to the graphs used in the current seminar are from *Book II: The Ego in Freud's Theory and in the Technique of Psychoanalysis* (S2, 1978/1988), where Lacan uses cybernetics to show how the symbolic order functions in the unconscious by highlighting the binary logic of absence and presence at work in machines. Machines are a product of symbolic activity, such that even 'the most complicated machines are made only with words' (S2, 1978/1988:47). They operate utilizing the binary logic of messages circulating in feedback loops (open/closed, access/closure, yes/no, presence/absence). In essence, the message circulating in a machine is a directed sequence of meaningless signs (viz., the horizontal movement of metonymy). It circulates, waiting for a reply, a yes or a no, that will allow it to exit its closed circuit and proceed. Lacan (S2, 1978/1988:89) points out that this process is analogous to what happens in the compulsion to repeat. Because he views the unconscious as the Other's discourse, he relates the functioning of these binary machines to unconscious operations as a network of relationally linked signifiers. The decentered subject operates within this play of symbols. In a literal sense, both structure and subject are byproducts of the symbolic. A network is a form of symbolic memory, where 'the signifier truly is the organiser of something that is inherent in human memory' (S4, 1994b/2021:228). The signifier mediates the subject by induction of signifying chains that represent the desires and expectations of others. Entrance into the symbolic itself constitutes desire, inaugurates fantasy, and operates as a cause of the unconscious. Here in condensed form is the formal and structural interpretation by Lacan of Poe's tale 'The Purloined Letter'.

The symbolic chain bestows continuity to imaginary effects by binding and orienting discontinuity. This binding occurs to the extent that 'the signifier's displacement determines subjects' acts, destiny, refusals, blindnesses, success, and fate, regardless of their innate gifts and instruction, and irregardless [*sic*] of their character or sex' (21, 3). The symbolic chain's functioning shows that something operates at its structural limits, something that symbolization resists, but nevertheless insists from within.[39] Lacan's use of cybernetics and the chain of pluses and minuses illustrates how chance becomes transformed into determination by the symbolic – that is, how symbolic chains limit and predetermine outcomes by syntax alone – by begetting the impossibilities and disallowing certain combinations 'until the compensations demanded by its antecedents have been satisfied' (Lacan, 1956c/2006:359). Within this symbolic memory model, 'the chain is found which *insists* by reproducing itself in the transference' (Lacan, 1956c/2006:431). What insists is the phenomenon of repetition that operates in the signifying chain's structure.[40] In 'The Purloined Letter', repetition mirrors the sequence of positions into which each of the characters inextricably places themselves.

The '1-3 Network'

The purpose of the instructions in the 1) 'Presentation', 2) 'Introduction', and 3) 'Parenthesis of Parentheses' are used to demonstrate the unconscious effects that formal language has on the subject, while simultaneously creating and determining the subject of the symbolic chain. From this perspective, the 'Presentation' seeks to lessen the analysts' preconceived notions 'in taking the psychologist's assurance down a notch' (32, 10). The 'Introduction' aims to give the 'audience practice in the notion of remembering implied by Freud's work' (34, 4). Lastly, the purpose of the 'Parenthesis of Parentheses' section is to elucidate the 'L Schema' through transcoding the symbols of the 'Introduction'.

In Bruce Fink's chapter on 'The Nature of Unconscious Thought' in *Reading Seminars I and II* (1996), he writes:

> The ideas presented in this afterword show the symbolic order or signifying chain… usurping even more of the functions usually assigned to the ego and the subject, and yet at the same time point to the limits of the symbolic order: the latter is shown to revolve around something else, to be centered or decentered in relation to some Thing which is not of the realm of meaning, being neither sign, symbol, nor signifier.
>
> (174)

The ideas presented in the '1-3 Network' section of this seminar focus on Lacan's conception of an unconscious that functions similarly to cybernetic models that were cutting-edge at the time.

The first step in demonstrating how the unconscious can function autonomously for Lacan is to list the number of random coin tosses one makes, i.e., '1, 2, 3, 4, 5, 6, 7'. The second step is to log the 'real outcome of the tosses being… left to chance [where] we see separate out from the real a symbolic determination' (38, 7). The logging of coin toss results occurs by assigning a symbol to heads (+) and a symbol to tails (−) and then writing it below the coin toss number. These tosses are a metaphor for a series of decisions on a broader scale, which will be 'loaded' by symbolic determination, such 'that imaginary factors, despite their inertia, figure only as shadows and reflections therein' (6, 3):

1	2	3	4	5	6	7	[Number of tosses]
+	+	+	−	+	+	−	[Heads/tails sequences]

(35–37) To meet the minimum prerequisites to represent an unconscious signifying chain, Lacan groups the pluses and minuses to illustrate the alternating concepts of presence (+) and absence (–) into triplets, where, as an element of the signifying chain, the subject 'plays the role of the little *pluses* and *minuses* in it' (S2, 1988:192).[41] These pluses and minuses are markers of the initial coupling of being and nonbeing that constitutes the evanescent subject's place in the symbolic network, with the subject being a 'purveyor of this absence' (S2, 1978/1988:192), and the symbolic network partly being the letter's movement in the unconscious. The radical subject's movement orients clinical work and emerges in both symbolic repetition and transference. This grouping can be considered the first out of four tiers, where presence (+) and absence (–) represent pure chance in the real and the minimum binary number of groupings required for a signifying chain. To put it another way, Lacan uses the act of flipping a coin to indicate that pure chance resides in the real alone. However, the child's assimilation of the symbolic, as a relatively autonomous structure, thereby supports not only the subject, but also the subject's lack. Entrance into language institutes the rules characteristic of the symbolic order. Whereas pure chance occupies the real, determination functions in the symbolic.

Returning to the '1-3 Network' (Figure 2.2) in the *Écrits*, Lacan transcodes the pluses and minuses by threes into the categories shown in the 'Numeric Matrix' (Table 2.1). (It is interesting to note that at least three elements are required for the structure of metaphor, in that it takes three signifiers to produce something called a signified.)

The opposition between symmetry (constancy, alternation) and dissymmetry (odd) becomes highlighted through these groupings. The determination becomes progressively evident, in that alternation cannot precede constancy

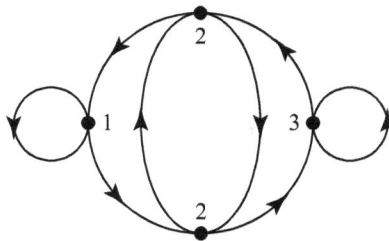

Figure 2.2 '1-3 Network' (35).

Table 2.1 'Numeric Matrix'

(1) (constancy)	(2) (odd)		(3) (alternation)
+ + +	+ + −	− + +	+ − +
− − −	− − +	+ − −	− + −

and vice-versa. These factors indicate that the rudimentary formations of possibility and impossibility emerge through the grouping of tosses into the three categories (1, 2, 3), four vectors (1, 2, 2, 3), and eight total possible groupings of the plus/minus triplets (+ + +, – – –, + + –, – – +, – + +, + – –, + – +, – + –), which is visualized in the illustration of the '1-3 Network' where these eight groupings imply movement between the vectors.

Note the impossibility of moving from 1 to 3 or 3 to 1 unless an odd number of 2s arises in the interval; the emergence of symbolic memory and law are created *ex nihilo*:

> In the series of the symbols 1, 2, and 3, one can observe, for example, that for as long as a uniform succession of 2s, which began after a 1, lasts, the series *will remember* the even or odd rank of each of these 2s, since this rank is responsible for the fact that this sequence can only be broken by a 1 after an even number of 2s or by a 3 after an odd number of 2s.
>
> (36, 1)

Concerning the relevance of such categories, Lacan states that 'it suffices to symbolize, in the diachrony of such a series, groups of three which conclude with each toss by defining them synchronically... for possibilities and impossibilities of succession to appear in the new series constituted' (35, 5). By way of illustration, the evolution of record tosses is transcribed as a series of numeric codes by the symmetrical and dissymmetrical groupings of these tosses into triplets, as illustrated in the 'Numeric Matrix'. Close examination of the application of these categorical groupings demonstrates that these constraints and the formation of new layers of symmetry and dissymmetry generate laws of succession and constitute a link between memory and law. Taking the string of tosses from the sequence of heads and tails and placing them directly underneath the categories of the 'Numeric Matrix' yields:

+	+	+	–	+	+	–	
		1	:	:	:	:	
			2	:	:	:	
				3	:	:	
					2	:	
						2	...

This expansion helps the reader unpack the groupings by simplifying the categories' placement in each overlapping group of the 'Numeric Matrix', which is illustrated directly below the toss results by Lacan in a footnote (47 n. 21) added ten years later to his original text, where he aims to simplify interpretation of the results:

+	+	+	−	+	+	−		[Heads/tails sequences]
		1	2	3	2	2	...	['Numeric Matrix' results]

The element of 'chance' involved in these coin tosses emanates from the order of the real. In contrast, the subject of speech feels they are conscious in their choices (e.g., *heads-tails, even-odd*, etc.), resulting in the above categories of the 'Numeric Matrix', which highlights the opposition between symmetry and dissymmetry emerging through the imaginary order:

> If man comes to think about the symbolic order, it is because he is first caught in it in his being. The illusion that he has formed this order through his consciousness stems from the fact that it is through the pathway of a specific gap in his imaginary relationship with his *semblable* that he has been able to enter into this order as a subject. But he has only been able to make this entrance by passing through the radical defile of speech, a genetic moment of which we have seen in a child's game.
>
> (40, 1; emphasis added)

Here it becomes evident that the trigrammatic assemblages of the symbolic chain involve 'degrees of ciphering' through reductive processes viewed as condensation – 'the superimposed structure of signifiers in which metaphor finds its field' (Lacan, 1957/2006:425). This ciphering refers to the coding and structural encryption of unconscious thought that leads to syntactic laws. This is further demonstrated by the subsequent grouping of elements in the upcoming symbolic matrices, which becomes the signifier's vocabulary.[42]

To denote the movement from symmetry to dissymmetry and vice-versa, Lacan transcodes the numeric sequence into a symbolic one consisting of four Greek letters: α, β, γ, and δ. This symbolic matrix is applied to the 'Numeric Matrix', where every possible triplet is assigned to one of four categories. In 'Kant with Sade', he emphasizes that the quaternary is fundamental: 'From the vantage point of the unconscious, a quadripartite structure...[is] always... required in the construction of a subjective ordering' (1949/1966:774). This further categorization is depicted in the 'Greek Letter Matrix I' (Table 2.2), which regroups the first level +/- triplets under four headings, each corresponding to a Greek letter.

Table 2.2 'Greek Letter Matrix I'[43]

α	β	γ	δ
(symmetry)	(symmetry-dissymmetry)	(dissymmetry)	(dissymmetry-symmetry)
1_1, 1_3	1_2	2_2	2_1
3_3, 3_1	3_2		2_3

Lacan states that the unities subsumed by each Greek letter represent intervals 'constituted by a transformation of the 1-3 Network' (48 n. 28).[44] In this second-level grouping into categories, the blank spaces indicate the movement of a denoted variable in the chain of signifiers. A subsequent regrouping determines the spaces in the middle of each triplet.

In an analogous manner to how the toss results were grouped initially into simple categories, the mappings of the expanded second-tier correspondences are below.[45]

	+	+	+	−	+	+	−	−	
		1	2	3	2	2	2		
				α	:	:	:		
				γ	:	:			
					β	:			
						γ	...		

Further abbreviations through the groupings of the 'Greek Letter Matrix II' (Table 2.3) occur by placing the symbols below each of the numbered categories, condensing the expanded second-tier correspondences:

+	+	+	−	+	+	−	−	+	−	−	−	−	−
		1	2	3	2	2	2	2	3	2	1	1	1
				α	γ	β	γ	γ	δ	γ	α	δ	α

By filling in these spaces and adding new ones to account for alternative groupings, the categories illustrated in the 'Greek Letter Matrix II' exhibit all the possible symbolic combinations of the first Greek Letter Matrix when filled out correctly (comprising 'the first finished form of a symbolic chain' (41, 3)).

Next, Lacan provides a diagram of a temporal distribution that shows how the first position always determines the third position during 'the succession of αs, βs, γs, and δs' (36, 5); in other words, it shows all possibilities in the succession of letters at the three moments designated as Times 1, 2, and 3. He calls this the 'AΔ Distribution' (Figure 2.3), where he explains that 'the symbols that are compatible from Time 1 to Time 3 line up here with each other in the different horizontal tiers that divide them in the distribution, whereas selection of any symbol can occur in Time 2' (37, 1). The underscores in 'Greek Letter Matrix I' denote Time 2 in the movement between Time 1 and Time 3.

Table 2.3 'Greek Letter Matrix II'[46]

α	β	γ	δ
(symmetry)	(symmetry-asymmetry)	(asymmetry)	(asymmetry-symmetry)
111, 123	*112, 122*	*212, 232*	*221, 211*
333, 321	*332, 322*	*222*	*223, 233*

$$\underline{\alpha, \delta} \quad \rightarrow \quad \alpha, \beta, \gamma, \delta \quad \rightarrow \quad \underline{\alpha, \beta}$$
$$\gamma, \beta \qquad\qquad\qquad\qquad\qquad \gamma, \delta$$

| Time 1 | Time 2 | Time 3 |

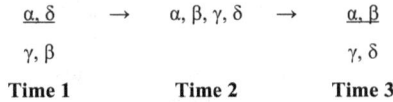

Figure 2.3 'A∆ distribution' (36).

Essentially, this shows that given either α or δ in Time 1, no matter what symbol follows at Time 2, the result will always be α or β in Time 3 (the same laws apply to the bottom terms of Time 1 and Time 3 if they are chosen instead). Lacan calls Time 3 the 'constitutive time of the binary' (36, 6), the term 'binary' referring to the first and third places in the initial categorical grouping of elements of the 'Numeric Matrix'. The 'A∆ Distribution' illustrates the linkages that provide 'the constitutive value for a primordial subjectivity' (37, 1), retroactive yet irreversible.

It is important to note that the Greek letter matrix categorization metaphorically marks the emergence of the symbolic order alongside the real and the imaginary:

> At the outset, subjectivity has no relation to the real, but rather to a syntax which is engendered by the signifying mark there. The construction of the network of αs, βs, γs, and δs has the property (or insufficiency) of suggesting how the real, the imaginary, and the symbolic form in three tiers, although only the symbolic can intrinsically play there as representing the first two strata.
>
> (38, 1-3)

In *The Object Relation*, he further elaborates on the purpose of the 'A∆ Distribution':

> In my text I indicated some of the sequential effects this entails, certain properties that are interesting in that they always bring out other phrases of the same form, laws of syntax that can be deduced from this exceedingly straightforward formula… in a such a way that they would be metaphorical… so that they would enable you to glimpse how the signifier truly is the organiser of something that is inherent in human memory. This is so to the extent that, by always implicating elements of the signifier in its weft,[47] human memory turns out to be structured in a fundamentally different way from any possible conception of vital memory, of the persistence or the effacement of an impression. How so? Because it's important to see that as soon as we introduce the signifier into the real – *and it is introduced into the real simply from the moment we start speaking*, less still from the moment when simply we count – everything that is apprehended in the realm of memory is taken up in something that essentially structures it in a way that is fundamentally different from anything that

can be conceived of in a theory that is founded on the theme of a vital property, pure and simple....

What I would like you to hold in your minds for a moment is simply that this means that as soon as there is a *graphia*, there is *orthographia*.

(S4, 1994b/2021:227–228; *emphasis added*)

In other words, there is a set of conventions, a collection of laws, that determine the rules of possibility and impossibility – created *ex nihilo* – because of the system of writing instantiated by the symbolic, which not only represents but organizes 'this something which is like a subject' (S2, 1978/1988:192).

In the next step, Lacan provides both 'Table Ω' (Figure 2.4 and Figure 2.4a) and 'Table O' (Figure 2.5) to help visualize the rules governing the 'AΔ

TABLE Ω

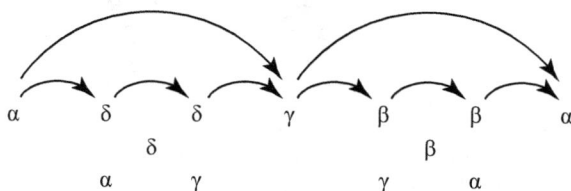

Figure 2.4 'Table Ω' (37).

TABLE Ω

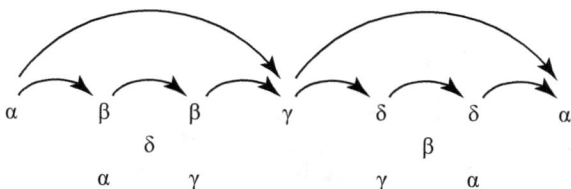

Figure 2.4a 'Table Ω'.[48]

TABLE O

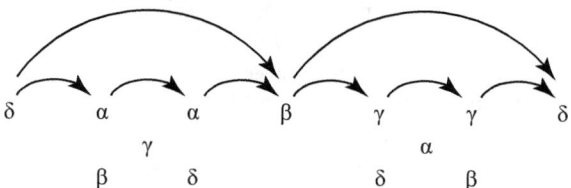

Figure 2.5 'Table O' (37).

Distribution', but with the addition of a Time 4. Lacan uses these illustrations to provide examples for the existence of 'impossible signifiers' and to show that 'by determining which term is to appear at Time 4, the one at Time 2 will not be indifferent' (37, 3). He calls Time 4 the 'point of arrival' because, like Time 2, a choice of any of the four symbols is once again possible.

(37–38) Lacan uses 'Table Ω' to show a structural contrast, 'that is, the direct or crossed way in which the exclusions' grouping (and order) subordinates by reproducing it in the order of extremes' (38, 8). By this, he means to illustrate a template that balances 'Table O' by providing a model where the other terms of the symbolic matrix become thrown off as the *caput mortuum* (literally, 'worthless remains' and 'impossible signifiers') instead.

The addition of 'Table Ω¹' modifies an error where the ordering of the Greek symbols was mirrored in the *Écrits*, resulting in a 'typographical error' that further confused the comprehension of the 'Introduction'. In other words, 'Table Ω¹' is a modified representation of 'Table Ω' because it was previously mirror imaged (inverted) in the *Écrits*.

In 'Table O', the first line tracks the Greek letters' movement from Time 1 (δ) to Time 4 (β), after which it continues along its trajectory. An essential aspect of 'Table O' is that it shows the excluded symbols cast-off as its course progresses, namely that between the letters δ and β, γ becomes impossible, and then between the letters β and δ, α becomes impossible. These excluded symbols occupy the second line down. Concerning this phenomenon, Lacan states that 'this could illustrate a rudimentary subjective trajectory, by showing that it is grounded in the actuality which has the future anterior in its present' (37, 6).

The essential point is that symbolic memory determines *what will have been* beforehand by dictating what is possible and impossible given its prior movements. The impossibilities become the *caput mortuum*, which makes a structural hole – a reservoir for what the symbolic chain excludes.

Before continuing, it is important to note that Lacan completely re-transcribes the original '1-3 Network' to the point where 'all the arrows have changed directions, and instead of finding the numbers 1, 2, and 3, we find the following combinations: 00, 01, 10, 11' (Fink, 1995:158). Thus, the original groupings of the 'Numeric Matrix' translate into the 'Binary 1-3 Network' (Table 2.4).

Because the resulting '1-3 Network' diagram is modified to become the 'Binary 1-3 Network' (Figure 2.6), there are now four categories (11, 10, 01, 00), four vectors (00, 10, 11, 01), and eight total possible groupings of the plus/

Table 2.4 '1-3 Network' translated into a 'Binary 1-3 Network'

(1)	(2)		(3)	→	11	10	01	00
+ + +	+ + −	− + +	+ − +		+ + +	+ + −	− − +	+ − +
− − −	− − +	+ − −	− + −		− − −	+ − −	− + +	− + −

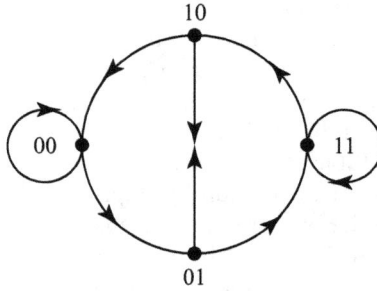

Figure 2.6 'Binary 1-3 Network' (48 n. 28).[49]

minus triplets (+ + +, − − −, + + −, − − +, − + +, + − −, + − +, − + −), which is more easily visualized in the following illustration:

For the 'α, β, γ, δ Network' (Figure 2.7), Lacan next splits the 'Binary 1-3 Network' into two parts, yielding the two steps of the diagram below, complete with both Greek and numerical associations. Specifically, in this fourth and final tier, Lacan correlates the Greek letters again with binary numbers. Given these Greek letters are two-sided in this modeling, Lacan transcodes them into the eight binary groupings, which are the result of the transformations in Table 2.5 below (α = 111, 100; β = 100, 110; γ = 000, 010; δ = 001, 011). These transformations culminate in the construction of the 'Chain L' (*la chaîne L*) in the upcoming 'Parenthesis of Parentheses' section, which is then

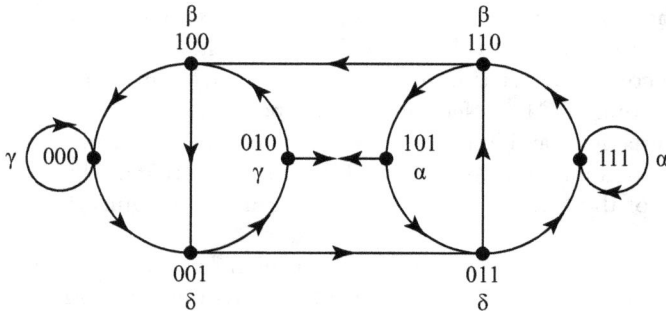

Figure 2.7 'α, β, γ, δ Network' (48 n. 28).

Table 2.5 Transformation from a 'Binary 1-3 Matrix' to a 'Binary Greek Symbolic Matrix'

11	10	01	00	→α	β	γ	δ	→α	β	γ	δ
+ +	+ +	− −	− + − +	111, 123	112, 122	212, 232	221, 211	111	100	000	001
− − −	+ − −	− + +	− + −	333, 321	332, 322	222	223, 233	101	110	010	011

70

further mapped onto the 'L Schema' (i.e., the intersubjective relations and structure of the subject during the 1960s).

What is herein termed the 'Binary Greek Symbolic Matrix' in the third transformation above follows the pattern Lacan supplies in the endnotes (48 n. 28), which essentially demonstrates the organization of the resulting matrix (e.g., α = 1_1, thus 111 and 101):

- 1.1 = α
- 0.0 = γ
- 1.0 = β
- 0.1 = δ

The two-step diagram in the 'α, β, γ, δ Network' illustrates the move from a three-slot combinatory to a four-slot combinatory, sometimes illustrated as a flattened cube. Lacan (1994a), in the French version of *Seminar IV – Séminaire, Tome 4: la Relation d'objet* – shows its transformation into a cube. That is, in *The Object Relation*, Lacan illustrates the further transformation of the 'α, β, γ, δ Network' into a 'Parallelepiped Formed of Vectors' at different times (Figures 2.8-8c):

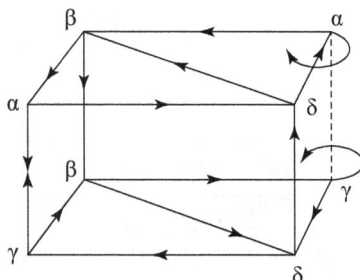

Figure 2.8 Parallelepiped formed of vectors.
Source: Lacan (S4, 1994a:337).

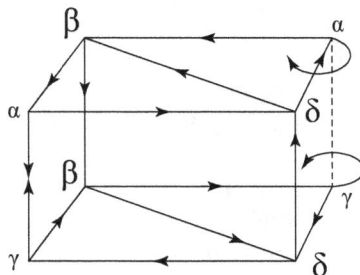

Figure 2.8a Parallelepiped at Time 1.
Source: Lacan (S4, 1994a:338).

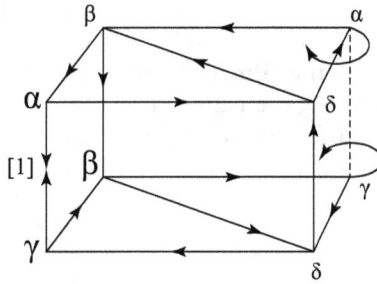

Figure 2.8b Parallelepiped at Time 2.
Source: Lacan (S4, 1994a:338).

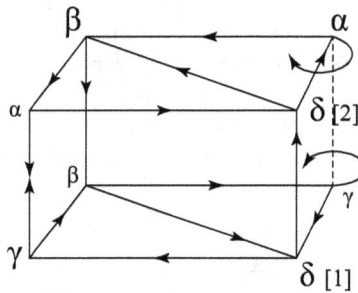

Figure 2.8c Parallelepiped at Time 3.

It's a matter of using the letters α, β, γ, and δ, to label a third series of symbols that is built from the second series. This is founded on the remark that when one knows the beginning and end term in the second series, the middle term is univocal. So, in order to define the terms α, β, γ, and δ, we take into account only the two extremes of the series. In a case like this one here, γ, you can see that it goes from odd to odd. Therefore the convention has been established whereby a sign is set down that captures within its range the five previous symbols from the first line. This will give the sign α when going from same to same, that is, from symmetrical to symmetrical, whether it is a matter of going from 1 to 1, from 1 to 3, or from 3 to 1. Going from odd to odd gives γ. Starting from the same to arrive at odd will give β. Coming back to the same from odd will give δ. These are the conventions.

On this basis, if we want to define all the possibilities by means of a network, we can construct it as a parallelepiped formed of vectors… This network provides an exhaustive summary of all the possible sequences. These are the only ones. A series that cannot be set into this network is an impossible series.

(S4, 1994b/2021:225)

72

Lacan continues:

> So, this network provides an exhaustive summary of all the possible
> sequences. These are the only ones. A series that cannot be set into
> this network is an impossible series... Everything I was representing
> and spelling out in my text was... a sort of opacifying of the mecha-
> nism for how the symbols play out. It would be a sort of creation that
> would make some kind of internal law emerge from within. This is...
> something that is introduced by the creation of the symbol and which
> goes beyond the pure randomness given at the outset. It's exactly that.
> And in one sense it can indeed be said that in the choosing of the
> symbols there is a certain ambiguity that is given at the outset, from
> the moment you set down the symbols, with the simple indication of
> an oddity, that is to say, asymmetry... There is something that you
> may call ambiguity, but be sure to tell yourself that this is precisely
> what one has to get a sense of. At every level, the symbol that is a +
> presupposes the −, and the symbol that is a − presupposes the +. The
> ambiguity is still there as we move further into the construction... It
> is precisely to the extent that the symbol harbours this ambiguity that
> what I have called the *law* becomes apparent.
>
> (S4, 1994b/2021:226–227)

Of particular interest in demonstrating the symbol's law, the *caput mortuum*
eventually represents the beyond of the symbolic order encircled by the drives.
The *caput mortuum* is not limited to the imaginary and symbolic orders but also
enters as the residue thrown off by introducing the symbolic into the real.[50] In
this way, the *caput mortuum* creates the hole that will later become the *object a*'s
origin, the impossible object that desire seeks but can never attain. The *object
a's* domain, with the *caput mortuum* as its avatar, is the real of the symbolic and
is subjectivized by the nonmaterial manifestation of phenomena. These phenomena include dreams, symptoms, anxiety, the return of the repressed, and
even perception itself.

In *Crucial Problems for Psychoanalysis*, Lacan explains how subjectivity is a
byproduct of the symbolic, emerging through the syntax it generates, and the
allowances and impasses that it engenders.

> The best proof that we could have of the existence of a subject in the
> starry heavens would be if some message with a minimum of four
> terms was found to correspond to the syntax that, in the introduc-
> tory chapter to Poe's *Purloined letter*, I tried to articulate as alpha, beta,
> gamma, delta which those who have read this little introduction know
> are composed from a sort of grouping of pure random selection, and
> that the fact of grouping them, of naming them in a certain unitary
> fashion, whatever it may be in fact, culminates at a syntax from which

already one cannot escape. If an analogous syntax were discovered in a succession of signs, we would have the assurance that what is involved there is indeed a subject.

(S12, n.d.:23.6.65:266)

Returning to the construction of the 'Greek Letter Matrix' structure illustrates that the excluded terms of the *caput mortuum* are distributed and situated into quadrants (48 n. 24), thereby forcing repetition, and inaugurating the trajectory of primordial subjectivity. Lacan's injunctions to study the chain and meditate on syntax derive from his desire to be taken literally – to steer the focus away from analysts' predominating tendencies to reify understanding and the ego in the analytic context.

(38–39) Lacan's subsequent remarks provide syntactical details of a 'recreational character' regarding the 'Greek Letter Matrix'. What is pertinent here are the essential features of the signifying chain that he highlights in his mainly formal analysis: chance, autonomy, syntax, memory, (over)determination, and the *caput mortuum*. Lacan elaborates on these conceptions of subjectivity in the 'Parenthesis of Parentheses' section, after a brief foray into how the 'L Schema' fits into his modeling of Poe's story. Before a quick recap of the 'L Schema', the 'R Schema', and the move into the upcoming 'Parenthesis of Parentheses' section, Lacan provides a short synopsis that helps elucidate the reasons why he gave this seminar precedence in the *Écrits*.

(39–40) Next, Lacan points out that repetition helps explain why free association is useful, especially since 'repetition is fundamentally the insistence of speech' (S3, 1981/1993:242).[51] Explanations can only occur by the 'autonomy of the symbolic' (39, 2) and not by any imaginary associations. He adds that conceptualization of unconscious desire can only occur through examples that illustrate the preservation of the symbolic chain. The main characteristic of repetition automatism is its insistence. This function of repetition is an essential point that one can grasp through this cybernetic model of structural determination. Repetition functions beyond neurology and affectivity, especially since the latter must submit to the constraints of symbolic logic. He denounces theories built on associationism ideas prevalent in philosophical and psychological circles, in that they reduce repetition and determination to principles of behavior conceivable in terms of operant conditioning or introspective analysis (e.g., behavioral psychology and cognitive psychology are examples of paradigms that employ these experimental methods).[52] Behavioral and cognitive psychology neglect symbolic determination in favor of 'imaginary inertia'. Moreover, the fields that operate under the heading of experimental psychology fail to account for 'the indestructible persistence of unconscious desire' (39, 4), a characteristic readily explained by the principles and autonomous operation of the symbolic chain.

(40–41) As observed in the *Fort-Da* example, the subject must first pass through the 'radical defile of speech' (40, 1) before entering the intersubjective dialectic. Speech initially sustains desire through negation using the prohibition of incest by the paternal signifier (*Name-of-the-Father*), derived from the logic of the Oedipus complex.[53] From this point forward, actions become motivated by a 'means for reproduction' (S7, 1986/1997:53) in the search for the lost object, which allows the split subject to mask the loss of being. It is usually the mother that facilitates displacement by offering the first signifier for an object always–already lost, one that the Other's discourse does not subject and subsume, namely the signifier of the mother's desire.

The 'L Schema' and the 'R Schema'

Lacan's introduction of both the 'L Schema' (Figure 2.9) and the 'R Schema' (Figure 2.10)[54] anticipates his use of topology to introduce his formulations and structural modeling of the psyche using non–intuitive representations (bypassing the limitations of three–dimensional imaginary models). Each schema has four points connected by vectors, indicating how these points relate. For example, in his modeling of the axes of *symbolic/unconscious* between Subject (*S*) and Other (*A*) and *imaginary relation* between Ego (*a*) and other (*a'*) in the quadripartite 'L Schema', the real of the drives had not yet been formulated as distinct from the imaginary order. On the other hand, Lacan's use of the 'L

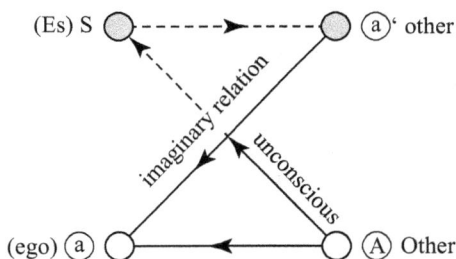

Figure 2.9 'L Schema' (40, 2).

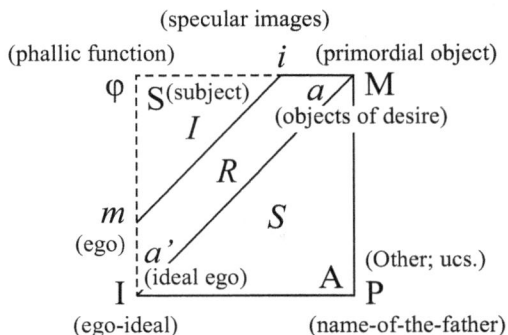

Figure 2.10 'R Schema' (Lacan, 1958/2006:462).

75

Schema' serves as a replacement for Freud's tripartite structural model of the id, ego, and superego, as mentioned briefly above.[55]

Although the 'R Schema' will show its significance as Lacan's final section moves toward topology, the primary focus will be on the 'L Schema'. On the 'unconscious' axis of the 'L Schema', A (*Autre*) represents the Lacanian Other, and S represents the pre-symbolic and incomplete subject, as well as the signifier. 'The subject, *in initio* [in the beginning], begins in the locus of the Other, in so far as it is there that the first signifier emerges' (S11, 1973/1981:198). The barred and divided subject (∃) emerges through inscription by the letter from the Other's locale, which is to say, through castration by the signifier. The unconscious axis of speech traverses from A unbroken until it encounters the axis of 'imaginary relation'.[56] The axis of the unconscious between Other (A) and subject (S) is also responsible for the insistence that is characteristic of repetition automatism (the 'imaginary relation' axis of a-a' responsible for resistance to unconscious repetition and inertia in general).

The dynamic between a and a' on the axis of 'imaginary relation' represents an exchange between ego and other. This dynamic primarily results from identification with the specular image that occurs in the mirror stage,[57] leading to the ego's subsequent projection in the narcissistic identifications arising within the intersubjective dynamic. The ego is the place of misrecognition, wherein fantasy operates to stave off the unimpeded transmission of the Other's discourse. It is essential to highlight that the ego possesses a dual structure with conscious and unconscious aspects and is again 'overdetermined' from the Freudian perspective.

In 'Kant with Sade', Lacan indicates these four points are the minimum prerequisites for the subject, despite Derrida's critique in *The Purveyor of Truth* (1975b) that Lacan fixates on using tripartite structures:[58] 'From the vantage point of the unconscious, a quadripartite structure can always be required in the construction of a subjective ordering' (Lacan, 1962/2006:653).

In *The Formations of the Unconscious* (S5, 1998/2017:142–143), the phallus is the fourth term of the intersubjective relation in the Oedipus complex (Figure 2.11).

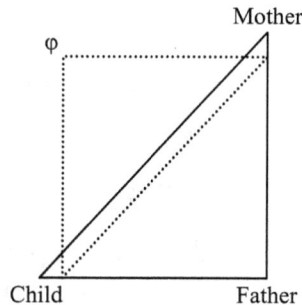

Figure 2.11 Phallus in the Freudian Economy.

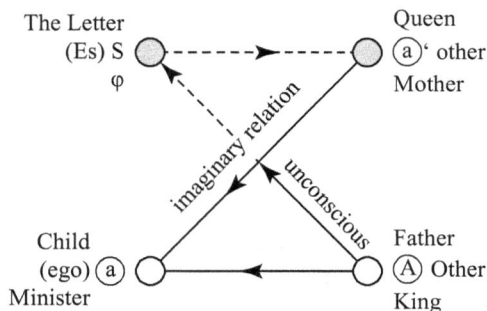

Figure 2.12 'L Schema' in the Oedipus complex and 'The Purloined Letter'.

Following Lacan in this seminar (S5, 1998/2017), Philip Dravers (2004:221) points out that not only can the primary figures of the Oedipal Complex be superimposed onto each of the four locales of the 'L Schema', but that the characters in Poe's story can also be inserted into this dynamic (Figure 2.12), alongside occupying the various positions of the 'R Schema' – especially since it conditions the *perceptum*, the object, insofar as these lines circumscribe the field of reality rather than being dependent on it.

To summarize, there are four primary characters in Poe's story depicted: the King, the Queen, the Minister, and the Letter. Each subject's power is not contingent on the letter's contents, but rather on its position in the symbolic circuit. It is worth reiterating that the letter governs the characters in the form of 'the essentially localized structure of the signifier' (Lacan, 1957/2006:418), that is, from the place of the subject:

> The letter here is synonymous with the original, radical, subject. What we find here is the symbol being displaced in its pure state, which one cannot come into contact with without being imme-diately caught in its play. Thus, the tale of *The Purloined Letter* signifies that there's nothing in destiny, or causality, which can be defined as a function of existence. One can say that, when the characters get a hold of this letter, something gets a hold of them and carries them along and this something clearly has dominion over their individual idiosyncrasies... They will be defined solely by their position in relation to this radical subject... For each of them the letter is his unconscious. It is this unconscious with all of its consequences, that is to say that at each point in the symbolic circuit, each of them becomes someone else.
>
> (S2, 1978/1988:196–197)

'Parenthesis of Parentheses'

(*Parenthèse des Parenthèses*)[59]

Given the difficulties inherent in fully understanding the 'Parenthesis of Parentheses' section, the goal here will be to provide a brief overview of its formalization, while focusing more on the purposes behind *why* Lacan presents this particular seminar at the forefront of his teachings on psychoanalysis. In brief, the 'Parenthesis of Parentheses' section, and ultimately the seminar itself, denotes a transitional period for Lacan that marks the beginning of his foray into topology. Lacan reimagines many psychoanalytic concepts in later seminars using topological figures (the Möbius strip, torus, Klein bottle, cross-cap, and so on). His later use of topology enlarges upon Freud's topographical modeling of the psyche, further incorporating the rigor of mathematics and logic into psychoanalytic practice and discourse. (For example, he later modifies the 'R Schema' to illustrate the subject's structure more accurately by using the middle of the figure as a Möbius strip to emphasize binary oppositions, such as inside and outside, as continuous instead of distinct.)

(41–43) Although difficult to comprehend and decipher, Lacan's 'Parenthesis of Parentheses' section, which was added approximately ten years (1966) after the original publication date of '*Le Séminaire Sur "La Lettre volée"*' (1956), furthers the work of the 'Introduction' by integrating the structure and concepts presented in the 'L Schema' into a variation of the network by using binary numbers and 'a parenthesis enclosing one or several other parentheses' (41, 5). He refers to the redoubled parenthesis as 'quotes' to emphasize the symbolic role of elements distributed both inside and outside the chain. He adds the 'Parenthesis of Parentheses' section to retranslate his 'L Schema' and highlight his evolving conception of the *object a* (by the time of its addition in 1966, the concept had gone through a series of evolutions, e.g., from the *caput mortuum* to the *object a* outlined in *Seminar X* (2004/2014)). In other words, he provides 'Chain L' to show its correspondence with the 'L Schema'.

Having located various connections between the vectors of the 'L Schema' and the three times of the 'AΔ Distribution', Lacan continues by highlighting the 'causal aspect' of the *caput mortuum*, the residue left behind by the signifier in its movement between the four vectors of 'Table O', 'Table Ω', and the 'L Schema'. For example, *S* represents initial redoubled quotes, (()), 'to cover the structure of the subject' (41, 7) in its division, and to also suggest its 'lining [*doublure*] function' (41).

Instead of reinventing the wheel and moving step-by-step through all Lacan's re-transcriptions, the remainder of this text will focus on the main points and purposes of these transformations.

'Chain L': (10. . . (00. . .0) 0101. . .0 (00. . .0) . . .01) 11111 . . .
(1010. . .1) 111. . .

Here is 'Chain L' translated into terms using the Symbolic Matrix:

'**Chain L**' (trans): βαγ. . . βγγ. . .γδ γαγα. . .γ βγγ. . . γδ . . .γαδ ααααα . . .
βαγαγ. . .αδ ααα. . .

'Chain L' is easier to work with after eliminating the ellipses.

'**Chain L**' (simplified): (10(000)01010(000)01)1111(10101)111

For example, the following simplification helps locate and illuminate the correspondences between 'L Schema' and 'Chain L' (Table 2.6), illustrated in the 'Chain L' and the 'L Schema' figure directly below the table (Figure 2.13). As Bruce Fink (1995) points out in *The Lacanian Subject*, 'it is this *twofold* structure – in other words, the double opening and closing parentheses, (()) – which is crucial here, as the stuffing (the αγ and γα pairs) can, according to Lacan, be reduced to nothing' (165). This 'stuffing' Lacan translates into 0s and 1s, which, as Muller and Richardson (1988) indicate, represent 'the binary language of absence/presence proper to combinatorial analysis' (72). These substitutions are reflected by and made to correspond to the binary groupings of 'Chain L' (Fink, 1995:166). While not evident by a cursory reading of the text, γ repetitions represent the 'silence of the drives' (42, 5). Further, αγ and γα combinations that repeat between parentheses (on the imaginary relations axis between the ego and the other in the 'L Schema') provide a 'value of scansion', which refers to the ending of a variable-length session at a point where it will have the most impact, as well as operations of punctuation and oracular interpretation as an analyst.

Table 2.6 Correspondences between 'L Schema' and 'Chain L'

(10	(000)01010(000)	01)	1111(10101)111
Ego(a)	(silence) Imaginary axis (silence)(a-a')	Other(a')	Unary trait and(Mvmt. of Drives)
The subject (Es)			Other (A)

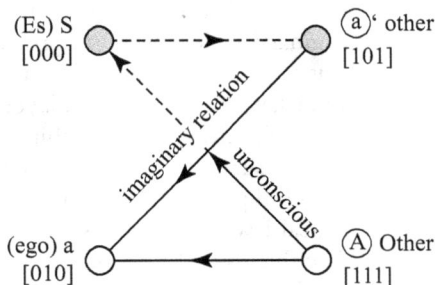

Figure 2.13 Simplified mapping of 'Chain L' and the 'L Schema'.

The only remainder required by this attempt is the formalism of a certain remembering [*mémoration*] related to the symbolic chain, whose law one could easily formulate with respect to the L chain. (This law is essentially defined by the relay constituted, in the alternation of 0s and Is, by the surmounting [*franckissement*] of one or several parenthetical signs and of which signs.) What must be kept in mind here is the rapidity with which a formalization is obtained that is suggestive both of a remembering that is primordial in the subject and of a structuration in which it is notable that stable disparities can be distinguished therein (indeed, the same dissymmetrical structure persists if, for example, we reverse all the quotes). This is but an exercise, but it fulfills my intent to inscribe therein the sort of contour where what I have called the signifier's *caput mortuum* takes on its causal aspect. This effect is as manifest when grasped here as in the fiction of "The Purloined Letter".

(42–43, 11)

Finally, Lacan introduces the last new concept of this seminar, represented by the 1s outside the leading parentheses (the S2s of the Other), which are repetitions of α as 'the times marked by the symbolic' (42, 8). He states: 'Repetition dominates there in the form of the 1, the unary trait' (42, 8). The unary trait (*einziger Zug*) explicated by Lacan in his seminar on *Identification* (S9, n.d.) refers to the signifier's hitching to the letter, language, and writing, which occurs through identification to establish the 'one' that marks the genesis of the subject. Further, the unary trait defines 'identity by the elimination of qualitative differences by reducing them... to a simplified schema: this is supposed to be the mainspring of this recognition characteristic of our apprehension of what is the support of the signifier, the letter' (S9, n.d.:6.12.61).

(43–45) In the final paragraphs of this seminar, Lacan revisits the game of even or odd that Poe introduces in *The Purloined Letter* (touched on earlier in the textual themes section). This game gives Lacan the example he needs to demonstrate the ascendancy of the symbolic and intersubjectivity over the concept of 'projection', and the principal focus on the 'dyadic relationship' (43) of the ego and narcissistic identification. Lacan advocates a position that abandons the usual strategies of the imaginary – identification, projection, mimicry, the assumption of a reflexive position – as insufficient because they do not have recourse to symbolic succession laws. 'Hence each player, if he reasons, can only resort to something beyond the dyadic relationship – in other words, to some law which presides over the succession of the rounds of the game' (44, 4). Thus, the most effective technique would be to hint that one follows a pattern: that there is some logical law behind one's choices. Then, whenever possible, to purposefully violate this law – 'the more this approach manages to free itself from real regularities that are sketched out *in spite of myself*, the more successful it will effectively be' (44, 6).

(45–46) In Lacan's modeling of symbolic (over)determination, the signifying chain is an autonomous structure that operates beyond any supposed conception of human subjectivity, where 'man is engaged with all his being in the procession of numbers, in a primitive symbolism which is distinct from imaginary representations' (S2, 1978/1988:307).

What is it that insists and repeats? In short, it is the repressed signifiers oscillating in a feedback loop that manifests through one's symptoms, speech, and in one's demand for recognition.

Lacan ends by informing the reader that the 'Seminar on "The Purloined Letter"' was constituted retroactively, and that his inclusion of subsequent theoretical materials was justified, given his eventual foray into topology in later seminars.

Concluding remarks

Lacan's excursion into cybernetics demonstrates the autonomy of the symbolic order and defines its limits. In looking at the material he presents regarding its purpose and relevance to psychoanalysis, he ultimately uses the operations of the 'Numeric Matrix', such as the '1-3 Network', and the symbolic 'Greek Letter Matrix II' to demonstrate that the 'primordial symbol constitutes the structures connecting memory to the law'. In conjunction with the 'Parenthesis of Parentheses' section, he indicates how the letter's play in the real determines the inmixing of subjects, thereby structuring the radical, decentered subject as a signifier within the symbolic network of the unconscious. Here one can visualize how Lacan's foray into cybernetics eventually led to his conception of the Borromean Knot, consisting of the *object a* (real), language (symbolic), and the ego (imaginary).

The point of the exercises included in this seminar is to demonstrate multiple features of 'unconscious thought' (later referred to as 'unconscious assemblies'). The following are the primary points Lacan illuminates in 'Seminar on "The Purloined Letter"': a) probability is unlikely when inserted into a cybernetic context (i.e., as a method of ciphering); b) symbolic matrices determine their own rules and laws on their own accord (viz. syntax, possibility, impossibility); c) the symbolic chain possesses a memory that keeps track of the preceding groupings that serve to determine future possibilities and impossibilities (where the memory of unconscious contents is '*eternal* and *indestructible*'); d) the unconscious has little, if anything, to do with meaning, the signified, or even signification itself; e) the *caput mortuum* institutes the hole as a void of absence that eventually evolves into Lacan's later formulation of the *object a*; f) the symbolic chain bestows the presence of indestructible unconscious desire, leading to the insistence of repetition automatism, a symbolic determination that can be pinpointed and encountered through effective analysis; and, g) an analyst must be adept at deciphering the unconscious, rather than attending to understanding and meaning, keeping in mind the important fact that speech remains.

'You can't help the play of symbols, and that is why you must be very careful of what you say' (S2, 1978/1988:179).

Notes

1 See Lacan (33, 44, and 48).
2 Cf. Cuellar (2010), Chapter 4.
3 Cf. *The Lacanian Subject* (Fink, 1995).
4 Cf. Chapter 1.
5 See Schneiderman (1991).
6 See Schneiderman (1991).
7 Cf. Fink (2014:70).
8 E.g., in *Seminar XX, On Feminine Sexuality, the Limits of Love and Knowledge* (S20, 1975/1998).
9 See Lacan (S20, 1975/1998); cf. O'Donnell (2004:47), Muller and Richardson (1988:91), and Lacan (1970:191).
10 See Chapter 5.
11 See Chatel (1995); cf. Fink (2007).
12 For example, Vappereau (2012); Prioteasa (n.d.); Fink (1996); and Dravers (2004).
13 Questions that the translation raises are also noted in some of the annotations available in 'Lacan's Seminar on "The Purloined Letter": Notes to the Text', written by John Muller and William Richardson as part of their collection of essays in *The Purloined Poe* (1988:83–98).
14 For more on Lacan's views on psychosis and foreclosure, see Lacan (S3, 1981/1993); Vanheule (2011); and Apollon, Bergeron, and Cantin (2002).
15 One may note that Lacan does not characterize Poe's first scene in *Seminar II* (S2, 1978/1988:195) as the 'primal scene'. Lacan, however, does cast the first purloining of the letter as the primal scene.
16 The libidinal flow of the drives is later reformulated by Lacan into the concept of *jouissance* – the 'substance of thought' as a continuous force that invests the links between signifiers in language, but that slips away from this process given that speech can never hold its own contents. Inertia comprises the metaphorical links in the chain of language that inhibit its transmission and articulation, occurring between articulation and *jouissance* (primary processes).
17 Cf. Fink (2007).
18 See Chapter 1.
19 The myth is variously told. See Felman (1987).
20 Cf. Fink (1996); Samuels (1993:10-21).
21 Cf. Dravers (2004), and Muller and Richardson (1988).
22 Cf. Lacan (1972:1.13.71).
23 See Dor (1998).
24 See Malone, 2012; cf. Lacan (1953/2006).
25 For more details, please see the reference to Heidegger's use of *Alethes* in the translator's notes (Lacan, 768).
26 As mentioned earlier, this is rendered in English as 'So fatal a scheme [design], /if not worthy of Atreus, is worthy of Thyestes'. Lacan changes *dessein* to *destin*, from 'design' to 'destiny', when he repeats the play's lines. In the above translation, *dessein* is rendered as 'scheme' instead of 'design'.
27 Cf. Fuks (2008).
28 See Cuellar (2010), Chapter 4; cf. Lacan (S2, 1978/1988:191).
29 Lacan's translation of *Wiederholungszwang* as *repetition automatism* employs the term *automaton* to refer to the network of signifiers and its probabilistic laws of repetition.

30   Cf. Lacan (S2, 1978/1988:218–219).
31   Freud theorized that separation occurs initially through attention, thereby instituting the division between the inner world (*Innenwelt*) and the outer world (*Umwelt*), which is formed alongside memory as a 'system of notation'.
32   Strachey's translation fails to account for the differences between *Instinkt* (instinct) and *Triebe* (drive), which are both rendered as 'instinct' in *The Standard Edition of the Works of Sigmund Freud*.
33   See Lacan (S11, 1973/1981:181).
34   In later works, Lacan describes repetition in terms of the insistence of the letter and speech.
35   It has been variously suggested that both *Gleichbesetzung* and *Besetzung* would be more accurately translated as 'invested' and 'investment' instead of 'cathected' and 'cathexis'.
36   See Lacan (S7, 1986/1997:39).
37   'Displacement' is often a translation of '*Entstellang*' too and even 'sometimes '*Verschiebung*' as well.
38   See Chiesa (2007:203).
39   See *Reading Seminars I and II* (Fink, 1996:174); cf. *The Lacanian Subject* (Fink, 1995:153–172).
40   See Lacan (S5, 1998/2017).
41   This foreshadows his later proclamation that 'a signifier is that which represents a subject for another signifier' (S11, 1973/1981:207).
42   Cf. Liu (2010:308).
43   See *Reading Seminars I and II* (Fink, 1996:178) for a variation of Table 2.2.
44   Cf. Lacan (S2, 1978/1988:193).
45   See *Reading Seminars I and II* (Fink, 1996:179).
46   See Lacan (S2, 1978/1988:178) for a variation of Table 2.3.
47   According to Walter Skeat's *An Etymological Dictionary of the English Language*, the term "weft" refers to 'the threads woven into and crossing the warp' (1910/2005:706)
48   Thanks again to Bruce Fink for pointing this out in Appendix 1 of The Lacanian Subject (1995:202), where he speaks of the typographical error in the illustration provided.
49   See The Lacanian Subject (1995:159), where he speaks of a typographical error in the illustration provided.
50   The *caput mortuum* is the inertia residing between articulation and *jouissance* as a modality of enjoyment.
51   In his later works, Lacan speaks of repetition in terms of *jouissance*.
52   See Cuellar (2010), Chapter 4.
53   The *Name-of-the-Father* refers to the fundamental signifier that serves to name and position the subject within the symbolic order.
54   See Lacan (S2, 1978/1988:243); cf. Lacan's simplified representation of the 'L Schema' in the *Écrits* (1958/2006:458).
55   Cf. Lacan (S2, 1978/1988:109).
56   See Lacan (S3, 1981/1993:161).
57   See Chapter 5.
58   Cf. Johnson (1975/1988:213) in Muller and Richardson (1988:213–251).
59   Besides the ambiguities present in the 'Parenthesis of Parentheses' section, there is also a typographical error present. Besides being one of the first to point out various typos in the text that serve to make its logical comprehension much more difficult, Bruce Fink's commentaries in *Reading Seminars I and II* (Fink, 1996:173–191) and *The Lacanian Subject* (1995:153-172) also clarify many operational ambiguities. For a detailed analysis of the 'Parenthesis of Parentheses' and its preceding sections, his texts on the seminar sufficiently clarify and simplify the operations and errors of the numeric and symbolic matrices in the 'Seminar on "The Purloined Letter"'. In other words, the advanced concepts of the '1-3 Network' and the 'Parenthesis of Parentheses' sections are not fully elucidated herein. Bruce Fink provides an insightful and thorough analysis of both in the aforementioned texts.

References

Apollon, W., Bergeron, D., and Cantin, L. (2002) *After Lacan: Clinical Practice and the Subject of the Unconscious.* Albany: State University of New York Press.

Burton, R. F. (2004) *The Arabian Nights: Tales from a Thousand and One Nights.* New York: The Modern Library.

Chatel, M. M. (1995) 'For a Practice of Particularity'. in *Clinical Studies: International Journal of Psychoanalysis,* 1(1), 99–108.

Chiesa, L. (2007) *Subjectivity and Otherness: A Philosophical Reading of Lacan.* Cambridge, MA: MIT Press.

Cuellar, D. P. (2010) *From the Conscious Interior to an Exterior Unconscious Lacan, Discourse Analysis, and Social Psychology.* London: Karnac Books.

Derrida, J. (1975a/1980) 'Le facteur de la vérité'. in *La Carte Postale de Socrate à Freud.* Paris: Flammarion, 439–524.

Derrida, J. (1975b) 'The Purveyor of Truth'. in *Yale French Studies, Graphesis: Perspectives in Literature and Philosophy.* trans. by Domingo, W., Hulbert, J., and Moshe, R. New Haven, CT, 31–113.

Derrida, J. (1981) *Positions.* trans. by Bass, A., and Ronse, H. Chicago: University of Chicago Press.

Dor, J. (1998) *Introduction to the Reading of Lacan: The Unconscious Structured Like a Language.* trans. by Fairfield, S. New York: Other Press.

Dravers, P. (2004) 'To Poe, Logically Speaking: From "The Purloined Letter to the Sinthome"'. in *Lacan: Topologically Speaking.* ed. by Ragland, E., and Milovanovic, D. New York: Other Press, 205–246.

Evans, D. (1998) 'From Kantian Ethics to Mystical Experience: An Exploration of Jouissance'. in *Key Concepts of Lacanian Psychoanalysis.* ed. by Nobus, D. London: Rebus Press, 1–28.

Felman, S. (1987) *Jacques Lacan and the Adventure of Insight: Psychoanalysis in Contemporary Culture.* Cambridge, MA: Harvard University Press.

Felman, S. (1988) 'On Reading Poetry'. in *The Purloined Poe: Lacan, Derrida, and Psychoanalytic Reading.* ed. by Muller, J., and Richardson, W. Baltimore, MD: Johns Hopkins University Press, 145.

Fink, B. (1995) *The Lacanian Subject.* Princeton, NJ: Princeton University Press.

Fink, B. (1996) 'The Nature of Unconscious Thought or Why No One Ever Reads Lacan's Postface to the "Seminar on The Purloined Letter"'. in *Reading Seminars I and II: Lacan's Return to Freud.* ed. by Feldstein, R., Fink, B., and Jaanus, M. New York: State University of New York Press, 173–191.

Fink, B. (2007) *Fundamentals of Psychoanalytic Technique: A Lacanian Approach for Practitioners.* New York: W.W. Norton.

Fink, B. (2014) 'A Brief Reader's Guide to "Variations on the Standard Treatment"'. In Fink, B. (2014) *Against Understanding, Vol. I: Commentary and Critique in a Lacanian Register.* New York: Routledge, 67–85.

Freud, S. (1895/1966) 'Project for a Scientific Psychology'. in *The Standard Edition of the Complete Psychological Works of Sigmund Freud, Volume I (1886–1899): Pre-Psycho-Analytic Publications and Unpublished Drafts.* ed. by Strachey, J. London: The Hogarth Press, 294–343.

Freud, S. (1897/1966) 'Letter 52: Extracts from the Fliess Papers'. in *The Standard Edition of the Complete Psychological Works of Sigmund Freud, Volume I (1886–1899):*

Pre-Psycho-Analytic Publications and Unpublished Drafts. ed. by Strachey, J. London: The Hogarth Press, 240–242.

Freud, S. (1900/1953) 'The Interpretation of Dreams'. in *The Standard Edition of the Complete Psychological Works of Sigmund Freud, Volumes IV–V (1900): The Interpretation of Dreams*. ed. by Strachey, J. London: The Hogarth Press, 1–621.

Freud, S. (1905/1958) 'Jokes and their Relation to the Unconscious'. in *The Standard Edition of the Complete Works of Sigmund Freud, Volume VIII: Jokes and their Relation to the Unconscious*. ed. by Strachey, J. London: The Hogarth Press, 8–236.

Freud, S. (1914/1958) 'Remembering, Repeating, and Working Through'. in *The Standard Edition of the Complete Works of Sigmund Freud, Volume XII: 'The Case of Schreber', 'Papers on Technique' and Other Works*. ed. by Strachey, J. London: The Hogarth Press, 145–156.

Freud, S. (1918/1966) 'From the History of an Infantile Neurosis'. in *The Standard Edition of the Complete Works of Sigmund Freud, Volume XVII: An Infantile Neurosis and Other Works*. ed. by Strachey, J. London: The Hogarth Press, 1–122.

Freud, S. (1919/2003) *The Uncanny*. trans. by McLintock, D. London: Penguin Books.

Freud, S. (1920/2003) *Beyond the Pleasure Principle and Other Writings*. trans. by Reddick, J. London: Penguin Books.

Freud, S. (1921/1955) 'Group Psychology and the Analysis of the Ego'. in *The Standard Edition of the Complete Psychological Works of Sigmund Freud, Volume XVIII (1920–1922): Beyond the Pleasure Principle, Group Psychology, and Other Works*. ed. by Strachey, J. London: The Hogarth Press, 67–143.

Fuks, B. B. (2008) *Freud and the Invention of Jewishness*. trans. Britto, H. H. New York: Agincourt Press.

Gallop, J. (1985) *Reading Lacan*. Ithaca: Cornell University Press.

Glynos, J., and Stavrakakis, Y. (2001) 'Postures and Impostures: On Lacan's Style and Use of Mathematical Science'. in *American Imago*, Vol. 58, No. 3. Baltimore, MD: Johns Hopkins University Press, 685–706.

Goethe, J.W. (1832) *Faust: Der Tragödie zweiter Teil in fünf Akten*. Berlin: Reclam.

Goethe, J. W. (1961) *Goethe's Faust*. trans. by Kaufmann, W. New York: Anchor Books.

Goethe, J. W. (1994) *Faust*. trans. by Swanwick, A. New York: Dover Publications.

Harries, K. (1967) 'Martin Heidegger: The Search for Meaning'. in *Existential Philosophers: Kierkegaard to Merleau-Ponty*. ed. by Schrader, G. A. New York: McGraw Hill, 61–208.

Heidegger, M. (1993) *Basic Writings*. San Francisco, CA: Harper.

Johnson, B. (1975/1988) 'The Frame of Reference: Poe, Lacan, Derrida'. in *Yale French Studies*, 55/56, 457–505.

Johnson, C. R. (2013) *Space-Time, Nonbeing, and the Void in the Field of Psychoanalysis*. Carrollton, GA: University of West Georgia.

Kierkegaard, S. (1843/1983) *Fear and Trembling / Repetition*. trans. by Hong, H. V., and Hong, E. H. Princeton, NJ: Princeton University Press.

Lacan, J. (n.d.) *The Seminar of Jacques Lacan, Book IX: Identification, 1961–1962*. trans. by Gallagher, C. For Private Circulation (unpublished).

Lacan, J. (n.d.) *The Seminar of Jacques Lacan, Book XII: Crucial Problems for Psychoanalysis, 1964–1965*. trans. by Gallagher, C. For Private Circulation (unpublished).

Lacan, J. (n.d.) *The Seminar of Jacques Lacan, Book XXIV: L'insu que sait de l'une bévue, s'aile à mourre, 1976–1977*. trans. by Gallagher, C. For Private Circulation (unpublished).

Lacan, J. (1953/2006) 'The Function and Field of Speech and Language in Psychoanalysis'. in *Écrits: The First Complete Edition in English*. trans. by Fink, B. New York: W. W. Norton, 197–268.

Lacan, J. (1956a) 'Le Séminaire Sur "La Lettre Volée"'. in *La Psychanalyse*, 2, 1–44.

Lacan, J. (1956b/1972) 'Seminar on "The Purloined Letter"'. in *Yale French Studies, French Freud: Structural Studies in Psychoanalysis*. trans. Mehlman, J. New Haven: Yale University, 38–72.

Lacan, J. (1956c/2006) 'The Freudian Thing'. in *Écrits: The First Complete Edition in English*. trans. by Fink, B. New York: W. W. Norton, 334–363.

Lacan, J. (1957/2006) 'The Instance of the Letter in the Unconscious'. in *Écrits: The First Complete Edition in English*. trans. by Fink, B. New York: W. W. Norton, 412–444.

Lacan, J. (1958/2006) 'On a Question Prior to Any Possible Treatment of Psychosis'. in *Écrits: The First Complete Edition in English*. trans. by Fink, B. New York: W. W. Norton, 445–488.

Lacan, J. (1960/2006) 'The Subversion of the Subject and the Dialectic of Desire in the Freudian Unconscious'. in *Écrits: The First Complete Edition in English*. trans. by Fink, B. New York: W. W. Norton, 671–702.

Lacan, J. (1962/2006) 'Kant with Sade'. in *Écrits: The First Complete Edition in English*. trans. by Fink, B. New York: W. W. Norton, 645–668.

Lacan, J. (1966a/2006) *Écrits: The First Complete Edition in English*. trans. by Fink, B. New York: W. W. Norton.

Lacan, J. (1966b/2006) 'Overture to the Collection'. in *Écrits: The First Complete Edition in English*. trans. by Fink, B. New York: W. W. Norton, 3–5.

Lacan, J. (1970) 'Of Structure as the Inmixing of an Otherness Prerequisite to Any Subject Whatever'. in *The Languages of Criticism and the Sciences of Man: The Structuralist Controversy*, eds. by Macksey, R., and Donato, E. Baltimore, MD: Johns Hopkins University Press, 186–194.

Lacan, J. (1971) 'Lituraterre'. in *Literature*, 3–10; republished in *Orincar?* 41, April–June 1987, 5–13.

Lacan, J. (1972) *The Knowledge of the Psychoanalyst, 1971–1972*. trans. Gallagher, C. For private circulation (unpublished).

Lacan, J. (1973/1981) *The Seminar of Jacques Lacan, Book XI: The Four Fundamental Concepts of Psychoanalysis*. trans. by Sheridan, A. New York: W. W. Norton.

Lacan, J. (1975/1998) *The Seminar of Jacques Lacan, Book XX: On Feminine Sexuality: The Limits of Love and Knowledge*. trans. by Fink, B. New York: W. W. Norton.

Lacan, J. (1978/1988) *The Seminar of Jacques Lacan, Book II: The Ego in Freud's Theory and in the Technique of Psychoanalysis, 1954–1955*. trans. by Tomaselli, S. New York: W. W. Norton.

Lacan, J. (1981/1993) *The Seminar of Jacques Lacan, Book III: The Psychoses, 1955–1956*. trans. by Grigg, R. New York: W. W. Norton.

Lacan, J. (1986/1997) *The Seminar of Jacques Lacan, Book VII: The Ethics of Psychoanalysis, 1959–1960*. trans. by Porter, D. New York: W. W. Norton.

Lacan, J. (1994a) *Séminaire, Tome 4: la Relation d'objet*. Paris: Seuil.

Lacan, J. (1994b/2021) *The Seminar of Jacques Lacan, Book IV: The Object Relation, 1956–1957*. trans. by Price, A. Cambridge: Polity Press.

Lacan, J. (2004/2014) *The Seminar of Jacques Lacan, Book X: Anxiety*. trans. by Price, A. Cambridge: Polity Press.

Lacan, J. (1998/2017) *The Seminar of Jacques Lacan, Book V: The Formations of the Unconscious*. trans. by Grigg, R. Cambridge: Polity Press.

Lacan, J. (2004/2014) *The Seminar of Jacques Lacan, Book X: Anxiety*. trans. by Price, A. R. Cambridge: Polity Press.

LaFont, J. (2004) 'Topology and Efficiency'. in *Lacan: Topologically Speaking*. ed. by Ragland, E., and Milovanovic, D. New York: Other Press, 3–27.

Laurent, E. (2007) 'Feminine Positions of Being'. in *The Later Lacan: An Introduction*. ed. by Voruz, V., and Wolf, B. Albany: State University of New York Press.

Liu, L. H. (2010) 'The Cybernetic Unconscious: Rethinking Lacan, Poe, and French Theory'. in *Critical Inquiry*, 36(2), 288–320.

Mabbot, O. (1988) 'The Text of "The Purloined Letter" with Notes'. in *The Purloined Poe: Lacan, Derrida, and Psychoanalytic Reading*. ed. by Muller, J., and Richardson, W. Baltimore, MD: Johns Hopkins University Press, 1–3.

Malone, K. (2012) 'Subjectivity and Alterity'. in *Journal of Theoretical and Philosophical Psychology*, 32(1), 50–66.

Milner, J. C. (1991) 'Lacan and the Ideal of Science'. in *Lacan & the Human Sciences*. Lincoln: University of Nebraska Press, 27–42.

Muller, J. P., and Richardson, W. J. (1988) *The Purloined Poe: Lacan, Derrida, and Psychoanalytic Reading*. Baltimore, MD: Johns Hopkins University Press.

O'Donnell, B. (2004) 'The Parmenides and the One'. in *The Letter (Dublin)*, 30, 31–43.

Pavón-Cuéllar, D. (2010) *From the Conscious Interior to an Exterior Unconscious*. London: Karnac Press.

Poe, E. A. (2004) 'The Purloined Letter'. in *The Essential Tales and Poems of Edgar Allan Poe*. New York: Barnes and Noble Classics, 362–379.

Poe, E. A. (2006) 'The Mystery of Marie Roget'. in *The Complete Tale and Poems of Edgar Allan Poe*. New York: Barnes and Noble, 455–493.

Prioteasa, M. (n.d.) 'The Paradox of Self-Inclusion in "The Purloined Letter"' http:// theroundtable.partium.ro/Current/2013/Literary/Mihaela%20Prioteasa%20-%20The %20Paradox%20of%20Self.pdf Accessed Dec 20, 2013.

Roudenesco, E. (1997) *Jacques Lacan: An Outline of a Life and History of a System of Thought*. London: Polity.

Roudinesco, E. (1993/1997) *Jacques Lacan: Outline of a Life, History of a System of Thought*. trans. by Bray, B. New York: Columbia University Press.

Samuels, R. (1993) *Between Philosophy & Psychoanalysis: Lacan's Reconstruction of Freud*. New York: Routledge.

Schneiderman, S. (1991) 'Fictions'. in *Lacan and the Subject of Language*. ed. by Ragland-Sullivan, E., and Bracher, M. New York: Routledge, 152–166.

Shane, A. (1997) 'Clinical Lessons from The Purloined Letter'. in *Anamorphosis*, 144–150.

Skeat, W. W. (1910/2005) *An Etymological Dictionary of the English Language*. Oxford: Dover.

Vanheule, S. (2011) *The Subject of Psychosis: A Lacanian Perspective*. Basingstoke, Hampshire: Palgrave Macmillan.

Vappereau, J.-M. (2012) 'The Two Moments Prior to Narcissism'. Workshop, Saturday, March 24, 2012. New York: Après Coup.

Žižek, S. (1992) *Enjoy Your Symptom!: Jacques Lacan in Hollywood and Out*. New York: Routledge.

3

ON MY ANTECEDENTS

Derek Hook, John Dall'Aglio, Sinan Richards, Stijn Vanheule and Benjamin Strosberg

Context

We can refer to the closing paragraphs of "On my antecedents" to establish an institutional context for this autobiographical écrits. Lacan names two institutions there that facilitated his development. The first of these is *Évolution Psychiatrique*, a psychoanalytic group founded in 1925 by French psychiatrist René Laforgue and the phenomenological psychiatrist Eugène Minkowski. This group deserves credit, says Lacan, for the fact that "psychoanalysis saw the light of day in [France]" (57, 1). In noting that "[p]resent generations of psychiatrists will find it hard to imagine that, at the time…[of] my residency, there were only three of us…involved in psychoanalysis" (57, 1), Lacan is both pointing to the dramatic changes that had occurred by 1966 in respect of how psychoanalysis had been received by psychiatry and also underlining his own contribution to the new cultural prominence of psychoanalysis in France. He goes on to describe the *Collège Philosophique* as "the major institution that offered me the opportunity to give several public lectures" (57, 4). The *Collège* was founded by Jean Wahl as an alternative to the Sorbonne. Wahl, a central figure within Parisian intellectual culture, is acknowledged for providing Lacan with an opportunity to speak and for his role in facilitating debates between various "intellectual fevers of the time" (57, 4). The fact that Lacan mentions, in an accompanying endnote, that one of his contributions to the *Collège Philosophique* was on the "Individual Myth of the Neurotic" is significant (see Lacan, 1979). That paper, says Lacan, highlighted "the beginning of a duly structuralist reference" (57, n. 5) in his work. Lacan is thus reiterating how structuralist ideas enabled him to break with many of the phenomenological precepts characterizing French psychiatry at the time.

"On my antecedents" is one of five short texts written specifically for the 1966 publication of *Écrits*. Its position in the text – at the opening of Section II rather than at the very beginning of the book – is itself perhaps a witty comment on *nachträglichkeit*, that is, on the retroactivity so crucial in any psychoanalytic treatment, or analysis. We might treat it thus as a delayed introduction,

DOI: 10.4324/9781003368649-4

indeed, as an alternative genealogy, one which breaks from what by 1966 would have been an established set of influences on Lacan's work – structural linguistics, Kojéve's Hegel, Henri Wallon's (1931) mirror test, etc. – so as to offer an alternative set of reference-points with which to navigate Lacan's most formidable collection of writings.

Commentary

It is commonplace within the histories of psychoanalysis to note that whereas it was hysteria that inspired Freud, it was psychosis – and more specifically, *paranoia* – that inspired Lacan. True as this may be, it begs the question: What existing theorizations most significantly informed Lacan's early thinking on paranoia and thereby psychosis? Lacan provides us with two sets of conceptual co-ordinates with which to take up this question. He directs us to consider "the surrealist environment" (the influence of René Crevel, and, more directly, Salvador Dalí's "critical paranoia" (51, 3)) and Clérambault's notion of mental automatism. We will take up each of these two important influences in turn after a brief description of Lacan's conceptualization of paranoiac knowledge.

Paranoiac knowledge

Lacan wastes little time in foregrounding his notion of "paranoiac knowledge", a concept that he, as "a physician and psychiatrist" (51, 2), introduced in his (1975/1932) doctoral thesis *De la psychose paranoïaque dans ses rapports avec la personanalité* ("On paranoid psychosis in its relationship with personality"). The thesis marked a break from the then-dominant empirical school of positivist psychiatry in France. In contrast to approaches that aimed to isolate the organic cause of mental alienation, Lacan opted to privilege the words and speech of psychotic patients to explore the details of their personal biographies and the material circumstances that related them to the society that had formed them.

   A central component of the thesis was the case of Aimée (Marguerite Anzieu), a railway clerk and author who, in a state of delusional paranoia, attacked a famous Parisian actress (Huguette Duflos) believing that her son's life was under threat. Lacan argued that Aimée's delusions began after a failed pregnancy and that her subsequent literary ambitions – she wrote two novels that were rejected for publication – were stirred by the onset of an anxious second pregnancy. Aimée's case was particularly fascinating because she appeared to make a full recovery after the attack on Duflos. Lacan saw in Aimée's behavior an instantiation of what he called "self-punishment paranoia", a condition in which the targets of the paranoid subject's aggression – those that they claim to be persecuting them – are in fact their own displaced ideal-ego. In attacking Duflos, Aimée was thus attacking an externalization of her own idealized self-image. Here then was the clue to the self-cure that Aimée managed to enact through assaulting Dulfos: the jealousy, erotomania, and persecutory ideation that had immediately preceded the act were no longer necessary because a punishment had actually been carried out. To this was added the fact – which of course echoes Freud's (1900) ideas regarding the unconscious need for punishment – that Aimée had secured for herself not only the status of being guilty before the law but of one punished by it. Hence the idea that it was through her violent act that Aimée facilitated a kind of spontaneous cure upon herself (Allouch, 1994; Cox-Cameron, 2000; Macey, 1988).

In short then, the originality of Lacan's approach to psychotic paranoia consisted in his foregrounding of the phenomenon of self-punishment, and in his insistence that those suffering from paranoia had been captured in the image of another. The underlying assumption – which of course anticipated much of what Lacan would go on to theorize in respect of the imaginary register – was that the foundation of paranoia consisted of a dual imaginary relation between the patient and the world. This dual imaginary relation is rooted in an identificatory process in which the ego is captured by ideal images: images from without that invade the patient's mind, thus installing an experience of intrusion that gives rise to unshakeable convictions (Vanheule, 2018). Whereas Lacan first qualified these convictions as "delusional knowledge" – *connaissance délirante* – he would later refer to them with the term "paranoid knowledge".

Evidently, Lacan's interest in paranoia predates his wholehearted embrace of psychoanalysis and therefore also his celebrated "retour à Freud". Significantly, "On my antecedents" is not the first text in *Écrits* where Lacan highlights the originality of the concept of paranoiac knowledge. In *Presentation on Psychical Causality* (discussed by Pavón-Cuéllar in this volume), Lacan remarks that paranoiac knowledge is "akin to...the reaction recognized by psychiatrists [as]...'transitivism'" (147, 4). Lacan had thus established a link between the psychological phenomenon observed by Charlotte Bühler (1935), that is, a state of confusion or overlap between one ego and another, and the more overtly psychiatric dimension pertaining to the designation "paranoiac".

Here it is worthwhile pausing for a moment to underscore an important but frequently overlooked distinction. This is between generally paranoiac (or, in today's vernacular, paranoid) phenomena, which can occur in almost any type of mental disturbance, which does not necessarily pertain to psychotic structure, and paranoia as a sub-category of psychotic structure, a "distinct diagnostic category involving the construction of a stable system of beliefs with a named persecutor" (Leader, 2011, p. 20).

A second important distinction should be stressed here, that between imaginary knowledge (*connaissance*), that is, *knowledge of the ego*, on the one hand, and symbolic knowledge (*savoir*), which is *knowledge of the subject*, on the other. This distinction is critical, not only because both terms (*connaissance* and *savoir*) are translated as "knowledge" in English but because psychoanalysis works to constantly undo the imaginary self-knowledge of the ego to reveal the dimension of symbolic knowledge of the subject that it impedes. *Connaissance*, which as Evans (1996) reminds us, can never be extricated from its necessary correlate, *méconnaissance,* is the imaginary knowledge a subject has of themselves, a type of *me-connaissance* that is constitutive of the ego. What we are dealing with here is not only a type of self-knowledge founded on mirage-like fantasies of wholeness, subjective/bodily integration, and self-mastery. "Imaginary knowledge", remarks Evans (1996), is called "paranoiac knowledge" by Lacan "because it has the same structure as paranoia (both involve a delusion of absolute knowledge and mastery), and because one of the preconditions of all human knowledge is the paranoiac alienation of the ego" (p. 95).

Before we move on to consider how Clérambault and Dalí influenced Lacan, it is worth noting how foundational the idea of paranoiac knowledge was in respect of Lacan's subsequent theorization of the mirror phase. This leads us to challenge the presumption, shared by so many texts on Lacan, that Lacan's intellectual legacy really begins with the theory of the mirror stage. That is to say: the notion of paranoiac knowledge can be said to be more foundational to Lacan's subsequent work than even the theory of the mirror stage. Or, differently put, it was precisely the early theorization of paranoiac knowledge (see Lacan, 2023) that lent breadth and complexity to Lacan's multiple re-elaborations of the mirror stage and the imaginary order.

Surrealism, Crevel, Dalí, critical paranoia

What though are we to make of Lacan's brief reference to the influence of surrealism? Well, Lacan credits "the surrealist environment" as enabling "a former link" – presumably a Freudian or psychiatric understanding of paranoia – to be "reestablished", reestablished, however, "on the basis of a new relay, including Salvador Dalí's 'critical paranoia'" (51, 3). While he does not particularly stress it, Lacan himself played a part in surrealism. He notes somewhat parenthetically that "my offspring can be found in the first issues of the journal *Minotaure*" (51, 3), the short-lived mouthpiece of French surrealism. He is referring here to the two articles he published in that journal, namely, "The problem of style and paranoid forms of experience" in the journal's first issue in 1933 (Lacan, 1933a) and "Motives of paranoid crime" in a subsequent issue later that same year (Lacan, 1933b).

We know that Lacan's thesis became a *cause célèbre* in surrealist circles (Macey, 1983). Cameron-Cox (2000) attributes this to Lacan's recognition that the writings he analyzed there – those of his psychotic patient Aimée – should be accorded a literary status and not be viewed merely as the symptoms of psychosis. It was this feature, she says, that was "seized upon by its first surrealist readers, and which gave to [the thesis]…a position in contemporary even avant-garde thinking" (2000, pp. 18–19).

While there is much speculation on the full extent of surrealism's influence on Lacan (Alexandrian, 1974; Constantinidou, 2012; Macey, 1983; Polsani, 2001) and Lacan's upon surrealism (Berressem, 1996), what seems beyond dispute is that Lacan found in surrealism a means of conceptualizing the processes of mental automatism and paranoiac association that differed significantly from theories of organicism that predominated in psychiatry at the time (Rabaté, 2002). Cox-Cameron observes that "the Dalínian *connaissance paranoïaque*... marked [Lacan's] thinking in the thirties and forties" (2000, p. 26). Before turning our attention to Dalí however, let us briefly consider Lacan's reference (51, 3) to René Crevel's (1932) *Le Clavecin de Diderot*.

René Crevel was a radical Marxist intellectual and a surrealist novelist who had little patience for Freudian psychoanalysis. For Crevel (1932), Freud's work represented a type of vulgar materialism, a naïve attempt at scientism. It seems then curious that Lacan cites *Le Clavecin de Diderot* as a significant influence especially given that it is in that work that Crevel outlines many of his dissatisfactions with Freud's psychoanalysis. It is not only psychoanalysis that comes in for critique in *Le Clavecin de Diderot*. Colonialism and scientism are likewise called to task in a work that, true to the Marxist commitments of its author, remains consistently scornful of any analytic perspective – including, of course, Freud's – that removed the individual subject from the concrete specifications of their social and historical situation. The critiques advanced in *Le Clavecin de Diderot* established, however, a basis for Crevel's (1933) subsequent praise, in the fifth issue of *Le Surréalisme au service de la Révolution,* for Lacan's radicalization of psychoanalysis. According to Roudinesco, Crevel saw "the old school of psychoanalysis as corrupt and steeped in bourgeois idealism...[yet he] saw Lacan as the spokesperson of a new spirit: his 'materialism'" (1997, p. 59). Lacan's citation of Crevel is thus less curious an inclusion than it may initially seem.

In his summary of Lacan's thesis from the fifth issue of *Le Surréalisme au service de la Révolution,* Crevel (1933) argues that Lacan was taking aim at the so-called objectivist empiricist positions in the psychiatric sciences. Lacan's contribution to psychiatry, by contrast, aimed to grasp the personality of the subject by trying to "illuminate both the inside and the outside" (1933, p. 50).

Whereas Freud is accused of a "relapse into mechanical materialism" (1933, p. 51), Lacan is seen as offering a properly materialist science via a psycho-dialectic approach that provided "detailed, precise, complete monographs" (1933, p. 51). For Crevel, Lacan's method as developed in his doctoral thesis was to seek as fastidious as possible a "clinical examination of certain typical cases" (1933, p. 51), which included an attempt to "socially situate their patients" and that necessitated study of "the relations of such and such a particular family with society in general" (1933, p. 51).

Crevel's enthusiastic endorsement of Lacan's work had much to do with the fact that it provided a viable means of linking the social and the individual and thereby – a hugely significant factor for a militant figure like Crevel – a way to read psychoanalysis with Marx. We should be cautious not to overlook Crevel's influence on Lacan in this respect: it was Crevel, insists Alexandrine (1974), who incited Lacan to develop a "psycho-dialectic" analysis (that is, a conjoined mode of psychoanalysis and Marxism) by associating Freud with

Hegelian phenomenology. With this background in place, we can see why Roudinesco (1997) argues – in what may initially seem an exaggerated claim – that for the surrealists, Lacan represented the future, and came to be "hailed as the leader of a school that combined Freudianism and Marxism and as the harbinger of the coming revolution" (pp. 59–60).

What though of Dalí's influence upon Lacan? Let us begin this discussion by noting the names of the articles that each contributed to the first issue of *Minotaure*. Lacan's text ("The problem of style and paranoid forms of experience" (Lacan, 1933/1988a)) followed directly after Dalí's ("Paranoid-critical interpretation of the haunting image of the Angelus of Millet" (Dalí, 1933)). Not only then were the two men intrigued by paranoia – paranoiac phenomena would of course prove in different ways, foundational to each of their careers – both, more specifically, were fascinated by the idea of paranoia as a type of delusional activity – or a state of delirium – that yielded *a systematic interpretation of reality*. The influence of Freud can be felt here. If such delirious interpretations or delusions are not dismissed as mere instances of "false reasoning" but are instead viewed as a stable system for the interpretation – or "systematization" – of reality, then paranoid delusion is not an illness *per se*, but is instead, as Freud suggested, a fundamental attempt at recovery. One recalls here Freud's remarks on the Schreber case: "What we take to be the pathological production, the delusional formation, is in reality the attempt at recovery, the reconstruction" (p. 71). The paranoid productions of delusion should thus be understood, as Constantinidou (2012) puts it, as "an assimilative fictional world created by the paranoid patient's ego in order to re-establish contact with reality" (p. 243). The delusions that emerge in paranoiac states are not thus inherently pathological, at least from a psychoanalytic standpoint, just as they are not fundamentally disordered, chaotic, or piecemeal in nature. Irrational as they might be, they nonetheless constitute a mode of thinking, one that adheres to a certain logic and that locates the subject in a world that is less chaotic because of the systematization of ideas brought about.

Let us return though to Dalí. We find in his writings of the late 1920s and early 1930s a clear if perhaps somewhat romanticized admiration for the complexity of the ways in which paranoid subjects make sense of the world. Dalí (1928/1998) was impressed by the speed and finesse of delusional interpretations which outstripped the capacities of "normal" (that is, "non-paranoiac") persons in the domains of both intelligence and creativity. He lamented that Freudian ideas had been diluted of their initial radicality and went on to stress – in terms which cannot but invoke Lacan himself – that his own agenda lay with restoring their "rabid and dazzling clarity" (Dalí, 1930/1998, p. 110). In his important essay, "The Rotting Donkey" (originally published in 1928), paranoia is characterized as a "mechanism of strength and power" that is able to contribute to a "total discrediting of the world of reality" (1928/1998, p. 115). The "new simulacra" that paranoid thought reveals – simulacra being Dalí's word for the new images or ideas of the world produced in a state of deliria – not only "have their roots in the unconscious" but might themselves be placed "at [it's] service" (p. 115). Interestingly, for Dalí the "force of paranoid power" is diametrically opposed to the processes of hallucination:

> As far as possible from the influence of sensory phenomena with which hallucination may be considered more or less connected, paranoid activity always employs controllable and recognizable material... Paranoia uses the external world as a means to assert an obsessive idea, with its disturbing characteristic of making this idea's reality valid to others. The reality of the external world serves as illustration and proof, and is placed in the service of the reality of our mind. (Dalí, 1928/1998, pp. 115–116)

For Dalí then, paranoid productions were unlike hallucinations not only because they are not primarily *sensory* in form (they are processes of *thought,* they are, at basis, *interpretative phenomena*), but also because they utilize existing verifiable, recognizable materials and do so in such convincing terms that the external world itself becomes the proof of – and thus potentially subservient to – the newly ascendent paranoiac ideas. Hence, as Dalí asserts in "The moral position of surrealism":

> [t]he particular perspicacity of attention in the paranoiac state must be insisted upon: paranoia [must be] recognized...as a form of mental illness which consists in organizing reality in such a way as to utilize it to control imaginative construction. (Dalí, 1930/1998, p. 112)

We understand better now Dalí's reference to "simulacra". The state of delirium produces a spiraling series of interpretative formations that have the potential to over-ride or replace prior understandings of the world, and to do so not merely as second-rate copies, but as vital, "living and breathing" schemas of comprehension that function in an adaptive and autonomous manner. Reality can thus be convincingly rearranged, reorganized.

While there is much in Dalí that Lacan would draw inspiration from – such as the insistence on the autonomous, non-deduced character of delusional thinking – we should, nevertheless, remain attentive to what differs in the conceptualizations of the two men. Bowie (1991) proves helpful here. He cites the Catalan artist's assertion in *The Unspeakable Confessions of Salvador Dalí* that "I believe my paranoia is an expression of the absolute structure, the proof of its immanence" (Dalí, cited in Bowie, pp. 38-39). In comparison with such a claim, Bowie continues,

> Lacan's vision of knowledge as inherently paranoiac seems modest... Lacan like Dalí talks about an immanent structure of the human world. Human knowledge [at the level of the imaginary] begins

from an illusion – a misapprehension...and constructs an inescapable autonomous system in its wake. Psychoanalysis is a "critical" interpretive system that seeks to reduplicate and modulate the subject's original delirium [of imaginary relations]. Unlike Dalí's paranoia-criticism, it vacillates interminably between mental registers, but its play of system upon system and delusion upon delusion is the closest approximation to truth that human beings can expect to achieve. (Bowie, 1991, p. 40)

There were then significant differences in how the artist and the psychiatrist sought to utilize paranoiac phenomena. Dalí aimed to use the interpretative deliria of paranoia in a central – if, admittedly, mimed or feigned – form so as to produce compelling and highly original imagery. Lacan, by contrast, was aware both of how inducing a mild or controlled form of paranoiac questioning might upset prior certainties of knowledge (thereby aiding the exploratory dimension of clinical work) and of how the deadlock of a paranoiac/imaginary rivalry could fatally capsize a treatment (i.e., the limitations of inducing a transference neurosis in cases of psychosis).

To recapitulate then, what we learn from Dalí – and what made Lacan and Dalí such kindred spirits at the time – is the idea that paranoia is a generative activity that depends not merely on distorting reality (i.e., "false reasoning") but on a systematic logic operating as a type of interpretative intelligence enacted upon the world. As Roudinesco puts it "a delusion is already an interpretation of reality...[just as] paranoia [is] a creative activity which does not depend....on deformation, but on logic" (1997, pp. 110–110). For Dalí, as Vanheule remarks, delusions

> do not emerge as a reaction against some primordial element, but autonomously constitute a mode of thinking that does not follow the rules of rationality. Paranoid thinking obeys a strict internal logic. It systematizes the confusion one is confronted with and produces simulacra about the world that reveal another side of reality than the one ordinary thought brings to the fore. (Vanheule, 2018, p. 213)

Dalí had formulated these ideas well before meeting Lacan, and it can "be assumed that [he]...inspired Lacan in stressing the autonomous, non-deduced character of delusional thinking" (Vanheule, 2018, p. 213).

In bringing this section to a close, let us ask: what was the real significance of surrealism for Lacan? There is a refrain that Lacan repeats several times over in "On my antecedents" that seems apt here. Formative as his engagement with surrealism may well have been, its true significance – at least from the perspective of Lacan of 1966 – was that it ultimately "led to Freud" (52, 8). It bears mentioning here that at the time that surrealism arguably exercised its greatest influence on Lacan – around 1932, when he was preparing articles

95

for *Minatoure* – he was also working on a French translation of Freud's (1922) paper "Some Neurotic Mechanisms in Jealousy, Paranoia and Homosexuality". We might say then, somewhat reductively, that in a three-way contest regards the relative influence upon Lacan of Freud, 19th-century psychiatry, and surrealism, Freud was always going to win out. This notwithstanding, we should recall that in 1948's *Aggressiveness in Psychoanalysis,* we hear Lacan invoking an echo of Dalí's paranoiac critical activity. In discussing how the ego should be approached in psychoanalytic treatment, Lacan remarks that instead of "attacking it head on, "the analytical maieutic adopts a detour that amounts in sum to inducting in the subject a directed paranoia" (89, 2).

Mental automatism

Having noted his debt to surrealism, Lacan identifies what he takes to be a more significant antecedent, namely, the work of Clérambault, and, more specifically, Clérambault's notion of mental automatism. At its most basic, mental automatism refers to fundamental disruptions in the processes of thought. True to form, Lacan does not define the concept, but instead invokes it in in somewhat vague terms (Lacan speaks of its "metaphorical, mechanistic ideology" (51, 5)), which alerts the reader to the fact that a somewhat creative exercise in citation might be at play. While Lacan makes a show of crediting the concept to his "only master in psychiatry" (51, 4), the way he will utilize and develop the idea is, at the risk of understatement, significantly different. That being said, Clérambault's concept remains of paramount importance for Lacan's intellectual project: it functioned as a kind of lever, enabling him to shift aside a series of longstanding psychiatric assumptions, thus creating the space for his own original account of paranoia and psychosis. Lacan intimates as much, noting that while the idea is "open to criticism", it nonetheless came closer "in its attempt to come to grips with subjective text" than any existing resource in French psychiatry, to what might "be constructed on the basis of a structural analysis" (51, 5).

What exactly though did Clérambault have in mind with the idea of "automatic phenomena"? For Clérambault (1925), the term referred to disorienting mental intrusions experienced by patients, to strange manifestations occurring within the intimacy of the subject's psychical functioning and self-understanding. He was interested in how thoughts, impulses, bodily sensations, actions, and utterances became disordered, and in how habitual modes of self-experience became incapacitated. A defining feature of the various forms of mental automatism for Clérambault is that they are experienced as exogenous. The subject undergoing such obtrusive effects views them as foreign elements intruding upon their usual psychological processes. Such effects incur reactions of bewilderment, confusion, and perplexity. Clérambault (1926) describes such phenomena as experiences of "dis-appropriation" and interference, stressing that there is a marked absence of any subjective sense of ownership; there is a lack, in other words, of a sense of "me-ness" or "mine-ness". Moreover, such "automatic phenomena" remain *non-ideational* and neutral; they are not inherently linked to a series of ideas, and they are viewed neither as intrinsically aggressive nor as attacks upon the person experiencing them. One begins then to intuit what would have appealed to Lacan about this theory of mental automatism. As in structural linguistics, it is not the apparent (experiential/ phenomenological) *meaning* that is most significant here but rather the effects of the rupture occurring on the level of *relationships between elements of psychical content.* That is to say, the perplexity mental phenomena produce is not a result of the mental contents (the specific thoughts, ideas, impressions, sensations) that the subject is confronted with but of the functional disruption in the formal structure of normal experience. Lacan's eschewal of content- or meaning-fixated approaches is apparent when he remarks on the contrast he perceived between "a hint of promise" in Clérambault's work and "the decline that could be seen in a semiology that was ever more bogged down in assumptions related to rationality" (51, 6–52, 1).

None of this is to suggest that the interferences mental automatism introduces into the subject's thought processes are not thoroughly disorientating. They most certainly are. They introduce troubling intrusions or blank spots in the subject's thought processes, hence Lacan's comment in *Seminar III* that what we find in mental automatism "is that which doesn't correspond to a train of thought" (1993, p. 6). Or, to put things in more explicitly Lacanian terminology: what we find in mental automatism is the experience of a "sudden emergence of an enigmatic signifier with non-sensical power". (It may help to note here that the concept in contemporary Lacanian clinical discourse which most closely approximates this idea is that of the elementary phenomena typically apparent at the onset of a psychosis, that is, intrusive, automatic interruptions in thought that overwhelm or incapacitate the subject who, accordingly, experiences a surplus of enigmatic meaningfulness).

What then were the key differences between Clérambault and Lacan's thinking? Well, for a start, Clérambault spent a good deal of time differentiating between different levels (ideo-verbal, motor, sensory affective), at which mental automatism occurred. Lacan's approach is notably more abstract and less concerned with categorization at various levels of psychical/physical functioning. Lacan focuses far more – as befits a generally structuralist orientation – on the relations between elements, that is, on the logical organization of such interferences. Clérambault moreover assumed that a strict parallel existed between clinically observable instances of mental automatism and the underlying neurological events taken to cause such disruptions. Indeed, Lacan's "master" consistently maintained a commitment to the biological nature of psychiatric breakdowns – he remained an organicist thinker throughout – viewing mental automatism as a reaction to a physical malady (intoxication, infection, tumors, etc.). Lacan, on the contrary, did not consider mental automatism to be a mechanical phenomenon determined by brain disturbances: "This is totally inadequate. It's much more promising to think of it in terms of the internal structure of language" (Lacan, 1993, p. 250).

To Freud, via Aimée

Having explained the notion of mental automatism – and how Lacan differed from Clérambault's articulation of this concept – let us now return to the letter of Lacan's text. Lacan, interestingly, offers a few reflections on Clérambault as clinician. Lacan's "master" is at once praised for achievements related to "the quality of his gaze", even though he is also critiqued as "a sort of recurrence of...a figure that dates back to the birth of the clinic" (52, 2). We can detect here a measure of respect for the influential psychiatrist's diagnostic interview skills and his abilities of clinical deduction. Yet the reference to Foucault's recently published *The Birth of the Clinic* highlights less commendable features of Clérambault's approach: it holds him up as an exemplification of the medical gaze in its psychiatric form. For Lacan, in other words, Clérambault appears to have been a remarkable psychiatrist (even if his "clinical genius" was allegedly inferior to that of Kraepelin (52, 3)). Nonetheless, Clérambault remained stuck in the mode of the medical gaze and was unable as such to move beyond the parameters of positivism or to transcend the organicism of the disease model of illness.

Now while Lacan is eager to strike some distance from the traditions that Clérambault represents (both, presumably, of French psychiatry and of the medical gaze), he is nonetheless forced to admit a degree of "faithfulness to the symptom's formal envelope" (52, 4). In other words, he still seems indebted to Clérambault's clinical orientation of remaining always attentive to the formal features of a patient's presentation. What though are we to understand by "the symptom's formal envelope", and why does Lacan move so quickly from this concept to the "literary effects" evident in his case of Aimée? Let us answer these questions one at a time.

Verhaeghe and Declercq (2002) provide a useful way of thinking about "the symptom's formal envelope", which takes us back to Freud's assertion that symptoms are made up of both the drive (in Lacanian terms, the real) and elements of the psyche (the symbolic). Conversion symptoms, they explain, can be studied from two perspectives: via attention to the symbolic dimension of signifiers/psychical representatives that are repressed, and by means of attention to the real dimension of drive impulses. The formal envelope of the symptom thus refers to the *symbolic constructions* built around the real of the drive.

The link to the Aimée case now seems easier to grasp, especially when we bear in mind that what Lacan analyzed in his doctoral thesis was not just Aimée's history and life circumstances but also the novels and various other literary works she produced which were "of high enough quality" to be considered instances of "involuntary poetry" (52, 5). This connection reflects Lacan's structural reading of pathology, specifically psychosis, with attention to the "function of ideals" (as exemplified in symbolic productions such as those of writing, speech, and language) over the "register of passion" (that is, the dimension of affects). Lacan isolates a moment from the Aimée case that captures this:

> the sort of gust effect that, in [Aimée], blew down the screen known as a delusion as soon as her hand touched, in a serious act of aggression, one of the images in her theater – who was doubly fictitious for her since she was also a star in reality – redoubled the conjugation of her poetic space with a gulf-like scansion. (52, 7)

Lacan's reference to the realms of the fictitious, the theatrical, and the poetic are significant here. They clearly reiterate his concern with the symbolic aspect of the symptom's "formal envelope" – a factor of considerable importance in his structuralist turn to language – just as they enable him to identify points of explanatory relevance that differ from the more usual recourse to affects, passions, and associated emotional factors.

Lacan's attention to "involuntary poetry", which we can understand here as itself an instance of mental automatism – an example, more specifically, of the *insistence of the signifier in psychosis* – contrasts markedly with a passion-based approach to delusions. This is a hallmark of a Lacanian approach: avoiding explanatory recourse to passions when a consideration of the role of the signifier (language, symbolic operations, symbolic ideals, etc.) yields a far more structurally robust account of psychical phenomena. One such example of the insistence or force of the signifier in Aimée's case is then immediately identified when Lacan remarks on the "function of ideals" – that is, to put things in more overtly psychoanalytic terms, the role of symbolic Ego-Ideals – which led to "a series of duplications" or repetitions in Aimée's life. A close attention to such ideals not only led Lacan to "the notion of structure" in the case, but to avoiding the rather uncritical reference to "the register of passion" (52, 6). We have here a tacit reference – soon to be picked up and developed – to the crucial psychoanalytic notion of identification.

Who or what does Lacan have in mind here with his reference to "the clinicians in Toulouse" (52, 6)? In Dany Nobus's (2022) reading of this passage, he argues that

> "*les cliniciens de Toulouse*" does not refer [as Bruce Fink's translation implies] to "the clinicians in [the city of] Toulouse", but rather to "Toulouse's clinicians", i.e. the psychiatrists working at Sainte-Anne Hospital under the direction of Édouard Toulouse [director of the Henri-Rousselle Hospital at Sainte-Anne]…Toulouse and his clinicians would have been at Sainte-Anne when Lacan was studying Aimée at the *Préfecture spéciale* under Gatian de Clérambault.

Nobus continues, remarking that while much that could be said about the conception of mental disorder developed by Toulouse,

> his outlook basically revolves around the (dys)functioning of a mental system of "auto-conduction", which is responsible for regulating the passions. In other words, even though Lacan doesn't explicitly refer to "auto-conduction" here, he is essentially saying that his notion of "structure", in all its abstraction, is more suitable than any notion that would have been used by clinicians working in the tradition of E. Toulouse, despite the fact that "auto-conduction" also suggests a certain degree of "structuring" of mental processes.

For Lacan then, what lies behind Aimée's delusion is not some untaken action that must be cathartically released via set of inflamed drives. Rather, an "involuntary poetry" is revealed that highlights the formal (and structuring) operations of the signifier. Indeed, while Aimée's "acting out" − or, to use the Lacanian concept that is more appropriate in this context, her *passage a l'acte* − certainly plays its part in tearing down the delusional screen, it does not resolve the psychosis; instead, it "redoubles" the "poetic space" (52, 7). Such poetics remain indexed to the problematics of passion and image without being reducible to them. None of this is to say that the dimension of the imaginary (i.e., "the images in her [Aimée's] theatre" (52, 7)) and the associated "stage machinery of acting out" (52, 8) are not crucial here. They certainly are, but they need to be situated in relation to Aimée's symbolic/literary productions and Ego-Ideal identifications, which were, in turn, made apparent via attention to the phenomena of "self-punishment". This concept had been variously approached by psychiatrists and criminologists; Lacan cites the "Berlin-style criminology...of Alexander and Straub", according it however little significance other than that it was through it that he was "led to Freud" (52, 8).

Resistance in theory and technique...and the role of psychosis

Let us retrace Lacan's steps so far. His beginning with Clérambault and Aimée indicates how his entry to Freud occurred via the means of psychosis. Indeed, the early seminars detail the problematics of psychosis by theorizing the ego and its relationship to the symbolic, insofar as the ego is structurally perturbed in psychosis. The next key stepping-stone he highlights in this *écrit* is his "mirror stage" presented to the International Psychoanalytic Association in 1936. He highlights the mirror stage as the "invention" that "brought [him] to the very heart of a resistance in theory and technique" in psychoanalysis (52, 11–53, 1). What exactly is the resistance he refers to here?

Well, we have seen how Lacan has drawn a line from signifier to psychosis, to mirror stage, which raises the further question of the nature of the relationship among these three. Later in this *écrit*, Lacan critiques Ego Psychology − "a theory of the ego" – for centering the ego around "a characteristic function of reality" (54, 3). This, it appears, is the "heart of...resistance...[the] ever more blatant problem" (52, 11–53, 1) in psychoanalysis. Such an approach, in Lacan's view, traces the ego back to Freud's (1921) *Group Psychology* – a text which, for Lacan, theorizes not the ego, but, far more crucially, the *mechanisms of identification*. One may keep this critique in play to explore something of the relationship between signifier, ego, and psychosis.

Lacan's position rejects a theorization of reality built upon the basis of "identicalness", a matching of identity between perceptual trace and what is found in reality (54, 6). This confuses "*Wirklichkeit*" and "*Realitat*" – the latter being "especially reserved for psychical reality" (54, 5). Lacan elaborates:

> If Freud reminds us of the relationship between the ego and the perception-consciousness system, it is only to indicate that our reflective tradition...has tested its standards of truth in this system. (54, 7)

Reflective consciousness – that is, the ego as indexed to the perceptual-consciousness system in Freud – aims to establish the identity of a trace with reality to judge "standards of truth" (54, 7). This, however, is not the reality that psychoanalysis is concerned with (see below).

For Lacan, *Group Psychology* is not the key reference for Freud's theory of the ego – "On Narcissism" (Freud, 1914) does a far better job of outlining the basic co-ordinates of the ego. Lacan opposes the "truth" of reality as something established via perceptual identity by delineating two dimensions of the ego in Freud:

> But it is in order to call these standards of truth into question that Freud links the ego, on the basis of a twofold reference, to one's own body – that is narcissism – and to the complexity of the three orders of identification. (54, 8)

The ego is not grounded in a reality-testing function, but rather in the narcissism of the body and the problematics of identification. It is here that Lacan places his mirror stage as "the watershed between the imaginary and the symbolic" (54, 9). The ego must be understood not only in its relation to drive (*jouissance*), but in terms of how it is caught up in images of the body via narcissism (Freud, 1914), as well as terms of identification with traits and signifiers of the social order (Freud, 1921). In this way, Lacan clarifies the mirror stage as not simply an imaginary operation but as a "watershed" or meeting-point of the imaginary and symbolic registers (and, insofar as narcissism is concerned with libido, one might add in addition, the register of the real; see more below). This is how Lacan interprets the Freudian ego as having roots in both *Group Psychology* and "On Narcissism". In neither case is the ego structured by the reality-testing of perceptual-consciousness.

Why does Lacan begin with the question of psychosis and transition into the mirror stage? One might suggest that Lacan is opposing standard psychiatric approaches to psychosis: delusions rooted in emotional passion; psychosis as a problem of being out of touch with reality. Insofar as the ego is structurally perturbed in psychosis, this perturbance does not principally concern some objective reality (which can be problematized in any case), but a disturbance regarding the body (as in "On Narcissism", where the imaginary relationship to the body is key) and identification (as in *Group Psychology*, where attention is drawn to the grounding signifiers of the symbolic, i.e., the unary trait).

The mirror stage, as the "watershed" between the imaginary and the symbolic, achieves a sort of binding or organizing between "images of the fragmented body" (55, 11) and signifier-automatisms. Indeed, Toulouse's idea of auto-conduction that Lacan referenced earlier describes a binding principle of various sensory inputs that was employed in psychiatry. This moves Lacan's mirror stage out of a purely imaginary interpretation, a point that Lacan is keen to emphasize by adding how, in the assumption of the image, what is also involved is "the exchange of gazes" of the child turning toward "the person who is assisting the child in some way" (55, 12–56, 1). The extra-imaginary reference here, the deferral to an Other who props up the body in the mirror, offers a significant extension of the earlier theorization of the mirror stage.

To return to the question of psychosis, Lacan demarcates his position as distinct from that of Ego Psychology as well as that of Melanie Klein. Insofar as psychosis is a disturbance of the mirror stage, we are dealing with more than merely a distance from reality testing (the lens of Ego Psychology) or simply a fragmentation of the body (the Kleinian account). Rather, there is the emergence of certain "mental automatisms" – "paranoiac knowledge", "involuntary poetry" – that indicate the operation of the signifier, the symptom's "formal envelope".

Revisiting "Beyond the 'Reality Principle'"

We need now circle back to the mid-section of "On my antecedents", where Lacan highlights the importance of his 1936 paper "Beyond the 'Reality Principle'". What we quickly appreciate here is that Lacan's criticism of accounts of psychosis grounded in measures of reality-testing extends to a more general critique of the idea of objective reality as typically construed. Lacan reminds the reader that Freud's (1920) *Beyond the Pleasure Principle* lays out a more fundamental tension than that of psychical reality and external reality. Such a tension would be epitomized in the infant's hallucinatory satisfaction of the breast that is not there in the world. Rather, Lacan places value on something outside of and more fundamental than the pleasure principle – the death drive – that thwarts and disrupts the pleasure principle. In his paper "Formulations on the two principles of mental functioning", Freud (1911b) had already recognized how the reality principle is really an extension of the pleasure principle. In 1920, Freud makes the point again:

the pleasure principle is replaced by the reality principle. This latter principle does not abandon the intention of ultimately obtaining pleasure, but it nevertheless demands and carries into effect the postponement of satisfaction, the abandonment of a number of possibilities of gaining satisfaction and the temporary toleration of unpleasure as a step on the long indirect road to pleasure. (Freud, 1920, p. 10)

For this reason, Lacan notes, Freud permits "reality to become established to the pleasure principle's satisfaction" (53, 6). The detour through reality runs under the guidance of the pleasure principle as the "watchman of mental life" (Freud, 1924, p. 159). Reality is not simply what corresponds with an objective external world. The reality principle operates by the postponement of discharge, the toleration of what the subject runs up against, in order to ultimately achieve pleasurable satisfaction.

Here, Lacan makes an "attempt to refute the misguided idea that there must be something, anything whatsoever, in the subject that corresponds to a reality system...to a characteristic function of reality" (54, 3). This rejects an emphasis on the opposition between pleasure and reality (as reality-testing), instead focusing on the issue of pleasure and the death drive.

the pleasure principle...takes on a still newer meaning by helping force open its traditional barrier related to a jouissance, a jouissance that is pinpointed at that time in masochism, and even opens onto [the question of] the death drive. (53, 5)

Freud noted that "masochism is incomprehensible" if the psychical apparatus is "governed by the pleasure principle" (Freud, 1924, p. 159). The death drive – and, for Lacan, the problematic of *jouissance* – arises at precisely this point of the weakness or fault-line of the pleasure principle.

Thus, the reality that psychoanalysis is concerned with is, for Lacan, not that of external reality or some function aligned to an egoic system of reality-functioning. Lacan states:

Let us simply say that it does not exaggerate the scope of psychoanalytic action [*l'acte psychoanalytique*] when it assumes that the latter transcends the secondary process to attain a reality that is not produced in it, even if it dispels the illusion that reduces the identity of thoughts to the thought of their identity. (53, 8)

The secondary process is transcended in psychoanalytic action, which is oriented toward "a reality that is not produced in it" (53, 8) – that is, a reality not produced in the secondary process of reality-testing. Analysis is oriented to the articulation of the specific co-ordinates of psychical reality, insofar as it is concerned with the deadlocks of desire, pleasure, and *jouissance*.

Importantly, reality is not simply to be ignored or deemed irrelevant. The key pieces of import for analysis are not the objective qualities of external reality, but rather specific pieces encountered in this reality that give shape to the circuits of pleasure and *jouissance*. Lacan makes this point precisely:

> the primary process encounters nothing real except the impossible, which in the Freudian perspective remains the best definition that can be given to reality [*réel*], the point is to know more about what Else [*d'Autre*] it encounters so that we can concern ourselves with it. (53, 9–54, 1)

We should pause here for a moment to shed light on the connection between "Else" and *Autre* in the above extract. "Autre" in French refers, of course, to the Lacanian symbolic Other. The close association with "Else" is made clear if we bear in mind that in French "quelque chose d'autre" translates as: "something else" or, less colloquially, "something Other", as we might put it.

Back though to questions of reality: the reality encountered in the primary process is the impossible, that which the primary process runs up against and bumps into. Lacan (2020) makes a similar and more detailed remark in *Seminar IV*:

> A no lesser paradox is found at the level of reality. Just as at the level of the pleasure principle there is, on the one side, the return to rest, but on the other, yearning, so too at the level of reality is there not only the reality that one bumps into, but also the principle of edging, of taking a detour through reality. (Lacan, 2020, p. 39)

Here, Lacan speaks again of a split at the level of the pleasure principle, specifically the tendency toward rest (how the pleasure principle is typically construed) and the fact of yearning and the tendency toward repetitive excess – that is, the *jouissance* of the death drive epitomized in the fore-pleasure of infantile sexuality. Likewise, there is a split on the side of reality. There is the "reality one bumps into" – the "impossible" that opposes the primary process – but also the "principle of edging, of taking a detour through reality" (Lacan, 2020, p. 39). Simply put, one might say that the "Else"/"something Other" encountered here in the detour concerns the "edging" of the drive, the contingency of the social order that marks the contours of the drive.

In terms of Lacan's register theory, we have in this écrit a critique of remaining in the imaginary register – the identicalness of perceptual-consciousness – as the guide toward a reality-oriented ego. Rather, the imaginary dimension of the ego is placed at the "watershed" with the symbolic: this is the ego with its dual-roots in the narcissism of the body and the orders of identification sketched out in *Group Psychology* (Freud, 1921). Pushing the symbolic dimension further, Lacan places psychoanalysis' concern not with objective reality as constructed in the secondary process, but rather with the "something Other" – the symbolic – that shapes the path of the drive, the real of *jouissance*.

This concern with the symbolic "something Other" hearkens back to the "symptom's formal envelope" that Lacan references at the start of this écrit. Likewise, the concern with *jouissance* links to the mirror stage and the dual-roots of the ego. Lacan here draws attention to the issue of the drive – its auto-eroticism and its primarily masochistic nature, the *jouissance* of the death drive – as one challenge that the narcissistic formation of the ego responds to.

Recall that Freud (1914) makes the point that one does not begin with a narcissistically cathected ego; rather, a new psychical action takes place that moves from auto-erotism to primary masochism. For Lacan, this new psychical action is the mirror stage. In this sense, and as emphasized in this écrit's careful clarification of the "watershed" of the mirror stage, this psychical action is a knotting of the real (*jouissance* of the drive, primary masochism), the imaginary (the narcissistic bodily ego), and the symbolic (identification, the Else encountered in the detour through reality).

Assailing the phenomenological

Lacan announces that one of the agendas in a proposed follow-up to his article "Beyond the 'Reality Principle'" – which never materialized – was "to assail Gestalt theory and phenomenology" (55, 2). In lieu of this, he had "constantly emphasized a moment in analytic practice", a *moment* which, importantly, "is not one of history" but instead one of "configuring insight" (55, 3). Lacan again here alludes to the mirror stage, which is afforded the qualification of having "emerged as a phase" (55, 3), an indication thus that it is *not* – crucially – tantamount to a critical developmental period.

What really prompts Lacan's line of commentary is that his various conceptualizations of the mirror phase had not as yet succeeded in ruling out phenomenological assumptions or conceptualizations about what he was theorizing. Thirty years after Lacan had proposed he would mount such an attack, it is now, finally, advanced. He wastes little time in extending the various facets of his argument. Can the mirror stage "be reduced to a biological crisis?" (55, 4), he asks. While Lacan, significantly, does not rule out the role of the biological here, his immediate response is to stress that the "dynamic of this phase...is based on diachronic effects: the delayed coordination of the nervous system related to man's prematurity at birth, and the formal anticipation of its resolution" (55, 4). There is, in other words, a diachronic factor, and more precisely, the factor of the adjoined temporalities of suspension and anticipation. The prospect of a head-long rush toward (imaginary) resolution takes on a fundamentally defensive quality here, as we shall see.

Lacan's questioning of a predominantly biological mode of explanation stems not only from the need to consider the dimension of psychical temporality and all its complexities; we find here also the crucial motif of rupture, discontinuity, non-harmonization, non-reconcilability (the factor, in other words, of the "real"). Hence Lacan's assertion: "to presume the existence of a harmony that is contradicted by many facts of ethology is tantamount to dupery" (55, 5). Interestingly, while biological explanation here is not permitted sole authority, it is not discarded. The remit of the ethological *does* constitute a viable set of explanatory reference-points, even if ultimately such references need to be understood alongside what has been learned from the psychoanalytic clinic.

We now come to what seems to be the overriding thrust of this section of Lacan's argument. Rather than the wishfully presumed harmonization – arguably essential to phenomenology apropos the (non-divided) relation constituted by its embodied consciousness – psychoanalysis insists that disjuncture, discordance, "splitness", must be asserted as more primary than assumptions of harmony, integration, wholeness, synthesis, adaptation, and so on. Having noted that the presumption of harmony amounts to a form of dupery, Lacan stresses now exactly what this dupery masks: "the crux of a function of lack" (55, 6). The function of lack is masked, furthermore, "with the question of the place that this function can assume in a causal chain" (55, 6). The reference to "place" here is significant: what is primary or structural for Lacan – be it disharmony or the function of the lack – has been demoted in phenomenological discourse to a more circumstantial status, to the role of a place (which, by implication, might be avoided). Lacan's argument here seems to be that other theoretical systems (Gestalt psychology, phenomenology, reductionist biological/evolutionary accounts), do not confront the "function of the lack" head on – but deal with it by displacing it, by locating it rather as an issue of secondary importance, making it, for example, a manageable crisis, something to be overcome. Lacan does not back away from or attempt to minimize the scale of the (conceptual and ethical) challenge posed by the function of lack: "far from imagining eliminating it...I currently consider such a function to be the very origin of causalist noesis" (55, 6). This is a bold claim, given that phenomenologically speaking, noesis refers to an intentional act in the most rudimentary and encompassing sense; lack thus features as a central category in any instances of human causality.

What is Lacan asserting here regards the position of psychoanalysis in relation to science? Johnston (2012) stresses that Lacan's critique of organicist biology in "On my antecedents" "is immanent and intra-scientific, rather than external and anti-scientific" (p. 37). Lacan's agenda is not to jettison the (natural or human) sciences but is, by contrast, to consider how science would be changed if it fully grasped the implications of psychoanalysis. Lacan's argument concerns

> the metaphysical bias of the modern sciences against the actual material efficacy of absences and lacks, a bias enshrined in what he refers to as

their "causalist noesis" (i.e. how they think the fundamental, science-grounding concept of causality); he diagnoses their constitutive blindness to fissures, gaps, negativities, and so on...Post-Baconian/Galilean scientificity, with its questionable *apriori* positivist presentism, tends to demand "eliminating" the "function of lack". Opposing this, Lacan tears aside the veils of a pseudo-scientific organicism tacitly leaning on non-empirical presentist presumptions...He does so through assigning a precise biological materialization of *manque-comme-cause* [lack-as-cause] (i.e. the absence of sufficient harmony and maturation intrinsic to the...bodily being of the newborn human organism) a crucial load-bearing position in the analytic architecture of his theoretical apparatus. (Johnston, 2012, p. 37)

In short, if it is the case that much within the epistemology of science pivots on presumptions pertaining to the substantiality of its objects – objects understood more on the basis of the actuality of their presence, as we might put it, than according to their inherent absences, disharmonies or "non-substantialities" – then such epistemologies will inevitably fall short when entering the realm of psychical processes where lack assumes a properly causal role.

It is worth stressing that the relation of disharmony that Lacan prioritizes here exists at several levels. This is significant because there are other theoretical standpoints that are willing to confront a modicum of disharmony so long as it can be displaced or partitioned to one register, one fixed domain, such that a picture of stable integration/harmonization can be retained at another level. For Lacan, the "real" of dis-harmonization goes "all the way down"; it pertains to all associated registers of experience such that (for example), the bodily, the psychical, and the social are all destabilized by the "real" of disjuncture, non-wholeness, non-integration. We might contrast here the Lacanian attention to disjuncture and dis-harmonization to the tendency in many phenomenological perspectives to foreground domains of harmonization (body in relation to consciousness, the embodied subject in relation to the world, etc.).[1]

Not only then must disharmony be located at all of these (bodily, psychical, social, etc.) levels, but it is, in an important sense, redoubled when we consider that the juxtaposition of the registers is itself fundamentally disjunctive. Consider the dilemmas of sexuation. Not only is it the case that both masculine and feminine positions are premised on a type of disjunctive impossibility (namely that of castration, lost *jouissance*). The illusory hope of some complementarity or wholeness being attained by the pairing of such impossibilities (the fantasy of the viable "sexual relationship") only leads to further impasses and deadlocks.

Given the omnipresence and unavoidability of lack, we can understand why Lacan asserts that "the subject's jubilation" occurs precisely – if only transiently – when lack is covered over (55, 8), as of course occurs in the mirror stage when the subject triumphantly assumes their mirror image.

We began this section by highlighting Lacan's critique of Gestalt theory and phenomenology. Our brief exploration of questions of scientificity has helped us to expand upon this theme, and yet there is more to be said here, both in terms of how we should qualify the idea of the body-in-pieces and in respect of the relationship between phenomenology and science. Johnston (2012) is again helpful. He reiterates how, for Lacan, the notion of the body-in-pieces – such a crucial aspect in the broader account of the mirror stage – can by no means be reduced "to a merely a phenomenological description of neonatal experiences of negative affects and the intentions they motivate" (2012, p. 38):

> Lacan's refusal of biologistic reductivism by no means drives him into the company of…phenomenological and/or existentialist neo-romantics. In fact…he insists that limiting the *corps morcelé* to being a non-biological experience of embodiment separate and distinct from the biological body implicitly concedes to the latter a wholeness and unity that the very biology of the human organism indicates it does not enjoy. (Johnston, 2012, p. 38)

This is a point that we anticipated above. The body-in-pieces is not merely psychological/phenomenological in nature – if it were, then we might retain the fantasmatic belief that the organic/bodily sphere permits some form of wholeness/cohesion/harmonious integration – but is disruptive at a series of conjoined (somatic, psychical, social) levels. The body-in-pieces is not merely thus a factor of experience; it must be seen instead as a crossing of registers, as the grafting of an emergent subjectivity onto a biological incompleteness, with the important proviso that neither such register represents a refuge of wholeness in respect of the other.

Johnston takes a further step here to offer the following conclusion with respect to Lacan's position regards phenomenology:

> Lacan's observations insinuate that, as regards modern science, phenomenology and its offshoots are simultaneously too radical (in their anti-naturalist turning away from the sciences) and not radical enough (in these turnings away, conceding "too much" to the fields thus abandoned). Psychoanalysis, on the other hand, promises the initiation of the pursuit of an immanent critique of modern science through which [it]…can be transformed significantly without, for all that, being indefensibly neglected or untenably dismissed. (Johnston, 2012, p. 38)

Lacan offers us a series of qualifications with respect to the phenomena of the mirror stage to stress that what is in question is not purely imaginary in nature. Imaginary identifications, for example, can be said to involve a part-to-whole dimension – particularly in the case of "so-called partial images" – which can be understood as enabled via the symbolic operation of metonymy (55, 11).

Lacan seems eager to set himself apart from "fantasies of the so-called paranoid phase in the phenomenology of the Kleinian experience" (55, 11) because psycho-analysis's ability to properly conceptualize psychical life would be fatally capsized if it remained solely at this level. He warns that psychoanalysis "would remain mythical were it to retreat to…the imaginary" (55, 10). Highlighting "the exchange of gazes" (55, 12), the "Other's field", and, crucially, the role of the Other's *desire* in processes of imaginary identification remains vital. Doing so situates imaginary identification within social and historical co-ordinates, that is, within the *symbolic* domain of given Ego-Ideals and phallic values. Hence the value of the example he sites, of a naked little girl viewing herself in the mirror – in what, we might naively imagine is a purely imaginary ego-to-mirror relation – and spontaneously gesturing in such a way that registers the dimension of the symbolic patriarchal gaze (realizing thus the dimension of "phallic lack" (56, 2)).

Just a few lines after differentiating his from a Kleinian perspective, Lacan – always willing to underscore aspects of Klein's work that affirm his own conceptualizations – notes that the "one or the other" logic of the "dyadic fascination" of imaginary ego-other rivalry corresponds to "the depressive return of the second phase in Melanie Klein's work…the figure of Hegelian murder" (56, 3). Having injected a critical – *symbolic* – sensibility regards how imaginary misrecognitions/identifications should be understood, Lacan seems suddenly intent on reminding us just how efficacious his theorization of the mirror stage was and remains. He calls to mind the right-left reversals ("inversions produced in planar symmetry") that occur when viewing mirror images as ourselves (as when one attempts to cut one's own hair when looking at a mirror) – something that he is surprised that philosophy has not taken more of an interest in. He seems to encourage his audience to consider what "a more in-depth discussion of spatial orientation" (56, 4) would yield in respect of such phenomena, an urging which indicates that the imaginary is not reducible merely to the visual field but pertains also to spatial parameters (one recalls here Lacan's descriptive reference to "gravel-pits and marshes", "fortified structures", "the…remote inner castle", and so on (78, 6) in "The mirror stage" paper). One suspects that Lacan has often needed to explain how the imaginary register cannot be collapsed into the perceptual domain of looking and seeing. "Even a blind man…knows he is an object of other people's gazes", Lacan avers, before evoking Molyneux's problem (i.e., Would a person, blind from birth, be able to immediately identify a shape previously made familiar to them only by touch, if they were suddenly able to see?). Molyneux's question is left unanswered, but Lacan brings the section to a close by stressing how "specular knowledge", that is, imaginary instances of misrecognition and identification (inclusive that is of paranoiac knowledge) "run…the gamut from subtle depersonalization to the hallucination of one's double" (56, 6). The imaginary register, in other words, is an irreducible dimension of human experience, and such phenomena do not, in and of themselves, provide a definitive basis for differential-diagnosis.

Texts of a future past

Having begun with a tacit reference to retroactivity, Lacan refers, in the closing section of this text, to a related but distinct psychoanalytic mode of temporality – that of the future anterior: "I find myself situating these texts in a future perfect: they will have anticipated my insertion of the unconscious into language" (56, 7). Not only does Lacan give his readers a suggestion for how his earliest writings – his "antecedents" – might be read today, i.e., as opening retrospective perspectives on his subsequent work. He also provides a clue in respect of how we might understand the curious arrangement of the current text, in which, conspicuously, has said little about his famous structuralist maxim according to which "the unconscious is structured like a language". This leads us to a question: Where, within this highly condensed account of the pre-history of Lacanian theory, do we find the "vanishing mediator" connecting all that is presented here to the subsequent influence of structural linguistics upon his work?

Richards (2023) offers a fascinating perspective on this question. We find at the outset of "On my antecedents" an emphasis on surrealism, indeed, on the value of automatic/paranoid/experimental writings on the one hand (as in Crevel's work), and the notion of a type of directed paranoiac activity (in Dalí's). Immediately following this there is a mention of Lacan's *Minotaure* articles, referred to by him as "my offspring" (51, 3). Five pages after the initial opening reference to these articles, after providing a complicated itinerary of his intellectual development, Lacan skips a line and again refers to "these texts" (56, 7), offering the line we have already quoted: "I find myself situating these texts in a future perfect: they will have anticipated my insertion of the unconscious into language" (56, 7). Lacan's apparent intimation then is that it was precisely the *Minotaure* articles ("my offspring", "these texts") that acted as the vanishing mediators in his own intellectual development, anticipating his understanding of the signifier's role in the functioning of the unconscious.

Note

1 A Lacanian approach thus provides a valuable analytical perspective in conceptualizing the various traumatic impacts of racism upon the body, the subjectivity, and the subject's relation to the world as so memorably described by Frantz Fanon's (1959) *Black Skin White Masks* (Hook, 2021). The implication of Fanon's analysis is that colonial racism derails all such prospective cites of subjective, social/structural, or even "ontological" harmonization.

References

Alexandrian, S. (1974). *Le surréalisme et le rêve*. Editions Gallimard.
Allouch, J. (1994). *Marguerite ou L'Aimée de Lacan*. Paris: E.P.E.L.
Berressem, H. (1996). Dalí and Lacan: Painting the imaginary landscapes. In W. Appolon and R. Feldstein (Eds.) *Lacan, Politics, Aesthetics: Divine Accommodation in Jewish and Christian Thought*. Albany: SUNY Press, pp. 263–296.

Bowie, M. (1991). *Lacan*. London: Fontana.

Bühler, C. (1935). *From Birth to Maturity: An Outline of the Psychological Development of the Child*. London: Kegan Paul, Trench & Trubner.

Constantinidou, D. (2012). When Lacan met Dalí: Lacan's "paranoid" reading of Saussure's theory of the sign. *Gramma: Journal of Theory and Criticism*, 20, 237–256.

Cox-Cameron, O. (2000). Lacan's doctoral thesis: Turbulent preface or founding legend? *Psychoanalytische Perspectieven*, 41/42, 17–45.

Crevel, R. (1932). *Le Clavecin de Diderot*. Paris: Éditions Surréalistes.

Crevel, R. (1933). Notes en vue d'une psycho-dialectique. *Le Surréalisme Au Service De La Révolution*, 5.

Clérambault, G.G. (1925). Psychoses à base d'automatisme – Premier article. In G.G. de Clérambault, *Oeuvres psychiatriques*. Paris: Frénésie éditions, 1987, pp. 528–544.

Clérambault, G.G. (1926). Psychoses à base d'automatisme – Second article. In G.G. de Clérambault, *Oeuvres psychiatriques*. Paris: Frénésie éditions, 1987, pp. 457–467.

Dalí, S. (1928/1998). The rotten donkey. In R. Descharnes (Ed.) *Oui: The Paranoid-Critical Revolution: Writings 1927–1933*. Cambridge, MA: Exact Change, pp. 115–119.

Dalí, S. (1930/1998). The moral position of surrealism. In R. Descharnes (Ed.) *Oui: The Paranoid-Critical Revolution: Writings 1927–1933*. Cambridge, MA: Exact Change, pp. 110–114.

Dalí, S. (1933). Interprétation paranoïaque: critique de l'image obsédanta: L'Angelu de Millet [A paranoid-critical interpretation of an obsessive im- age: The Angelus of Millet]. *Minotaure*, 1, 65–67.

Fanon, F. (1967). *Black Skin White Masks*. New York: Grove Press.

Freud, S. (1900). The interpretation of dreams. In J. Strachey (Ed.) *The Standard Edition of the Complete Psychological Works of Sigmund Freud*, Vols. 4 & 5. London: Vintage.

Freud, S. (1900). The interpretation of dreams. In J. Strachey (Ed.) *The Standard Edition of the Complete Psychological Works of Sigmund Freud*, Vols. 4 & 5. London: Vintage.

Freud, S. (1911a). Psycho-analytic notes on an autobiographical account of a case of paranoia (Dementia Paranoides). In J. Strachey (Ed.) *The Standard Edition of the Complete Psychological Works of Sigmund Freud*, Vol. 12. London: Vintage, pp. 1–79.

Freud, S. (1911b). Formulations on the two principles of mental functioning. In J. Strachey (Ed.) *The Standard Edition of the Complete Psychological Works of Sigmund Freud*, Vol. 12. London: Vintage, pp. 213–226.

Freud, S. (1914). On narcissism: An introduction. In J. Strachey (Ed.) *The Standard Edition of the Complete Psychological Works of Sigmund Freud*, Vol. 14. London: Vintage, pp. 67–102.

Freud, S. (1920). Beyond the pleasure principle. In J. Strachey (Ed.) *The Standard Edition of the Complete Psychological Works of Sigmund Freud*, Vol. 18. London: Vintage, pp. 1–64. Hogarth Press.

Freud, S. (1921). Group psychology and the analysis of the ego. In J. Strachey (Ed.) *The Standard Edition of the Complete Psychological Works of Sigmund Freud*, Vol. 18. London: Vintage, pp. 65–144.

Freud, S. (1922). Some neurotic mechanisms in jealousy, paranoia and homosexuality. In J. Strachey (Ed.) *The Standard Edition of the Complete Psychological Works of Sigmund Freud*, Vol. 18. London: Vintage, pp. 221–232.

Freud, S. (1924). The economic problem of masochism. In J. Strachey (Ed.) *The Standard Edition of the Complete Psychological Works of Sigmund Freud*, Vol. 19. London: Vintage, pp. 155–170.

Hook, D. (2021). Racial ontologizing through the body. In L. Laubscher, D. Hook & M. Desai (Eds.) *Fanon, Phenomenology and Psychology*. London & New York: Routledge.

Johnston, A. (2012). Reflections of a rotten nature: Hegel, Lacan, and material negativity. *Filozofski Vestnik*, 33, 2, 23–52.

Lacan, J. (1932/1975). *De la psychose paranoïaque dans ses rapports avec la personnalité, suivi de premieres écrits sur la paranoïa*. Paris: Seuil.

Lacan, J. (1933/1988a). The problem of style and the psychiatric conception of paranoid forms of experience. *Critical Texts: A Review of Theory and Criticism*, 5, 3, 383–388.

Lacan, J. (1933/1988b). Motives of paranoiac crime: The crime of the Papin sisters. *Critical Texts: A Review of Theory and Criticism*, 5, 3, 389–399.

Lacan, J. (1979). The neurotic's individual myth. *Psychoanalytic Quarterly*, 48, 405–425.

Lacan, J. (1993). *The Seminar of Jacques Lacan, Book III: The Psychoses, 1955–1956* (edited by Jacques-Alain Miller, translated by Russell Grigg). New York and London: W.W. Norton.

Lacan, J. (2020). *The Seminar of Jacques Lacan, Book IV: The Object Relation* (edited by Jacques-Alain Miller, translated by Adam Price). Cambridge: Polity Press.

Lacan, J. (2023). *Premiers Écrits*. Paris: Éditions du Seuil.

Leader, D. (2011). *What is Madness?* London: Hamish Hamilton.

Macey, D. (1983). Fragments of an analysis: Lacan in context. *Radical Philosophy*, 35, 1, 1–9.

Macey, D. (1988). *Lacan in Contexts*. London: Verso.

Nobus, D. (2022). Personal communication. Email of 11 March.

Polsani, P. (2001). The image in a fatal kiss: Dalí, Lacan, and the paranoiac representation. *Bucknell Review*, 45(1), 159–174.

Rabaté, J.-M. (2002). Loving Freud madly: Surrealism between hysterical and paranoid modernism. *Journal of Modern Literature*, 25, 3/4, 58–74.

Richards, S. (2023). Personal communication. Email of 9th February.

Roudinesco, E. (1997). *Jacques Lacan*. New York: Columbia University Press.

Vanheule, S. (2018). From De Clérambault's theory of mental automatism to Lacan's theory of psychotic structure. *Psychoanalysis & History*, 20, 10, 205–228.

Verhaeghe, P., and Declerq, F. (2002). Lacan's analytic goal: *Le sinthome* or the feminine way. In L. Thurston (Ed.) *Re-Inventing the Symptom: Essays on the Final Lacan*. New York: Other Press, pp. 59–82.

Wallon, H. (1931). Comment se développe chez l'enfant la notion de corps propre. *Journal de Psychologie*. November–December, 705–748.

4

BEYOND THE "REALITY PRINCIPLE"

David Pavón-Cuéllar

Au-delà du 'Principe de Réalité' was written and published in 1936 in *L'Évolution Psychiatrique,* volume 3, pages 67 to 86. At that time, Lacan was 35 years old. He was a licensed forensic psychiatrist and held a *Doctorat D'État,* awarded four years earlier for his thesis *On Paranoiac Psychosis in Relation to Personality* (Lacan, 1932/1975), which was acclaimed by the surrealists. He was also an associate member of the *Société psychanalytique de Paris* (SPP), having been elected in 1934. In the same period, he began to work as an analyst, though still involved in a long – and rather tricky – training analysis with Rudolph Loewenstein that lasted from 1932 until 1938, and allowed Lacan to become a full member of the SPP.

Lacan began to write *Beyond the 'Reality Principle'* in August 1936 while attending the 14th Congress of the International Psychoanalytical Association in Marienbad. It was on that occasion that, while presenting his paper on the Mirror Stage (Lacan, 1949/2006), the congress chairman, Ernest Jones, interrupted him before he had concluded, 'right in the middle of a phrase' (Roudinesco, 1993/2009: 1643). Deeply offended, Lacan marched out of the Congress to go and watch the Berlin Olympic Games. He returned to France to spend the end of the summer season with his wife, Marie-Louise Blondin, who was five months pregnant with their first child, on the island of Noirmoutier, on France's Atlantic coast. There Lacan finished writing this essay, which was intended to be the first part of a trilogy that should have included two other texts, though these were never written: 'part two', on the 'notion of the image' (71, 4), and 'part three', with a critique of the Freudian metapsychological theory of the 'reality principle' (74, 6). Instead of completing the trilogy, Lacan accepted Wallon's invitation to write *The Family Complexes* for the *Encyclopédie Française* (Lacan, 1938/2001).

Beyond the 'Reality Principle' echoes the title of Freud's essay, *Beyond the Pleasure Principle,* which represented a turning point in the history of psychoanalysis, as it added the idea of *Thanatos,* the death drive, to *Eros,* the sexual instinct, in its explanation of human behaviour (Freud, 1920/1961). Just as Freud went beyond the explicative domination of the pleasure principle, so too

DOI: 10.4324/9781003368649-5

Lacan wished to move beyond the theoretical centrality of the reality principle by elaborating a critique of the Freudian concept. As this ambitious critique was planned for the end of the aforementioned unfinished trilogy, it was not really accomplished, but the will to go *beyond the reality principle* did become a central aim of Lacanian psychoanalysis, especially in the 1950s, when Lacan began his questioning of Ego-psychology. Earlier, in 1936, the first part of the trilogy constituted nothing less than Lacan's first essay on psychoanalysis (Miller, 2011), as well as the beginning of his reflections on the 'problem of perception' (Soler, 2006: 130), and the first important step in his 'tribute to Freud', which must not be confused with a 'return to the master', as it reveals, from the first, the Lacanian 'ambition of originality' (Marcos, 2002: 85).

Lacan's essay offers a rich plethora of contributions: a critique of the notion of objectivity in science, a differentiation between scientific reality and psychological truth, an immanent critique of associationist and empiricist psychologies, a historization of psychoanalysis, a phenomenological description of the psychoanalytical experience, a preliminary questioning of Freudian biological metapsychology, a correlative affirmation of the importance of the social and the relational in psychoanalysis, an examination of the function of language in analysis and an introduction to the Lacanian theory of the image. In addition to these significant achievements, the essay also sheds new light on key psychoanalytical notions such as *identification, free association, transference, interpretation, id, ego* and *superego,* the *libido,* the *complex* and the *abstinence rule.* Here we also find Lacan's first theoretical elaborations of the concepts of *the symbolic, the imaginary* and *the real, reality* and *the truth, the image,* and *the subject of knowledge.*

The second generation of Freud's school can define its debt and duty in terms of a fundamental principle of his doctrine: The reality principle

Lacan begins by historicizing psychoanalysis and distinguishing two successive generations of analysts. In the first, which corresponds to those who followed Freud from the 1900s to the 1920s, the immersion of people into psychoanalysis is disapprovingly described as a disruptive and pathological or irrational 'conversion' that entailed an 'affective striving' and provided seductive forms of 'compensation' (58). In contrast, the second generation, which included Lacan's contemporaries or immediate predecessors, is characterized by its rationality and indebted and imperious attachment to the Reality Principle, which stands for reality in the Freudian representation of the psyche (Freud, 1915/1984).

It is almost as if Lacan placed the early analysts under the Pleasure Principle, and their successors under the Reality Principle. To be sure, aside from limiting their horizon to what is perceived as the more-or-less realistic relation to the outer world, the analysts of the 1930s overcame their impulsive and passionate commitment to Freud's doctrine. This is how they may have begun to approach psychoanalysis 'from a normal point of incidence', under 'normal' conditions, and from the point of view of something presupposed as 'normality', which enabled the psychoanalytical doctrine to legitimize itself and attain its place among the existing 'disciplines' (58).

Freud was still alive when Lacan began to perceive how psychoanalysis was passing through a sort of normalization that we may understand retrospectively, and from the 'mature' Lacanian perspective, as a deplorable process of stabilization, standardization, trivialization and domestication – even deactivation – of the Freudian subversive discovery. However, according to the young Lacan of 1936, this process was not necessarily to be deplored. In reality, the normalization of psychoanalysis had the advantage of allowing its acceptance, revalorization and validation by psychology, which could only have been deemed a positive step at that time. It was later, in the 1940s and 1950s, that one could see that such a reconciliation between psychoanalysis and psychology might lead to the assimilation of the former by the latter, as occurred, in fact, in Ego-psychology, which would be tirelessly attacked by Lacan in the 1950s (e.g. 1953/2006, 1955/2006, 1956/2006).

It is true that in 1936, before undertaking his long struggle against Ego-psychology, Lacan already seemed suspicious of what may be described today as *the psychologization of psychoanalysis*. But his suspicions, which become evident – though just barely – later in the text, do not entail any general opposition to either psychology or the second generation of analysts with their focus on the criteria of normality and the reality principle. Far from this, Lacan only discusses particular conceptions of psychology, normality and the reality principle, and seems to maintain a relatively positive opinion of his contemporaries. In fact, as Roudinesco (2004) has pointed out, Lacan sees himself in this essay 'as the spokesman' of the new generation '*vis-à-vis* the pioneers of the first French generation' (p. 31).

Psychology was constituted as a science when the relativity of its object was posited by Freud, even though it was restricted to facts concerning desire

Critique of associationism

This section and the following one offer an assessment of traditional psychology and include several ideas that may still be effective for critical psychology and for the critique of the psychological discipline in general. These ideas constitute one of the most elaborated critiques of psychology in Lacan's work. But why criticize psychology in an essay whose central aim is to describe psychoanalysis? The answer is provided from the first lines when Lacan denominates the birth of psychoanalysis as a revolution, the 'Freudian revolution', whose meaning emanates from a 'context' assimilated to late 19th-century psychological ideas (59, 1). The revolutionary disruption of this context *is* the founding gesture of psychoanalysis, which can thus only be comprehended through a contextual understanding based on a critical analysis of that 'disrupted' traditional psychology.

After justifying the need for a critical analysis of psychology, Lacan presents a subtle, yet profound, methodological elucidation of the way in which he would critically analyse psychology. And his elucidation may still be invaluable for those interested in the potential of the Lacanian perspective, not only for critical psychology, but also for epistemological enquiry, for sociology, for the archaeology of knowledge and for the history and philosophy of the human and social sciences. What Lacan proposes and clarifies thus goes far beyond the purely psychoanalytical frame of reference, as it is a general method of critical work in the historical study of 'facts of knowledge'[1] as 'facts in history' (59, 1).

While recognizing the fundamental need to interpret and explain the literal texts through which traditional psychology has developed, Lacan announces that he will focus on a 'moment of critique' that he considers 'the essential'[2] of this 'basic work' of 'exegesis' with its 'historical method' (59, 1). We must consider seriously the fact that the historical-exegetical task of interpretation and explanation, as conceived by Lacan, comprises the critical approach as its essential moment. This supposes that without critique, any historical exegesis will turn out to be not only partial and unfinished, but unessential, superfluous, empty and superficial, bereft of critical essence.

Why is critique essential for Lacanian exegesis? We could say, in a response that may seem redundant at first glance, that critique is essential because of the way Lacan understands it as an *immanent critique*, a critique that involves the deepest knowledge of its objects, since it must proceed from their perspective and under their own criteria, so that it 'remains immanent in the data recognized by the method' (59, 1). It is well known that this form of critique reverses the transcendent critique developed by Kant (1781/1998), that its origins can be traced back to Marx and Engels (1846/1970), that it has been systematically used and elucidated by Adorno (1973, 1982) and that its importance for critical theory is such that it has been considered the 'central mode of critical theoretical analysis' (Antonio, 1981: 30). What is perhaps less well known, however, is the crucial theoretical function of the idea of immanent critique in structuralism, as can be appreciated in 'the immanent critique of the consciousness' in Althusser (1965/2005: 143), and in Lacan's own work (1958/1998), which advocates a critique from within and in accordance with the 'interrogations' and 'articulation' of what is criticized (p. 473). This prescriptive idea of critique in the structural immanence of the Other, and in the absence of a transcendent Other of the Other, is consequent with other Lacanian descriptive and prescriptive structuralist notions that exclude the Other of the Other, such as the absence of metalanguage (Lacan, 1960/2006) and the rebuttal of comprehension (1956/1981). All these latter notions have their direct precedent in the method of immanent critique that we find in *Beyond the 'Reality Principle'*.

Unlike other methods of immanent critique, the Lacanian version not only proceeds from within its object but also through the intrinsic reflexivity of what is criticized. Lacan actually conceives his critique as 'grounded in the secondary order', in the 'element of reflection', inherent in what is interpreted and explained (59, 1). It is as if the object of critique turned towards itself through its own immanent critical reflection. For instance, in the case of late 19th-century psychology, Lacan takes its own theoretical reflexivity as expressed in its claim to be scientific in 'its apparatus of objectivity and its profession of materialism', in order to demonstrate that it 'failed to be positive, excluding from the outset both objectivity and materialism' (59, 1).

It is by placing psychology reflexively against itself that Lacan develops his immanent critique in this section and the one that follows. To be more precise, this critique would reveal the inherent reflexive contradictions of a specific form of psychology, the one that predominated in the late 19th century, and that Lacan describes as being 'based on a so-called associationist conception of the psyche' (59, 2). This conception was sustained in the very target of the Lacanian critique of psychology, a critique that in reality turned into a *critique of associationism*, as indicated in the title of this section.

Associationism, as we know, is the idea that all, or most, complex mental activity operates through the association between simpler mental states, an idea that can be traced back to Plato and Aristotle but was only systematized – first – in modern philosophical empiricism and – later – in contemporary psychology, especially in the behavioural tradition. However, it is important to note that the proponents of these systematizations offer completely different versions of the idea of association. Let us examine some examples that will prove to be useful for analysing Lacan's critique of associationism. Hobbes (1651/1929) describes reasoning as a 'train of words' or 'mental discourse' that depends on an association with, and between, 'images' or 'motions within us, relics of those made in sense' (pp. 18–19), while Berkeley (1732/2008) considers that 'one idea may suggest another to the mind' when 'they have been observed to go together', even 'without any demonstration of the necessity of their co-existence, or so much as knowing what it is that makes them to thus co-exist' (p. 11). Hume (1740/2012) speaks of 'the principles of union or cohesion among our simple ideas', and finds here 'a kind of attraction, which in the mental world will be found to have effects as extraordinary as [those] of the natural [world], and to show itself in as many and as various forms' (p. 9). Hartley (1749/1801), in turn, explains mental activity, 'ideas, opinions and affections', by the association of physical 'vibrations' in the nervous system with the corresponding psychic 'sensations', which 'may be said to be associated together when their impressions are either made precisely at the same instant of time, or in the contiguous successive instants' (pp. 65–72). John Stuart Mill (1843/1994) claims that the mind plays an active role in forming associations and that a complex thought, as an effect and not as a sum of its associated parts, must 'be said to result from, or be generated by, the simple ideas, not to consist of them' (p. 40). In the behavioural tradition, Pavlov (1924/2003) elucidates 'conditioned reflexes' through 'association' between different stimuli, and between stimuli and responses (pp. 49–50), while Watson (1913: 174) explains all kinds of behaviours, including 'higher thought', by the 'serial order' of 'associative mechanisms'.

We can see here that all associationist theories decompose the totality of mental activity into its supposed parts, for instance, images, sensations or simple ideas. However, those elements, according to Lacan, are not objective things discovered in 'psychical reality' by psychological research, but, rather, ideological or theoretical deposits, remains from 'scholastic psychology', residues of 'centuries of philosophy' or non-objective 'products of a sort of conceptual erosion'[3] that detaches, isolates, solidifies, reifies and objectifies them, presenting them as a 'guarantee of truth', as undeniable evidence for psychology, as if they were objective things (59, 2). And it must be said that some part of this simulacra of objects still constitutes the basic psychological processes studied in current psychology, especially in the cognitive tradition, despite its shift from association to structure (Mandler, 1962). After all, this shift may be seen, from a Lacanian point of view, as a merely rhetorical reconceptualization of *associations of simulacra* into *structures of simulacra*.

Be they structured or associated, the 'objects of psychology' are simulated, as they are something non-objective, 'not positive', of which psychology should be 'cleansed' (60, 1). It is of the utmost importance to understand that such purification is not an imperative that Lacan imposes upon psychological theories from without, from the Lacanian psychoanalytical perspective, but a necessity that logically results from an immanent critique developed from within modern psychology itself, and through its intrinsic positivist-associationist reflexivity, which cannot accept any kind of not-positive impurities, especially when these have 'metaphysical implications' (60, 1-2). However, as Lacan demonstrates in the succeeding pages, metaphysics is implied in associationism itself and cannot be eliminated from it. This is so because associationism is not dominated by a 'function of the real', but by a 'function of the truth'[4] (60, 2) that is based on the metaphysical 'search for truth', a search undertaken by 'mystics' and 'moralists', and situated 'under the heading of the spiritual' (63, 4).

In order to demonstrate the metaphysical implications of psychology, Lacan takes two fundamental concepts of the psychological associationist perspective, namely, that of the *engram*, the hypothetical idea of a psychophysical trace that would serve to explain memory, and that of the *associative link*, which enables the association of engrams and other simple mental states in order to constitute complex mental processes. These two concepts are submitted to an immanent critique that demonstrates how they are projected onto reality rather than being discovered in it. In the case of the engram, it is not found there, but theoretically constructed through both a questionable notion – the 'hypothesis' of its 'passive production' – and a refutable assumption: the 'postulate' of its 'atomistic nature', which leads psychologists to ignore the organization of the engram's 'form' by the subject (60, 3). Likewise, the idea of the associative link is based on the assumption of the 'mental form of similarity' that enables the association between similar things, as if this form of similarity were distinguishable from the form of the associative link (60, 4). In reality, for Lacan, association seems to explain similarity, which therefore can only circularly explain association. This vicious circle, just like other 'mirror explanations' in psychology (Janet, 1929/2005: 21–22), excludes any kind of effective 'explanation', for this can only be made possible through what the young Lacan proposes under the designation of 'phenomenological analysis' (61, 1).

As Jacques-Alain Miller (2003: 17) points out, when Lacan said 'phenomenological' in 1936, 'that came from Husserl', and was 'a matter of identifying the data of experience' and 'trying to put prejudices to one side in order to describe what appeared as such'. The young Lacan valorized this Husserlian phenomenological description as the necessary condition of an objective account in the discipline of psychology. Here the object could only be extracted through what Husserl developed as a phenomenological analysis of either transcendental subjectivity (Husserl, 1913/1931) or intersubjective experience (1931/1960). Therefore, without phenomenology, allegedly objective psychology would be unable to attain any real form of 'objectivity' (61, 2). This is how immanent critique may conceive the lack of a phenomenological analysis as a deficiency of objective psychology from its own objectivist perspective.

Lacan is convinced that the shortcomings of objective psychology have been 'inherited', through associationism, from 'Locke's so-called empiricist formulations' (61, 3), particularly the definition of mind as *tabula rasa* or a blank sheet, 'white paper, void of all characters, without any ideas', and the conception that 'all ideas come from sensation or reflection', from 'external sensible objects' or 'internal operations of our minds' (Locke, 1689/1836: 50–52). In their Lacanian reinterpretation, these formulations anticipated the psychological notions of the *engram* and the *associative link*. The idea of the engram was implied in the general empiricist-sensualist claim that 'nothing is in the intellect which was not first in sense' [*nihil est in intellectu quod non prius fuerit in sensu*], a claim that reduces the origin of all knowledge to a 'blind spot of knowledge', to a 'point of contact with pure sensation' in which 'nothing is recognized' (61, 3-4). Recognition only occurs in the mental sphere, and through the 'uncriticised implications' of the associative links, when the 'pure mind' recognizes the object 'at the same time that it asserts it' (61, 3-4). This 'true moment of knowledge' (61, 3), which remains implicit in empiricist and associationist psychology, becomes explicit through the rationalist affirmation with which Leibniz (1704/1921) completes the empiricist formulation: 'nothing is in the intellect which was not first in sense, except the intellect itself' [*excipe: nisi ipse intellectus*], an intellect that 'includes being, substance, one, same, cause, perception, reasoning, and many other notions which the senses cannot provide' (p. 70).

Among *the notions that the senses cannot provide*, we find the empiricist *associative links* that are necessarily established in the intellect, in the domain of ideas.

Here we confirm that associationist and empiricist psychology paradoxically presupposes 'a fundamentally idealist theory of knowledge phenomena' (61, 4-5). Lacan illustrates this psychological idealism through Taine's definition of the 'exterior perception' as a 'veridical hallucination', an 'idea', a 'sensation' that is a 'simulacrum taken for the object' (Taine, 1868: 44–46). Here the real object remains inaccessible, imperceptible and unknowable. Conversely, the simulacrum, the idea or the sensation, is the only object of supposedly materialist and objectivist psychological research. This clarifies that psychology 'fails to constitute its object in positive terms, failing all the more fatally in that it receives these concepts emptied of the reflection they bring with them' (61, 6).

Reflection remains confined to philosophy, while its products – concepts emptied of their inherent reflection – are adopted by psychology and treated as its objects. Hence the importance of reconstituting reflexivity through an immanent critique like the one proposed by Lacan. Without reflexivity, the objects of psychology are nothing but simulacra or veridical hallucinations, which are obviously, as *hallucinations*, not defined as something real but, rather, as *veridical*, distinguished 'as a function of their truth' and 'on the basis of value' (62, 1).

Psychology valorizes perceptions and sensations, understood as veridical hallucinations, because they are true, just as it does not assign any value to other hallucinations because they are not true. This is how hallucination comes to be reduced to an 'error of the senses' (62, 2) through the same psychological evaluation that reduces 'the image', the 'most important phenomenon in psychology', to 'its function as an illusion' or as a 'weakened sensation' (62, 3). Both image and hallucination are regarded as debilitated or fabricated sensations, as false or meaningless psychological states, and thus judged 'to signify nothing' (62, 4), and rejected 'either to the nothingness of neglect or to the emptiness of epiphenomena' (63, 1).

Empirical-associationist psychology differentiates epiphenomena from normal phenomena. On the margins, abnormal or irrational epiphenomena, such as dreams or delusions, feelings or intuitions, belong to an 'illusory reality', and require an explanation based on an 'organic' determinism (63, 2-3). At the centre, normal phenomena belong to a 'true reality' of 'rational knowledge' and merit an 'associationist analysis' that assimilates them into a 'system of references' constituted by tangible mechanisms in the physical sciences and utilitarian motivations in the natural sciences (63, 2-3). This assimilation of psychical phenomena to the system permits the verification of the system, of its truth, and confirms that psychology, as a 'function of this truth' of the system, is not 'a science' of the real (63, 3).

The truth of psychology and the psychology of truth

Lacan ended the precedent section by making a point that might seem paradoxical, inconsistent or perhaps even absurd, as he argued that psychology could not be a science because it is a *function of the truth*. For this young Lacan, to put it plainly, truth is not the goal of science, for science is about the real, not about the truth. It is almost as if science had nothing to do with the truth.

In this section, Lacan unmistakeably asserts that 'science need know nothing about truth', and justifies this affirmation by explaining that truth is 'a value' that 'remains foreign to the order of science' that concerns our 'lived experience' of 'uncertainty', and the search for which motivates all manner of religious, moral and other non-scientific deeds and facts, such as 'the mystic's flights and the moralist's rules, the ascetic's progress and the mystagogues's finds' (63, 4-5). It is indeed here, 'under the heading of the spiritual' (63, 4), that the psychologist's discipline is situated by the young Lacan, who in subsequent years would continue in the same line of critique by relating psychology to pious 'beliefs' and 'obscurantism' (Lacan, 1953/2001: 143), 'religion' and 'spirituality' (1954/1998: 394–395) and even 'judicial astrology' (1960a/2006: 676).

In any case, the psychological or parapsychological search for the truth has nothing to do with science, which searches not for the truth, but for something different. Lacan concedes that science may circumstantially adopt the truth as its 'object', may be proud of its 'alliances with truth', and may have been conditioned by the 'moral attitude' towards the truth in 'an entire culture', but none of this refutes the fact that science 'cannot in any way identify truth as its own end' (63, 4). This is why scientists do not wonder, for example, 'whether the rainbow is true' (64, 1). They are not precisely interested in 'the truth of the rainbow', but in the real cause of its 'illusion or mirage created by drops of water in the atmosphere' (cf. Grotstein, 2003: 223). Their research deals with something real that is not evident at all, that cannot be approached without disappearing, and which lacks all the attributes of the truth, i.e. confidence, assurance and consistency.

In reality, as evidenced in the 'dizzying relativisms' of 20th-century physics and mathematics, especially general relativity and quantum mechanics, scientific discoveries are becoming more and more *uncertain, enigmatic* and *paradoxical* or *contradictory*. Even if they still need to be *communicated* through jargons and formulas, *reported* in experiments and *integrated* into theories (64, 1), they are not necessarily oriented by the three main logical principles of the search for truth, namely, *certainty, self-evidence* and *non-contradiction* (63, 5), all of which are still fundamental to philosophy and the human and social disciplines, including psychology.

Unlike mathematicians, physicists and other authentic scientists, psychologists still cling to such feelings as the firm conviction that their findings are true (*certainty*), the perception of the truth of their propositions through simple comprehension of their meaning (*self-evidence*) and the reassuring idea that two contradictory statements cannot both be true in the same sense at the same time (*non-contradiction*). Even if these feelings have nothing to do with science, they may give us the impression that we are doing science, and so may be used to make a phenomenological description of our experience of what we think science is. The experience of our idea of 'science' is actually deepened and intensified by the 'practical successes' of science and its resulting 'brilliant prestige for the masses' (64, 2). This is how science finds itself 'in a good position to serve as the ultimate object of the passion of truth', which Lacan designates as 'scientism' (64, 2).

From the Lacanian point of view, we may say that scientism is the characteristic relation of psychologists with science. Indeed, we may go so far as to say that psychology is a kind of scientism and not a science, for the very good reason that psychologists do not *make* science, but rather *love* and *venerate* science, especially their own science, and 'are only interested in the act of knowing, that is, in their own activity as scientists' or, rather, as 'scholars' (64, 2). The same could be said of psychiatrists, philosophers and other intellectuals or academics. In that same year, Lacan (1936c) denounces them in a commentary on Minkowski for being more interested in 'being intelligent' than in 'being informed' (p. 66), a condition that led them to 'the eternal pedantry that mutilates what they are able to grasp of reality, because they do not realize how much their truth is relative to the walls of their tower' (64, 2).

Instead of acknowledging the subjective experience of their truth, psychologists present this experience as an objective account of reality. The real is thus usurped. A similar usurpation would explain the 'contempt for psychical reality' that Lacan finds among physicians at the time of Freud, and which was expressed 'both in the biased nature of observation and in hybrid conceptions like that of *pithiatism*' (64, 3).

The notion of *pithiatism* may be helpful to fully appreciate what Lacan seeks to elucidate here... But what is pithiatism? This notion was proposed by a contemporary of Freud, the French-Polish neurologist Joseph Babinski, who preferred the term *pithiatism* (from the Greek πειθώ, *peitho*, 'persuasion', and ιατος, *iatos*, 'curable') to *hysteria* (from the Greek ὑστέρα, *hystera*, 'uterus'), as he was convinced that hysterical disorders could be reproducible and curable through persuasive suggestion, and, therefore, in a certain sense, reducible to a manifestation of suggestibility. In Babinski's words, suggestion played 'the essential part in the production of hysterical manifestations', which were 'absent or very rare in circumstances unfavourable for suggestion', and 'very common under the opposite circumstances, their frequency, intensity and duration depending on the conditions which are suitable to producing and maintaining suggestion' (Babinski & Froment, 1918: 46). This idea seems to be an eloquent example of the reduction of *the real of hysteria* to *a truth of suggestion* that was not the truth of the hysteric's desire, of course, but the truth of the physician's 'pedantry' (64, 2), the truth of his 'contempt for psychical reality' (64, 3), that is to say, the truth of *considering himself able to cure hysteria through suggestion*. In this respect, it is significant that curing, according to Babinski, depended on 'confidence in the doctor', on 'the conviction' that he had 'the power to cure' (Babinski & Froment, 1918: 224–225). We know that this power of suggestion is precisely what would be questioned and subverted by Freud's discovery, by his 'fruitful step' (64, 3), which made him move from hypnotic suggestion towards talking cures and free association (Freud & Breuer, 1895/2004).

Freud's revolutionary method

According to Lacan, what distinguishes Freud is his 'attitude of observation, of conquest of the real' (Lacan, 1936c: 66), which is essentially an 'attitude of submission to the real'[5] (65, 1). This attitude contrasts with the mutilation of, and contempt for, the real that Lacan found in late 19th- and 20th-century philosophers, psychologists and physicians, and even in phenomenological psychiatrists such as Eugène Minkowski, whom Lacan accused of preferring an 'abstract' phenomenology rather than 'the real and the living' in the same year that *Beyond the Reality Principle* appeared (Lacan, 1936c: 66).

While Freud's contemporaries reduced the real to conceptions such as the engram, associative link, true hallucination and persuasive suggestion, Freud limited himself to listening carefully to the subject's own words, and thus witnessed the emergence of the real of psychical phenomena. But why does this real emerge through the subject's words? Lacan's answer is astonishing: the subject's words 'provide the most usual access' to 'the social relations' function' to which 'the majority of psychical phenomena in man are apparently related' (65, 1).

Between the words and the psychical phenomena there lies the social relations' function. It is because of the social that Lacan initially gives such importance to language as a medium to reach the real of the psyche. This methodological weight of words is a consequence of the theoretical weight of social relations. We may even conjecture that the essential connection between society and language, as recognized by Lacan in 1936, is at the origin of the centrality of language and the symbolic, of words or signifiers, in later Lacanian theoretical developments. This is all the more significant when we consider that those developments tend to conceive society as nothing more than language, assimilating social relations to relations between signifiers (Pavón-Cuéllar, 2013).

In addition to anticipating what would become the symbolic, Lacan offers a prefiguration of what he would later identify as the real and the imaginary. We have already seen how the real is ignored, excluded and even mutilated by the discipline of psychology, thus turning the psychological domain into 'the field of the *imaginary* in the sense of the illusory' (65, 2). Thereafter, Lacan would identify the 'imago' as the 'object of psychology' (1946/2006: 153), enclose psychological facts within the imaginary 'frame of narcissism' (1964/1990: 216–217) and even say that 'psychology is nothing but the confusing image of our own body' (1976/2005: 149). All this would confirm that psychology is *the field of the imaginary.*

In this imaginary psychological field, something real, such as the symptom, cannot be recognized as really psychological; instead, it is 'distinguished from the ordinary register of psychical life by some discordant character' (65, 2). Psychologists begin by 'choosing' (65, 3), but their mutilating choices imply omissions and systematizations, and can only be avoided through the psycho-analytical rules of *non-omission* and *non-systematization* (65, 4) that Freud synthe-sizes in the law of *free association* (66, 1). These rules would allow psychoanalysis to approach something real that could not be approachable through psychol-ogy. And this brings us to a crucial idea that would be incorporated into Lacanian theory: some 35 years later, in his 17th seminar, Lacan (1970/1991) was still appealing to 'the real' in order to distinguish the 'Freudian enuncia-tion', with the real at its 'centre', from psychology, which is not 'conceivable' in relation to the real (pp. 143–144)

A phenomenological description of the psychoanalytic method

The relation to the real might explain, precisely, that psychoanalysis creates 'a relationship that is so simple that it seems to evade thought's grasp' (66, 2). Here Lacan is ironically asserting that the ungraspable, unthinkable nature of the analytical relationship lies in its simplicity, the plainness of words, of 'language' as the 'pre-given' (66, 3). In a sense, language is so simple that it can only be spoken, unconsciously articulated, but never consciously thought without complicating itself and thus betraying its simplicity.

Lacan opposes the simplicity of language to the complexity of think-able meaning in language: 'How complex is the problem of what it sig-nifies, when the psychologist relates it to the subject of knowledge; that is, to the subject's thought?' (66, 3). Hence, it is the psychological insist-ence on thought that uselessly complicates the simple question of language. Simplicity vanishes when psychologists try to go beyond words, away from the signifiers of language, and make them thinkable at the level of mean-ing, signification, cognition, information or mental processes. At this level, the speaking subject fades behind the 'subject of knowledge' (66, 3), a psy-chological notion that in later Lacanian conceptual clarifications would be clearly distinguished from the psychoanalytical idea of the 'subject of the signifier' (Lacan, 1967/2001: 579).

Despite his early critique of the subject of knowledge, the young Lacan of the 1930s does not yet propose a subject of the signifier. While it is true that his notion of the subject already stresses the importance of the signifier, this signi-fier is still clearly subordinated to 'social relations' (66, 4) and to the 'function of social expression' (67, 1). The signifier 'signifies to someone', represents the 'man who speaks' (66, 4), not 'to another signifier', as in later Lacanian theory (Lacan, 1960b/2006: 713).

Lacan would subsequently disclaim some of the ideas on the signifier, dis-course and language that he sustained in 1936. A case in point would be the rather psychologistic recognition of a subjective 'intention' in 'the meaning of discourse' (66, 4). Thirty years later, in 1966, the Lacanian conception of discourse would exclude any 'pure and simple intentionality', or 'more or less good intention', capable of 'surmounting' the 'effects of the unconscious' (Lacan, 1966/2001: 224). Perhaps we should attempt – retrospectively – to detect these effects in the intentions enumerated here by the young Lacan: 'a demanding intention, a punitive intention, a propitiatory intention, a demonstrative intention, or a purely aggressive intention' (66, 4). But just whose intentions are we talking about? Those of the subject or those of the Other? This is the key question, and Lacan indeed glimpses it when he explains that 'intention turns out to be unconscious insofar as it is expressed and conscious insofar as it is repressed' (67, 1). In other words, the real intention can only be thought by being denied, in 'the form of negation', and can only be articulated through the 'form of symbolism', which is necessarily unconscious and implies a 'moral anonymity' (66, 4-67, 1). We know that this place of anonymity will soon be occupied, in Lacanian theory, by the 'Id' as 'anonymous discourse' of the Other (Lacan, 1957: 22).

It seems that anonymity of discourse excludes the real presence and not only the name, the symbolic representative, of those who cannot meet one another through words. Instead of the encounter between the subjects in their transparent communication, there is a sort of mirror 'monologue' in which each one meets an 'image' that 'replaces' the other subject (67, 2-3). Lacan paradoxically explains that a psychoanalyst can only stop such a 'monologue' by refusing to play the role of 'interlocutor', that is, by 'remaining silent' and 'hiding everything including his facial expressions' (67, 2). In classic psychoanalytical terms, 'treatment must be carried out in abstinence' (Freud, 1915/1993: 177). The strict observance of the Freudian *abstinence rule* should initially provoke all manner of reactions in the analysand, such as 'imploring, imprecations, insinuations, provocations, and ruses' (67, 3). But these reactions will ultimately reveal the image with which the analysand has replaced the analyst, and which may constitute 'a reflection of the subject himself' (68, 1), the 'very image that the subject makes present through his behaviour, and that is constantly reproduced in it', even if it is 'ignored by him' (68, 2).

By using the 'power' derived from their imaginary starring role (68, 3), psychoanalysts operate on the 'two registers of intellectual elucidation through *interpretation* and handling affect through *transference*' (68, 4). The effective application of both processes, a matter of 'tact' and 'technique' (68, 4), should enable analysands to free themselves from the 'image's suggestion' (68, 5). But without this suggestion, the analyst's power decays and becomes 'useless' (68, 5). We thus arrive at the end of analysis, which is still implicit, as in the famous conclusion of the *Mirror Stage*: 'the point where the true journey begins' (Lacan, 1949/2006: 81). We still need to wait until 1953, the year of the rupture with the *Société Psychanalytique de Paris* (SPP) and the *International Psychoanalytical Association* (IPA), to obtain an explicit postulation and justification of the 'termination of an analysis' (Lacan, 1953/2006: 264).

Discussion of the objective value of the experience

Even though Lacan does not explicitly propose and explain the end of analysis in 1936, he nevertheless offers a representation of psychoanalysis as a terminable and closed process, one with both a beginning and an end. The process begins with the assimilation of the 'diffuse and broken' image to 'the real' and ends with its disassimilation from 'the real'[6] and restoration 'to its proper reality' (69, 1). The reality of the image is thus clearly differentiated from the real. This differentiation would be highlighted by Pellion (2009), who sees here an antecedent of the distinction between 'the real' and the chimerical 'objectivity assumed by Ego-psychology in the idea of adaptation to reality' (p. 101).

While Ego-psychologists would accept their image of objective reality as *the reference* for the analytical process, Lacanian psychoanalysis presents itself, from the very beginning, as 'a constant interaction between the observer and the object', a 'subjective movement' without a 'fixed reference' and 'based on conditions that are diametrically opposed to objectivity' (69, 2-3). An apparently objective 'observation'[7], for instance, may involve the 'personal stake' of the observer in what is observed (69, 4). In that same year −1936 − Lacan insisted that 'an object has an existence and a value only as long as it has a meaning that is inseparable from the subject's affective life' (Lacan, 1936a: 25). The subject appears in the core of the object. The most objective may be the most subjective, and the frontier between subjectivity and objectivity will depend on the very process of analysis.

It might seem that Lacan differentiates psychoanalysis from a scientific activity that would not have any problem with the frontiers between subjectivity and objectivity, the real and the imaginary, nature and culture, the human and the non-human. In this point of view, nature would 'no longer reveal itself in any sort of human form' (69, 5). The human and the natural would have been definitively separated in modern science... Far from it! Lacan points out that even 'physical science, as purified as it may seem in its modern progress from any intuitive category, nevertheless betrays, indeed all the more strikingly, the structure of the intelligence that constructed it' (70, 1). To support this idea, Lacan mentions the French-Polish chemist and philosopher Émile Meyerson, who showed in his *Essays*, published precisely in 1936, how the development of science implies diverse psychological factors, such as the need to identify phenomena, to 'transform diversity into identity', eliminate differences and find identities between different things (Meyerson, 1936: 21). The psychological-intellectual 'identification' would underlie the objective 'identities' between causes and effects, antecedents and consequents of changes, atoms and their smaller constituent parts, and successive states of matter, according to the principle of conservation (pp. 21–105). All these objective, identical things would be subjectively constituted by psychological identification. There would then be a psychological formation and evolution of physics.

Lacan accepts and generalizes Meyerson's idea of the psychological constitution of science and finds a 'psychological anthropomorphism' everywhere in nature; for example, in the physical notion of 'force', which is interpreted as 'the projection of human intention' into the outer world (70, 2). Projections such as this, coupled with the use of 'artificial tools' (70, 3), would lie behind what Lacan describes as 'the anthropomorphism of the myth of nature' and 'the subversion of nature implied by the *hominization* of the planet' (70, 4–71, 1). It goes without saying that hominization must be understood here as an epistemological-psychological phenomenon, at the level of human knowledge, and not as an ontological-physical phenomenon, in connection with the constitution of humanity, as in the theory of hominization proposed by Teilhard de Chardin (1956).

The object of psychology is defined in essentially relativistic terms

Having dismissed the possibility that science could ever be completely cleansed of its humanity and anthropomorphism, Lacan returns to the discussion of the reference and objective reality in psychology, postulating that psychological concepts must not be 'subjective, but relativistic', as their object and method have to be circumscribed to 'the specific reality of interpersonal relations' (71, 2). We may conjecture that, in the development of Lacanian theory, this early *relativism of interpersonal relations* would pave the way for the future *structuralism of signifying relations*, of an 'intersignifiance' that explicitly excludes any kind of interpersonal 'intersubjectivity' (Lacan, 1971/2007: 10).

The Lacanian conception of interpersonal relativism proposed in 1936 does not dismiss objectivity. However, 'the objective value' of research does not reside in what is researched, but in the research itself and in 'the efficacy of its progress' (71, 3). Thirty years later, Lacan might have said that this efficacy would retroactively demonstrate the objectivity of the research. So the research will be objective *après coup*, *nachträglich*, thanks to its efficacy.

The young Lacan finds efficacy in the psychoanalysis of his time, and by placing Freud among the psychologists, insists on his superiority, later confirmed by the progress of psychoanalytical research. So here psychoanalysis *is* a form of psychology. We are still far away from the sharp Lacanian demarcation with respect to psychology that we may trace to the 1950s, when Lacan began to insist upon 'the distance' between psychology and psychoanalytical 'praxis' (1951/2006: 178), concluding that 'there is no compromise possible with psychology' (1959/2006: 588).

Yet, in 1936, psychoanalysis was still not distinguished from psychology as such, but rather from other forms of psychology, since it was *better*, which means, in this context, that it shows *greater efficacy in its progress* and therefore has a *higher objective value*. This value of the Freudian form of psychology was illustrated significantly through Freud's theory of the image, an essentially psychological theory. According to Lacan, Freud would have demonstrated the 'informational function' of the image 'in intuition, memory, and development' (71, 4), as well as its function in 'discovering through analytic experience the process of identification' (71, 5).

When focusing on the identificatory process, Lacan begins by examining the difference of identification with respect to imitation, in which he follows the example of Freud, who also stressed this difference when he introduced the concept of identification with reference to hysterical psychic contagion. Freud (1900/1950) made it clear that identification was not 'simple imitation', but 'assimilation on the basis of a similar aetiological pretension' (p. 145). Lacan takes up this difference between the simplicity of imitation and the assimilatory character of identification, considers what Freud (1921/2004) developed in his mass psychology, and adds two important specifications: imitation is 'partial and groping', while identification is 'global' and 'structural' (71, 5).

Lacan is especially interested in the structural aspect of identification. According to him, identification involves not only a *global assimilation of a structure*, but also a *virtual assimilation of development* implied by that structure in a still undifferentiated state' (71, 5). This twofold assimilation takes place mainly during childhood thanks to an ensemble of mutually related characteristic features that distinguish children from adults; namely, their great 'immediate perspicacity', the absence of 'conventional categories that censor them' and their capacity to perceive 'the essential meaning of the situation' and to develop the 'germ' of the 'social interaction' that gives the situation its shape (71, 6–72, 1). For Lacan, it is the situation and its intrinsic social interaction, expression of a 'certain social structure', that will be maintained through identification with a parent, and then reflected by 'man's behaviour' and by 'his personality', conceived as a 'particular form of his human relations' (72, 2-3) – just as the Marxian 'human essence' defined as 'the ensemble of the social relations' (Marx, 1845/1969: 14).

It is hard not to be astonished by the importance of the social and the relational in the early development of Lacanian theory. Human relations are deployed by personality. Behaviour is an actualization of social interactions. The social structure is reproduced through the identificatory process. Identification is not just with an individual role, but with a transindividual plot that will organize an ensemble of 'psychic relations', a 'complex' whose 'concrete' and 'fruitful' conception Lacan opposed to the 'inadequate' and 'sterile' notion of 'instinct' (72, 4).

Lacan gives a picture of the complex through the metaphor of the *commedia dell'arte*, an Italian theatrical genre characterized by masked personages who represent fixed social types and offer improvised performances based on sketches or scenarios. Like actors in this form of the theatre of the 17th and 18th centuries, the individual performs the complex by obeying 'a typical framework and traditional roles', but also 'improvises it and makes it mediocre or highly expressive depending on his gifts' (72, 5). However, unlike actors in the *commedia dell'arte,* each subject is the sole actor in her/

his psychic drama and must alternatively perform all the roles or images provided by the complex.

After having praised the social-relational Freudian concepts of the complex, the image and the identificatory process, Lacan ends the last section with an introductory critique of psychoanalytical metapsychology. His critique focuses on the notion of 'libido', which is not a social-relational concept but a problematic biological notion that Freud attained when he moved beyond 'culture' and 'interpersonal relations' (73, 1). This movement is precisely the first problem with the libido, and with Freudian metapsychology in general; a problem criticized by Lacan during a debate that same year, when he questioned the biologism of a Freudian metapsychology in which 'the genius did not suffocate the biologist' with his 'passion for connecting everything to an infrastructure that often remains mythological' (Lacan, 1936b: 57–58). The second problem of the libido, as Lacan sees it, is the confusion between two different uses of the biological notion: on the one hand, outside psychology, the notion of libido implies a 'substantialist hypothesis' on matter (73, 2-3) that is based on the 'correlation' between psychical disorders and physical sexual irregularities (73, 4-5); on the other, inside the field of psychology, the energetic concept of libido is just a 'symbolic notation' that expresses the equivalence between the 'dynamisms' or 'efficacies' of different images (73, 6–74, 2).

The symbolic-psychological notion of libido is the only one that Lacan accepted, finding it necessary to compare and connect diverse objects that seem to be autonomous and incommensurable in the 'reality' constituted by 'knowledge' in conventional psychology (74, 3). For instance, how to relate erotic love and social cohesion, romanticism and nationalism, neurosis and morality? The unitary psychological account of these concrete objects requires the common denominator of libido just as it also needs the organizing idea of *complex*. The same is true for theoretical entities such as *the id*, *the ego* and *the superego*, which are described by Lacan as the 'imaginary posts that constitute personality' (74, 4).

Finally, though we have gathered the unitary account of concrete objects and theoretical entities, of imaginary posts and identificatory processes, we still need to answer two questions evoked by Lacan at the end of this section. The first regards the way 'images' constitute the 'reality' for knowledge, while the second concerns the way 'identifications' constitute the 'I' for the recognition of the subject (74, 5). As Lacan points out, Freud answered both questions by invoking the notion of the 'reality principle', which is as 'metapsychological' as that of 'libido' (74, 6).

Lacan sees the libido and the reality principle as questionable notions because of their metapsychological nature. If only they could be comprehended by psychology! Unfortunately, they are not psychological, but metapsychological, and it is here that their weakness lies.

It is at least perplexing to discover how the young Lacan so closely approaches the Ego-psychological tendency that led in due course to Merton

Gill (1976), who wished to purify psychoanalytical 'psychology', understood as an analysis of 'intention and meaning', of 'metapsychological propositions', which 'deal with force, energy, and structure' and were relegated to 'the realm of the natural sciences' (p. 71). We know that this psychologistic standpoint was diametrically opposed to the mature Lacanian project of adopting psycho-analytical 'metapsychology' for the purpose of going 'beyond psychology' and surpassing 'psychological prejudices' (Lacan, 1954/1998: 173–180, 259).

The later development of Lacanian theory would give critical significance to the Freudian conception of metapsychology (Orozco-Guzmán & Pavón-Cuéllar, 2014). And it is this significance that would allow Lacanian metapsy-chological theory to oppose psychology and turn this French psychoanalyst into a 'barred psychologist' (Parker, 2003), a *metapsychologist* who has proven to be very useful in current critical approaches to psychology (e.g. Parker, 2004; Hook, 2008; Owens, 2009). But we must not forget that Lacan began by criti-cizing psychology from within, through its immanent critique, which must be the central operation of what we currently call critical psychology.

Notes

1 The French *'faits de la connaissance'* was translated by Bruce Fink as 'facts of conscious-ness'.
2 The French *'le moment de la critique qui nous semble l'essentiel'* was translated by Fink as 'what seems to me to be an essential moment on critique'.
3 The French *'érosion conceptuelle'* was translated by Fink as 'conceptual decline'.
4 The French *'fonction du réel'* and *'fonction du vrai'* was translated by Fink as 'function of truth' and 'function of reality'.
5 The French *'attitude de soumission au réel'* was translated by Fink as 'attitude of submission to reality'.
6 The French *réel* was translated by Fink as 'reality'.
7 The French *'observation'* was translated by Fink as 'case study'.

References

Althusser, L. (1965/2005). *Pour Marx*. Paris: La Découverte.
Adorno, T. W. (1973). *Negative Dialectics*. New York: Continuum.
Adorno, T. W. (1982). *Prisms*. Boston: The MIT Press.
Antonio, R. J. (1981). Immanent Critique as the Core of Critical Theory: Its Origins and Developments in Hegel, Marx and Contemporary Thought. *The British Journal of Sociology* 32 (3), 330–345.
Babinski, J., & Froment, J. (1918). *Hysteria or Pithiatism and Reflex Nervous Disorders in the Neurology of War*. London: University of London Press.
Berkeley, G. (1732). An Essay Towards a New Theory of Vision. In Clarke, D.M. (2009) (ed.) *Philosophical Writings* (pp. 1–66). New York: Cambridge.
Freud, S. (1900/1950). *The Interpretation of Dreams. Standard Edition of the Complete Psychological Works of Sigmund Freud 4–5*. London: Hogarth Press.
Freud, S. (1915/1984). *On Metapsychology: The Theory of Psychoanalysis*. New York: Penguin.

Freud, S. (1915/1993). Observations on Transference-Love: Further Recommendations on the Technique of Psycho-analysis III. *The Journal of Psychotherapy Practice and Research* 2 (2), 171–180.

Freud, S. (1921/2004). *Mass Psychology*. London: Penguin UK.

Freud, S., & Breuer, J. (1895/2004). *Studies in Hysteria*. London: Penguin.

Gill, M. M. (1976). Metapsychology is not Psychology. *Psychological Issues* 9 (4, Mono 36), 71–105.

Grotstein, J. S. (2003). 'East is East and West is West and Ne'er the Twain Shall Meet' (Or Shall They?). In J. D. Safran (Ed.), *Psychoanalysis and Buddhism: An Unfolding Dialogue* (pp. 221–230). Somerville, MA: Wisdom.

Hartley, D. (1749/1801). *Observations on Man*. London: Johnson.

Hobbes, T. (1651). *Leviathan*. Oxford: Clarendon, 1929.

Hook, D. (2008). Absolute Other: Lacan's Big Other as Adjunct to Critical Social Psychological Analysis. *Social and Personality Psychology Compass* 2 (1), 51–73.

Hume, D. (1740/2012). *A Treatise on Human Nature*. New York: Courier-Dover.

Husserl, E. (1913/1931). *Ideas. General Introduction to Pure Phenomenology*. New York: Macmillan.

Husserl, E. (1931/1960). *Cartesian Meditations*. The Hague: Nijhoff.

Janet, P. (1929/2005). *L'évolution psychologique de la personnalité*. Paris: Harmattan.

Kant, I. (1781/1998). *Critique of Pure Reason*. Cambridge: Cambridge University Press.

Lacan, J. (1932/1975). *De la Psychose paranoïaque dans ses rapports avec la personnalité*. Paris: Seuil.

Lacan, J. (1936a). Intervention sur l'exposé de D. Lagache « Passions et psychoses passionnelles » au Groupe de l'Évolution Psychiatrique. *Évolution Psychiatrique* 1, 25–27.

Lacan, J. (1936b). Intervention sur l'exposé de P. Mâle « La formation du caractère chez l'enfant – la part de la structure et celle des événements ». *Évolution Psychiatrique* 1, 57–58.

Lacan, J. (1936c). Intervention sur l'exposé de E. Minkowski « La psychopathologie son orientation, ses tendances ». *Évolution Psychiatrique* 3, 66.

Lacan, J. (1938/2001). Les complexes familiaux dans la formation de l'individu. Essai d'analyse d'une fonction en psychologie. In *Autres écrits* (pp. 23–84). Paris: Seuil.

Lacan, J. (1946/2006). Presentation on Psychical Causality. In *Écrits* (pp. 123–158). New York: Norton.

Lacan, J. (1949/2006). The Mirror Stage as Formative of the I Function. In *Écrits* (pp. 75–81). New York: Norton.

Lacan, J. (1951/2006). Presentation on Transference. In *Écrits* (pp. 176–185). New York: Norton.

Lacan, J. (1953/2001). Discours de Rome. In *Autres écrits* (pp. 133–144). Paris: Seuil.

Lacan, J. (1954/1998). *Le séminaire. Livre I. Les écrits techniques de Freud*. Paris: Seuil (poche).

Lacan, J. (1955/2006). The Freudian Thing or the Meaning of the Return to Freud in Psychoanalysis. In *Écrits* (pp. 334–363). New York: Norton.

Lacan, J. (1956/1981). *Le séminaire. Livre III. Les psychoses*. Paris: Seuil.

Lacan, J. (1956/2006). The Situation of Psychoanalysis and the Training of Psychoanalysts in 1956. In *Écrits* (pp. 384–411). New York: Norton.

Lacan, J. (1957). Entretien avec Madeleine Chapsal. *L'Express* 310, 220–222.

Lacan, J. (1959/2006). In Memory of Ernest Jones: On his Theory of Symbolism. In *Écrits* (pp. 585–601). New York: Norton.

Lacan, J. (1958/1998). *Le séminaire. Livre V. Les formations de l'inconscient*. Paris: Seuil.

Lacan, J. (1960a/2006). The Subversion of the Subject and the Dialectic of Desire in the Freudian Unconscious. In *Écrits* (pp. 671–702). New York: Norton.

Lacan, J. (1960/2006). Position of the Unconscious. In *Écrits* (pp. 703–721). New York: Norton.

Lacan, J. (1964/1990). *Le séminaire. Livre XI. Les quatre concepts fondamentaux de la psychanalyse.* Paris: Seuil (poche).

Lacan, J. (1966/2001). Petit discours à l'ORTF. In *Autres écrits* (pp. 221–226). Paris: Seuil.

Lacan, J. (1967/2001). Première version de la Proposition du 9 Octobre 1967 sur la Psychanalyse à l'École. In *Autres écrits* (pp. 575–591). Paris: Seuil.

Lacan, J. (1970/1991). *Le séminaire. Livre XVII. L'envers de la psychanalyse.* Paris: Seuil.

Lacan, J. (1971/2007). *Le séminaire. Livre XVIII. D'un discours qui ne serait pas du semblant.* Paris: Seuil.

Lacan, J. (1976/2005). *Le séminaire. Livre XXIII. Le sinthome.* Paris: Seuil.

Leibniz, G. W. (1704/1921). *Nouveaux Essais sur l'entendement humain.* Paris: Flammarion.

Locke, J. (1689/1836). *An Essay Concerning Human Understanding.* London: Tegg & Son.

Mandler, G. (1962). From Association to Structure. *Psychological Review* 69 (5), 415–427.

Marcos, J.-P. (2002). Subversion de l'image. Contribution à une lecture d' «Au-delà du principe de réalité» (1936). *Essaim* 9, 65–85.

Marx, K. (1845/1969). Theses on Feuerbach. In *Marx/Engels Selected Works, Volume One* (pp. 13–15). Moscow: Progress.

Marx, K., & Engels, F. (1846/1970). *The German Ideology.* New York: International.

Meyerson, E. (1936). *Essais.* Paris: Vrin.

Mill, J. S. (1843/1994). *The Logic of the Moral Sciences.* Peru, IL: Open Court.

Miller, J.-A. (2003). Lacan's Later Teaching. *Lacanian Ink* 21, 4–41.

Miller, J.-A. (2011). L'être et l'un. Notes du cours 2011 de Jacques-Alain Miller. 18 mai 2011. 13° cours de Jacques-Alain Miller. Tripartition de la cause lacanienne. http://disparates.org/lun/2011/05/cours-de-jacques-alain-miller-18-mai-2011/

Orozco-Guzmán, M., & Pavón-Cuéllar, D. (2014). Metapsychology. In Thomas Teo (Ed.), *Encyclopedia of Critical Psychology.* New York: Springer.

Owens, C. (2009). Lacan for Critics! *Annual Review of Critical Psychology* 7, 1–4.

Parker, I. (2003). Jacques Lacan: Barred Psychologist. *Theory & Psychology* 13, 95–115.

Parker, I. (2004). Psychoanalysis and Critical Psychology. In D. Hook (Ed.), *Critical Psychology* (pp. 138–161). Cape Town: UCT Press.

Pavlov, I. P. (1924/2003). *Conditioned Reflexes.* New York: Dover.

Pavón-Cuéllar, D. (2013). Lacan and Social Psychology. *Social and Personality Psychology Compass* 7 (5), 261–274.

Pellion, F. (2009). Jacques Lacan vers le réel (1936–1962). *Revista Latinoamericana de Psicopatología Fundamental* 12 (1), 99–115.

Roudinesco, E. (1993/2009). *Jacques Lacan. Esquisse d'une vie.* Paris: Pochotèque.

Roudinesco, E. (2004). The Mirror Stage: An Obliterated Archive. In J.-M. Rabaté (Ed.), *The Cambridge Companion to Lacan* (pp. 25–34). Cambridge: Cambridge University Press.

Soler, C. (2006). Lacan en Antiphilosophe. *Filozofski vestnik* 27 (2), 121–144.

Taine, H. (1868). *Les Philosophes classiques du XIXe siècle en France.* Paris: Hachette.

Teilhard de Chardin, P. (1956). *Le phénomène humain.* Paris: Seuil.

Watson, J. B. (1913). Psychology as the Behaviorist Views it. *Psychological Review* 20, 158–177.

5

THE MIRROR STAGE AS FORMATIVE OF THE *I* FUNCTION AS REVEALED IN PSYCHOANALYTIC EXPERIENCE

Calum Neill

The *mirror stage* is a conceptual framework elaborated by Jacques Lacan in his seminal essay *Le stade du miroir comme formateur de la function du Je telle qu'elle nous est révélée dans l'expérience psychanalytique*. This essay, as it appears in *Écrits* is a significantly revised version of a paper Lacan presented at the 14th International Psychoanalytic Congress in Marienbad in August 1936. The later and better-known 'version' of the essay was itself originally presented at the 16th International Psychoanalytic Congress in Zurich in July 1949 and subsequently published in *Revue française de psychoanalyse* later that year. It is worth noting the unusual time lapse between the first and ultimate version of the essay. At a mere eight pages, the essay appears to have been a work in progress for over 13 years. This should alert us to the centrality of the work and the ideas contained within it to Lacan's project. While Lacan had been building an impressive reputation before the final version of the essay appeared, we might understand it as the publication that announced his arrival as a major figure on the world stage.

The *mirror stage* does not, then, of course, erupt suddenly from nowhere. Many of the ideas presented here are adumbrated in some fashion in earlier works. As early as his doctoral thesis (1932), Lacan is considering the complex of identification in terms of the misfit of mirrored reflection, describing his subject, Aimee, in terms which clearly pre-echo the ideas of 'The Mirror Stage', noting, for example, that she relates to her contemporaries simultaneously as ideals and as objects of aggressivity (Lacan, 1932: 225). A short while later, in his early essay 'Beyond the Reality Principle' (1936), he discusses at some length the centrality of the image and of identification in the psychical and social life of humanity in ways that explicitly prefigure 'The Mirror Stage'. More explicitly still, his 1938 text 'Family Complexes in the Formation of the Individual' contains a section titled 'The Mirror Stages', which Lacan suggests covers similar ground to the lost 1936 presentation (150–151).

It is also important to note that even after the publication of the essay in 1949, Lacan continued to refer to and refine the core ideas presented therein. Thus, the term *the mirror stage* has come to commonly refer to both the essay

DOI: 10.4324/9781003368649-6

itself and the central concept expounded within it and subsequently developed in Lacan's seminars. This central concept itself is inspired in part by the work of the French psychologist Henri Wallon. Wallon (1931) observed, through a procedure he termed 'the mirror test', that both human and chimpanzee infants were capable of recognising themselves in a mirror at around six months. What Wallon found significant here is that while the chimpanzee would quickly lose interest, the human infant becomes fascinated and will spend some time entranced by the phenomenon of the mirror image, exploring the apparent connections between their body and the reflected image. For Wallon, what is significant here is that the child has succeeded in distinguishing what we might call two levels of the visual. The child can see (parts of) itself in the flesh and it can see (parts of) itself reflected in the mirror. That the child seems to distinguish between these two sights can be understood to point towards some transition from an imagistic (or imaginary) grasp of the world to a representative (or symbolic) one. The argument Lacan develops out of Wallon's point here is that the encounter with the mirror is pivotal in the emergence of the child's identity. We come, to put it simply, to identify ourselves on the basis of an external, reflected image.

A number of commentators have taken issue with Lacan's arguments here, arguing that the phenomenon on which he bases them is unscientific or untestable and, seemingly more cuttingly, that Lacan's own appeals to science and psychology in the essay are misleadingly selective at best. Perhaps the best-known such critique comes from Michael Billig (2006), who argues that Lacan effectively misuses psychology in his paper. Without dismissing the fascinating insights of Billig's work, we need to pause here and consider what the use value of psychology might have been for Lacan. To claim that someone has misused psychology is to suppose that there is a proper use to which psychology might be put and, then, an improper one. Lacan clearly does deploy psychology unconventionally, in that as his citations are often vague and imprecise. Insofar as we understand Lacan to be building a theory of child development and insofar as we would understand Wallon, Köhler and Baldwin to be adequate foundations for such a project, we might understand Billig's critique to hit home. These suppositions are, however, rather wide of the mark and, arguably, miss the many points of Lacan's essay. Part of the problem here is a tendency to reduce Lacan's argument to two points and, moreover, to posit the second point as reliant on the first.

These two points are that children at a certain point in their development will forge the beginnings of an identity when they recognise a reflected image as themselves and, subsequent to this, they will, as they mature and become adults, continue to forge identities in similar ways. What this simplistic reduction misses is the connection or relation between the two modes of the mirror stage. Why, we might ask, if the child establishes its identity in the first moment, would the second moment be necessary at all? The important point here is that the process of identification evoked in each dimension here is necessarily a failure. Moreover, it is not simply that the continuing, lifelong mirror staging is a consequence of an initial failure. Rather we should read the failing dimension of what appears to be a second stage as already entailed within what only appears to be a first stage.

The logic here is apparently not only complex but it is one which is radically incommensurate with the conventions within which critics such as Billig would like to remain. To appreciate what Lacan is doing in the essay, it is necessary to look at it much more closely and less selectively.

More coherent and insightful accounts of 'The Mirror Stage' do, of course, exist. Among the best and worth mentioning here are Dany Nobus's 'Life and Death in the Glass: A New Look at the Mirror Stage' (Nobus, 1998) and Elisabeth Roudinesco's contribution to the *Cambridge Companion to Lacan*, 'The Mirror Stage: An Obliterated Archive' (Roudinesco, 2003). 'The Mirror Stage' is also widely referenced and commented upon in a myriad of books and articles and is undoubtedly the most read, best known and most influential of Lacan's works. This is in part due to its appearance in many anthologies, particularly from within literary and film studies. Through this dissemination, the idea of the mirror stage has become fairly commonplace in an impressive range of disciplines, from the aforementioned literary and film studies and psychology to the wider social sciences and cultural studies. In becoming rather widely known, the concept of the mirror stage can be understood to have become somewhat fixed and conveniently oversimplified. The dominance of a particular, if not terribly precise, understanding of what the mirror stage is and means can then be understood to already infect the understanding of one who reads the essay itself. That is to say, when you come to read the essay, you are likely to already be reading it through a number of received interpretations and this, encouraged by the characteristic density of Lacan's writing, can lead to expedient glossing of the text.

In addition, as already noted, the concept of the mirror stage is not restricted to this one piece from Lacan's writings. He had already written on the concept before 1949 and he continued to refer to and develop the concept for decades to come. Here, however, the attempt has been made to focus on *The Mirror Stage* as a piece of writing, rather than to assume to extract from this and other pieces of writing a developing concept. Only after we have read the initial essay carefully might we be in a position to consider the *mirror stage* as a concept.

The text

Lacan opens his essay (75, 1) with a little contextualisation and a reference to the earlier version, remarking not only on the time which has lapsed between his 1936 presentation and the 1949 presentation, but also on the significance his conception of the *mirror stage* has taken on for what he refers to as 'the French group'; i.e. his own circle. He then clearly states his core motivation for revisiting the concept of the *mirror stage* and, consequently, the core concern of the current essay. He is concerned with the function of what he terms 'the I' (or, in French, simply *je,* without any article) and he is concerned with this specifically as it is experienced within a psychoanalytic context. This focus is already evident in the expanded title of the essay (the 1936 version was simply called *La stade du miroir,* 'The Mirror Stage'), emphasising the productive dimension of 'I', to which he is referring as a function, not an essence or a substantial entity as such.

The reference to 'the experience psychoanalysis provides' suggests that the focus of the piece is to be clinical. As we read on it will become evident that this is not exactly the case. This underscores a crucial dimension to reading this *écrit,* which may then be generalised throughout Lacan's work. He is a psychoanalyst and he is concerned with teaching psychoanalysts and, thus, with the clinical practice of psychoanalysis. He is also always drawing on a wider body of cultural and philosophical texts and thus engaging in a dialogue which necessarily exceeds the bounds of the clinic. When he says that he is concerned with the function of the 'I' as we experience it in psychoanalysis, he is, of course, referring to the understanding of the 'I' as evident in clinical practice but he is also suggesting that this conception of the function of the 'I' is something we need to take outside the clinic.

This point is made in the final and forceful sentence of the first paragraph (75, 1) where Lacan declares that the experience of (Lacanian) psychoanalysis, and subsequently his theory, is such that it positions us in opposition to any philosophy directly issuing from the *Cogito.* This claim performs a number of functions. First, it draws our attention to Descartes and thus situates the theme or focus of Lacan's intervention. It tells us that what we are about to read is concerned with fundamental questions of subjectivity and self-knowledge and locates such questions in a modern, i.e. post-enlightenment, context. Second, it situates Lacan and this essay in relation to the then–current intellectual climate of Paris.

In 1946, Jean-Paul Sartre published his famous tract *L'existentialisme est un humanisme.* Here Sartre argues that 'the subjectivity which we thus postulate as the standard of truth is no narrowly individual subjectivism, for as we have demonstrated, it is not only one's own self that one discovers in the *cogito,* but those of others too' (1973). Sartre's argument, while constituting a radical departure from Descartes' solitary individualism and drawing on a certain Hegelianism, does not, to Lacan's mind, go far enough. Sartre's problem with Descartes is that his philosophy shuts us off from others. He wants to maintain a solidarity, a social dimension at the core of subjectivity. Lacan's issue with this is that it does not go far enough, that it still accepts the basic self-identity of Cartesianism. Sartre famously declares in his essay that 'existence precedes essence' (Sartre: 22). For Lacan, there is no essence.

The thing to keep in mind, however, is that Lacan is not simply rejecting Cartesianism. Lacan returns to Descartes again and again (see the opening chapter of Neill, 2014). We should read this claim then with an emphasis on 'directly' (75, 1). Lacan is fascinated by Descartes' basic operation but argues that he gets it wrong. Lacan refashions the cogito as 'I think where I am not, therefore I am where I think not' (Lacan, 1977: 166). This is a complex manoeuvre. Thinking occurs in language but language can never capture it all. I therefore think in a realm which is other to me, while at the same time, I am not a possibility outwith this realm. I exist in a constant tension between being and meaning. On the simplest level, Descartes, according to Lacan, only establishes the ego. The mistake is to assume that the ego is all. This also, then, extends Lacan's criticism to ego psychology and what we would now refer to as mainstream psychology.

We can then see that in the short opening paragraph, Lacan announces his targets. He refuses the conventions of Cartesian subjectivity, the supposed subject of modernity and, with it, modern science. But more than this, he refuses the apparently radical and certainly chic existentialism of the Left Bank. For Lacan, it is not that radical at all. His project, over the next few pages (and, to be fair, over the next few decades) will be to explore and reconfigure how we think about ourselves and how we think an idea of ourselves into existence. He is not concerned with finding a pre-existent self but rather he is concerned with exploring the contradictions and ramifications of our conception of ourselves.

In the second paragraph (75, 2), Lacan links the concept of the mirror stage, at least in its earlier formation, to an observation from Wolfgang Köhler's work with chimpanzees (1925). Köhler is understood to have demonstrated that at a point in infanthood when a child seems less developed than a chimpanzee a striking anomaly is evident. Despite the chimpanzee's superiority in terms of its instrumental intelligence, the human infant appears more developed in one significant way; it is able to recognise itself in a mirror. Not only does the human infant recognise itself but it marks such recognition with what we might term a *eureka!* moment. This moment can be understood as the beginning of the child's ability to situate itself in the context of the world.

This is an extremely complex operation. Even in adulthood, we simultaneously perceive the world and experience ourselves. To achieve this recognition, we need to perform the complex and imaginative operation of synthesising these two experiences. That is to say, we have to imagine ourselves in the world.

Lacan refers to this process as situational apperception, a term he credits to Köhler. In the context of Gestalt psychology, the term situational apperception might simply be understood as something like contextual apprehension; that is, the ability to conceptually grasp oneself in space. Given the preceding paragraph's invocation of Descartes, however, we might also see the term apperception as resonating with a philosophical sense. The term apperception (*appercevoir*) is in fact introduced by Descartes in his *Les Passions de L'âme* (1649), although it is most often translated simply as perception, indicating, as

Leibniz (1992) has pointed out, that Descartes did not adequately distinguish the two. Leibniz argues that Descartes conflates (conscious) thought and perception and thus excludes the possibility of a perception of which we are not conscious. Seeking to clarify, he distinguishes apperception, as conscious, from simple perception, which is continuous but not conscious. Kant (2007) further utilises the term apperception in the construction of his epistemological theory, distinguishing between transcendental and empirical apperception. The former refers to the necessity, in Kant's schema, of a unifying consciousness which would hold together all experience. The latter refers to one's awareness of oneself in the moment, the sense of self which would accompany any activity of thought. Clearly, there is a spatial significance to the mode of apperception to which Lacan refers here and we might understand the qualifying 'situational' as intended precisely to refuse Kant's transcendental apperception. For Lacan, there is no unity of self in consciousness.

Curiously, while Köhler is brought in here in relation to the notion of situational apperception, the whole paragraph could be understood to orbit around this proper name. Köhler, as well as being one of the founders of Gestalt psychology (1929), worked for six years with primates in Tenerife, particularly investigating problem solving. In relation to problem solving in human subjects, Köhler observed that we often solve problems when we are not actively or consciously thinking about them. Probably the most famous example of this phenomenon is Archimedes' discovery of displacement when, following his wife's suggestion that he stop working and relax, he took a bath. His famous cry of 'eureka' is one way in which we might translate Lacan's *Aha-Erlibnis*. Köhler was also a phenomenologist (indicating a theoretical link with Sartre) and the German term *Erlibnis* is one favoured by phenomenologists to describe what we might render in English as 'lived experience'. The child's intellect may grasp something in its encounter with the mirror but the intellectual moment here follows from a lived experience.

This knotty configuration of unobvious references renders the short paragraph incredibly dense, signalling a variety of meanings, associations and points of departure. This example, early in the essay, should alert us to the unusual use of references throughout. Proper names are cited where the referent is not at all clear. References are alluded to with no name flagged. What we need to perhaps ask in each of these many incidences is what are the effects? What echoes are triggered? Rarely are we going to encounter anything as simple as a direct, conventional citation.

Returning to the chimpanzee (although Lacan now refers to it as a monkey), while it may recognise itself, or at least register its image, it will soon lose interest (75, 3). The child, on the other hand, is captivated by the reflection of its movements and the apparent relationship between these movements and the reflected movements and their reflected backdrop. The reflection of the backdrop, the environment in which and against which the child's reflected movements appear is important to keep in mind. The two worlds – the mirror world and 'reality' – appear connected. Added to this, it is not only going to be the room, the furniture, toys and so on which are reflected in the mirror but, crucially, there will most likely be other people too.

Lacan suggests that it is commonly accepted that this mirror recognition will occur after six months of age (75, 4). In articulating this claim to the psychologist Mark James Baldwin, who does not appear to have made the claim himself, Lacan might be understood to be invoking earlier theorists of the social self, such as William James, George Herbert Mead and Charles Horton Cooley (the theorist of the 'looking-glass self'), as well as Baldwin himself, who did advance the idea that one's sense of self develops through imitation or mirroring of the other (Baldwin, 1895). The social dimension is certainly what Lacan wishes to emphasise, pointing as he does to the fact that before the child has independent movement – before it can walk or even support itself – it will need to be held in front of the mirror. Whether the child is held by a parent or sibling, or is held up by a baby walker, it will require support that is external to itself. This raises a number of important points. First, it emphasises the intrigue the child displays. According to what appear to be Lacan's own observations, the child will lean into the mirror, hold its own gaze and, resisting the constraints of its support, will respond with 'a flutter of jubilant activity' (76, 1). This in turn emphasises that, despite the mirror containing a reflection of the room, its contents and any other persons there, the focus of the child's attention is likely to be firmly on itself. We should not ignore, however, the social dimension implied here. While the child may be fixated on its own reflection, the experience is most commonly going to be one in which it is accompanied by another. Not only does this already mark one's initial recognition of one's self as already socially mediated but it also implies the disjuncture of the fact that there are, for example, suddenly two mothers with which to contend.

The child's reaction points to a libidinal dimension of the mirror encounter. The child is not merely curious but is jubilant. An element of desire is evident here. Lacan also claims here that this scenario underpins his assertion that all human knowledge is paranoiac. The experience of the child before the mirror points, he says, to 'an ontological structure of the human world that accords with my reflections on paranoiac knowledge' (76, 2). It is worth noting here that Lacan refers to the 'human world' rather than simply the world. This emphasises the mediated nature of what is at stake here. The world we encounter is not the world as is but the world as we encounter it, the world already constructed through the prism of human knowledge or, in Lacan's later terminology, the world structured through the symbolic. More than this, however, Lacan wants to emphasise that such knowledge is not somehow emotionally neutral but is always affected by a paranoiac tension. Lacan holds that paranoia is not something that develops or emerges gradually, but rather that it is precipitated by certain 'fertile moments' (Lacan, 1993: 17) that involve 'external relationships' (Ibid: 18). An element from outside is internalised on the basis of what it is thought to illuminate about the subject's being. This is the process Lacan terms *meconnaissance* and it is the same process we see in the mirror stage, thus suggesting that paranoia is structurally commonplace (see Vanheule, 2011: 16).

The theme of paranoiac knowledge is elaborated upon in the essay 'Aggressiveness in Psychoanalysis', which follows 'The Mirror Stage' in the *Écrits*, despite being published a year before this final version of 'The Mirror Stage', and in 'On My Antecedents', which appears earlier in the *Écrits*, despite only being composed at the point of the publication of the volume in 1966. This is then clearly a theme of central importance not only for this point in Lacan's development of his theory but still 17 years later (see relevant commentaries in this volume).

Lacan goes on to say that the mirror stage describes an identification, emphasising the process of identification rather than identity as a fixed state (76, 3). This identification is the result of a transformation of the subject as it takes on an image. The sense of a transformation here should perhaps resonate with the idea of metamorphosis and, subsequently, with the tale of Narcissus from Ovid's *Metamorphoses* (2004). Narcissus is transformed. He takes on a new form as a result of his encounter with a reflection. In psychoanalytic terms, the product of identification would be termed an *imago*, a Latin term that also denotes a developmental stage of maturity such as the butterfly in relation to the caterpillar, as well as, in ancient times, referring to a death mask. The term *imago* would also connote an idealised image as in *Imago Dei*, an image of God. Lacan appears to be drawing on these multiple senses to paint a picture here of a process of identification which marks the distinct movement to another phase or stage of experience through the internalisation of an idealised but fabricated idea. The identification which takes place, then, is not an identification with what is.

The mirror experience is the exemplary case of human self-experience. This underscores the point here that we are not only dealing with a developmental stage but with something which will repeat throughout our lives. It is easy to see with a baby that the image they begin to identify with is quite different from the bodily experience they live. Babies cannot control their own bodies – just note the frequency with which a child will bop itself on the head with a toy or reach out to grab one thing and collide with another. Babies are utterly dependent on their caregivers. The difference, then, between the image in the mirror and the uncontrolled lived experience is itself what gives rise to a jubilation as the infant assumes the image as itself. Lacan's use of the term 'assumption' here is significant (76, 4). In assuming the reflected image, the child is taking it on, in the sense that one might assume a title, but the child is also mistaking the image as itself, in the common sense that one might make an assumption prior to the facts. Third, we might hear here an echo of the Christian notion of assumption wherein a body is transposed from one realm to another. Typically, this would be from earth to heaven. Here it is from one side of the mirror divide to the other. Taking all three notions of assumption together allows us to grasp the simultaneous emphases being placed here on the body, on transition, on language and on error. What is assumed is not only 'taken from', 'taken on' and 'taken to mean', it is also 'mistaken as'. One key point which arises out of this is that the mirror stage being presented here is not something that can be located exclusively in childhood. After this assumed initial event, after we exit the apparent animal existence of infanthood and move more explicitly and fully into culture, social identity and language, we still continue to experience a mismatch between our idea of ourselves and our experience of ourselves. This idea we have of ourselves is what Lacan is refer-ring to as the *I*.

Immediately, Lacan expands on this to clarify that the *I* as he is referring to it here would be equivalent to what in Lacanian terminology would usu-ally be referred to as the Ideal-I (76, 5). The ideal-I or ideal-ego refers to our idealised image of ourselves and is in part the basis of libidinal identifications with others. What is crucial here is the fact that the ideal-I, based on misrecog-nition, is fictional, not real. This is then to situate the whole of what Lacan refers to as the 'ego function', the internalisation of a quasi–coherent sense of self, as fictional and, given the astatic nature of the ego, as an unfolding fiction. This means there is always going to be a mismatch between the experience of subjectivity and the ego. They will never coincide. They remain asymptotical; coming close but without the possibility of ever actually coinciding.

This mismatch is seen clearly through the fact that what the child is identify-ing with is a mirror image. While in everyday usage we may take the mirror image of something to be a reasonably accurate representation of what it is, Lacan wants to draw our attention to the illusion in such a move. A mirror image is always, by definition, inverted. You move your right hand, the mirror image moves its left hand. Perhaps less obviously, it is also always partial, dis-torted and smaller. Moreover, in the current context, it is crucial to acknowl-edge that it is only a shape or form (76, 6). The German term Lacan uses here, *Gestalt*, which literally means form, immediately also brings to mind the school of Gestalt psychology, as previously flagged in the reference to Köhler. Gestalt theory, which is primarily concerned with perception, argues that what we first perceive is the whole form (*Gestalt*) and from this we discern parts, rather than perceiving parts and composing them into a greater whole. This is the point Lacan is making when he says that the form is 'more constitutive than constituted' (76, 6). What is also crucial here, for Lacan's point, is that the form is merely that, a shape or an image. It has no interiority, no spirit or personality. We project onto or into this form our sense of self, much in the same way as we might project characteristics onto a statue or an automaton.

Having begun by warning us against proceeding directly from Descartes (75, 1), Lacan appears here to be making a direct reference to the *Meditations*. In his second meditation, Descartes looks down into the street from his win-dow at the people walking below. How, he asks, can he know that what he sees are really people like himself rather than automata beneath hats and coats

(Descartes, 1993: 22). Descartes feels certain of himself but cannot be sure of the reality of others. Lacan is extending this very point to make the case that we cannot even be sure of ourselves. Just like Descartes' consideration of the automata, we start from an exterior image and imagine an interiority. It is not, however, simply the fact that there is a mismatch here, that the mirror image is not the same as the figure that stands before it. The mirror image appears to maintain a coherence and consistency which is absent from the child's bodily experience. In seeing before it an image of itself which is more capable than it experiences itself to be, the child encounters the future, albeit in a fantasised form. This underscores a key force of the mirror stage; it is concerned with a futurity, an anticipation but an anticipation for a future self which will never arrive, which is always to come. Such an anticipation is then also a projection. Encountering the other that is the mirror image as a more advanced manifestation leads the subject to posit itself as inferior. This then situates the subject as permanently under the shadow of the fantasy, but it also sets in motion a certain creative trajectory. The child is not adequate to the image before it, but neither is the image actually what the child mistakes it to be (76, 6).

Lacan appeals to clinical experience to support the idea that the image of oneself is fundamental to experiencing the world. The image of ourselves pervades our psychic life, in dreams, in hallucinations (77, 2). Body parts, bodily failure, the otherness of the image we take to be ourselves; all of these appear to become fundamental to our experience of ourselves in the world. We relate to the world in terms of our image of ourselves despite the fact that this image is 'only' an image. In fact, the very idea that something is *only* an image is itself delusional. Images have effects as the structural anthropologist Claude Lévi-Strauss discussed at length through his concept of symbolic effectiveness (Lévi-Strauss, 1963: 167–205).

Lacan appeals to zoology to support the notion that the encounter with an image can have such profound effects (77, 3). Some pigeons require the presence of another pigeon to mature sexually but this other pigeon can be a mirror image (Matthews, 1939). All it takes, then, is for the pigeon to encounter an image for a real biological effect to take place. Similarly, locusts, according to Lacan, will change their social nature simply by exposure to the correct image. Lacan appears to want to argue here that homeomorphic identification, the identification with something of the same form, plays a fundamental role in both human and animal relations with the world.

Extending the significance of visual identification, Lacan raises the question of mimicry wherein an animal appears to engage in a form of identification with something which is other than itself by adopting its form. The mirror stage encounter might be understood to sit between these two, homeomorphic and heteromorphic identifications, insofar as it describes the encounter with something which, on the one hand, we take to be the same and, on the other, is not the same. Lacan is keen to stress here that this function cannot simply be reduced to a mode of adaptation (77, 4).

In addition to the liminal location of the mirror stage encounter between same and other, Lacan wants here to emphasise the fact that the encounter always takes place in a space. As indicated earlier, the focus of attention may appear to be on the image the child takes to be itself but we cannot ignore the context that accompanies this. It is not only the form with which one identifies which shapes our developing idea of self but also the environment in which we find ourselves. Ultimately, the two cannot be separated. Lacan refers here to Roger Caillois's concept of *legendary psychasthenia* (77, 4), the phenomenon whereby an animal, such as a praying mantis, blends with its surroundings (Caillois, 2003). What is significant about *legendary psychasthenia* here is that it illustrates that the separation between an individual and its context, between *me* and the world in which I find myself, is not so absolute.

Echoing the point made earlier about the paranoiac character of human knowledge, Lacan here argues that even prior to the socialising effects which would be understood to engender such a paranoiac structure, human beings are going to be tipped in this direction due to their insufficiency (77, 5). It is not simply that at the point of the mirror stage in infanthood, when we are less than two years old, we are incapable of surviving or even moving about on our own. Lacan argues that we are always organically insufficient or inadequate and can never become anything other than organically insufficient. The human condition is not and cannot be a natural one. The very notion of nature is a construct posited from a position of knowledge which would, by definition, be beyond nature.

The mirror stage can thus be understood as a particular example of how the *imago* works to establish a relationship between an organism and the world around it (78, 1). The specific terms Lacan uses here, *Innenwelt* and *Umwelt*, are taken from the German biologist Jakob Johann von Uexküll. In Uexküll's usage, *Umwelt*, which might commonly be translated as surroundings or environment, does not denote the environment in an objective or neutral sense. Rather, Uexküll argues, each individual organism maps its environment as a field of significance and it is this meaning-laden version of the world, which necessarily situates the individual in question at its centre, that is described by the term *Umwelt* (Uexküll, 1926: 79). *Innenwelt*, on the other hand, refers to the immediate sensory data the individual takes in. When Lacan parses this distinction as a relationship between the organism and its reality, he is thus making the point that what he terms reality is not a neutral field but is rather a symbolically mediated context which is inseparable from the individual in question. The relation between the two, then, is the relation between the raw sensory data and the symbolic field onto which this might map. Crucially, such mapping will always entail a gap; the gap introduced by meaning. Significant here is the fact that Uexküll, as a biologist, is not specifically writing about speaking beings, which is to say, in his usage, the semiotic dimension indicated here would not be reducible to language. Heidegger takes up Uexküll's use of *Umwelt* in *Being and Time* where the term becomes central and is used to denote the specifically human world of ready-to-hand entities (Heidegger, 1962: 101). Lacan's use of the general term organism would suggest he is drawing more on Uexküll than Heidegger, but given his familiarity with Heidegger, we should perhaps not ignore this layer of significance.

Pulling us more to the Heideggerian side in the subsequent paragraph, Lacan reminds us that the experience of human beings is distinct from other organisms due to the fact that we are born too early. Where other animals can function reasonably independently from a very early age, human beings are not born ready to survive. A foal, to use a most obvious example, will usually stand and start to walk within an hour of being born. A human baby will usually take at least a year. We are born premature, incomplete, uncoordinated (78, 2).

Embryologists refer to the fact of the extension of human infancy as *foetalisation* or pedomorphism (see Bolk, 1926; Gould, 1977). This, it is argued, is what gives rise to the relatively larger and superior form of the human brain. Parts of the cortex in human beings are notably larger than in primates such as gorillas and chimpanzees. This is said to account for greater initiative and future orientation in human beings and, according to Lacan, might be understood as something akin to an intra-organic mirror, the locus of our imagining ourselves as well as our anticipatory projection of ourselves (78, 3).

Lacan is working to capture a complex temporal logic here, what he refers to as a temporal dialectic (78, 4). The child sees what it simultaneously takes to be itself but perceives to be more coherent and complete than itself. Subsequently the child aspires to become this image it sees before it but, crucially, it is also then aspiring to become that in the image which was only ever imagined to be in the image. In this curious toing and froing, there is strictly speaking no beginning, no point of origin, no original or authentic self. The very formation of the individual, as an identity, is only ever something which would be posterior to this confrontation. Here we have the first echoes of Hegel in 'The Mirror Stage' essay. The use of the term dialectic, the sense of an individual being formed in relation to history. These references ought to bring to mind Hegel's famous 'Master-Slave Dialectic'. This section of *The Phenomenology of Mind* concerns the advent of consciousness through the interaction of two beings. This is precisely what Lacan is trying to articulate with his theory of the mirror stage. As with Hegel, prior to the encounter, there is no full consciousness. It is only through the encounter with the other being – or with the mirror image – that consciousness and an idea of self could be seen to emerge. Importantly, it is what *could be seen to* that is in play here. The formation of the individual is not something which is experienced in history but rather projected into history, where history itself is posited as an artifice into which the mistake of the ego is read.

This leads Lacan to one of the central declarations of the essay: 'the mirror stage is a drama whose internal pressure pushes precipitously from insufficiency to anticipation' (78, 4). The mirror stage, he tells us, is a drama. In describing it as a drama, we should understand resonances of performance and action but also acting, artifice and scriptedness. The mirror stage is a construct, but it is a constructive construct. The movement of this drama is from insufficiency, that of infant motor incapacity but also the defining dehiscence of human life, to anticipation. Not to accomplishment. We are incomplete but the mirror offers us the promise of a completion to come. This instantiates the movement of our lives.

This experience is often reflected in fantasies and dreams both of incompletion and completion (78, 5). The notion of the body in pieces is common enough, both in clinical experience and in culture. Children often draw themselves and others with limbs disconnected or, in the world of art, we might take the example of Hans Belmer with his curious but enduringly compelling dolls with malcomposed body parts. Similarly, culture abounds with images of the reinforced body, from Robocop to Ironman. These images, both of fragmentation and orthopaedic reinforcement attest to Lacan's point here. Our identity is as fundamentally bodily as it is fundamentally impossible. The struggle to verify and maintain one's identity is destined for repeated failure and is, therefore, unending. Moreover, the identity we choose, the identity with which we so strongly identify (if we can express this in such a tautology) because it is not what we are, is necessarily alienating. We feel the need for the protective shield of an identity which is always other but, precisely because it is always other, we are alienated in wearing it. It functions then not simply as a protection but also as a constraint, a limitation. Our entire mental development is thus conditioned by the limited nature of the identity we adopt. Importantly here, it is not that we would somehow be better off were we to select a 'better' or less limiting identity. It is rather the fact of identity itself which is limiting. This adoption of a rigid identity can be understood as the rupture of the continuum of inside and outside and it is this, and the ill-fitting nature of the identity so adopted, which necessarily then gives rise to an unending self-accounting. It cannot end because *I* am not that.

From a clinical perspective, Lacan argues that fantasies of the body in pieces are indicative of internal aggressive disintegration, echoing points he has covered in *Aggressiveness in Psychoanalysis*. Such fantasies tend to manifest as ideas of disjointed limbs, internal organs presented on the outside of the body, burgeoning wings or battling internal forces. Lacan himself points to the quintessential example here as the work of Hieronymus Bosch (78, 5), presumably referring to the triptych, *The Garden of Earthly Delights*, the central panel of which is dominated by a bisected, hollowed-out torso whose arms become trees while little people climb inside him. Such schisms are apparent too even in the base bodily experience of psychotic and hysteric subjects.

The complex of this oscillation from insufficiency to anticipation means that the fantasy of the body in pieces is going to find its correlate in fantasies of completion. Thus, we also encounter the fantasy of the ego in dreams of fortresses and stadiums (78, 6). Importantly, Lacan draws our attention here to the fact that where there is ego, there is also necessarily id. The unconscious knows this. The point here is that we dream of fortification precisely because we are not fortified. It is a defence mechanism.

There is a danger in the recourse to the images Lacan has evoked here. Commonplace as these images are, they appear to suggest an entirely subjective experience and this runs counter to the point Lacan is trying to make (79, 2). Recall that, at the outset, Lacan was clear that we should resist the lure of Cartesianism. That is to say, where for Descartes and much of modernity, the subject is atomistic and self-enclosed, for Lacan such self-enclosure is never more than a fantasy. The stadium of the previous paragraph is a key metaphor here; and stadium is also one of the meanings of the French *stade* of the title of the *écrit*. The self-enclosure of the Cartesian *I* is already a reaction formation against the experience of fragmentation and insufficiency. This being the case, the proliferation of repeated images in our culture should not be seen as coincidental subjective manifestations, the products of this or that artist's or patient's particular imagination. Rather, they should be understood as articulations conditioned by a particular grammar, that of the unconscious. And the unconscious for Lacan is transindividual, not individual. In advocating a 'method of symbolic reduction' (79, 2), Lacan is already advancing his emphasis on linguistics and adumbrating his later suggestion that 'the unconscious ... is structured like a language' (737, 2).

The process of mirror identification can help to locate particular problems such as hysteria and obsession insofar as these would relate to different stages in the process (79, 3). Lacan is not appealing to any natural norm as all human development requires a movement through this process and thus a move towards culture. In this sense, he is largely repeating Freud's points with regard to the psychosexual stages. What Lacan is adding is the claim that, as different ego defences are evident in different clinical structures, and these different defence mechanisms, as Anna Freud had hypothesised, follow a certain sequence, the emergence of defence mechanisms can allow the clinician to ascertain something of the aetiology of the clinical structure of the analysand. He has already articulated the link between paranoia and the nascent formation of social identity through the notion of a constitutive paranoiac knowledge. Here he suggests that this paranoiac knowledge would emerge at a later point than obsessive inversion and that, in turn, would emerge at a later point than hysterical repression. It is this paranoiac alienation which marks the subject's emergence in the social world, the world of the Other, and of language.

Here we come to what we might understand as a transition moment in the essay where Lacan talks of the end of the mirror stage. This would have to be understood to refer to the moment in infanthood where misrecognition ushers in the process of identification. Lacan here refers to the image in the mirror as a counterpart, emphasising the alterity at the heart of this process (79, 4). In identifying with this counterpart, as Lacan has already made clear, we do not have anything like a reduction to one. Rather, in the midst of identification, we establish a relationship of jealousy comparable to the psychologist Charlotte

Bühler's phenomenon of transitivism, i.e. the attribution of one's own psychic and physical experiences to other persons or things. Transitivism points to the fact that our *Umwelt* is not only very much a part of what we are but also emphasises that the *Umwelt* contains other people. This indissoluble connection between the becoming subject and the world of others points to the fact that the end of the infant mirror stage is the movement into socialisation.

As we come to find ourselves in a social world, we are forced to relate to ourselves and the world through the medium of the desire of the other. Again, we appear to be in Hegelian territory here. In Alexandre Kojève's famous reading of the Master-Slave Dialectic (Kojève, 1980), the encounter is understood in terms of each player's desire to be desired by the other. In the world of psychoanalysis, the key example of this would be the Oedipus complex wherein the child largely relates to the desire of the mother (79, 5). This should be understood in a number of ways. Not only does the child desire to be the object of the mother's desire, it also comes to model its desire on the fact of the mother's desire. Beyond this, the child has to face the fact that it is never adequate to the mother's desire, she always desires something more, something else, something elsewhere, something other. This introduction of desire as opposed to instinctual needs means that the latter presents as threatening to the subject. Again, Lacan is emphasising the fact that for the human subject, there is no natural. For a human child to mature, it is necessary to abandon the domination by instinct and negotiate culture, to negotiate desire.

The experience of the mirror stage Lacan has been describing up until this point appears, he suggests, to accord with what Freud termed primary narcissism, i.e. an initial and ubiquitous self-love which reflects and allows our self-preservation instincts. Prior to and as detailed in Freud's famous 1914 paper 'On Narcissism: An Introduction' the name of Narcissus had been borrowed extensively to refer to auto-libidinal perversions (by Näcke in 1899) and psychological tendencies (by Ellis (2011) in 1898) and had already entered the psychoanalytic vocabulary by 1909 before Otto Rank's paper 'A Contribution to Narcissism' (1911). Ovid's tale of the fated youth who, entranced by the beauty of his own reflection in a stream, perishes and, in the moment of death, is transformed into a flower, had already echoed through Western literature and, in doing so, had come to be equated rather simply with self-love. In constructing his idea of the mirror stage, Lacan is very obviously drawing a line back to Ovid but in so doing he wants to emphasise the scopic dimension, which seems to be lost in the reduction of Narcissus to a shorthand for self-love or self-infatuation. There is, he claims, a semantic latency in the choice of the term *narcissism* in that, appealing as it does to the story of a youth entrapped in the gaze of his own reflection. Already, he implies, psychoanalysis and its forbearers pointed to the theory he is only now extrapolating in full; the theory of the mirror stage (79, 6).

Ovid's tale from *Metamorphosis* also pre-echoes the Freudian notion of the death drive. Narcissus seeks stasis and remains locked, gazing at his own reflection until death takes him and he is transformed into the perennial flower that bears his name. The mirror stage, similarly, describes the snare of narcissistic libido, a self-love which excludes the other. The cathexis here has its counterpoint in an unabating aggressivity towards the other. Even apparently altruistic acts are, Lacan argues, imbued with aggressive intent. In the simplest of Good Samaritan scenarios, a hierarchy is established which presents the Samaritan, the one bestowing help, in a favourable light. There is an unavoidable egoism at play here but also, Lacan argues, an aggressive dimension. To bestow charity is already to look down. This allows us to appreciate that Lacan is also here positing an anti-consequentialist ethics. We need to look beyond the superficial effect of a deed and understand the narcissism from which it springs (79, 6).

In isolating the phenomenon of narcissism, Lacan argues, psychoanalysts encountered a negative, destructive core to human experience. This does not seem so different to the then, at the time of Lacan's writing, fashionable stance of existentialism. Lacan had begun the essay with a swipe at Sartre and the existentialists and here he takes up this opposition once again (79, 7).

Like Sartre, Lacan is asserting the negativity of self-experience, the idea that I never fit, the idea of the disjuncture between the self and the world. The problem with existentialism, however, is that it does not go far enough. Sartre and his ilk, as alluded to in the opening paragraph of the essay, are still caught in the trap of the self-identical *cogito* and, like Descartes, they equate the self with consciousness. The problem with this, for Lacan, is that it effectively means equating the self with the ego. The core message of the 'Mirror Stage' essay is to describe how the ego is established on the basis of a misrecognition. Far from being the site of autonomy or something like an authentic kernel, the ego is nothing but a mistake. This would then mean that the autonomy of the self, which is so central to the existentialist project, is, from Lacan's perspective, grounded on an illusion (80, 1).

In seeking to combine psychoanalytic teachings with the existentialist perspective, the work of figures like Otto Rank and Viktor Frankl is scarred with a fatal contradiction. If the self is only ever produced through and on the basis of an encounter with something other, then the always partial and distorted idea of self which is introjected cannot be the ground of an autonomous being in the world.

Modern life, for Lacan, is characterised by a deadening utilitarian perspective (80, 2). We should understand this both in the Millian sense of a domination by a consequentialist striving for maximum happiness, as well as in the simpler sense, already implied in Bentham and Mill's writings, that the world can and should be understood in terms of use functions. This reduction of the world to utilitarianism has an obviously devastating effect on man's relation to the world in which he finds himself. For the existentialists, the condition of modern man is not unlike life in a concentration camp; dehumanised, debased, unfree. This picture of contemporary life is illustrated through a number of existentialist texts that attest to the popularity of the perspective but which also all illustrate a profound contradiction. As represented in Viktor Frankl's 1946 account of life in an actual concentration camp *Man's Search for Meaning* (Frankl: 2004), the existentialist perspective suggests that true freedom can be found even, and especially, in the most apparently constrained of circumstances. Sartre's own 1938 novel *Nausea* (2000) conveys the idea of the individual's commitment in the face of his impotence against the world. Similarly, Henry Miller's *Tropic of Cancer* (1934) and *Tropic of Capricorn* (1939) present the individual's pursuit of a form of freedom through the idealisation of sex. A number of Dostoyevsky's characters resort to suicide, most significantly, in this context, Kirillov from *The Devils* (1973), who maintains that the only true way to overcome fear of death is to embrace suicide. Finally, Lacan evokes Camus's *Outsider* (2000), drawing a link back to Hegel's Master-Slave dialectic and the notion that one can only attain full consciousness through engaging in a battle to the death with the other. Each of the examples illustrates a core contradiction. Frankl's freedom is clearly rather constrained. In a less obviously extreme way, Sartre's narrator is constrained by the world in which he finds himself. What is perhaps most remarkable about the sexual pursuits of Miller's narrative alter-ego is the alienation and distance the encounters evoke. The brute contradiction of self-realisation through suicide is perhaps self-evident. The final reference to Hegel underscores the irony here. In Hegel's myth, the battle that actually results in death is a literal dead end. If the potential master actually kills the potential slave, then they both lose.

Insofar as psychoanalysis refuses the reduction of the ego to perception-consciousness and sees it stretching beyond the reach of the reality principle, it is radically incommensurate with existentialism (80, 3). Rather, psychoanalysis suggests, as Lacan is suggesting throughout this essay, that the ego is essentially an effect of *meconnaissance,* of a process of misrecognition. As such, the dominant character of the self is going to be denial. When this unconscious dimension manifests, it is apparent that the ego is not all, as the force of the id is felt.

Caught in an inadequate misrecognition, the contemporary subject retreats into the death drive. This is not, contrary to common interpretation, simply defined by risk-taking and destruction, it is not only evident in the temptation to jump out of an aeroplane, go bungee jumping and go to war. The death drive is primarily concerned with repetition and stasis. The death drive is inertia, the tendency towards nothingness, stillness, death, repeating. In the mirror, we are seduced and captivated by the image in which we misrecognise ourselves and cannot move. Such stasis and captivation can be found in quintessential images of the madhouse; the patient who rocks themselves endlessly, catatonia, the thousand-yard stare. But, Lacan argues, it is not only evident in the madhouse, it is evident in the madness that is our society, a madness that is characterised by a 'sound and fury' (80, 4) and, lest we forget, as Macbeth tells us, sound and fury 'signify nothing' (Shakespeare, 2007).

For psychoanalysis, the mad – the neurotic, the psychotic – offer an insight into the apparently normal (80, 5). There is no real normal for Lacan. Even more than Freud, he sees us all as beset with 'issues'. Encounters with neurotic and psychotic analysands, Lacan argues, betray something important about the human condition, something which is less evident in the apparently sane world, characterised as it is by denial and a deadening of passion. This goes some way to explaining the popularity of existentialism compared with the hostility society feels towards psychoanalysis. Existentialism perpetuates a comfortable fantasy. It is psychoanalysis, and particularly Lacan's version of psychoanalysis, which demands a difficult confrontation.

In conclusion, Lacan's theory allows us to grasp the complex relation of nature and culture and how we come to find ourselves in this already cultured and linguistically mediated way. We are enchained by the imaginary captivation of ego identification, but it is fundamentally a form of alienation. Only love, of which psychoanalysis is a form, can help. The key mode of operation of psychoanalysis is the transference effect that Freud equates with love. Transference is the connection between people and thus the best alternative to crippling and confounding alienation.

We should not delude ourselves here, however, and see the aim of psychoanalysis as some happy cure which leads us all to a lovely life. An easy cure is always a dangerous illusion. The goal of psychoanalysis is rather a journey of discovery and acceptance of our 'darker' impulses, our aggression as well as our love (80, 6 - 81, 1). This is no utopian quest Lacan is inviting us on.

Lacanian psychoanalysis works by taking the subject to the point of confronting its condition, the mistake of the ego, the illusions of identification and thus, ultimately, to the point of what Lacan calls 'subjective destitution' (Lacan, 1995). This, however, Lacan tells us, is only really the beginning. From there it can never be anything other than the subject's responsibility (81, 2).

References

Billig, M. (2006) `Lacan's Misuse of Psychology: Evidence, Rhetoric and the Mirror Stage' *Theory, Culture & Society* 23(4), 1–26.

Bolk, L. (1926) *Das Problem der Menschwerdung.* Jena: Fischer.

Caillois, R. (2003) 'Mimicry and Legendary Psychasthenia' in *The Edge of Surrealism: A Roger Caillois Reader.* Ed. Claudine Frank. Durham: Duke University Press. pp. 89–103.

Camus, A. (2000) *The Outsider.* London: Penguin.

Descartes, R. (1993) *Meditations on First Philosophy*, trans. D. A. Cress. Indianapolis: Hackett.

Descartes, R. (1649) *Les Passions de l'âme.* Paris: Henry Le Gras.

Dostoyevsky, F. (1973) *The Devils.* London: Penguin.

Ellis, H. (2011) *Autoeroticism: A Psychological Study.* London: Tebbo.

Frankl, V. (2004) *Man's Search for Meaning.* New York: Rider.

Freud, S. (2001) 'On Narcissism: An Introduction' in *The Standard Edition of the Complete Psychological Works of Sigmund Freud, Volume XIV (1914–1916): On the History of the Psycho-Analytic Movement, Papers on Metapsychology and Other Works.*

Gould, S. J. (1977) *Ontogeny and Phylogeny.* Cambridge: Belknap.

Hegel, G. W. F. (1967) *The Phenomenology of Mind*, trans. J. B. Baillie. New York: Harper and Row.

Heidegger, M. (1962) *Being and Time*. Oxford: Blackwell.

Kant, I. (2007) *Critique of Pure Reason*. Trans. M. Weigelt. London: Penguin.

Köhler, W. (1925) *The Mentality of Apes*. Trans. E. Winter. London: Kegan Paul, Trench, Trubner & Co.

Lacan, J. (1949) *Le stade du miroir comme formateur de la function du Je telle qu'elle nous est révélée dans l'expérience psychanalytique* in Lacan, J. (1966) *Écrits*. Paris: Editions du Seuil.

Lacan, J. (2007) 'The Mirror Stage as Formative of the Function of the I as Revealed in Psychoanalytic Experience' in *Écrits: The First Complete Edition in English*. Trans. B. Fink. New York: Norton.

Lacan, J. (1995) 'Proposition of 9th October 1967 on the Psychoanalyst of the School'. Trans. R. Grigg. Analysis Number Six, 1995.

Lacan, J. (1993) *The Psychoses: The Seminar of Jacques Lacan, Book III, 1955–1956*. Trans. R. Grigg. London: Routledge.

Leibniz, G.W. (1992) 'Monadology' in *Discourse on Metaphysics and Other Essays*. Trans. D. Garber and R. Ariew. New York: Hackett.

Lévi-Strauss, C. (1963) *Structural Anthropology*. Trans. C. Jacobson and B. Grundfest Schoepf. New York: Basic Books.

Mathews, L. H. (1939) 'Visual Stimulation and Ovulation in Pigeons' *Proceedings of the Royal Society*. B 126, 557–560.

Miller, H. (1934) *Tropic of Cancer*. Paris: Obelisk.

Miller, H. (1939) *Tropic of Capricorn*. Paris: Obelisk.

Näcke, P. (1899) 'Die sexuellen perversitäten in der irrenanstalt' *Weiner Klinische Rundschau* (27–30).

Neill, C. (2014) *Without Ground: Lacanian Ethics and the Assumption of Subjectivity*. London: Palgrave.

Nobus, D. (1998) 'Life and Death in the Glass: A New Look at the Mirror Stage' in *Key Concepts of Lacanian Psychoanalysis*. Ed. D. Nobus. New York: Other Press. pp. 101–138.

Ovid, O. (2004) *Metamorphoses: A New Verse Translation*. Trans. D. Raeburn. London: Penguin.

Rank, O. (1911) 'A Contribution to Narcissism' *Jarhbuch für Psychoanalytische und Psychopathlogische Forshungen* 3, 401–26.

Roudinesco, E. (2003) 'The Mirror Stage: An Obliterated Archive' in *The Cambridge Companion to Lacan*. Ed. J. Rabaté. Cambridge: Cambridge University Press. pp. 25–34.

Sartre, J. P. (2000) *Nausea*. Trans. R. Baldick. London: Penguin.

Sartre, J. P. (1973) *Existentialism and Humanism*. Trans. C. Macomber. London: Methuen.

Shakespeare, W. (2007) *Macbeth*. London: Penguin.

Uexküll, J. J. von. (1926) *Theoretical Biology*. New York: Harcourt, Brace & Co.

Vanheule, S. (2011) *The Subject of Psychosis: A Lacanian Perspective*. Basingstoke: Palgrave MacMillan.

Wallon, H. (1931) 'Comment se développe chez l'enfant la notion de corps propre' *Journal de psychologie*. November–December, 1931, 705–748.

6

AGGRESSIVENESS IN PSYCHOANALYSIS

Calum Neill and Tom Eyers

Context

The 'Aggressiveness in Psychoanalysis' paper is often, and rightly, linked with Lacan's more famous 'Mirror Stage' essay. While the 'Aggressiveness' paper was presented at the 11th Congress of the *Psychoanalystes de langue française* in Brussels in May 1948, a little over a year before the 'Mirror Stage' paper was presented in Zurich, thematically the former appears to follow the latter. That the 'Mirror Stage' essay had a long gestation, perhaps accounts for this. Certainly, the two essays connect and appear to emerge from a similar theoretical consideration. The theme of narcissism is obvious in the 'Mirror Stage' essay and the same theme is carried through 'Aggressiveness in Psychoanalysis'. Where the 'Mirror Stage' essay is required to perform a complex role as it stages Lacan's intervention into existentialism and Parisian intellectual culture while seeking to ground a new approach to psychoanalysis, 'Aggressiveness in Psychoanalysis' is afforded a little more focus and allows Lacan to extend some of the considerations of narcissism which provide more of a framework than an object of discussion in the 'Mirror Stage'. Rooted in narcissism, however, both essays, taken together, can be helpfully understood as the theoretical bedrock of what Lacan would, a few years later, come to term and explicitly theorize as the 'imaginary' (Lacan, S1).

The basic argument of 'Aggressiveness in Psychoanalysis' is that psychoanalysis is nothing without a coherent theory of the subject and that, insofar as the subject is always in tension with its various others, aggression must be a foundational affect for the subject as it is understood by psychoanalysis. Lacan considers that, clinically speaking, aggression manifests in the subject's sense of its own bodily disconnection, especially in the fragmentary nature of the body in fantasy. The interrelation between aggression, narcissistic self-identity and the body allows the psychoanalyst to ascertain more general social maladies connected to this formative subjective violence.

Commentary on the text

The paper, as it appears in the *Écrits*, opens with a reference to the 'Mirror Stage', making explicit the fact that both papers are linked by a concern with

DOI: 10.4324/9781003368649-7

aggressiveness (82/1). Lacan sees the current essay as an attempt to test the value of his arguments and, specifically, to ascertain whether or not a refined and clinically operational concept of aggressiveness can be established. He refers to Freud as the foundational author, as would be recognized by all psychoanalysts, but he wants to make the further point that the path that Freud founded was never completed (82/2). Just as Freud needed to add to the wealth of concepts he continued to develop, so now Lacan continues this work. Freud utilized the term *Todestrieb* or 'death instinct' (or 'death drive' as it is more usually rendered in English) to describe or theorize something of humanity's aggressive tendencies (82/3). The concept of *Todestrieb* went through various developments as Freud extended, questioned and, ultimately, rethought its meaning (Freud, 1955b and 1955d). Lacan notes that Freud's thinking around the concept of 'death instinct' and its relation to the register of biology encountered an aporia, or impasse. Rather than having been resolved in the work that has been produced since Freud, this aporia remains and, moreover, can be understood as central to the very notion of aggressiveness (82/4). It is the aporia which accounts for both the unresolved arguments around humanity's tendency to aggression and for the contradictions which abound in such arguments and theories (82/5).

Lacan introduces his own arguments by suggesting that he will make a few modest comments based on his experience and reading. Echoing some of the comments he makes in the 'Mirror Stage' and 'Beyond the Reality Principle', he articulates his current endeavours negatively in relation to the disciplines of experimental psychology and psychotherapy. It appears Lacan feels that psychoanalysis bears some responsibility for the readdressing of the misconceptions to which these disciplines have given rise. Specifically, he argues that both experimental behaviourism and certain popular forms of psychotherapy root themselves in a misreading of psychoanalytic theory or a misapplication of psychoanalytic categories (83/1).

Lacan presents his argument in five theses.

Thesis one

As in the previous chapter of the *Écrits*, Lacan emphasizes the experience of psychoanalysis (83/2). Psychoanalysis is not merely a theory but consists in a very particular experience. This experience is rooted in the analysand speaking in the clinic (83/3). Through this speech, the analysand, or subject, produces him or herself to or for the analyst. Two important points emerge here. First, the subject cannot be considered to be something which precedes the clinic. The subject is produced in the clinic through what is said in the clinic. Second, this saying has to be said to someone. Sitting in a room alone with a recording device would not have the same effect (83/4).

While a recording device can record sound, it cannot record meaning (83/5). Meaning implies and requires a person, or a subject, as Lacan puts it.

The fact that the analysand presents him or herself as being potentially understood, then means, for Lacan, that they appear as a subject with the potential to be understood. This does not necessarily mean that they will be understood or that they will be understood in the same way as they want to be understood. It is also not to suggest that the meaning they convey or the position they come to occupy through speaking is something which precedes the fact of speaking. It is through speaking that the subject comes to formulate themselves and in so formulating themselves, to emerge within the realm of meaning. Once again, Lacan contrasts this open and difficult understanding with the reductionist perspectives advanced by psychology. Where psychology fixates on the isolated utterances of the patient, psychoanalysis strives to understand the dynamic of dialogue (83/5).

It was in response to this endeavour to grasp an emerging discourse that always implies an interaction that Freud developed the techniques of psychoanalysis (83/5). It may, and has been, argued that this body of techniques does not, and cannot, constitute a science (83/6). Lacan argues that it can, as long as it can be verified by everyone. The verification Lacan appeals to here is that which is evident through analytic training. While the apparently dyadic confines of the clinic might suggest that what goes on in the clinic remains hidden in the clinic, Lacan is suggesting that we focus on the process, not the content. The process, the efficacy of the technique of psychoanalysis, uncoupled from any particular subjective experience, is what is ultimately transmitted and what can be said to be verifiable, at least potentially, by everyone.

Thesis two

Lacan's second thesis is that aggressivity in the clinical context manifests and is clinically effective as both an aggressive intention and an image of bodily dislocation (84). The term intention (it is the same term in French) may be understood here in a double sense. It should be read in its everyday sense, which would be to say that the aggressiveness apparent in analysis is not necessarily fully enacted but merely intended. Intentionality is also, however, a technical term from phenomenology, a school of thought which was widely influential in France at the time and which still, at this moment, bore some significant influence on Lacan's thinking. For Husserl, the father of phenomenology, intentionality refers to the directed aspect of thought. Where thinking denotes consciousness, intentionality is denoted by thinking about something. To say then that 'aggressiveness presents itself in analysis as an aggressive intention' (84/2) is, phenomenologically speaking, to say that aggression in the clinic is always directed at something. It is not merely a state of mind, an emotional eruption or even tendency, but should be understood as directed at something and (often) directed against the (idea of the) self.

Lacan argues that once the analysand has succeeded in pushing beyond those defence mechanisms, which serve to decouple the symptoms from lived experience and personal history, it is possible to discern aggressivity in their symptoms. That is to say, they become apparent in those unconscious mechanisms which are the stuff of psychoanalysis; disavowing declarations, mistakes, fantasies and dreams (84/2). More particularly, Lacan lists the specifics in which we might adduce the analysand's aggressivity: their demanding tone of voice, their pauses, hesitations, inflexions, slips, contradictory recall, failure to follow rules, lateness, absence, recriminations, reproaches, fantasmatic fears, angry reactions, and intimidating displays. The aggression that manifests in the clinic is, Lacan says, unlikely to do so in the form of direct violence. This, he argues, is due to the circumstances which will have led the analysand to be in the clinic in the first place and to the acceptance of the conventions of the clinic that stipulate that the medium is one of dialogue (84/3).

Turning to the effect of intentional aggression, Lacan draws our attention to the fact that it often appears to be directed against those the subject sees as being dependent upon them. Such intentional aggression, Lacan says, has a destructive force. The precise terms Lacan uses here are illustrative; 'it gnaws away' (ronge), it mines (mine), it breaks apart (désagrégé), it castrates and leads to death. What is curious, beyond the vividness of the language through which Lacan illustrates the aggression, is the question it raises about the location and origin of the aggression. It is not immediately clear whether the effects of the aggression are felt on the aggressor or on the one at whom the aggression is directed. Indeed, it is not clear who exactly the aggressor is or who is present. Lacan exemplifies his point with reference to a mother who aggressively dismisses her son as impotent after he tells her of his homosexuality. Here he notes that 'her permanent aggressiveness' had taken its toll. However, we are left uncertain as to whether the mother or the son was the one in analysis. That is to say, is the mother an element of the son's speech, or is the son an element of the mother's speech? Lacan's point here appears to be to remind us that, while the convention of the clinic is a dyadic encounter, it can become rather crowded and, in this context, aggression is brought into the clinic through multiple routes and its effects can be dispersed (84/4). This also then allows Lacan to broaden his discourse to the expression of aggressivity outside the clinic. While aggressiveness may be constrained, whether within or outwith the clinic, by conventions of appropriacy, it is still effectively expressed through manner and mood. Often less is more. A parent can have control over a child simply by being present, or by evoking a punitive other. The imagined aggression is much more effective than any immediate corporal punishment (85/2).

Swiping at psychology (85/3), Lacan recapitulates an argument he'd first outlined in the 1930s, initially in his doctoral thesis and then in an encyclopaedia entry he wrote on the family (Lacan, 2001). That argument circulates around 'imagos', defined here as images connected with the instincts, or drives. As Lacan glancingly mentions, the term 'imago' has a Latin root, literally meaning 'image', but is specifically used in two contexts. In ancient times it referred to a death mask, which would commonly be displayed in the homes of the descendants. The death mask would be fashioned from a mould taken from the corpse but would then be modified, or touched up, and the masks would often end up being copies of copies. The point here is not simply that the imago is not accurate, but that it lends itself to a certain cultural styling. The masks then become typified. The other common usage of imago is in modern biology, where it concerns the final developmental stage in the life of an insect. The term then functions not only to differentiate Lacan's concept from the more common-sensical usage of 'image', but also connotes something of maturation, metamorphosis, death and artifice.

At this stage in his thinking, Lacan thought that such images present as evidence, at the level of unconscious fantasy, of primal sexual drives, drives that underpin and reinforce processes of narcissistic identity formation. Lacan is especially concerned with images of 'castration, emasculation, mutilation, dismemberment, dislocation, evisceration, devouring, and bursting open of the body' (85/4), images of the fragmented body that he especially associates with the phenomenon of aggressiveness. Such 'imagos' can then be found at the social level in the practices of tattooing and circumcision but also, Lacan adds, in fashion, which underscores the point that what is being addressed here is the alteration of the image of the body, a practice which, for Lacan, emphasizes that the idea of the natural form of the human body is itself a construct. The human's relation to their own body is always, then, fundamentally one of alienation (85/5).

We can see this, Lacan reminds us, in the activities of young children, who delight in pulling off a doll's head or bursting open a teddy bear (85/6) and also, in fantasmatic detail, in the paintings of Hieronymus Bosch, whose 'Garden of Earthly Delights' Lacan has already referenced in the 'Mirror Stage' essay. Specifically, here, Lacan draws attention to the externalization of the oral, anal and reproductive organs, images, like the imago, derived from insects and the narcissistic exhibitionism on display in the painting. Such images are not unique to Bosch's paintings, but, Lacan says, are common to dreams. He illustrates this with an example of an analysand who saw himself in a dream in a car with his lover being chased by flying fish that resembled a half-full bladder (86/2). These images point to the symbolic dimension of aggressivity (86/3).

All of this is intended to remind Lacan's audience of the centrality of an affect, aggression, that had otherwise been lost in what he takes to be the neutralizing effects of American 'ego–psychology', an influential current of analytic practice in 1948 and, indeed, today. Lacan thought that American analysts, in particular, had downplayed Freud's late emphasis on the death drive in favour of an increasingly positivist, even idealist, emphasis on the ego. By contrast, Lacan takes the ego, including the domain of aggressive identification that is its *raison d'etre*, to be the seat of illusion, of the necessary narratives of self-identity that nonetheless conceal the truth of the self in the unconscious. As Lacan clarifies, these images of aggression, tied as they are to those movements of identity and self-identification, are part of an 'imaginary function' (86/4).

From 1953 onwards, the 'imaginary' will take its place alongside the 'symbolic' and the 'real' as one of three registers of the subject, and we can see Lacan here moving towards that fundamental breakthrough. Both after 1953 and in its use in 1948, the 'imaginary' names the domain of self-identity, the routing of our sense of self through images of significant others, a domain saturated with the alienated aggressiveness at issue in this *écrit*.

Thesis three

The third thesis is that the sources of aggressivity are what provide the rationale which underpins the psychoanalytic technique (86). This claim is strikingly bold. Lacan seems to be suggesting no less than that aggressiveness, previously considered one of many crucial affects that help define the psychoanalytic clinic, in fact, provides the key for successful psychoanalytic technique *tout court*. How could this possibly be justified? Lacan begins by emphasizing the dialogic character of the analytic scene, compared here with a Platonic dialogue. He makes particular reference to Thrasymachus's somewhat aggressive claim in Book 1 of Plato's *Republic* (1992) that justice is effectively what is in the interests of the strongest. It is perhaps the angry, or what Lacan terms "mad" (86/5), nature of Thrasymachus's intervention in the dialogue that serves to underpin Lacan's point here: whatever renunciation of aggression is implied in the compact to undertake dialogue, it often re-emerges in that dialogue (86/5). More than in any other social practice, psychoanalysis provides the patient with a forum within which to speak at will, and without the artificial constraints that other social spaces would impose. But this is not, again, to say that the psychoanalytic dialogue is a placid one. Indeed, much of this section of the article is given over to emphasizing the fundamentally agonistic quality of the psychoanalytic scene, the crucial forms of hostility that inevitably impact upon the process and that the analyst must successfully manage.

The compact of the analytic session is that the analysand's position and purpose are central. Unlike most dialogues in which we engage, which social convention would dictate would entail some reciprocity, in the psychoanalytic clinic it is all about the analysand and their 'cure' (86/6). There is, however, an element of blind faith here insofar as the analysand has no idea of the ends of the analysis from the vantage point of the beginning (86/7).

The analysand speaks but the duration of their speaking is determined by the analyst. What the analyst refrains from doing, however, is providing advice or guidance, which is precisely what many analysands would expect or wish from an analyst (86/8).

In many respects, analysis requires that the analysand is in dialogue with a blank screen, with an interlocutor who tolerates the patient's speech without *supporting* it, without providing them with the verbal assurance that might prevent the properly antagonistic aspects of the transference from emerging, and without divulging aspects of themselves onto which the analysand might latch (87/1). This subjective effacement might help the analyst themselves to put aside their personal feelings and minimize the intrusion of personal perspectives that could affect their understanding and treatment of the analysand. It also allows any intervention that they might make to take on an enigmatic tone, insofar as it gives the analysand little by way of clues as to how it might be interpreted (87/2). These benefits, however, are in many ways secondary to the greater function of helping the analyst to avoid being ensnared by the analysand and their wish for the analyst to take on their suffering (87/3). The silence of the analyst then functions to solicit a key aggressive reaction from the analysand, one that Lacan describes in a term borrowed from the 17th-century writer François VI, Duc de La Rochefoucauld; '*amour-propre*'. This phrase has often been glossed as self-love, egoism or even vanity, but it arguably carries a more specific sense. Rousseau contrasts *amour-propre* with *amour de soi* (Rousseau, 1911). While the two terms appear rather synonymous, Rousseau uses the former to refer to a self-love which is supported through the approval or esteem of others, as opposed to *amour de soi*, which is self-supporting. Lacan's use of *amour-propre* in this context would seem, then, to precisely point to this place of the other.

With a typical ambivalence, the analysand, according to Lacan, cannot 'bear the thought of being freed by anyone but [themselves]' (87/4), yet, at the same time, they expect the analyst to somehow share their suffering. The trap here is a challenging one and Lacan is keen to warn analysts of the dangers of assuming to help or of offering oneself as a model, as the ego psychologist might (87/6). Charity, he reminds us, both invites an aggressive reaction (87/5) as well as, itself, being understandable as an aggressive impulse (87/7), insofar as it positions the receiver in a subservient position to the benefactor.

Such dangers notwithstanding, the elicitation of aggression is a necessary moment of analysis, in that it is this that instigates the negative transference which creates the relationship that mobilizes the analysis (87/8).

But what is the specific nature of the aggression unleashed by the analyst's agnostic stance? In an argument that will become less literal and more deeply inflected with the slipperiness of the signifier as his career unfolds, Lacan speculates here that 'imagos' placed in the unconscious may, through an 'accident of repression', attach themselves to the analyst through the transference, thus giving the aggression in question its particular subjective colour (87/9). Stealthily, Lacan reclaims the notion of an underlying unconscious symbolic logic, from its heretofore usual place in Jungian analysis, through an appropriation of the notion of the 'archetype', now figured as the specific – rather than universal – content of the repressed image as it is reactualized in the analytic setting (87/9 and 88/1). It requires, Lacan argues, only the most seemingly innocuous opportunity to ignite an aggressive response which can have the effect of resurrecting the imago and bringing into the clinical session the intentional affect which attaches to it (88/2).

Lacan argues that this process often proves to be fairly straightforward in cases of hysteria (88/3) but can be considerably more challenging in obsessive neurosis (88/4). Recounting a case of a hysteric who was unable to walk or stand, Lacan describes how, following her identifying him with her father, he was able to facilitate the resolution of her symptoms simply by commenting on her father's refusal to support her. The implication here is that through the transference process, the knot of the symptom can be addressed without the analysand being aware of what has transpired. Such a resolution is much harder to achieve in cases of obsessional neurosis precisely because the obsessive guards against expressions of aggressivity (88/4). In cases of phobia, on the other hand, aggressiveness is already very active and evident (88/5) and, thus, Lacan warns against seeking to further stimulate it (88/6).

It can, then, Lacan is arguing, be productive to provoke a repressed aggression (88/7) but only insofar as the aggression does not unwittingly find a support in the ideas the analysand has already concocted about the analyst, particularly when those ideas are shaped through the kind of ego defences that are common in the psychoanalytic experience (88/7). In invoking the ego, Lacan is careful to emphasize that he is not referring to the ego as a synonym of pre-consciousness but rather to the ego as it is most evidently manifest in the clinic, which, according to Lacan, is in its force of negation (88/8). It is important to emphasize the place of the ego here precisely because the ego is the site of conflict and ambiguity that characterizes the emergence of subjectivity. The ego is not the subject, but the misrecognized form of what the subject is taken to be (89/1).

This is to say, then, that the analysand will tend to erect certain ideas of the analyst which are shaped negatively by their (the analysand's) own misconstrued idea of themselves. As this defensiveness typically manifests in 'opposition, negation, ostentation, and lying' (88/7), the provocation of aggression here is likely to merely accentuate or intensify both the defensiveness and the projected ideas of the analyst which will only prove, then, to be counterproductive.

Conversely, the analyst, Lacan argues, needs to subtly encourage a kind of paranoia in the analysand, but a paranoia which is structured and very carefully managed by the analyst (89/2). This structuring entails isolating certain aspects of what the analysand presents. Lacan articulates this notion both in terms of imaginary space – mobilizing metaphors of islands, blind spots and alien bodies, that is to say, with demarcated and apparently autonomous entities within the subject (89/3) – and in terms of time, which he relates to anxiety, whether this is overtly manifest or latent (89/4).

What Lacan is talking about here is the danger of the analyst becoming something like a mirror for the analysand (89/5). Were the analysand to succeed in so 'trapping' the analyst – as, Lacan tells us, often does happen with inexperienced analysts – the result is likely to be an aggressivity which is so excessive, even if in the form of an extreme anxiety, that it blocks the possibility of transference (89/6).

Thesis four

Following from this, Lacan's fourth thesis is that aggressivity correlates with the narcissistic identification that structures the subject's ego and, by extension, their world (89).

To begin to theorize aggression or aggressive tendencies within the psychoanalytic context, we necessarily shift away from the specific experience of the specific analysand and abstract to a more general level of a metapsychology (89/8). While necessary in order to allow any shared, theoretical discussion of the phenomena, such a move cannot but entail a certain flattening of the specifics (89/9). As such distinct states such as fear, anger, sorrow and even fatigue can or even must be brought together under the single construct of aggressivity (89/7).

Such aggressivity is particularly significant in cases of paranoid psychosis (90/2), where, Lacan asserts, the specifics of the aggressivity that manifests can themselves be indicative of the extent of development of the delusions harboured (90/3). In this sense, we might categorize aggressive reactions in a series that ranges from violence to belligerence to stalemates. This series of reactions runs in parallel with a series of fantasies, which Lacan lists at some length, ranging from poisoning and evil spells to various forms of control, such as telepathy and coercion, to intrusion, of either the body or one's secrets or privacy, and beyond (90/4).

And so, what is initially only the moment of the formation of the ego becomes a temporal and spatial feature of all subjective experience (90/5), which although it is demonstrated in its most exaggerated form in paranoid psychosis is present too in such everyday phenomena as ungrounded suspicion of one's partner, in violent shifts of mood, even in cultures of litigation and blame. The various assumptions and accusations of harm (90) that derive from this can appear in such stereotypical forms that it has the effect of suspending the possibility of any intersubjective resolution (90/5). For all the apparent Hegelianism of this period of Lacan's teaching, the aggressiveness in question stalls any dialectical resolution or closure as much as it incites the development of new attempts at the construction of a stable identity.

Lacan acknowledges his debt to Pierre Janet, the influential French depth psychologist, who had shown how feelings of persecution were phenomenologically discernible in observable moments of social life (Janet, 1926). Lacan, however, draws attention to what he argues was missed in Janet's theory; the fact that the feelings of persecution themselves are also constituted in such moments, when the moment becomes frozen in the subject's mind, much like when a film is stopped suddenly and the actors' faces are caught in the oddest poses (90/6), an experience which has become all the more familiar through Zoom and Teams meetings.

This tendency to introject a fixed moment is, Lacan argues, not so unusual and should remind us of such typical processes as ego formation and the fixing or constitution of the objects to which the ego attaches. That is to say, unlike the flux that characterizes our existence in the unpredictability of the world, we tend to assume a permanency to the ego and its select objects. Among other things, this distinguishes us from animals (90/7). It allows the human, through a marked distinction between an inner and outer-world, to imbue its psychic objects with a more extensive significance and resonance, and even to utilize them as an aggressive/defensive structure (91/1). This can work both to enable subjective raids on the image of the other and to allow the establishment of self-identity that protects the subject from the intrusion of what, just a few years after the publication of 'Aggressiveness in Psychoanalysis', Lacan will call the 'real' (S1) – the contingency of trauma, the terrifying truth of one's own unconscious investments.

This paranoic knowledge can then be understood to mark the moments of the subject's mental development, with each frozen element corresponding to a specific stage of identification (91/2). This structure is attested to in the work of a number of prominent psychologists, notably Charlotte Buhler, whose work on transitivism will form a key reference in the 'Mirror Stage' essay. Buhler's ideas were subsequently developed through application in the field of pedagogy by Elsa Köhler and in sociology and criminology by the Chicago School. These developments and applications of the theory, however, worked towards generalization, as tends to be the case in empirical domains. The psychoanalytic context, with its properly subjective focus, is, Lacan argues, unique in allowing us to not only witness the specifics of this intersubjective process as it pertains to the subject in question but it also, importantly, allows the analyst to work with the subject on this material (91/3).

As is recounted in the 'Mirror Stage' essay, the infant first begins to experience itself as a discrete entity through the encounter with something – an image, another – in the external world. The apparent paradox, which is central to a Lacanian understanding of identification, is that the child only starts to identity itself on the basis of a recognition in something else. Where the 'Mirror Stage' essay focuses on the encounter with the mirror image, here Lacan focuses on the child's mirroring other children. In what might be understood to be a concession to something like developmental psychology, Lacan delimits this stage to a particular age and, moreover, insists on the children in question being within a few months of each other. Where the children's interactions lead to hitting, which is then copied, Lacan warns against dismissing this as mere playfulness. What is transpiring, he argues, is rather a shift of the child's physical functioning from a self-concerned biology into a domain that is governed by sociality. To put this into a phenomenological register, we could say that the child starts to become *for the other* (91/4). This then marks an emotional and mental development which ushers the beginning of the urge to conceptualize the self as a whole at a point where the child's immediate experience of its body still very much emphasizes the lack of any such wholeness (91/5).

Rehearsing key elements of the mirror stage, Lacan re-emphasizes the point that the child, while entranced by the image and given to fits of joy at this recognition, is, at this stage, still markedly less developed, in most other ways, than a chimpanzee (92/1), allowing Lacan to characterize the human infant as constitutively pre-mature (92/2).

It is the capture in and by the idea of the human as form, the human as image, which then dominates the child at this age. The child is not displaying empathy or understanding in their interactions with other children so much as experiencing themselves mirrored. This is then seen in episodes of transitivism, where a child fails to distinguish adequately between itself and another. This may manifest in various forms, such as a child crying as if it had hurt itself, when it sees another child hurt or believing itself to have been hit when they were actually the one doing the hitting. Such transitivism, Lacan claims, never entirely leaves us and can form the basis of certain parasitic modes of social relation, an actor playing on an identification with the audience, a seducer relying on points of identification with the object of their seduction or, in what we might read as a reference to Hegel, the slave identifying with the master (92/3).

What, however, does this account of the formation of the ego or self have to do with aggressivity? For Lacan the two are bound together in the inadequacy of self-identity – the fact that the child has modelled itself on an exterior image which is not only not itself but which also appears to be more self-sufficient – and the feelings to which this gives rise. It is the structuration of these feelings which forms the basis of the ego and the fact that these feelings have arisen in the face of what Lacan elsewhere terms a rivalry (see 'On My Antecedents' earlier in this volume), indicates a certain aggressivity at their core (92/4).

The ego itself then is predicated on a conflict that has its support in the social world, the world of others (92/5). Desire, which we might understand as definitive for the human subject here finds its model in the desire perceived in the other. The child then finds itself or constitutes itself in a triangle entailing its becoming idea of itself (ego), the other and the object of the other's desire. So dominant is this dynamic at this point that it colours the whole of the child's understanding of the world, to the extent that it is not uncommon for children at this age to not recognize someone with whom they are very familiar if they appear in an unusual context. The emotional grasping, that is, overshadows the specular (92/5). This idea that the ego is, from the start, constituted with an aggressive relating at its core (92/6) suggests that this aggressivity is likely to emerge at each point in the subject's development. As the ego changes, the aggressive impulse which is embroiled in its formation is necessarily implicated (93/1). As the ego is never reducible to the person, or to the identity the person assumes for themselves, it is bound to find itself as under attack as it experiences itself as inadequate. As the ego is not self-contained, such moments tend to manifest as a reversion wherein the ego and the other are castigated or punished (93/2). These two moments are, however, experienced as one (93/3). This, then, shows the ego as paranoid in its very structure. Lacan points out that this is analogous to what Freud had named as the three delusions: jealousy, erotomania and interpretation (Freud, 1955c). The ego of the modern human has, as Lacan repeats in *The Function and Field of Speech*, taken on the form of the beautiful soul, who assumes to denounce the very disorder they project onto the world (93/3).

The ambivalent aggressiveness which sits at the core of subjectivity tends to manifest in our own culture in the form of what Nietzsche called *ressentiment*. Distinct from the commonplace English language concept of resentment, which would define a certain mode of hard feeling or bitterness, Nietzsche's *ressentiment* is meant to describe the characteristic stance of our age, what he also calls slave morality (Nietzsche, 1998: 21). Opposed to the yea-saying that Nietzsche champions, the nay-sayer of slave morality bitterly accepts and even revels in a position of weakness precisely because it allows them to castigate the other for having put them in this position. So embedded is this sentiment in our culture that we can already see it at play in the very young. Lacan quotes St Augustine of Hippo (whom, he pithily remarks, is able to make this observation because he is not yet hampered by the discourse of behaviourist psychology) who recounts a story of a baby demonstrating jealousy before it even mastered speech (Augustine, 2008: 90). Lacan sees in Augustine's angry child a progenitor of the resentful children he observes in the clinic. While there is perhaps something a little fanciful in this interpretation of Augustine's words, it does clearly illustrate the silent drama that Lacan reads as crucial to the emotional life of the infant (93/4), one that will carry over into the modes of identification that will define adult relationships. And yet the boldness of Lacan's comments here covers not only this implied extension of the structures of formative resentment into adulthood, but even more importantly they speak to the insights to be located in the very earliest months of an infant's life. Such insights are situated far earlier than suggested by the psychoanalytic orthodoxy dictated by Freud's focus on the Oedipus complex, that familial imbroglio occurring much later in the life of the child, dated usually between the ages of three and six. Lacan will, in his seminars, have critical words to say about Melanie Klein's contemporaneous psychoanalytic innovations (Lacan, 1998), but here he duly recognizes that she, like him, has had the insight to recognize the importance of the very first months of life to subsequent psychic perturbances (93/5).

Klein allows us to appreciate the function of a particular imago, that of the enclosing maternal body (93/6). Here the mother, in her imagined and internalized form, becomes a site of dispute and contest (94/1). Klein also allows us to appreciate how the trace of 'bad internal objects' persists in the subject, connected to apparently unrelated ideas through an association that Lacan is eager to emphasize is organic and thus unpredictable, as opposed to the notion of association popularized by the philosopher David Hume, for whom

163

associations of ideas are fixed at the point of perception (Hume, *An Enquiry Concerning Human Understanding*). This allows us, then, to see how obviously the invocation and questioning of characters or personae from someone's past may destabilize them, insofar as the personae in question may have become fixed in a particular manner and have been tied to an initial identificatory moment. That is to say, in questioning the imagined point of identification, the sureness of the ego itself is called into question (94/1).

Lacan praises Klein for allowing us to appreciate that the roots of the identifications, the roots of the formation of the ego occur much earlier than was previously thought (94/2). We should be careful, however, not to over-extend this theory and blur the specificity proper to what Lacan is calling aggressivity (as opposed to the tension experienced in guilt, oral destructiveness, hypochondrial fixation or primordial masochism). The specific aggressivity Lacan is interested in is the aggressivity linked to narcissism and the misrecognitions and objectifications that characterize ego formation (94/3).

What we might understand as the archetype or prototype of this ego formation is both alienating and satisfying. It is alienating because it is based on external elements – what is most me in me, is based on something from outside of me. It is satisfying because it achieves a certain order from disorder. This satisfaction appears to presuppose a rupture in the subject, an opening onto a natural world of chaos which is assumed to precede harmony, much as the pre-Socratic philosopher Heraclitus had proposed (94/4). It is here that we might locate the narcissistic source of energy which propels the Freudian reality principle (94/5), despite the seeming contradiction this might suggest. That this contradiction duped Freud, who failed to identify the 'narcissistic passion' that fuels this reality principle is, Lacan chides, due to his still being under the sway of the pseudo-objectivity of conventional psychology. This error led Freud to assume as occluded what is in fact repressed (94/6). We can see a corollary here between the irrational oppression of the superego, which actually underpins our sense of moral conscience and this irrational passion which underpins the ego's most rational caution (95/2).

This idea of aggressivity as being bound into the narcissistic formation of the ego shines a light on a number of seeming anomalies and peculiarities (95/3) but can also be adduced in the functioning of the most central of psychoanalytic moments, the Oedipal complex (95/4). Typically, the unbridled passions, which Lacan is arguing underpin the formation of the ego, are sublimated in the course of the Oedipal drama. The infant who will have initially assumed an identification with the mother is forced to reshape its identity with the intervention of the father (95/4). Curiously, Lacan here refers to a process of secondary identification based on the imago of the parent of the same sex, which would suggest that he has in mind Freud's account of male Oedipalization. The version of the Oedipal complex that Freud fashions to account for female identification is, as is well-known, more complicated. A few years after this essay, Lacan will begin to formulate the Oedipal complex in structural terms

(Lacan, 1998), a move which, among other things, allows him to sidestep the gendered conundrum that stimies Freud. While his comments here seem more aligned with the Freudian narrative of Oedipalization, there does appear, perhaps, to already be an embryonic hint of Lacan's later thinking, or at least a questioning at work, in the non-specificity of the sex of the infant in question.

While a biological source may be assumed for the erotic energies discussed here, the articulation of these energies to the process of identification and ego formation requires us to think of the process in terms of a specific structuration which cannot be reduced to the biological. Lacan suggests that the rivalry/identification, which is central to the Oedipal drama, would have to be prefigured by another more primary rivalry/identification: that of the subject with themselves (95/5). As is recounted in the 'Mirror Stage' essay, the infant's emerging identification is determined in part by a certain anticipation inspired by the exterior image, and the unfavourable comparison the child makes between itself and this more coherent spectacle. The significance of this ideal aside, Lacan's focus here is more on the ego-ideal, the emergence of a socialization through the internalization of the father, which establishes both a libidinal and cultural normalization. Here Lacan makes a reference to Freud's myth of *Totem and Taboo* (1955a).

Freud's myth concerns a supposed pre-cultural moment wherein there is a troop of proto-human beings who are dominated by an alpha male. This alpha male figure, the primal father, has exclusive access to the females of the troop. Unhappy with this situation, the other males of the troop band together and defeat the father, freeing access to the females for themselves. However, having killed the father they are overcome by feelings of remorse and, rather than avail themselves of the females, they now choose instead to institute a prohibition. This prohibition against incest is the first rule and, as such, comes to institute law, culture and society. Concomitant with the emergence of law, then, is the emergence of guilt. The myth, importantly, reads in two modes. On the one hand, it accounts for (or rather, properly speaking, covers over the impossibility of accounting for) the emergence of culture. On the other, it describes the possibility of the emergence of the subject as subject of language and culture. Noting the circularity of Freud's story, Lacan simultaneously acknowledges the absurdity and brilliance of Freud's reading back of the function of the modern bourgeois father to an imagined point of pre-history; absurd, perhaps, for its elevation of a specific iteration of paternal authority to a universal norm, brilliant, surely, in its acknowledgement that psychic history functions outside the empirical demands of history 'proper'. For Lacan, at this point, however, the key focus is on the emergence of subjective guilt (95/5).

Lacan's reading of Freud's myth here is that the identification with the father, which is achieved through his consumption, is itself actually based on the need for a collective action that will neutralize any potential rivalry between the brothers. In this sense, Oedipal identification can be understood as a secondary form of identification which transcends the aggressivity that is formative of a prior self-identification (95/6). This secondary form of identification has the benefit of allowing a certain separation of the self from others and, as such, is then constitutive of the possibility of a productive sociality (96/1).

In the 1880s, the German anthropologist Karl Von Den Steinen travelled to northern Brazil where he studied various tribes, including the Bororo. The Bororo are a totemic tribe from the Xingu area who take as a totem the ara or macaw (as featured in Blue Sky Studios' 2011 film *Rio*). In the course of his research, the tribespeople explained to Von Den Steinen that they were aras. That is, they did not envisage their identification with the totem as metaphorical or indicating some as yet unattained future state, such as, for example, the idea that they would become aras after they died or that aras were the incarnation of their ancestors. Rather, they believed that they were, there and then, already aras. Von Den Steinen apparently found this claim very difficult to believe and equated it to a caterpillar believing that it was simultaneously a butterfly (Levy-Bruhl, 1910). In a somewhat mocking tone, Lacan dismisses Von Den Steinen's disbelief as a product of modern obsession with objectification, arguing that the Bororo's claim is really no more difficult to fathom than the commonplace claims we hear when people identify with their profession or country. A more logically problematic claim, for Lacan, is evident in the statement, 'I am a man', which, taking a Hegelian perspective, Lacan sees as somewhat circular. To say that 'I am a man' would entail identifying with someone who I recognize as a man but in order to recognize this other as a man, I would need to posit them as someone capable of recognizing me as a man. The point here can be summarized in Arthur Rimbaud's famous phrase from his 1871 letter to Paul Demeny, where he declares, '*Je est un autre*' (Rimbaud, 1986: 9). Novel as this claim – that I is another – may be for the poet, it is, Lacan says, rather obvious for the psychoanalyst (96/2). Its value lies in its condensation of many, if not all, of the crucial propositions that define Lacan's reinvention of Freud in the 1940s, but also throughout his career. Most importantly, for this particular instance of that long trajectory, perhaps, is the notion that the ego, the 'I', is not to be identified with the subject proper. If the 'I' – all its claims to sovereignty and inviolability aside - is made up of images of others, as we've seen, then the truth of the subject is to be located elsewhere, in the singularity of the unconscious that subtends the fragile 'I' or ego that is constituted and sustained in acts of aggressive appropriation.

The equation of the subject with 'I', Lacan argues, is merely a reflection of our particular culture. Echoing a point made by Nietzsche in *Beyond Good and Evil*, Lacan suggests that we confuse the grammatical subject with the agentic subject (or subject in the psychoanalytic sense of the term), much in the way that Descartes's famous *cogito ergo sum* is taken to have proven the existence of the I which it already, grammatically, assumes (96/4). *Cogito*, meaning 'I think', already contains the first person singular as the subject of the sentence. When Descartes concludes that *ergo sum*, 'therefore I am', he has done little more than repeat what was necessarily assumed at the beginning of the statement (96/3). Or, as Nietzsche puts it, he is duped by language (Nietzsche, 2001: 18).

Lacan remarks that having pursued an understanding of the formation of the ego so far, with particular reference to the Oedipal drama, it is perhaps not surprising that analysts have tended to present 'successful resolution' as the norm, which it is difficult not to see as a moral judgement (96/4). Here Lacan makes reference to the term '*oblativité*', a term which in standard French means something like altruism but which in psychoanalytic theory is usually used with the modifier 'genital', as in 'genital oblativity', to refer to harmonious sexual union (96/5). Lacan's invocation of the word should probably be read as combining both these meanings, as he wants to question both the reality of harmonious sexual union and the assumption that it is towards that which we should aim. Ignoring the obvious heteronormativity implied by the theory of genital oblativity, if harmonious sexual union is not actually possible, then to hold this up as a goal would seem somewhat perverse. This essay was written some 23 years before Lacan coined his famous phrase, *il n'y a pas de rapport sexuel*, but the sense of this impossibility appears already to be here.

Rather than valorize sexual union as an end in itself, Lacan claims it is obvious that genital libido exceeds any individual desire and 'blindly' pursues the propagation of the species. As Freud has already argued, the sublimation of desire in the Oedipal experience, the renunciation of desire for the mother and the assumption of a new object choice, is entwined with a bigger question of socialization (96/5).

Folding the moralism implied in the conventional adherence to the notion of genital oblativity in on itself, Lacan suggests that there is already an aggressivity at work in the normative impulse this notion implies. Lacan's point here is really two-fold. He is having a characteristic swipe at other traditions in psychoanalysis but, more significantly, particularly in the context of this essay, he is making the point that not only is the harmonious union of the sexual relation a fantasy but, moreover, the very desire at work here necessarily entails both a narcissism and an aggressivity (97/1). He illustrates this, humorously, by paraphrasing La Rochefoucauld, who in his Maxime 113, states 'There may be good but there are no pleasant marriages' (2013). This echoes a point that Lacan will extrapolate upon some years later in his seventh Seminar, where he talks at length about the distinction between the service of goods or the maintenance of order, on the one hand, and desire on the other (Lacan, 1992: 319).

While it may well be the case that a certain social conformity is achieved through either a 'successful' trajectory through the Oedipal complex (96/3) or the work of psychoanalysis to reduce symptoms, it is important not to imagine that either route results in the eradication of aggressivity. Even the most functional or apparently benevolent social convention will continue to induce aggression at the level of the subject (97/2). The idea that the ego can be reabsorbed or transcended, as certain theological writers of the Middle Ages had argued, Lacan suggests, is but a fantasy (97/3).

Narcissism, as Lacan has argued through the essay, is foundational of the very possibility of the subject, insofar as the ego, the *I*, is riven in its very constitution. This is evident, albeit in different ways, at every single stage of development and through quite radically differing conceptions of the subject and their relation to others. The subject may overcome infantile libidinal frustrations through Oedipal sublimation, but the ego remains thwarted and aggressivity is thus maintained (97/4). This centrality of aggression can be seen across various operations in which the subject creates obstacles to their own development or progress, particularly, Lacan says, in terms of those significant life stages such as the psychosexual stages of weaning, toilet training, the whole Oedipal drama and what follows. This is, Lacan says, already obvious in that it was the very failures to resolve the Oedipal conflicts that first brought this process to the attention of Freud and his followers (97/5).

Despite having emphasized the ongoing nature of the aggressivity which arises through the constitutionally conflictual formation of the ego, Lacan here introduces the notion of a specific narcissistic phase (97/6). Such a phase may be understood to describe the period before any Oedipal resolution, the pre-socialized phase when narcissism is more overt. This should not then be understood as suggesting that narcissism is somehow resolved and surpassed but rather to emphasize that it is, to a degree, sublimated (95/4). It is in this before of sublimation that we can discern the emergence of the partial drives and, Lacan argues, the theory of aggressivity he has been expounding allows us both to better appreciate the ambivalence of these drives and the conventional forms of aggressivity we witness in their effects, particularly insofar as it pertains to the manners in which the subject constructs or internalizes their relations with others (97/5).

An important dimension of this, Lacan notes in conclusion, is the bodily strictures the process of socialization entails. It is not simply that we learn what is or is not acceptable in terms of practice or behaviour. The formation entailed in the process of Oedipal sublimation is a formation of the body, which can manifest, Lacan suggests, in something as seemingly innocuous as the conventions of a preference for right-handedness (and the perceived aberrance of left-handedness) as well as in sexual preferences. This can be seen very obviously in the ancient Greek conjunction of the notions the beauty and good, as exemplified in the exalted position of gymnastics and the glorification of the athletic body (98/1).

Thesis five

Lacan's fifth thesis seeks to conclude his discussions by bringing the focus to what we might term the modern condition of man and, explicitly, the role this plays in what Freud had termed the *Unbehagen* of civilization, the malaise in civilization or, as it is conventionally translated into English, *Civilization and Its Discontents*. Lacan also draws explicit attention in the thesis to the category of space, remarking that it is especially insofar as the role of aggressivity in the formation and sustenance of the ego relates to space that it allows us to discern something of its role in modern neurosis and the unease in what we take to be civilization (98). For Freud, of course, human civilization as such was out-of-joint, a product of sublimations and repressions for which no final point of equanimity or normativity could be found. The English 'discontent' does not really fully articulate what we might call the uncanny flavour of the German *Unbehagen* or the bodily dimension of the French *malaise*, both of which point to something ungraspable or beyond conscious thought. Applying this to the wider scope of civilization, Freud is seeking to articulate the tenacious worm in the apple that forever alienates human societies from any form of natural, thoroughgoing harmony. Just as, at the individual level, as Lacan has been discussing, the subject is alienated from itself, sundered from any unmediated access to its instincts by virtue of its immersion in language, so civilization itself must protect against its own, uncanny and irresolvable status.

The evocation of 'space' in this final thesis explicitly locates the phenomenological value in the aggressive movements of identification that have been discussed throughout. Insofar as the subject must route itself through the image, movements and comportment of another in order to gain any identity whatsoever, that routing creates the space that defines and limits the subject's horizon or *lebenswelt*. On a different scale, those processes form and contain the spatial sense of whole cultures, through the projection outwards of individual processes of identity formation. It is Lacan's aim here, he says, to touch briefly on some of the conclusions that psychoanalytic experience makes possible with regard to wider society (98/2).

The fact that aggressiveness is often taken to be a sign of strength is, Lacan argues, sign enough of its ubiquity and status. In a world where the ego is seen as paramount, we often see a certain aggressivity as advantageous, as a necessary and virtuous trait which allows us to succeed. So embedded is this idea that one would need to step entirely outside of modern Western thinking in order to really grasp its particularity, the fact that this is not simply the way things naturally are (98/2). We can see this, Lacan suggests, in the widespread acceptance of Darwin's theory of natural selection, which promotes the idea that aggression will not only prevail but that it is necessary for survival. Lacan suggests that this Darwinian perspective projects the already prevalent aggression evident in Victorian society, in the form of colonization and industrialization, onto the natural world. Far from attesting to our successful evolution, human aggression is actually likely to destroy the planet and subsequently ourselves (98/3).

Rather than Darwin, Lacan would prefer to lean on Hegel who, he says, before Darwin came along had already given us an unparalleled theory of the indissoluble function of aggressivity in human beings. In his famous 'Self-Consciousness' chapter of the *Phenomenology of Mind*, Hegel (1967) presents his myth of the master and slave (or Lord and Bondsman as it is more commonly translated in English). This myth, Lacan declares, captures the essence of both

169

subjective and objective human progress. It allows us to grasp the trajectory of human history, and see how struggles resolve in, but are also then preserved in, a certain development (98/4).

Hegel's myth concerns the burgeoning of what he terms self-consciousness and mirrors much of what Lacan has been seeking to say about ego formation. In Hegel's story, the pre-self-conscious being is seeking a confirmation of its identity. It finds the potential of such recognition in another like itself but here meets an impasse. The first being must minimally recognize the second being as worthy or capable of bestowing the sought-after recognition but if it confers this recognition, it will have placed itself in a subordinate position. It wants to be recognized without giving recognition. This leads to a deadlock which then gives rise to aggression. Each of the beings seeks to bludgeon the other into submission and thus attain the recognition they desire without giving the recognition that would subordinate them to the other. The obvious catch here is that bludgeoning your opponent is likely to lead to their death and dead people are not very helpful when it comes to giving recognition. What turns the tale is that eventually one of the fighters is likely to submit short of death. They face death, Hegel tells us, and decide that submission and servitude are preferable. This encounter with death, the fear it inspires, has, however, another effect, which is to locate the subservient being in relation to death, what Heidegger would later call a being-towards-death (1967). This being-towards-death, coupled with the labour on the world which follows, is the ultimate source of recognition and thus self-consciousness. It is in this sense that we can refer to death as the absolute master (98/5).

Lacan encountered Hegel through the Russian philosopher Alexander Kojève, who famously introduced many of the Parisian intellectuals of the time to Hegel's work. Not only does Kojève give particular emphasis to the master-slave dialectic, as it is often referred, he also places a particular emphasis on desire. The pre-self-conscious being desires recognition from the other. Lacan, here, extracts a salient point from this reading of Hegel to state that human desire can only find satisfaction when it is mediated either by another's desire or when it is mediated in work. While the focus of Hegel's myth is arguably the former, the desire for recognition from another human being, Lacan is keen to draw attention to the fact that both the satisfaction of recognition and the satisfaction of work indicate a negation of nature (99/1).

It is, for Hegel, the slave who is the ultimate victor, due to their encounter with a fear of death and their transformative labour on the world. Although Hegel seems to be talking about feudal servitude rather than the more common conception of slavery we might have now, Lacan wants to show an echo of Hegel's point in the emancipation movements of the 19th century and the concurrent expansion of colonial empires. The slave attains a certain freedom but the aggressivity of humanity is unabated (99/2).

The level of barbarous aggression we can see in our civilization is, Lacan argues, due to the absence in modern life of traditional manifestations and embeddings of the functions of the superego and ego–ideal. We can see these traditions in the cultures we document precisely as we destroy them, whether they take the form of the rites of quotidian relations or festivals and ceremonies. As living cultures, though, such examples only persist in their watered-down form (99/3).

Lacan laments the demise of what he calls the 'cosmic polarity of the male and female principles' and attributes to this lack what he calls the contemporary 'battle of the sexes' (99/3).

Through all of these facets, Lacan argues, the modern condition is such that we have, through the widespread endorsement of schools of thought such as utilitarianism, promoted narcissistic individualism. We are consequently situated in an aporia between a free rein of the passions and their narcissistic levelling, a situation that can only result in the negation of the soul (99/3). In a moment of startling prescience, Lacan wonders if the flip side of this narcissistic isolation is the emergence of an alienating technology, the ultimate slave turned master that will eclipse us entirely. We may imagine self-driving Teslas in Lacan's prediction of automated racing drivers or the robodogs from the *Black Mirror* episode 'Metalhead' (2017) in his 'guards for regulating power stations' (99/4).

The importance of the spatial in the formation of the ego, the fact that the ego emerges from an encounter with that which is exterior, that which is in the world, demands further theorizing which Lacan only hints at here. We know from zoology that some species map their territory collectively in such a way that the individual's position is determined in relation to the group. What is unique in the human realm is the manner in which our conceptualization of ourselves in a space, conjoined to and informed upon by the existence of others, is then folded into each other's conceptualization of a space that includes them. It is a little like Yayoi Kusama's *Infinity Mirror Rooms* (2021) and the effect, just like Kusama's, is, Lacan says, kaleidoscopic (99/5). This is the space of the imaginary, the space in which the ego emerges as already informed upon by and already connected to external reality (99/6).

Though the current essay was composed some 12 years before Lacan coined the term *extimité* in his seminar on the *Ethics of Psychoanalysis*, we can already see the thinking of this concept at play here. The ego is both internal and external and yet, as such, properly neither. The point is not only, however, that the ego is extimate. This particular, and infinitely refracted, nature of the relation of the ego to its spatial context cannot but tie into the aggression which is constitutional of the ego. This may then explain humanity's ceaseless hunger for spatial exploration and expansion, whether in terms of colonialism or space travel. Such external expansion, however, is, by definition, endless. In another adumbration of Lacan's later thinking, we might say that spatial expansion cannot be exhausted, not only because of the posited infinity of the reach of the universe but also because our grasp of what we encounter is never complete (100/1).

Regardless of the actual specifics of the circumstances, it appears that war is the go-to response when our civilization meets some obstacle, and it is then war that shapes our social structures and directions. The homogenization of culture in this regard is, Lacan says, striking, whether this is brought about by a perception of necessity or it is a matter of one culture being tipped towards an emulation of what it sees or grasps, just as Francesca and Paulo are supposedly inspired to kiss each other after reading about Guinevere and Galahad (Alghieri, 1993: 68) (100/2).

Whatever parallels we may draw between the individual and broader society or nations, Lacan suggests that there is a performative contradiction that arises insofar as the individual is too emotional and thus inefficient for the level of aggression that the machine of war requires (100/3). The individual's tendency to flight notwithstanding, the idea that self-preservation prevails is not convincing. Psychoanalysis allows us to appreciate two crucial limits to this supposed instinct. Both our urge for spatial domination and our narcissistic attachment to our own bodies appear to overshadow any fear of death, despite what Hegel claims (100/4).

That the subject finds itself in a double tension, through its inconclusive, but necessary and constitutive, emergence in a spatial dimension and through its difference from itself also points to a temporal disjunction. Here Lacan mentions by way of possible further illustration and exploration of this temporal tension the philosophies of Henri Bergson and Soren Kierkegaard. Bergson conceives of the subject as split between a superficial self, the bodily aspect of the subject, the part which would occupy space, and a profound self, which more or less equates with the mind. This division is then replicated in terms of conceptions of time, which can be said to have a continuous form when viewed objectively but consists of durations when viewed subjectively. The two conceptions cannot, then, be conjoined in one conception (Bergson, 2019: 122). Kierkegaard, similarly, propounds an idea of the subject as inadequate to itself, a subject forever propelled in a state of becoming which is mobilized through a constellation of contested intersubjective relations (Kierkegaard, 1992) (100/5).

The human subject's fractured status, which Lacan has discussed at length through the essay, is, he says, only to be properly grasped by the subject at the intersection of these tensions between what Lacan will go on to call in the 'Mirror Stage' essay, the *Innenwelt* and the *Umwelt*, the inner-world and the outer-world. It is here that we should locate the death drive (100/6). This split, as it is foundational, marks every aspect of the subject's existence. It constitutes an irresolvable aggression of self against self and we can see it in the self-flagellation of neurosis, in hypochondria, in inhibitions, psychological isolation and in social failure and criminality. It is when the subject falters in this division and flounders on the impossible demands of society that psychoanalysis seeks to help, despite the impossibility of this task (100/7).

This modest conclusion notwithstanding, the essay 'Aggressiveness in Psychoanalysis' has delivered, at a minimum, a significant number of the co-ordinates within which Lacan would build his revision of Freud. What would become the 'Imaginary' is established here through a meticulous reconstruction of the early formation of the ego, an emphasis that simultaneously distances Lacan from Freud in its location in the pre-Oedipal miasma. The essay also provides a tentative recognition of what would, by 1953, become a central concern for Lacan, namely the formativity of the symbolic in the life of the subject. Further, the essay presents an ambitious extrapolation of intersubjective dynamics in the service of a historical, civilizational diagnosis. While the terms in which these claims are made will radically mutate throughout Lacan's career, the ambition remains constant. What is here offered up via speculation and conjecture would, by the time of his 17th Seminar (Lacan, 2007), become a set of social 'discourses', presented there with algorithmic ambition and standing as a testament to the power of Lacan's revamped Freudianism in sharpening our understanding of fundamental cultural and political truths. It is for this reason, among others, that the relative neglect of the 'early' period of Lacan's teaching, of which 'Aggressiveness in Psychoanalysis' is surely the capstone, is to be regretted, all those requisite citations of the 'Mirror Stage' notwithstanding. Too often, this *écrit* and those written contemporaneously have been brushed off as merely preliminary, Hegelian appetizers to be overlooked in favour of the full, structuralist main course. A reconsideration of these powerful essays, however, potentially enriches both our theoretical and clinical treatments of intersubjective dynamics.

References

Alighieri, D. (1993) *The Divine Comedy*. Oxford: Oxford University Press.

Augustine. (2008) *Confessions*. Trans. H. Chadwick. Oxford: Oxford University Press.

Bergson, H. (2019) *Time and Freewill: An Essay on the Immediate Data of Consciousness*. Trans. F. L. Pogson. London: Grey Rabbit Publishing.

Freud, S. (1955a) 'Totem and Taboo' [1913] in *The Standard Edition of the Complete Psychological Works of Sigmund Freud Volume XIII*. London: Hogarth Press.

Freud, S. (1955b) 'Beyond the Pleasure Principle' [1920] in *The Standard Edition of the Complete Psychological Works of Sigmund Freud Volume XVIII*. London: Hogarth Press.

Freud, S. (1955c) 'Some Neurotic Mechanisms in Jealousy, Paranoia and Homosexuality' [1922] in *The Standard Edition of the Complete Psychological Works of Sigmund Freud Volume XVIII*. London: Hogarth Press.

Freud, S. (1955d) 'Civilization and Its Discontents' [1930] in *The Standard Edition of the Complete Psychological Works of Sigmund Freud Volume XXI*. London: Hogarth Press.

Hegel, G. W. F. (1967) *The Phenomenology of Mind*. Trans. J. B. Baillie. New York: Harper and Row.

Heidegger, M. (1967) *Being and Time*. Trans. John Macquarrie and Edward Robinson. Oxford: Blackwell.

Janet, P. (1926) *De l'angoisse à l'extase, Vol. 1: Un délire religieux*. Paris: Félix Alcan.

Kierkegaard, S. (1992) *The Concept of Anxiety*. Trans. R. Tompte with A. B. Anderson. Princeton: Princeton University Press.

Kusama, Y. (2021) *Infinity Mirror Rooms*. Tate Modern.

La Rochefoucauld, F. (2013) *Reflections Or, Sentences and Moral Maxims*. Project Gutenberg. [Available at https://www.gutenberg.org/files/9105/9105-h/9105-h.htm#link113] [Accessed 03/03/2023]

Lacan, J. (2001) 'Les complexes familiaux dans la formation de l'individu' [1938] in *Autres écrits*, ed. Jacques-Alain Miller. Paris: Éditions du Seuil.

Lacan, J. (2006) 'The Mirror Stage as Formative of the Function of the 'I' as Revealed in Psychoanalytic Experience' [1949] in *Écrits*, trans. Bruce Fink. New York: W.W. Norton.

Lacan, J. (1992) *The Seminar of Jacques Lacan Book VII: The Ethics of Psychoanalysis*. Trans. D. Porter. New York: W.W. Norton.

Lacan, J. (2007) *The Seminar of Jacques Lacan Book XVII: The Other Side of Psychoanalysis*. Trans. Russell Grigg. New York: W.W. Norton.

Levy-Bruhl, L. (1910) *Mental Functions in Lower Societies*. Paris: Alcan. pp. 61–62.

'Metalhead'. Series 4, Episode 5. (2017). Dir. David Slade. Netflix.

Nietzsche, F. (1998) *On the Genealogy of Morality*. Trans. C. Diethe. Cambridge: Cambridge University Press.

Nietzsche, F. (2001) *Beyond Good and Evil*. Trans. J. Norman. Cambridge: Cambridge University Press.

Plato (1992) *Republic*. Trans. G. M. A. Grube. Indianapolis: Hackett.

Rimbaud, A. (1986) *Collected Poems*. Trans. O. Bernard. London: Penguin.

Rio (2011) Dir. Carlos Saldanha. Los Angeles: 20th Century Fox.

Rousseau, J. J. (1911) *Emile: Or Education*. Trans. B. Foxley. London and New York: J.M. Dent & Sons.

7

A THEORETICAL INTRODUCTION TO THE FUNCTIONS OF PSYCHOANALYSIS IN CRIMINOLOGY, WITH MICHEL CENAC

Carol Owens

Overview

The essay on criminology is one of only two papers in the *Écrits* presented at the Conference of French-speaking Psychoanalysts; the other is the essay on 'Aggressiveness in Psychoanalysis' given at the 11th Conference in May 1948.[1] The essay on 'Criminology' is the only collaborative piece in the *Écrits*, and the collaborator in question is Michel Cenac. Originally presented at the 13th Conference of French-speaking Psychoanalysts on 29 May 1950, it was published in the *Revue Française de Psychanalyse* (1951) along with other contributions to that conference by Karl Abraham, Marie Bonaparte, and Daniel Lagache, together with a discussion paper of themes arising from the conference of which Lacan wrote a further six pages constituting his response to the *Discussion des rapports theorique et Clinique* section of the conference.[2] The conference was opened by Sacha Nacht, the president of the *Société psychanalytique de paris* (SPP) at the time, and in his opening address he put forward the position of psychoanalysis as supporting the view that there is only a difference in degree, not of essence, between normal and anti-social conduct, and that there isn't an impenetrable barrier between normal and so-called abnormal behaviour (1951, 5). Nacht remarked that the 13th Conference of French-speaking Psychoanalysts had chosen for its theme – psychoanalysis and criminology – in view of the fact that a few months later the Second International Congress on Criminology would be held in Paris.

Michel Cenac (1891–1965) was a French psychiatrist and psychoanalyst and member of the SPP. He was awarded the *Croix Guerre* and the Legion of Honour during the First World War and later studied medicine and psychiatry. Originally working as an intern at the *Asiles de la Seine*, he later became head of the clinic. His doctoral dissertation was entitled: 'The Languages of the Mentally Ill' ('*Langages crées par les aliénés*'). He was in supervision with Rudolf Lowenstein in 1928 and joined the SPP in 1929. In 1934, he published a monograph entitled '*Ce que tout médecin*

     DOI: 10.4324/9781003368649-8

doit savoir de la psychanalyse' ('What every doctor should know about psychoanalysis'). In 1936, he set up a psychoanalytic clinic with John Leuba (Bourgeron, 2005). In 1943, during the occupation, he took in Eugène Minkowski's daughter as a refugee, and is somewhat renowned for being the only psychoanalyst in Paris to publish an article in the *Annales medico-psychologiques* using the term 'psychoanalysis' during the years 1941–1944 (Roudinesco, 1999, 153; Kutter, 2013, 78). After his collaboration with Lacan, he went on to conduct several studies related to the field of criminology, as part of his work at the psychiatric infirmary of the Paris Prefecture of Police, including a study on witnesses in 1951, recidivism in 1956, and juvenile delinquents in 1961 (Bourgeron, 2005). After the split in the SPP of 1953, Cenac stayed with the SPP having been one of the members to oppose Lacan during the heated meetings of 1953, leading to Lacan's resignation from the SPP as president and as a member (Nobus, 2000; Kutter, 2013, Zafiropoulos, 2010).

By way of a gloss on this radically innovative essay, I hope to indicate how it brings together Lacan's emergent psychoanalytic conceptualisations, his observations about how the changing form of the family and its place and function in society condition human subjectivity, and his thoughts about what psychoanalysis can teach to other disciplines and fields of research concerning the human condition. In it, we find the track and trajectory of his early thinking just prior to his incontestably Lévi-Straussian epoch denoted most emphatically by his 'Rome discourse'. The essay is hallmarked with references to Hegel and Marx belying his connection with the 'College of Sociologists'[3]; it bears the significant imprint of his early discoveries about paranoia, delusion, and alienation, and how these come to be understood as the effects of identification and constitutive of, as well as inherent to, ego formation; and moreover, testifies to his massive interest and curiosity in his world, a world not long after a war whose ravages still haunt and condemn.

The Nuremberg trials, the Indo-China war in Vietnam, and the rise of industrial and technological capitalism were all features of Lacan's life at this time. His essay on criminology is breathtakingly broad in its range, both historically and culturally, as well as highlighting Lacan at his most Marxist, making scathing comments about humanism, totalitarianism, and the psychology of his time, dedicated as it was, to a conservatism and developmentalism that he abhorred. It also has a poetic dimension sharing with many of his essays of the 1950s a tendency for poetic irony as conclusion. In it, there is a generosity of scholarship in his acknowledgement, positive appraisal and meta-analysis of the early psychoanalytic contributions to the field of criminology, and a stunning panoramic wealth of research from the fields of anthropology, literature, mythology, penology, philosophy, psychology, and sociology. This is Lacan before his 'return to Freud' per se, but indicating as well as foreshadowing the serious commitment he would make in following Freud's recommendation that psychoanalysis should involve the study of the history of civilisation, mythology, the psychology of religion, literary history, and literary criticism. Lacan was later to add to this list that the psychoanalyst should study rhetoric, dialectics, grammar, and poetics (238, 5). In this essay on the functions of psychoanalysis in criminology, Lacan does all of this and more.

At this point, I will sketch out and explain some of the key motifs in Lacan's early work which will help guide the reader in the references Lacan makes to that work as well as to the arguments he constructs in the essay for what psychoanalysis can bring to criminology.

In his 'Antecedents' paper he writes:

> My students occasionally delude themselves into thinking that they have found "already there" in my writings what my teaching has only brought out since then. Is it not enough that what is there did not bar the way to what came later? (53, 3)

The trouble with reading Lacan in our time is that we still risk fomenting a similar type of delusion with which Lacan's students were diagnosed in 1966. But on the other hand, focusing on a paper from 1950 with respect to what was 'already there' is a far less delusional opportunity. In the same paper of 1966, he announces his own (Lacanian) scene as opened up via the notion of 'paranoiac knowledge', which he had expounded in his doctoral thesis in his examination of the case of Marguerite Anzieu née Pantaine ('Aimée') and which informed the two papers he published in *Minotaure* a year later – '*Le problème du style et la conception psychiatrique des forms paranoïaques de l'expérience*' and '*Motifs du crime paranoïaque: Le crime des soeurs Papin*'. In fact, we can say – along with Lacan himself – that a 'crime scene' inaugurates Lacanian psychoanalysis!

Lacan's 'first criminal' was the woman he called 'Aimée' after a protagonist in a novel she had written.[4] Incarcerated on the night of her attempted murder of the actress Huguette Duflos, 10 April 1931, Marguerite Anzieu would spend over a year in the company of Lacan who met her on 18 June at the Sainte Anne asylum where she had been transferred after a stay in the women's prison at Saint Lazarre (Roudinesco, 1999, 32–35).[5] Having translated Freud's 1921 paper 'Some Neurotic Mechanisms in Jealousy, Paranoia, and Homosexuality' in the same year that he published his doctoral thesis, a point of aggregation can be seen to crystallise around his (Freudian) study of jealousy, his (Dalinean) engagement with surrealism with the notion of the 'double image' as paranoid process, and the influence of Jaspers' notion of delusional jealousy and psychic process.[6] Indicating how Aimée's delusional system was comprised of delusions and hallucinations related to events and conflicts in her life, Lacan argued that her attack on the actress had allowed Aimée to deflect onto her the hatred she felt for her myriad female 'persecutors', and 'behind' them, the direct object of her hatred, her sister Elise (who in turn had 'functioned' as substitute for Aimée's mother).[7] These women had all represented 'ideals' for Marguerite: Lacan advanced the crucial thesis that in striking at her (symbolic) ideals (women who enjoyed freedom and social power and whom she hated, as embodied in Duflos that evening in April), Aimée was able to protect her sister and mother (her real objects) from her hatred. The ideal functioned as a double: on the one hand, as an image she emulated, on the other hand, as the object of her hate. As such, there was *meaning* in Aimée's madness.[8] By means of symbolic substitution, Aimée had succeeded in externalising as 'symbols' her internal enemies. But at the moment of stabbing Duflos, Aimée effectively turned her persecutor into a victim, and having been 'found guilty' by the law, her delusions disappeared.[9] Only when punished directly by the law did Aimée come to realise that ultimately the real object of her attack was herself. In her paranoid structure, a *paranoid knowledge* in which there was lodged a hate of negligent mothers (after her own mother, but ultimately, also, herself) was produced in a *paranoid form* expressed in the sense of being persecuted. According to Lacan, once she was punished for her act, she realised that the motivation for attacking Duflos was her wish for self-punishment, in order to deal with her own guilt over neglecting her son.[10] However, the mechanisms underpinning the drive to self-punishment are unconscious and therefore Lacan had to go to Freudian doctrine' to elucidate them (Cox-Cameron, 2000, 40). Categorised by Lacan as the separate clinical category of the 'self-punishing paranoia', this new psychosis owed much to Freud's concept of criminals from a sense of guilt. Freud had described how criminal acts can bring about the conditions for the provision of relief for subjects who suffer from oppressive feelings of guilt before the crime, much like the way a child misbehaves in order to provoke punishment and feels better afterwards (Freud, 1917, 333). In his thesis, Lacan also went on to link Aimée's various conflicts to her psychical structure and personality development, to a certain moment of superego formation where a fixation had taken place: the stage when the subject is assimilating the constraints and ideals of his/her parents and substitutes (Benvenuto & Kennedy, 1986, 44). According to his own view, his doctoral thesis allowed him to theorise the *'function of ideals'*, *'acting-out'*, and *'self-punishment'* (52, 8). According to Roudinesco, his thesis was welcomed by the Paris avant-garde in the 'joint name of surrealism and communism', supporting a materialist philosophy derived from Hegel, Marx, and Freud (Roudinesco, ibid, 61).

The following year saw his publication of the article in *Minotaure* about the Papin sisters' double murder, in which he advanced the same theoretical arguments he had applied in the case of Aimée, but with new terminology borrowed from Marx and Hegel.[11] Lacan's 'second crime' took place on 2 February 1933 in the town of Le Mans, where two servant girls Christine and Léa Papin brutally murdered their employers Mme and Mlle Lancelin (mother and daughter), gouging out their eyes, and hacking up their bodies. The girls were interviewed by three psychiatrists to whom they confessed their crime, and were pronounced sane and responsible for their actions, both were subsequently charged with unpremeditated murder, with a sentence of death for Christine and a life imprisonment sentence for Léa (Roudinesco, 1999, 62). However, in the Papin crime, numerous competing opinions contested their 'responsibility'. On the one hand, their confession mobilised the idea of reason and hence rational culpability, but on the other, the servants admitted under questioning that they had not held any grudge against their victims (therefore pointing to the hidden meaning of an act they did not understand). For Lacan, the elements that seasoned this crime with the same flavourings as Aimée's violent attack on Duflos were the apparent lack of motivation, social tension, paranoia, and self-punishment. Lacan sought once more to show how a paranoid structure through which the murderer strikes at an ideal *within* herself externalised in an other was the real motive for the crime, as he put it: *'cette sœur dont notre malade a fait son idéal'* (Lacan, 1933, 28).[12] Appignanesi has suggested that the 'self-punishment' element emerges from the notion that the girls may have been surprised in a sexual act together when their mistresses returned home that fateful day, and in an enactment of murderous punishment for their own sins (of homosexual, incestuous desire), went ahead and blinded and castrated their employers.[13] Lacan doesn't exactly say this in his paper but he does go beyond calling their bond an *'attachement singulier'* and identifies it as sharing characteristics of a homosexual relationship based on a dual adoration and hatred of each other (Lacan, 1933, 25). However, there was a further element which Lacan took on board: although the Papin sisters' crime appeared to reflect the social reality of class hatred and tension, it also reflected another reality, *paranoid alienation*. Roudinesco (1999, 64) points out that in his writing on the Papin sisters, Lacan had already discovered the work of Hegel via Koyré's articles, and this explains why their crime was interpreted through the lens of the *master-slave dialectic* tied to the struggle between minds or consciousness.

With these two early pieces of *criminal investigation*, the stage is already set, and the scene prepped for Lacan's first theory of subjectivity revolving around the ego as an imaginary construction, corresponding to the subject's identifying alienations in the (imaginary) other.[14] In his 1953 paper on the ego, Lacan remarked that by studying 'paranoiac knowledge', he had been led to consider the mechanism of paranoiac alienation of the ego as one of the preconditions of human knowledge (Lacan, 1953, 12).

Between these two crimes, which first led Lacan to discover the mechanism of paranoiac alienation, and the 'Oedipal crimes' whose symbolic coordinates are conditioned by the family constellation and the family's 'place' within the social structure in the essay on Criminology, there is the further development of his conceptualisation of the ego against the background of his ideas about the relationship of the individual with 'nature' and 'culture' (Lacan, 1936, 72; 1938, 6 and 72–78).[15] In his 'Presentation on Psychic Causality' some 14 years after 'Aimée', he pulls together the strands of his thinking on his early conceptualisation of 'paranoiac knowledge' and the effects of psychic doubling which he identified in both Aimée and the Papin sisters as the essential characteristic of 'the general structure of misrecognition' (Lacan, 2006, 139). He elaborates on his 'Mirror Stage' theory as the very means by which he was able to outline the 'psychological genesis' of psychical causality insofar as it is grounded in the operation of identification of the individual with his/her semblables (ibid., 154). In his 'Mirror Stage' theory (originally prepared in 1936 for presentation at the conference in Marienbad, later published in his Écrits), he had emphasised the importance of regarding the ego in its function as *misrecognition* – in other words, via identification, the subject assumes an image which is always already, other (76, 3). Therefore, this operation founds the ego as alienated, and dialectically at odds with the subject ('*je est un autre*'). His observation that the dialectic linking the split alienated subject to his/her social reality (i.e., mediated by the 'other's desire'), foregrounds a rivalrous, competitive social bond is furthermore precipitous of his intrusion complex outlined in the article on 'The Family Complexes' where we can see that the 'fraternal complex' sketched in Aimée and the Papin sisters finds a new footing.[16]

Recapitulating a prevailing motif in 'The Family Complexes', his long article of 1938, he links the Oedipus complex in its function as bringing a psychical cycle to a close, with the 'family situation', insofar as qua institution, it marks the 'intersection of the biological and the social in the cultural' (ibid. 150). In his 1938 article, he remarked that the family is to be understood as a sociological institution (following Durkheim's sociological method). As a sociological institution, it organises modes of familial authority; the transmission of laws of progeny, parenthood, and marriage; inheritance and succession (Lacan, 1938, 6). But he observed that 'the modern family' has evolved as a 'reduced group' and must be understood as a contraction of the institution of the family. Moreover, he argues that the profound restructuring which has led the institution of the family to its present-day form can be attributed to the dominant influence marriage has assumed (ibid. 10).[17] After Durkheim, he refers to this modern family constellation as the 'conjugal family' and argues that a 'degraded form of the Oedipus complex' was characteristic of this conjugal form of the family (ibid. 72). He goes on to advance the idea that three successive complexes revolving around the functions of three different imagos dictate the subject's early social interactions in the context of his/her family: these are the weaning complex, the intrusion complex, and the Oedipus complex (Lacan, 1938, 14–40). In the 'Presentation on Psychical Causality', he refers to the complexes as revealing the functions of imagos as 'ideal identifications' (ibid, 15). The complexes were to be understood as playing the role of organisers in psychic development. Each complex occurs in succession and each one represents a bio-psychical crisis, resolved in the form of a dialectical structure. A vital tension at each stage, Lacan theorises, is resolved into a mental intention (Lacan, 1938, 17).[18] As such, the complexes relied on a notion of psychical 'development' immanent in the idea of a 'resolution', where a stagnation or fixation in a complex indicated particular pathological consequences (Lacan, ibid, 14–40 and 72–85). The problem was that the Oedipus complex itself was seen to be increasingly degraded as a consequence of newer forms of family, i.e., the conjugal family as a variation of family constellation was characteristically anomic (Lacan, 1938, 72). As such, this degraded form of the Oedipus complex featured an incomplete repression of desire for the mother and a narcissistic bastardisation of the father which for Lacan marked the essential aggressive ambivalence immanent in the primordial relationship to one's fellow man. Moreover, the degradation of the Oedipus complex was coordinated with the rise of the character neuroses, which in turn related to family structures because of the roles that parental objects have in the form of the superego and ego-ideal (Lacan, 1938, 78). In his paper on 'Aggressiveness in Psychoanalysis', he develops this idea further. He argues that the function of the 'normal' Oedipus complex is sublimation, which brings about the identificatory reshaping of the subject via the (pacifying) introjection of the (same sex) ego-ideal, and an opportunity for a transcending of the (rivalrous/jealous) aggressiveness constitutive of the ego at the Mirror Stage (95, 4).[19] However, 'the increasing absence of all the saturations of the superego and ego-ideal' is correlated for Lacan with mid-twentieth century ideas of democracy, liberalism, and the blurring of gender-role difference in the movement towards gender 'equality', all of which lead to the degradation of the 'normal' Oedipal functions of superego and ego-ideal (99, 3). As such he argues that:

> between a democratic anarchy of the passions and their hopeless leveling out by the "great winged hornet" of narcissistic tyranny, it is clear that that promotion of the ego in our existence is leading, in conformity with the utilitarian conception of man that reinforces it, to an ever greater realization of man as an individual, in other words, in an isolation of the soul that is ever more akin to its original dereliction. (99, 3)

For Lacan, in this 1948 paper, the effects of the degradation of superego and ego-ideal functioning together with the promotion and idealisation of the ego lead to a 'formidable crack' at the very heart of being, leading to the emergence of self-punishing neuroses, hysterical/hypochondriacal symptoms, obsessional and phobic anxieties, and the social consequences of failure and *crime* (101, 2).

We have arrived at the point where we can marshal together all of these early moments in Lacan's work up to the essay on criminology and see how they are worked into the essay. We have seen how it all begins with a criminal act which indicates intentionality at a symbolic level, from there we see how the notions of paranoiac knowledge, psychic doubling, and misrecognition figure in the assemblage of conceptual raw material for the theorisation of the ego via mirror stage identification and alienation. The influence of Marx, Hegel, and Durkheim, and later Mauss, through his connections with the field of sociology, indicate Lacan's interest in what constitutes 'social reality', and the area of criminality marks a meeting ground par excellence for the theorisation of the intersection of the individual, the cultural/symbolic and the social. Finally, his innovative theorisation of the individual within the sociological institution of the family allows him to consider the effects of the changing face and form of the family on the individual psyche; and his claim that certain symptoms were the consequence of the degraded Oedipus complex, itself the effect of the rise of the conjugal family unit, with its dehiscence from the wider social network, can be seen to be applied in his remarks about the rise of 'narcissistic tyranny' and crime (101, 2).

In Part I of the essay, the nature and method of the search for truth in the field of criminology are outlined as implying a possible affinity with the dialectical method that Lacan identifies as inherent in the search for truth by the psychoanalytic method. The paper is framed from the outset as doing something other than showing how psychoanalysis can contribute to the study of delinquency: rather it will involve 'rethinking' it. Here we see already, with the references to dialectical materialism and the business of 'truth' as revealed in dialectic, Lacan's debt to Hegel immanent in his theorisation of the Papin crime, and explicit in his theorisation of subjective becoming in 'The Family Complexes'. With the splitting of the object of criminology into 'the crime' and 'the criminal', an essential deconstruction takes place which foregrounds the idea he has brought out in the theorising of the ego in his 'Mirror Stage' as revealing a dehiscence at the core of subjectivity, and in his work on 'The Family Complexes' a dehiscence of the conjugal family with respect to the social bond.

Part II firmly locates the content of the paper as commensurate with the field of sociological investigation. The relationship between crime and law is designated as constituted by society, and punishment for transgression of the law is argued to be predicated upon subjective assent. However, punishment signifies within society a function of the way that 'responsibility' is defined therein. While psychoanalysis is limited to the study of the individual case, and sociology's scope involves the whole set of forces operating in society, psychoanalysis nonetheless discovers in the analytic dialogue, the encapsulated relational tensions that demonstrate the discontents of civilisation. In this way, psychoanalysis appears to extend the reach of anthropology as it finds in the subject's speech, the intersection of the subject's particularity with the universal. In his theorisation of the Aimée case and the Papin sister's crime, he had found meaning where none was apparent, but precisely he had found this 'meaning' in the speech of the perpetrators in each case. In addition to finding the *scanding* of social tensions articulated in each case, he also discovered the function of self-punishment, in other words, the signification of punishment with respect to responsibility and its correlate, subjective assent. Moreover, the influence of Durkheim at work in his piece on 'The Family Complexes' is also apparent here in his treatment of crime, law, and punishment as social institutions (the 'forces operating in society'), and in his attendance to the intersection of the subject with the 'social' and the 'cultural'.

Parts III, IV, and V take the psychoanalytic concepts of Superego, Ego, and Id in order to rethink criminality in relation to the newly emergent form of the family and its effects upon psychical structure.

In Part III, the Freudian Oedipus complex is introduced as the dramatic crisis at the centre of human subjectivity in which the transgression of law (incest) and murderous crime (parricide) are essentially inscribed, and later resolved in the psychical structure. The complex is understood to be pathogenic: guilt and the superego are o outlined as the effect and agency associated with its structuring effects. The superego initially conceptualised as an agency which organises repression of incestuous desire, is seen to be increasingly connected with an array of new 'morbid' symptoms – character neuroses, sexual and social failure. In a time of increasing liberalism, secularisation, and weakening of traditions, far from viewing crime as a jubilant turn to amorality and nihilism, Lacan advances the view that criminal acts instead reveal the law of the superego insofar as they ensure a commensurate punishment. In fact, there is revealed here, the very logic of 'self-punishment'. Crimes which appear to be 'unmotivated' on closer inspection reveal an Oedipal interpretation with a 'symbolic' character. The very structures of society may be regarded as symbolic and while normal subjects use these structures in their real behaviour, those who are mentally ill use them in symbolic behaviour. The expression of this symbolism is moreover to be seen as connected to the psychopathological effects of Oedipal tensions, and for Lacan, an index of the extent to which the family unit as the place where the Oedipus complex is played out is radically altered. Numerous studies demonstrate the effects of the structure and form the family unit has upon psychical development, and psychoanalysis is able to demonstrate that crimes understood as caused by the superego, itself the result of the changing form and sociological status of the family unit, reveal their symbolic and imaginary motivations, thereby deconstructing a monolithic understanding of crime. This radical innovation allows for the de-essentialising of the crime as a discrete nosological category, but also reveals the 'criminal' in a new light, i.e., as a subject for whom a particular act is meaningful, even if not lawful. In sum, the superego is a manifestation in the individual of the social conditions of Oedipalism: but the criminal tensions in the family situation only become pathogenic in societies where the family unit's function has disintegrated.

In this advancement of the superego as the causal factor of crime, we can see a number of earlier theoretical elements harnessed together. In particular, we see again the reference to his work on 'The Family Complexes', here reworked in his comments on the decline of the traditional family unit and connectedness to the wider social kinship network; to the degradation of the Oedipus complex associated with the rise of the conjugal family unit; and to the function of the superego as immanent in the signification of (self)-punishment. There is the Durkheimian and Maussian reference to institution, social force, and use of symbol, and an axiomatic formula explains that according to psychical structure, a subject behaves differently with the symbolic. This reminds us that in Aimée's case, it was argued that she took the symbolic for the real when she attacked Duflos as a substitute object. Again, the notion that crime is constitutive and revealing of symbolic 'meaning' follows the trajectory begun with Aimée and taken up further in the Papin case examination, as does the idea that the superego is involved at the very beginning in organising the necessary psychical conditions for morbidity.

Whereas Part III of the essay effectively deconstructed crime, laying out its constituent parts of unconscious yet meaningful symbolic function and indexing, the effects upon the psyche as entirely caught up with the social structure of the family, Part IV examines the dialectical formation of the ego and the consequences of its interruption at the level of the individual, as well as the correlative functions of identification and alienation that articulate the 'criminal's reality'. The whole business of who, or what, in the criminal is at work in the criminal act is traced according to the rise of the sanitary conception of penology, understood as a product of the humanitarian turn in the human sciences and law, as well as to the evolution of how the probation of crime has been tested. Article 64 of the penal code of 1810 allows for the admission of a force at work upon the criminal that he or she is incapable of resisting. Psychoanalysis locates the source of this coercive force *within* the subject, Lacan indicating the way that repression testifies to the Freudian split subject, and anthropological studies testify to the constancy of dissimulation of the 'truth' in human subjectivity. Only the psychoanalyst has a proper understanding of this split subject since only they have a dialectical experience of the subject. The dialectic can be seen at work in the very formation of the ego as a series of unfolding of thesis, antithesis, and synthesis of the crises of early human subjectivity. Each crisis is resolved by means of a new identification, but identification is the operation by which the human subject is ever more alienated from her/his being. Indeed, the criminal's identifications are revealed in the 'calling-card' or 'signature' they leave behind at the crime scene, indicating at what moment of ego identification a crucial repression occurred. However, a dialectical negativity experienced and demonstrated as aggressive tension is commensurate with the operation of identification and can become criminogenic according to whether and how this particular psychical mechanism is interrupted. The fundamental aggressiveness corresponding to every alienating identification within the context of the changes in the family's function in the social order, and modalities of work under mid-century capitalism, suggest to Lacan a variety of consequences with sociological, political, and philosophical relevance. He argues that the social assimilation of the ideal of individualism, coupled with the passion for power, possession, and prestige at the level of the social, will mobilise a form of criminality that will riddle the social body; will lead to the inclusion of a criminal type within the set of ideals which value the isolated characteristics of the lone subject; and the social signification of crime will be reduced to the fostering of normative transgressions perpetuated by advertising.

Here in Part III then we find the outcomes of Lacan's Mirror Stage theorisation manifest in the social and criminal domain. The early theorising of psychic doubling and alienation present in the Aimée case and the discussion of the Papin sisters is brought to bear on the nuancing of the 'criminal's reality' as conditioned by the ego. The conceptualising of the ego as founded on the operation of identification in which the image of one's semblable is assumed, marks out a terrain of 'an alienating identity that will mark his entire mental development with its rigid structure' (78, 4). Now, in Part III, we see how the entire mental development can be 'marked' with the branding of the criminal according to how the dialectical process involved in the formation of the ego proceeds. The inherent aggressiveness constituted at the moment of the 'Mirror Stage', finds new purchase in the fraternal, and later, intrusion complex in 'The Family Complexes' and here in the essay on criminology gains yet new traction in Lacan's reflections on the consequences of the promotion of individualism, the fostering of a kind of friendly fascism in the workplace, and the homogenisation of desire.

Part V concerns the Id and the radical negation of the notion of the 'born criminal'. Having de-objectified both 'crime' and 'the criminal', Lacan takes the opportunity to dispel the illusion that crime involves an eruption of instincts: the fact that humans torture and kill their fellows supports not the idea of an innate atavism, but rather the essential Hegelian discovery of the 'fight to the death for pure prestige' in which one human wins recognition from another. Neither is the Freudian discovery of the drives answerable for some excess of libido which leads to the production of a criminal. The Id is a lot closer to the idea of the repetition automatism and whose functionality can be seen in all sorts of fateful choices that appear in a crime in often revelatory fashions. Indeed, what is often revealed is that there is no guarantee whatsoever that the repetition automatism associated with the Id brings about a satisfaction; far from it, as what seems to be an index of the Id at work in the subject is the repeated failure to satisfy. This suggests for Lacan, a field of enquiry where criminal 'satisfaction' could be examined. There is no absolute crime, there are only subjects – to be evaluated case by case – according to psychoanalytic practice.

I – On the motor force of truth in the human sciences

The business of 'Truth' is introduced as inescapably caught up with, and problematised by, the investigations of the 'human sciences' (102,1).[20] The 'physical sciences'– driven by what Lacan is calling 'the motor force of knowledge' – pursue the investigation of their 'objects' within the terms of the scientific paradigm (whose objectives include the search for 'pure' knowledge, and whose adherence to the scientific method involves the maintenance of 'internal coherence'). However, the object in question in the investigations of the human sciences must be considered differently. The human sciences in taking the specifically human subject as their object of study, take the *behaviours* of that object as the very variables (independent and dependent, we could say) that constitute what counts as 'knowledge' of that object. However, the behaviour(s) of the human subject cannot be considered apart from meaning-making, and hence, truth.[21]

His first mention of 'dialectic' in this essay is framed here as a sideways reference to 'dialectical materialism' (102, 2). Karl Marx and Friedrich Engels' fusion of philosophical materialism and the notion of dialectical thought had formed the (Marxist) foundation for a view of human reality as constantly changing in a dialectical process. This way of thinking about human reality appears juxtaposed by Lacan with the scientific drive to discover pure knowledge (i.e., deducible by reason and logic, and therefore implying a more 'idealist' position).

Psychoanalysts know very well (however) that the true value of a revelation *in psychoanalysis* is the power or ability of (subjective) truth to produce or bring about a desired/therapeutic effect (102, 3).

In criminology, the search for truth both constitutes its object as belonging to the field of the law, as well as bringing together the two sides of criminological truth: the truth of the crime itself which concerns the police (the 'whodunnit' of the crime: who is the perpetrator, how was the crime committed, what constitutes the crime scene, etc.,), and the truth of the criminal, what Lacan calls 'the anthropological facet' (why did the perpetrator do it, what does the crime mean for this perpetrator and so on) (102, 4).

The question Lacan poses in this context is what can psychoanalysis contribute to the search for truth(s) in criminology, or again, what can be taken from the techniques the analyst deploys in psychoanalytic 'dialogue', and from the concepts which belong to the psychoanalytic clinic, when 'rethought' with a 'new object' (102, 5).

II – On the sociological reality of crime and law and on the relation of psychoanalysis to their dialectical foundation

It makes no sense to try to conceptualise crime or criminals outside of their sociological context (103, 2). Saint Paul's assertion in his *Epistle to the Romans* (7:7) that 'I can only know sin by means of the Law', and his claim that if it were not for the Law ordaining what is prohibited, he would never have thought to covet what the Law forbade, sets up for Lacan an observable fact: just as every society lays down a set of laws, every society experiences transgressions of these laws which come to be defined as crimes (103, 3). In his note on Lacan's remarks about the existence of 'positive law' in every society (103, 4), Fink (2006, 776) makes the clarification that according to the *Tresór de la Langue française – loi positif –* positive law, designates written law as opposed to unwritten (natural) law. However, he further clarifies that Lacan would appear to be referring to what in English is known as positive law (existing law created by legally valid procedures), or indeed to substantive law (the positive law that creates, defines, and regulates rights and duties of parties). Fink claims this is probably the intention of Lacan's use of the term, i.e., underscoring both the notion of law as 'written' and the idea of regulatory and defining rights and duties, as his remarks following his use of the term criticise a more ethnological theory or understanding of why members of social groups follow the rules of those groups. Lacan claims that it is a myth – perpetrated by ethnology, to think of primitive 'man' obeying the rules of the social group because of some kind of unconscious, forced, or intuitive obedience.

The signification of punishment – as the manifestation of the relationship between crime and law – relies upon 'subjective assent'. Regardless of whether a punishment must be inflicted by the criminal on himself (sic) or be carried out within the institutions of the social system, the ways in which punishment is understood by, and 'inflicted' upon the criminal, constitute an index of how the notion of 'responsibility' is defined in a society (103, 6). In other words, the signification of the criminal act and its sanctions, as well as how those sanctions are to be carried out, are correlated with beliefs around individual responsibility. Lacan refers to Malinowski's discussion of incest between matrilineal cousins on the Trobriand Islands as an example of the self-infliction of the punishment of suicide as a particular manifestation of the relationship between crime and law.[22] In his *Crime and Custom in Savage Society* (Malinowski, 1926/1985), Malinowski had indeed reported a case of a breach of exogamy where the young man guilty of the breach committed the act of suicide (1985, 78–79).

Next, Lacan outlines some of the consequences of the non-equivalence of 'responsibility' with regard to punishment (103, 7). Responsibility is after all quite a slippery notion: there is not always a neat one-to-one mapping of individual responsibility with either punishment or (social) restitution (103, 8). The fact remains, Lacan remarks, that sometimes societies are so 'destabilized' or 'impaired' by the action of one of its members that no equivalent punishment 'satisfies' the law (104, 2). In other words, holding that member individually responsible doesn't adequately 'punish' and thereby restore order, and in these situations, the law demands more: either the member's partisans or group are held 'responsible' and punished in some way too or there is recourse to scapegoating. Even in the case where only the perpetrator of the crime is punished, how he is judged responsible relies upon which court is making the judgment (104, 3). Lacan points out that answering for one's acts in front of the Holy Office (formerly the Inquisition) compared with standing up in front of the People's Court (the special court set up in 1934 by Adolf Hitler operating outside the constitutional framework of the law and according to which acts of treason against the Third Reich were punishable by death) points to the different agencies (with)in the individual, or functions, for which he can be held responsible. Indeed, the example of standing charged of heresy is an interesting one as the crime of heresy attracted a punishment which was itself intended not merely for 'the correction and good of the person punished, but for the public good in order that others may become terrified and weaned away from the evils they would commit'.[23]

On the other hand, psychoanalysis, because it distinguishes different agencies and functions in the individual, can comment on and help explain how notions of responsibility have become tied to or connected with (even constructive of) a particular way of objectifying crime (104, 4).

Despite psychoanalysis's experience being limited to working with the individual subject (one by one, case by case), it manages nonetheless to discover in that very experience – as it gets articulated by that individual subject – the tensions that permeate that individual subject's relations, tensions that somehow epitomise the 'discontents of civilization' (104, 5). As such, although the object of psychoanalysis differs from the object of sociological enquiry and knowledge (groups/social forces/universals), the subject who speaks in the psychoanalyst's consulting room lays bare the meeting point of nature and culture. For this reason, the human sciences and criminology in particular, can make use of psychoanalytic discoveries once certain adjustments are made. In fact, just as the subject's confession, and his reintegration into the social community, are to be understood as underpinning the objectives of criminology in its enquiry and in its application, these very operations – confession and reintegration – are per excellence immanent in the psychoanalytic dialogue since it is here that the intersection of the individual subject with what is universal becomes articulated (104, 6). It is in this way that we can regard psychoanalysis as an extension of anthropology because the technique of psychoanalysis allows for the exploration in each individual of 'the import of the dialectic' that 'scands' society's creations, which include ('crime' and) 'the law'. This neologism – 'to scand' – is introduced by Bruce Fink here to properly distinguish Lacan's use of the verb – *scander* – from the usual translation into English as scanning. Lacan's use of the term denotes not the practice of scanning, skimming a text rapidly, or indeed, more contemporaneously, passing text or images in digital form into a computer, but rather, the method of scanning verse, or its division into metrical feet (Fink, 2006, 776).

This leads Lacan to refer to another dialectic, this time as it appears in Plato's dialogue 'Gorgias', which according to Lacan recounts 'the deeds of the hero of dialectic' (105, 1). The subtitle: 'On Rhetoric; Refutative' is considered as a treatise on the motives of the Just and the Unjust.[24] In fact, it is Gorgias, the title character, who makes the statement that rhetoric deals with what is just and unjust (454b, Lamb).

In a dense, yet highly nuanced paragraph, Lacan manages to condense Plato's entire dialogue into some snippets about that work allowing him to say something else about the signification of punishment and more implicitly, about the nature of responsibility (105, 2).[25] There are two reasons why Plato's Gorgias may be of special interest to Lacan here. But we should read the entire paragraph in which it is cited as one of Freud's dreams recounted in *The Interpretation of Dreams* (Freud, 1900), that is to say, as a massively over-determined writing. To begin with, there is the whole business of the dialectic as the method per excellence of discovering the truth, and of the Socratic method in particular suggesting a parallel with the psychoanalytic method or dialogue as he has been referring to it until now in the paper. Second, the content of Gorgias as a set of dialogues, pivots around debated notions of responsibility, belief, truth, and myth, culminating in the strong statement of Socrates that rhetoric is to be used for the single purpose of pointing to what is just (527c, Lamb). We may perhaps read in the implied message to the reader who may be sceptical of the value of psychoanalysis to criminology, or the 'uncultivated contemporaries' of the preceding paragraph, that they like Callicles, would also do well to heed Socrates' words when he says that, 'it is disgraceful that men [...] should put on a swaggering, important air when we never continue to be of the same mind upon the same questions' (527e, Lamb).

So what is Lacan taking from his reading of Plato?

Through Socrates' refutations of his various interlocutors' positions (via the maieutic or dialectic method),[26] he brings about the conditions for Callicles (the Athenian),[27] and Gorgias and Polus (the rhetoricians) to recognise how rhetoric is tied to power and constitutive of injustices carried out in the name of law (or in the name of the just). Lacan makes rather short work of the dialectical transformations or shifts in the dialogue, but he claims that Socrates eventually convinces Callicles to see how punishment can be understood as a way of making amends and setting an example for the group.[28] Lacan further remarks that Socrates accepts his own destiny according to the 'universal' he explains in the dialogue. This is a reference to the fact that Socrates was found guilty and put to death some 19 years before Plato wrote the Gorgias. There is an interesting moment in the dialogue, all the more for its retroactive construction, where Callicles is busy trying to persuade Socrates that if he isn't careful he will wind up dragged into a law court by a paltry rascal (Lamb, 521c), and Socrates conceding this, claims that it could only be a villain who would prosecute a good man and that yes it was entirely possible that he could be put to death by such a villain (ibid., 521d). Socrates goes on to say (in keeping with his beliefs that the good and the bad are dealt with accordingly in the nether world) that no (good) man should fear dying, rather it is doing wrong that one should be afraid of, for 'to arrive in the nether world having one's soul full fraught with a heap of misdeeds is the uttermost of all evils' (ibid., 522e). In referring to Plato's Gorgias, wherein the business of rhetoric is exposed and subjected to the dialectic method, Lacan is able to emphasise the dialectical foundation of crime and law and their relation to punishment, the very themes which characterise Part II of the essay.

The next reference is to Freud's essay 'The Future of an Illusion'. His statement quoted here, recalls, for Lacan, Socrates saying to Callicles 'Philosophy always says the same thing' (105, 3). This is an interesting and underplayed moment. In fact, in 'The Future of an Illusion', Freud himself takes up a somewhat Socratic posture and method. He proceeds in this essay to imagine that he has an opponent who follows his arguments with mistrust and to interject some remarks from time to time (Freud, 1927, 21). Tarrying with his interlocutor leads him to a position of refuting his interlocutor's opinions on religion while advancing his own defence that science – far from being the illusion his interlocutor claims – promises to produce a greatly beneficial knowledge (ibid., 55). His remark that the voice of the intellect is a soft one, not resting until it has been heard, follows on from an insistence upon the primacy of the intellect over the 'instinctual' (ibid., 53). In addition, and this is something which Lacan surely observed but for some reason did not emphasise: at a certain point in Gorgias, Socrates is urged to continue arguing with himself (having exhausted and frustrated his interlocutors, 505e). He rises to this challenge but not before remarking that if things are to proceed in a monologue, his interlocutors must still interrupt and refute him, and vie with him in an attempt to know what is true and false (506a). This is so close to Freud's acknowledgement of the dangers of a monologue without refutation (ibid., 21).

In Gorgias, Callicles having suffered the dialectical twists and turns of Socrates' maieutics, has become backed into a corner with his own hotheaded arguments, and finds himself in the indefensible position of having agreed that (since) the wisest man is the best, and that the best deserves the most, therefore even the shoemaker (who logically is better at making shoes) deserves the biggest and largest number of shoes (490e). In his exasperation, he gives out to Socrates for talking about cobblers and cooks and doctors and for repeating himself, whereupon Socrates agrees and moreover emphasises that he not only repeats himself but he repeats himself on the same subjects (491a).[29] Wolff (2014) comments that Kierkegaard quoting this passage some 2000 years later, made the point that although the essence of the Aesthetic is novelty, the essence of the Ethical is repetition.[30] As what counts as truths in matters of morality never change, when we speak of morality, it's not surprising that we should be saying the same things and in the same ways. Lacan here takes Socrates for saying that 'Philosophy always says the same thing' but Fink (2006) makes the point that this statement can also be rendered as 'Philosophy is always true'. Are we to take from this passage the idea that Lacan is blue in the face trying to get a certain message across? Perhaps! But clearly, in matters of morality, on questions of what comes to count as criminological acts and what comes to signify as punishment, the psychoanalyst concerned with the ethics of the subject qua dialecticised, may after Freud, have to repeat himself ad infinitum before he is finally heard.

III – On crime as expressing the symbolism of the superego as a psychopathological agency: Although psychoanalysis unrealises [irrealise] crime, it does not dehumanise the criminal

In Part II, the *sociological* reality of crime (and its relation to law) was considered to be related to psychoanalysis via their dialectical foundation. Lacan begins Part III by claiming that the *concrete* reality of crime cannot be understood without seeing how it is related to a 'symbolism', one whose pathogenic effects psychoanalysis has discovered to reverberate in individuals to a far-reaching extent (105, 4).

Freud's 'depth psychology'[31] inaugurated a form of psychology that examined the earliest signifying relations of the individual and their effects upon their subjectivity and lived experiences (105, 5).

The 'psychogenic effects' that psychoanalysis (i.e., the 'depth psychology' it came to be known as at a certain time) studies, and that are the effects of 'this first symbolism' and its meaning, were designated by psychoanalysis by the name of the 'feelings' associated with it, i.e., guilt (106, 1).

The pathogenic effect of guilt, thanks to Freud's discovery of it as such, has been taken up and studied in the field of psychology, demonstrating psychology's debt to Freud, but as it has been taken up it has become framed within the conceptual (and 'empirical') apparatuses of behavioural experimental (and behavioural geneticist) psychology so as to be unrecognisable from its Freudian form (106, 2). Behaviourist experimentalism with its emphasis on animal studies experiments, on their 'learnt' and observable behaviours, with no theory of mind or consciousness, and regarding subjective human experience as merely epiphenomenal, had thereby managed to reduce the study of affect to only that which was overtly observable and in any case upon which theorising could at best remain speculative.[32]

Thanks to Freud's discovery of guilt arising from a moment in early human relational development, and the import of this moment into the field of psychology, psychology has been afforded the opportunity to study the moment that gives rise to guilt as a dramatic crisis (not as mere relationship dynamics), one whose resolution is actually constitutive of psychical structure (106, 3). This early crisis is none other than the Oedipal complex, understood as giving rise to the (fantasies of) crimes of incest and parricide.[33]

Just as the Oedipus complex is invented by Freud to describe the moment in early subjectivity that explains for him why all little boys harbour the wish to kill their father and take his place with their mother (Freud, 1900, 260–267) and feel guilty for this wish thereafter, his Totem and Taboo is invented to explain why in 'the collective mind' mental processes occur just as they do in the mind of the individual, and that a sense of guilt for an action has persisted in the collective mind for many thousands of years and remained operative in generations without conscious knowledge of that action (106, 4).[34] In other words, Freud draws from the social realm of law and prohibition in order to make sense of individual desire and guilt and then draws from the individual realm of repression and affect to establish a universal sociological fact. Notwithstanding the criticisms of his methodology in Totem and Taboo, Freud nonetheless makes the essential claim there that man begins with law and crime (i.e., with submission to the paternal law and the law prohibiting incest), and the significations of this relationship (as remarked upon by Lacan in Part II) is foundational for the human subject of the images (imagos and ideals) he constructs (as another, and for the other). How the human subject views their self and its value to the other is one function of the agency of the Superego in the human psyche.

Although the term Superego was introduced by Freud in 1923 in 'The Ego and The Id', his conceptualisation of the Superego undergoes various phases and is present in various modalities in his early work as Strachey points out (Freud, 1923, 9). Somewhat condensing the moments in the evolution of the concept and theorisation of the Superego, it is nonetheless nuanced succinctly by Lacan (106, 5).

The 'self-critical faculty' and its correlative 'sense of guilt' were connected by Freud in his early theorisation of obsessional neurosis. Indeed, that the characteristic 'self-reproach' of the obsessional could be unconscious was implicit in 'The Neuro-Psychoses of Defence' (1896) and then explicit in 'Obsessive Actions and Religious Practices' (1907). In his On Narcissism paper (1914), he posits a special 'psychical agency' whose task it is to watch over the ego and call it to task according to how it measures up to the ideal ego or ego-ideal. Numerous functions were attributed to the agency including conscience, dream censorship, and paranoic delusions. However, in his Mourning and Melancholia paper (1917), he went further, arguing that the agency of the Superego was responsible for the pathology of mourning (melancholia). In his chapter on The Ego and the Super-Ego (Freud, 1923), Freud explains the psychogenesis of his invention as well as its function in the dissolution of the Oedipus complex: while the superego retains the character of the father (as ideal), the more powerful the Oedipus complex was and the more rapidly it succumbed to repression (under the influence of authority, religious teaching, schooling, and reading), the stricter will be the domination of the superego over the ego later on – in the form of conscience or perhaps of an unconscious sense of guilt (Freud, 1923, 34–35).[35]

In an ironic reflection, Lacan remarks here that contrary to the vision of modern humankind imagined by late nineteenth-century thinkers (both libertarians and moralists alike) – as liberated, uninhibited, and freed of religious and other conservative traditions and bonds – the modern subject is shackled by unconscious guilt for the crimes of his/her Oedipal beginnings (106, 6). The first reference to Dostoyevsky is to his novel 'The Brothers Karamazov' (2003) – the family tragedy centred around a father and his three sons.[36] At a certain point in the story, Fyodor Karamazov (the father) asks/suggests 'if God is dead, then everything is permitted?'[37] The Brothers Karamazov is considered – among other things – to be Dostoevsky's commentary upon the struggle for faith and anti-religious ideas that pose a threat to society. Perhaps not incidentally, Dostoyevsky was regarded by Freud as a 'creative artist, neurotic, moralist and sinner', and his novel 'The Brothers Karamazov', the most 'magnificent novel ever written' (Freud, 1928, 177). The second reference to Dostoyevsky is to his short story published in 1877, 'The Dream of a Ridiculous Man'. In this story, a man wanders the streets of St Petersburg filled with thoughts of his own ridiculousness and the meaninglessness of his life and plans to take his life by shooting himself with a revolver. A chance encounter with a little girl however, changes the course the story later takes.[38] The reference to Nietzsche is to his novel *Thus Spake Zarathustra* in which the *Übermensch* (superhuman) is configured in order to oppose a nihilistic (some would say Dostoyevskian) response to the death of God. If God is dead, and the idea of God can no longer provide meaning or values then there arises the need for a solution to the problem of meaninglessness. The *Übermensch* would function in order to create new values within the moral vacuum of nihilism.[39] In relation to this, the point Lacan is making here is that the modern human subject, enslaved to the law of Superego, far from enjoying an unbridled, unlimited, freedom from the law of God, and far from restoring a restitutive set of values in its place, in his words and in his acts demonstrates something very different. In the absence of the old ties and bonds to religion and tradition, the modern Oedipal subject lives as if 'nothing is permitted' any longer.[40]

As such, the modern subject's words and acts testify to a demonstration of the meaning of self-punishment (107, 1).[41] Since no one can say that they are ignorant of the law, and everyone knows what is the outcome of transgressing that law, hence breaking a law that carries a penalty is equivocal with punishing oneself.[42] This is the characteristic mode of punishment carried out by superego. The singular recognition by psychoanalysis of superegoic crimes and offences creates the conditions for examining how far such an understanding can be of service in anthropology (and by extension, criminology) (107, 2).

Now Lacan mentions the work of Franz Alexander, Hugo Staub, and Marie Bonaparte (107, 3).[43] The point common to all case examples is the highlighting of what they are calling 'the morbid structure' of the crime/offences which indicates that in each case, the subject was unable to resist a force coercing them into a certain act or deed. Even though the individual aspects of the crimes/offences are judged incomprehensible, they are, however, comprehensible if interpreted as Oedipal crimes. Indeed, what makes them truly 'morbid' is their symbolic character (107, 4) (what they represent, and how it is represented). And now Lacan introduces the notion that it is not in the criminal situation that we can find the psychopathological structure of criminal behaviours, but rather, in their *unreal* mode of expression (i.e., their symbolic mode of expression [see paragraph 109, 5 for further elaboration of the use of this term 'unreal']).

To fully bring out this point, Lacan gives the example of another type of crime. He refers to the practice during war-time of the rape of women in the 'enemy civilian population' by soldiers in the presence of an older, powerless male (107, 5). Lacan remarks that it isn't significant to think of the perpetrators of these crimes as somehow morally different to the rest of the male population of which they are members. He seems to suggest that such a crime may be underreported by the media and even trivialised as a 'random news event', but he considers it to be a *real* crime, committed in an Oedipal (symbolic) form. Even so, the fact remains that the perpetrators of such crimes often go unpunished as their acts are explained away as pertaining to the responsibility of their group and in any case carried out under extreme conditions (108, 1).

Referring to, and concurring with Marcel Mauss's formulation that the structures of society are symbolic, 'normal' individuals use these structures in 'real' behaviours, whereas those who are mentally ill, (use) express these structures by symbolic behaviours (108, 2).[44]

What can be symbolised (in an act, in a crime) at best can only be piecemeal. But it is useful to think of it as signalling the appearance of a kind of fault line for the subject, indeed as indicating a subject position (where things break down or go wrong in their social network). Still though, even if something of the structure of these fault lines is revealed in psychopathological manifestations (his 'Maussian' point), it is worth remembering that this structure is only one element among others (108, 3).

While psychoanalytic theory does indeed offer something distinctive to the field of criminology, the problem is that other *less rigorous* theorisations of psychopathological manifestations continue to attempt to base their claims on 'analytic theory', even going so far as to extrapolate from its 'data' (108, 4).

What *is* indicated by the symbolism revealed in psychopathological manifestations, as discovered by psychoanalysis, indicates for Lacan, the social signification of Oedipalism, as well as the scope of the notion of the superego for all the human sciences (108, 5).[45]

Indeed, most of the psychopathological effects of Oedipalism indicate for Lacan, how at the very heart of society something has happened to the family as a structure (108, 6). He claims that this 'dehiscence' of the family unit is expressed as psychopathology (the metaphor is perhaps in keeping with his previous point (108,2) of how something becomes expressed symbolically at the 'breaking point/fault lines' in the individual's 'social aggregations'). The family has become ever more reduced to its nuclear (conjugal) form, and as such, has occupied an ever more formative and exclusive place in a child's early identifications and discipline.[46] In this way, the individual is ever more under the power of the nuclear family unit even as that unit is less and less powerful at the level of the social.

By way of contrast with the nuclear family units under discussion, Lacan refers to societies whose 'structures' are matrilineal (recalling the Maussian reference in 108, 1). He cites the examples of the Zuni and/or Hopi Indians whose matrilineal, totemic, exogamous societies inscribe their children in complex kinship systems whereby each child is fitted into an intricate and closely knit social organisation (108, 7) (cf. Mead, 1937).[47] In his chapter in Mead's book, *Cooperation and Competition Among Primitive Peoples*, Irving Goldman remarks that the matrilineal household typical of the Zuni Indians is crowded with the mother, her husband and children, her daughters and their husbands and children, not to mention some divorced, separated or unmarried sons. In an aside, but as ironic testimony to what Lacan is attempting to bring out in this paragraph, Goldman notes that the Zuni individual 'lacks that privacy we seek out in our civilization' (Goldman, 1937, 322).

However, it is already a redundant exercise to regard matriarchal family structures more favourably than the modern version of patriarchy in terms of the kind of superego they might constitute in the individual (no doubt a less cruel one). All that remains of the patriarchal model, as far as Lacan is concerned here, is the trait of authority 'reserved for the father' (109, 2). However, that very authority is ever more unstable to the point of being practically obsolete. The impact of this obsolescence of authority embodied in the father, and the decline of the function of the (patriarchal) family, is on the one hand the effect of loosening of the individual from family and kinship ties and bonds, and on the other, a commensurate ambivalence (around the figure of the father as an 'ideal' with whom an identification is formed).[48]

Lacan refers to Aichhorn's work with juvenile delinquents and his positing of the notion of latent delinquency (Aichhorn, 1935), and then to Friedlander's understanding of delinquency as correlated with the formation of a 'neurotic character' (Friedlander, 1947). Lacan comments that even the best critics of the 'neurotic character' concept (e.g., Edward Glover) cannot find in it a way to distinguish between the criminogenic aspect of the neurotic character and the (ordinary) neurotic (whose symptoms symbolically represent his/her neurosis) (109, 3).[49] Lacan is referring here to the debate sketched by Glover in his 1925 article around what constitutes neurosis, and what is to be distinguished as 'neurotic character'. Glover had argued that whereas the non-neurotic's solution to a situation of instinct tension arising within was to do something to bring relief (i.e., by using the 'autoplastic method', an example would be of meeting sexual needs by masturbation), the neurotic encounters a conflict here, faced with methods of gratification that are forbidden, which contravene the 'imperative injunctions' of the superego, and therefore produces a symptom – an illness. On the other hand, the 'neurotic character' is somehow able to take advantage of social conditions to disguise his/her solution to drive tension (Glover, 1956, 54).

By contrast, and to properly distinguish one from the other, Lacan explains how he thinks that 'neurotic character' is nothing other than the asocial, isolated, position of the modern family unit mirrored in the individual's behaviour (i.e., the 'conjugal family' type), whereas neurosis expresses the family unit's own structural variations (i.e., how a particular family is composed) (109, 4). The reference to Daniel Lagache's 'conduite imaginaire' is actually to the paper Lagache read at the meeting of the SPP in March 1948. In it, Lagache refers to the term 'imaginary behaviour/conduct' as one part of an attitude associated with 'criminal behaviour/conduct': he argues that external reality provides the material for the actualisation of fantasies under the sway of the pleasure principle (Lagache, 1948, 569). Lagache had in fact delivered a paper on 'Psycho-criminogenesis' at the Second International Congress on Criminology in Paris in 1950 just a few months after he and Lacan had given papers at the 13th Conference of French-speaking Psychoanalysts, both being published in the *RFP* of 1951. So the snippet Lacan refers to here of Lagache's work would certainly not have been the only aspect of Lagache's work on criminology of which Lacan was aware. In fact, Lagache had his own fairly thoroughly developed notion of a di-phasic genesis of criminality, heavily influenced by Eissler's early deprivation theories of criminality (see fns 58, 59, and 80).

So in lending a bit of support to Lagache, Lacan appears to be saying that the point is not only to frame an investigation of the criminal as in some way stuck in a situation where he can only 'act out' his 'fantasies', but rather that the focus should really be on the 'symptoms' that (symbolically) express something of the family constellation and/or family unit qua sociological institution in the criminal's act.

Understood sociologically, the 'neurotic character' qua concept tells us more about the social conditions for a psychogenetic pathway towards crime. The Oedipal structure is short-circuited in these cases and the subject remains arrested (fixated) at a certain developmental moment (i.e., at the early stage of superego formation) (109, 5). 109, 5–6

In so far as psychoanalysis approaches an understanding of crimes as caused by the superego, it performs a crucial twist in the way that crime is considered (109, 6). Lacan says that psychoanalysis 'unrealizes' crime: perhaps we can usefully think of it as a 'de-realizing', or along with Fink as a troubling of it as an objectifiable 'thing' in itself without imaginary or symbolic motives or intentions (Fink, p. 776).[50] But even the penologists gradually came to realise that crime cannot simply be approached as categorically utilitarian, that indeed some crimes cannot be understood as motivated in the same way, even if the final outcome of the crime is similar (109, 7). Lacan goes on to give the example of English penal practice punishing the perpetrator of a petty crime that ends in homicide with the same penalty as the perpetrator of a premeditated murder (110, 1).[51] Indeed the saying 'might as well be hung for a sheep as for a lamb' hails from late 1600s England where the death penalty was in place for the theft of either lamb or sheep.[52]

A brief look at the history and evolution of penology allows Lacan to indicate how penologists have variously responded to the 'dim recognition' that crime cannot be approached as merely utilitarian.[53] If some crimes suggest 'motives' that are other than utilitarian (i.e., consciously motivated), the question posed to penology was thus answered in curious and sinister ways. Beginning with Lombroso's attempts to relate criminality to physiology and biologically isolatable characteristics, we can see how such an understanding of criminality would have satisfied a certain ideology at the time (i.e., 'dominant class' concerns) (110, 2).[54] Lombroso's claims were gradually invalidated – war-time revealed that atrocities could be carried out by men with different (biological/physiological) characteristics, that, in other words, man did not have to be atavistic in order to (be able to) torture or kill another man (110, 3). In addition, the whole study of criminals and criminology began to take place within the more 'respectful' conditions of the human sciences. Lacan refers to the work of William Healy as an important landmark in 'the return to principles' by virtue of the way he approached the study of criminology (110, 4). Healy's 'multi-factor' approach to studying the causes of delinquency introduced the notion that a single case could be commented on by a variety of specialists, thereby shifting away from the dominant 'genetic factors' approach in European criminology at the time. In addition, he emphasised that 'every case will always need to be studied by itself' (Healy, 1915, 5).[55] Psychoanalysis's *monographic* emphasis on knowledge as produced in dialectic contributes in a similar way to the study of criminology.

Constituting another landmark, what psychoanalysis resolves then is the question of how to think about crime as differentially motivated. By restoring the unconscious (symbolic) dimension to criminal motivation, it de-realises crime as a discrete nosological category. At the same time, it doesn't de-humanise the criminal – reducing him/her to the sum of his/her atavistic and/ or biological instincts, seeking instead to understand criminality as a psychopa-thology derived from Oedipal/superego formation (110, 5).

It is even the case that in the transference, psychoanalysis is able to access the imaginary world of the criminal (his/her unconscious identifications, etc.,), and this in turn mobilises the possibility for the criminal to gain access to a footing in reality previously unavailable (110, 6).

Lacan reflects on the manifestation of transference as it develops between a criminal and a presiding judge. He comes up with the example of Hans Frank (the Governing General of Poland during WWII) giving evidence at the Nuremberg Trials under the British judge Geoffrey Lawrence and remark-ing on his elegance and dignity (this Lacan deems worthy to comment on no doubt because it seems at odds with Frank's barbarism and responsibility for sending thousands of Jews to perish at Dachau) (110, 7).[56]

Returning to the point made at 110, 5 – Lacan hails the progress Melitta Schmideberg was able to make with major criminals in treatment with her.[57] He bemoans the fact of there being obstacles to what can be written up about psychoanalytic cases (110, 8).

Lacan insists that criminal cases that indicate an Oedipal psychogenesis should be passed to the psychoanalyst without any limitations placed on the treatment (nor presumably the publication of any results) (111, 1).

Why not allow psychoanalysis to prove its claims about the causes and explanations of crime? As things stand, the claims made by penology don't hold water as can be seen in the reaction by juries to cases even where there would appear to be little cause to debate criminal motivation (as is demon-strated by the case written up by Grotjahn where the guilty party is acquitted of the crime that was apparently, overwhelmingly, proven)[58] (111, 2).

The argument that Lacan has been mobilising until now culminates here in a strong statement about the theoretical consequences commensurate with the notion of superego as the key agency in criminality. The superego must be understood as an *individual* manifestation knotted to the *social* conditions of Oedipalism (111, 3). The particular *social* condition under scrutiny in this paper

– the dehiscence of the family unit, and its reduction to the conjugal nuclear triangle – is seen to be productive of pathogenic (criminal) tensions. It is the superego which reveals these tensions, functioning as a barometer of family disintegration qua social phenomenon (111, 4).

However, Klein's view (from her theory and practice of psychoanalysis with children) that the agency that detects and experiences Good and Bad objects is present in infancy may appear to somewhat problematise the view that the superego emerges as a structural condition of Oedipus rather than as a precedent (111, 6). Well, not necessarily, according to Lacan. The retroactive significations attributed by Klein to superegoic function in infancy and early childhood far from indicating an incompatibility with Lacan's thesis, in fact, can serve to indicate support (and clarification) for Lacan's idea of the misery that attends the human infant's physiological and biological prematurity as itself knotted into the psyche marking the human subject as pathetically dependent upon his/her 'human' (social) milieu (111, 7). As such, some individuals will express this dependence earlier rather than later in their signifying behaviours (111, 8).[59]

On the meeting ground of nature and culture, the discovery of the tyrannical agency at work in the human psyche, manifesting as psychopathology, opposes the Kantian ideal of acting in accordance with moral law as duty. Since the superego is pure pathology, and the Kantian option demands that our pathological inclinations are traversed in order to pave the way towards the incentive to duty towards the moral law, there would appear to be a contradiction between superego as moral law and Kant's Categorical Imperative (112, 1).[60]

The superego is manifest in the individual in his/her psychopathology (symptom) recreating each one's private (fantasmatic) world of wrongdoing (112, 2).[61] As such, although we find the distillation of the social world in the subject's own (Oedipal) symptom, we do not reverse the logic and find in the social world a collective superego, as an index of the pulse of the individual psyche. In fact, the only way a 'collective superego' is thinkable is in terms of one which brings about a complete disintegration of society (where mass sacrifice testifies to the universalising of an ideal) (112, 3).[62]

IV – On crime in relation to the criminal's reality: If psychoanalysis provides its measure, it [also] indicates its fundamental social mainspring

It isn't possible to think about the notion of 'responsibility' outside of notions of humanity – in a given time and place (112, 4). Fink reminds us that the French 'responsabilité' renders up a particular signification: the 'obligation to endure punishment for one's acts' (cf. Fink, p.778). It is obvious that this meaning attached to the notion of responsibility insists throughout this essay.

As such, as civilised societies become ever more utilitarian in their modes of production (and as Lacan argued in Part III, *utilitarianism* is not the most effective rule of thumb for considerations of crime, criminality, and criminal motivation), the signification of punishment (and hence responsibility) as a method of (subjective) atonement for the human subject becomes less and less comprehensible (112, 5). Whereas punishment was once considered as functioning as a warning to others not to carry out crime, it has become absorbed as a function into its other goal, i.e., its correctional aspect. But the effect of this absorption is to change the way that crime and punishment are (thought to be) related.

One of these changes is that 'the ideals of humanism have become dissolved into the utilitarianism of the group'. As such, uncertainty and doubt as to whether the foundations of its laws are just (to all humankind) leads to a reliance on humanitarianism in order to mobilise a universal benevolence, i.e., one that includes the potential for expression by both the exploited and exploiter of its effects. Lacan calls this an 'ideological antinomy' which reflects an underlying social malaise. The turn to science by way of psychiatry in order to (try to) sort out this problem and to determine both what is required in order to prevent crime as well as how to guard against recidivism, marks for Lacan nothing other than an attempt to inscribe a sanitary (humanistic) conception of penology, i.e., whereby what is at stake is a diagnosis of criminality (now indexed by the presence of madness or reason).

This was already attempted at the Nuremberg Trials (112, 6). On the one hand, by bringing in the psychiatrist to interview the Nazi war criminals – there was the generating of what could come to count as a certain 'expert testimony' – were the Nazis mad or just plain bad? At the same time, there was the putting into operation of the humanitarian ideal of treating even the *barbarian* with the dignity and respect accorded to any 'human object'. Doubtful though, Lacan shrewdly remarks, whether there was any actual sanitising of the very effect the trials sought to suppress (112, 1).

In turn, the way that the meaning of punishment has evolved can be seen as corresponding to the way that the 'testing' of a criminal's act (its proof) has evolved (113, 2).[63]

To begin with, in religious societies, the guilty person was identified by means of the sworn oath or confession (113, 3). However, as the notion of a 'juridical personality' comes more to the fore, how the accused person is identified came to demand more from the individual in the process of confession. Lacan refers here to the spread of torture as a method for extracting confessions in Bologna as entirely commensurate with the humanist evolution of Law in Europe.

Rajali (2007) points out that in the late Middle Ages, Europe had undergone a major legal revolution. The church had banned ordeals (such as trials of water and fire) and replaced them with a new system of proof in which lawyers evaluated evidence and put them together in a case. In this new 'inquisitional' system, judges and prosecutors prized written documents and confessions. To this end, they revived the Roman practice of torture to general additional evidence. While originally the citizens of city states (such as Bologna) were protected from the practice of torture, by the early 1200s, the spread of its practice to high-ranking citizens led to the creation of the Statutes of Bologna 1288 (see Fink, 2006, 778; Rajali, 2007). In Bologna, a citizen had been protected up to that point by membership of a guild society and it is interesting to note that the University of Bologna arose around these guild societies of mainly non-Bologna citizens called 'nations' who invited scholars from the City to teach them.[64]

It is of crucial significance then for Lacan that the emergence of the specifically humanist notion of law and its universal application was contemporaneous with the use of torture – not as a means of punishment in itself but rather as a means of extracting the proof of the crime, its 'probation', to use Lacan's term here.[65]

The fact is that as yet, people haven't quite understood what consequences this moment in the history of the constitution of crime and punishment continues to have for penology. Lacan appears to suggest that the ideals of humanism continue to legitimate the idea that justice is enforceable (by means of oppression even if it involves torture) since that notion of justice is based upon an ideology that the regard for human life is shared, universal (113, 4).

Lacan claims that the juridical practice of torture was abandoned not because of some kind of social or cultural improvement. Indeed, the picture of social reality in the nineteenth century suggests no such improvement of this kind. It was abandoned as such he claims, because the promulgation of human rights rested upon an abstraction of the human subject – i.e., the human subject considered outside of his/her social reality (and a rational, measurable individual abstraction at that). The human subject no longer understood as a 'sinner' could hardly be expected to be responding to sin's unique relationship to the Law (the Pauline assertion no longer carrying water at this point). The crucial twist in conceiving of what could underlie criminal intentionality thus changed from the idea of the subject as a sinner to the subject as 'motivated' to carry out a crime. But, as Lacan remarks, such motivations had to be comprehensible to everyone (113, 5).[66]

The reference to Gabriel Tardé's work is to his theory of Moral Responsibility (in his *La Philosophie penale* from 1890). Tardé, an influential French sociologist and magistrate for 27 years, advanced the view that in order to judge an individual to be responsible for a criminal action two conditions were necessary. In the first place, Tardé contested the prevailing Kantian view of free will underpinning moral responsibility, claiming instead that the assumption of 'individual identity' rather than liberty of will is the more practical guide to causality and action. As he put it: 'if I am and as long as I am, it is but a farce to seek any cause for my acts other than myself' (Tardé, 2001, 87). But the knowledge that the individual is the 'identical author' of his action isn't sufficient in itself to judge responsibility. A second condition, that of 'social similarity' is required. Tardé explains:

though I might have brought the same judgement of identity to bear in the case of a murder committed on a European by a savage of a newly discovered isle yet I would not have the same moral indignation and virtuous hatred as a similar act carried out by one European on another [...]. Therefore one indispensable condition for the arousing of the feeling of moral and penal responsibility is that the perpetrator and the victim of a deed should be and feel themselves to be more or less Country-men from a social standpoint, that they should present a sufficient number of resemblances of social [...] of imitative origin. This condition is not fulfilled when the incriminating act emanates from someone who is insane, or from an epileptic at the moment he is seized by a paroxysm or even from one addicted to alcoholism. (Tardé, ibid, 88–89)[67]

As far as Lacan is concerned, this (notion of causality linked to motivation) led to the installation of the psychologist's role and function in the criminal court (113, 6).

Increasingly, the situation of the accused person on trial highlights how irreconcilable truths collide in the courtroom (113, 7).[68] On the one hand, the prosecution and the defence debate in terms that the jury will comprehend (speaking of emotions with which they will identify and so on), on the other, the expert witness presents so-called 'objective' facts and testimony. A testimony Lacan criticises for always failing (or perhaps not having the nerve) to capture a judgement of non-responsibility (in the sense of mental deficiency; Fink, 2006, 778).

It is even the case that expert witnesses bear testimony to this incommensurability of discourse in their own unwillingness to serve up anything but a scant cursory examination of the accused, preferring to hide behind the Code of Law where possible (114, 1-2).

Even so, expert witnesses have discretionary power over how severe a sentence may be passed according to Article 64 of the Code (114, 3). The Code in question is the French Penal Code of 1810; article 64 states that:

There can be no crime or delict where the accused was in a state of madness at the time of action; or when he has been constrained by a force which he had not the power to resist.[69]

And this same article of the code doesn't explain anything about the coercive nature of the force at work upon the accused. Nonetheless, it does point to what *in* the subject suffers the coercion (114, 4).

But the psychoanalyst can explain the coercive nature of the force that leads the subject to the criminal act. This is because only the psychoanalyst has the experience of the human subject as dialecticised (divided, conflicted) (114, 5).

What the psychoanalyst discovers in the dialectic experience of the subject is how the ego functions in order to disguise the subject's truth from him/herself.

Freud recognised that the operation of *verneinung* (negation) was the character-istic form of the subject's repression in his/her speech (114, 6). Moreover, the content of a repressed idea or image can only make its way into consciousness on condition of its being negated (Freud, 1925, 235).

Indeed, there is a whole manner of forms in which subjective truth(s) have been protected (historically and cross-culturally). Lacan refers first to the Jesuits, as moralists (descended from the Christian Humanist tradition) for which use of intellectual suppression they have long been reproached (114, 7). This is most likely a reference to the Galileo scandal when Jesuits were charged with the attempted quashing of Galileo's heliocentrism, since Galileo's claims threatened their Aristotelian worldview.[70] The next reference is to Gobineau's discovery of the 'ketman'. Ketman is regarded as a time-honoured principle of Islam, dating back to ancient Persian culture, the term having its roots in the Persian language. According to the principle of Ketman, Muslims are entitled to conceal their true faith and temporarily adopt a false one in the face of grave danger to their dignity and life.[71] Gobineau had emphasised the pleasure and satisfaction of those cunning and daring enough to cheat the deeply oppressive system of thought and action, while secretly practising their faith or philosophy (Donski, 2008). The last reference is to the Chinese refusal rituals, the principal function of which is to preserve mutual honour in an elaborate, yet rule-bound face-saving system.[72] Ritual refusals are a codified way to say something other than what is desired.

From this diverse choice of examples, Lacan concludes that, in Western society, it rather looks as though the profession of innocence and sincerity is most frequently asserted and/or privileged by the subject. This reveals a para-dox then, wherein the dialectic in search for truth encounters its main obstacle in the very speech of the subject: a first principle of disguising or negating (i.e., Lacan's Freudian point), the truth of intentionality (115, 1).

Having already introduced the idea of the ego as dialectically founded, Lacan mounts an essentially Hegelian argument in favour of understanding the ego as formed and shaped out of a series of syntheses emerging (produced) following a series of subjective crises (weaning, intrusion, Oedipus) (115, 3).[73] Francois Regnault (1998) has remarked that Lacan's use of Hegel in the early 1950s demonstrates how Hegel explains for him the essential law of human becom-ing.[74] It is of note in this regard that Henri Wallon published a paper the year after Lacan's paper on criminology was presented, entitled 'Psychology and Dialectical Materialism' in which he presented a strong argument in favour of a (Marxist) dialecticist materialist position as against an idealist position in psy-chology.[75] Lacan here claims that the ego (and its systems) are produced in this series of dialectical operations, culminating in performative syntheses for the human subject, and further remarks that the form which each synthesis takes is that of an alienation (in which the drives are frustrated) predicated upon an identification. The concept of identification is emphasised as the most funda-mental psychical phenomenon discovered by psychoanalysis.[76] Remarking that its formative power is also seen in the biological world is no doubt a reference to Wallon's paper of 1931 (in which he had observed and compared the behaviour of the chimpanzee with an infant of the same age, i.e., one of the strands that leads to Lacan's theorising of the Mirror Stage (Lacan, 1949) but also to data coming from animal ethology (Laplanche & Pontalis, 1988, 251). Upon resolution of each successive crisis, the object of the drive comes under the domination of a particular libidinal structure. The reference to Fritz Wittel's work is a nod to his argument that at puberty there is a 'second edition' of the phallic phase (Wittel, 1949, 46). During this second edition, according to Wittel, the anxiety incumbent to castration fears is felt for the first time by the youth. Wittel argued that such anxiety regularly attends the first experience of orgasm (via masturbation or other circumstances).

Referring to his own concept of the Mirror Stage and the core idea of the infant identifying with his/her specular image at once alienated from their being, and thereby caught up in a series of (lifelong) rivalrous positions with a counterpart is simultaneously the bedrock of Lacan's theory of ego formation, as well as the foundation of his theory of imaginary at this time (115, 4). Lacan's idea of identification involves both the operation by which subjective crises are 'resolved', as well as the imaginary lure of the specular by which and in which the counterpart or image offers the experience of jubilant accord and/or of aggressive discord. Identification isn't merely an operation that gives rise to aggressiveness because of drive frustration, rather it arises because of the very discordance associated with alienation (the famous *Je est un autre* – 'I is somebody else' – from the poet Rimbaud makes explicit this alienation of the identifications of the ego).[77]

As an exemplar of this phenomenon, Lacan references Pavlov's 'circle-and-ellipse' experiment and its effects (115, 5). Described by Keehn (1979, 31) as a method for producing an experimental neurosis, Pavlov's (1927) experiment begins as an exercise in fine-differentiated-conditioned response. At the beginning of the experiment, a luminous circle is projected before a dog followed by a piece of food in the standard procedure of conditioning of the alimentary (salivation) response. After this, an ellipse is projected as an inhibitory stimulus through being consistently not followed by food. The shape of the ellipse is gradually rounder in appearance and a point arrives at which the dog is no longer capable of discriminating between the circle and the ever rounder ellipse. The dog has been conditioned to salivate at the sight of the circle and conditioned not to respond to the ellipse but as the ellipse image appears more and more like a circle (becoming more and more 'ambiguous' as Lacan puts it), the dog's behaviour changes. It shows its teeth and refuses to eat the meat which is presented in order to condition the salivation response to the image of the circle, and finally, after three weeks of persistently trying to evoke a differentiated response, Pavlov reported that the original differentiation deteriorated until it disappeared completely. Furthermore, he reported that the dog's behaviour included biting off the laboratory apparatuses, and tearing and destroying other elements in his surroundings as well as barking violently on entry into the experimental room (Wolpe, 1958, 38).

Lacan uses Pavlov's experiment to suggest that the conflict the dog undergoes – where he becomes hostile and aggressive as he receives (identifies) conflicting signals – is a good way to understand how something similar is at work in the human subject's formation of the ego as dialectically constructed (e.g., 'like another for another'). Freud recognised this inherent 'negativity' of the ego with his term 'death instinct' (death drive) (116, 1).

Whereas he has been concentrating on the successive conflicts of the ego and their part in the ego's syntheses, Lacan goes further here to say that 'every form' of the ego embodies this negativity; which we might interpret as meaning on the one hand, every 'stage' of ego formation, and on the other hand, every modality of the ego (ego–ideal, superego) (116, 2). Both renderings are applicable and compatible. The reference to the 'Moiroi' or apportioners of fate in Greek mythology (Clotho the spinner, Lachesis the allotter, and Attropis the unturnable), known in English as 'the fates' or incarnations of destiny, suggests that in tandem they control our destiny even though each one has its own special function. Perhaps like the different functions of the ego as Lacan is attempting to spell them out here.

Like Pavlov's dog, the human subject is capable of turning aggressive when the 'other' doesn't correspond to what one expects or hopes for, and in this ruptured identification, a criminogenic 'object' is produced (116, 3).[78]

Lacan had already theorised the way in which a criminogenic object was produced in the case of Aimée and in the case of the Papin sisters, and suggested how the object's structure had a functional role, and a delusional proximity (Lacan, 1932, 1933 op.cit.). The functionality of the 'object's structure' was its lending itself as material for symbolic substitution, and via paranoiac (deluded) knowledge, the expression of ambivalence (see above discussion). Cases such as these prove that only the psychoanalyst can demonstrate that crimes are not simply the result of someone's social context (116, 4).

In the same way, Anna Freud, Kate Friedlander, and John Bowlby also show in their work as analysts how they discover various object structures testifying to the work of a symbolism and the correlation of each object structure with a 'type of reality' (116, 5). Common to each of these analysts was the idea that if early object-love relationships were 'disturbed' in some way, whether through neglect, abandonment, instability (etc.,), these disturbances would become manifest in some form of delinquency in later life. Part of their work has consisted of an educational (rehabilitational) effort to unbind the subject from his alienating identifications (116, 5).[79]

Acknowledging the pioneering work of Aichhorn here, Lacan draws attention to his work with so-called 'aggressive groups' (Aichhorn, 1935) (116, 7). Aichhorn founded an institution in 1918 for the care and treatment of boys who had been severely deprived and horrifically abused. He set out to create a positive caring environment where the aggressiveness of the boys was not met with counter-aggression. This break in the pattern of what the boys were accustomed to created the conditions for the emergence of a 'corrective experience' and over time mobilised outbursts of frustration and misery and the expression of guilt.

The scope and impact of this kind of work are utterly at odds with the genetic psychology approach (and presumably, how this approach has influenced educational systems). The latter is charged with relying upon flawed methods – aptitude testing using abstract adult mental categories – in order to claim results of epistemological status (116, 8). Fink remarks that the reference here is to Piaget (Fink, 779). Piaget's (cognitive) theories had implications for the whole field of educational psychology. His claims that children's thinking develops in invariant sequential stages, with scientifically observable quantifiable differences between younger and older children's thinking, and children's and adult thinking paved the way for the construction of modern educational curricula.[80]

Establishing the facts of a child's 'reality' via the methodology of the genetic (epistemological) psychologist is pedantic according to Lacan (and perhaps, because of the reference that follows, considered also to be fascist!). The reference to 'Long Live Death' is the slogan made famous by the Franco supporter José Millán-Astray in favour of fascism under Franco in Spain as a healing force for Spain, exterminating the Catalans and the Basques as 'cancers on the bodies of the nation' (Thomas, 1961) (117, 2).[81]

In contrast to the pedantic opinion of the genetic psychologist, the '*expert*' opinion that psychoanalysis offers on the reality of crime is based upon the examination of the ego's negativistic techniques (as described earlier) (117, 3). The 'techniques' of the ego's negativism form an 'entire chain' of elements, which Lacan remarks, contains 'structural anomalies' that analysts may think of as 'landmarks on the path to truth'. This chain includes therefore a list of conditions that the ego brings about, and from which the human subject 'suffers'. Lacan begins with the notion of the exhaustion (inanition) of spatial and temporal perspective (this may very well be a reference to Wittgenstein's idea of the self as perspectival point from which the world of objects is present to experience, or following Kant and Husserl, the self as a perspective from which objects are known). Lacan comments that this is the starting point of utilitarian *hedonistic* penology ('if I have lost my bearings in relation to the world and its objects, I will operate only in utilitarian terms').[82] The next element is a diminished interest in the field of object temptations ('objects no longer tempt me *in the same ways*'). Loss of perspective and loss of interest is followed in this 'chain' by loss of conscious awareness of the situation (Lacan calls it a kind of sleep-walking) leading to the criminal act. Finally, there is even a loss of the 'subject' (qua conscious rational agent), since what is present in the criminal act is the coordination of all the unconscious fantasies and unconscious manifestations characteristic of the very alienated reality constituted by the ego's formations.

In so far as there may be anomalies observed in this chain of a structural nature, psychoanalysts will find and attach meaning to these and other paradoxical traces left behind by the criminal. In particular, there is what is called the criminal's 'calling-card' or signature, which far from denoting a carelessness, or 'imperfect' crime, signifies instead – for the psychoanalyst – the very moment of ego identification at which a repression occurred (117, 5). The function of this repression means that, on the one hand, the subject cannot answer for his crime (he/she is not consciously present), and on the other, he/she remains attached to the repression in its negation.

Lacan refers here to Jacqueline Boutonier's article in which she describes the case of an adolescent boy killing an older woman in order to rob her (117, 6).[83] At a certain moment he realises that he is covered in her blood and washing it from his face he sees his image spattered with blood in the mirror. From this, he recognises the possibility of making up a story about having been attacked himself. Boutonier remarks that the boy encountered 'a blood-covered double in the mirror who made tangible for him the presence of an assassin' (in Fink, 2006, 779) and that the boy could not reconcile the idea of himself as the assassin he had become with the 'image' of himself as a child loved by his mother. We could say though that strictly speaking, there are two crimes: the murder and the 'cover-up'. While the murder itself may speak to some of the chains of negativistic techniques Lacan mentions earlier (117, 3), the 'cover-up' speaks to the signing of the act, its signature as redolent of the moment of ego identification revealed in that particular awakening/misrecognition in the mirror, and testimony to the repression that has taken place.

Given that it is repression that dissimulates much of the criminal act, would it not be a good idea to use some kind of method (narcosis) to induce a 'lifting of the censorship' involved (117, 7)? Well, no! First, because repression doesn't merely indicate the censorship of a truth waiting to be discovered. Only the psychoanalyst knows that truth is dialectic in motion, not pre-given (118, 1). Furthermore, and harking back to his point at the very beginning of the paper (102, 3), Lacan maintains that psychoanalysts understand very well that the true value of a revelation in psychoanalysis is not the bringing of repressed unconscious material to consciousness (118, 2). In addition, the reality of the crime should not be sought using narcosis (Fink suggests that Lacan is thinking about 'truth serums'), since, like the practice of torture, it has its limits: the subject cannot confess to something he/she doesn't know anything about (118, 4). Moreover, if the subject has a psychotic structure, such a procedure can be enough to trigger the onset of a psychotic delusion (118, 3).

Paolo Zacchia was an Italian physician, teacher of medical science, medico-legal jurist, philosopher, and poet. He is said to have been the personal physician to Pope Innocentius X and Pope Alexander VII. Zacchias was also a legal adviser to the Rota Romana, the highest Papal court of appeals, and head of the medical system in the Papal States. His book, *Quaestiones medico-legales*

(1621–1651) established legal medicine as a topic of study. In addition, he developed a schema for clinical examinations using the idea that mental symptoms reflect disturbances of one of the elementary mental functions.[84]

According to Lacan, Zacchias' work has paved the way for an understanding of how the unity of the personality is disturbed by illness (118, 5). Psychoanalysis is then, the very means of examination of the point at which nature and culture are linked: namely of what in the 'personality' constitutes the synthesis of neurological functioning (and dysfunction) at the pole of identification, with the subject's experience of group relations (and tensions) at the pole of alienation.

Sociology could learn a thing or two from the psychoanalyst who has discovered the criminogenic functions of advanced Western society. As society becomes ever more complex and is organised along increasingly hierarchical lines in keeping with the objectives of mass production, the 'ideals' proposed to its subjects require of them that they identify with each other ('collaboratively') (118, 6). However, there are side effects of this formulation. On the one hand, individualism is raised to its highest value, yet on the other hand, each subject competes with another for each of the objects in which these ideals are incarnated or embodied (118, 7). It follows then that given the inherent aggressiveness correlative to every alienating identification, in this phenomenon of social assimilation, there will be a point at which aggressive tension will be precipitated, as Lacan says here, 'the mass will break apart and become polarized' (118, 8–119, 1).

As an example of the way that advanced society capitalises upon the subject's tendency to identify with his/her counterpart (i.e., his point at 118,7), Lacan refers to the 'Hawthorne Effect', so-called because of the Western Electric Company research carried out in Hawthorne, Illinois, between 1924 and 1933. Originally designed to study worker productivity under certain conditions, the researchers discovered that, in fact, any change (even for the worse) increased worker productivity. The fact of their being studied had increased group identity and awareness, and ultimately, their productivity as working units (119, 2).

It is interesting that the Hawthorne studies have become known in the social sciences as having discovered desirable outcomes by accidental means, and maybe it is within this context that Lacan defines the objects of study about which psychoanalysis can offer – to the ones who gather and analyse such data – the 'correct coordinates' from which to begin measuring things (119, 3). So what should be studied, and what are its coordinates? First, the separation of the subject and the subject's family (its dehiscence) from the wider symbolic systems and networks (within which the family must survive), its socioeconomic structure. Lacan cites poor old Mr Verdoux – the character played by Charles Chaplin in the film of the same name – a family man who upon losing his job as a bank clerk takes to seducing rich widows and murdering them for their money. Second, the way that ideals are promoted and circulated at the level of the image in such a way as to nurture desire but homogenise satisfactions. Finally, the fostering of the competitive passions for power, possession and prestige when it comes to social ideals.

Aimed at the sociologist, nonetheless, these objects of study together with their co-ordinates, will be of use to the politician and the philosopher too. Lacan points up a certain type of criminality, a certain type of criminal, and a certain type of crime, correlative with (American) society and 'mores' (119, 4). The high point of aggressivity is standardised within the (American) goal of high achievement; rivalry, competitiveness, and alienating identifications are sanctioned within the normalisation of the (American) individual success story; and the meaning of 'crime' is reduced to the fostering of normative transgressions perpetuated by advertising ('because you're worth it!').

On the other hand, and as Plato argued, democracy can degenerate into tyranny (119, 5). These very observable structures (which Lacan sees as tied to advanced Western democratic society[85]) appear reversed when viewed through Plato's formalisation of regimes. For Plato, each regime (Aristocracy, Timocracy, Oligarchy, Democracy, and Tyranny) succeeded the one before and was typified by a certain type of personality (Republic, Book VII, 544–545). In Democracy, the individual is consumed with unnecessary desires and has the freedom to act in whatever way is pleasing, including breaking the law. In Tyranny, the tyrant is consumed by lawless desires which allow him to do terrible things including, according to Lacan's witticism, ensuring that individuals no longer count.

Although leaders of totalitarian societies are judged to be *criminal* and *responsible* for acts testifying to an objective guilt, i.e., which indicates full deliberation and consent, the sanitary conception of penology successfully effaces these judgements and their penalties (as previously argued above 112, 4–5). It isn't the rebel judge who will decide who gets locked up in the concentration camp after all. Instead, it is the dynamic operating in the social group which is the decisive factor in determining how the aggressiveness inherent in the social bond, constituted by a fundamental alienation founded on identification with another, doles out justice or injustice (119, 6).[86] Hegel's critique of Kant's Categorical Imperative emphasises that although the 'law of the heart' is supposed to be a law that works as a universal, it fails because others cannot recognise themselves in the laws of the other's heart (120, 2). In this way, Kantian morality always results in an alien situation, one that always establishes a law that is not our own even if we are the very ones to institute it (Kain, 2005, 102).

V – On the non-existence of 'criminal instincts': Psychoanalysis stops short at the objectification of the Id and proclaims the autonomy of an irreducibly subjective experience

Psychoanalysis also has something to say about the so-called 'innate factors' at work in criminals (120, 3).

It is an illusion, one which is necessary to dispel, that crime is due to an irrupting of instincts breaking through the moral forces that normally keep it in check (120, 4).

Indeed, if instincts are to be understood as humankind's animal nature, then how is this animal domesticated in some people and not in others (120, 5)? *Homo Homini Lupus* – 'man is a wolf to man', implies that man/humankind is most cruel to his/her own species. However, it is necessary to also understand that the human subject targets his/her semblable. What psychoanalysis discovers is that in targeting the semblable (fellow being, the other, the counterpart, the image of her/himself) (120, 6), the human subject demonstrates what Hegel had identified as the 'fight to the death for pure prestige' (Kojeve, 1969, 7).

On the other hand, instincts are also understood to mean atavistic behaviours, a phylogenetic throwback to our primitive ancestors whose necessity to use violence was in keeping with the circumstances of his/her survival. Understood in this way, instincts are bottled up primitive urges (120, 7).

Psychoanalysis does indeed have a theory of instincts, and moreover, it is the first 'verifiable' theory of the human subject (121, 2). Almost immediately Lacan moves from speaking about 'instincts' to speaking about 'drives', for him, the preferred way to translate Freud's term *Triebe*.[87] Paraphrasing somewhat Freud's theorisation of the drives in his 'Instincts and their Vicissitudes' (Freud, 1915), he explains that for psychoanalysis, the 'drives' make up a system of energetic equivalences to which are related psychical exchanges in so far as they symbolise or dialectically incorporate the functions of the organs in which these exchanges appear (i.e., oral, anal, and genito-urinary).[88] The formulation of the organ, aim, and object of the drives is compared with the Jeannot knife whose parts may be endlessly exchanged.[89] Moreover, as the drives cannot be pre-assessed as more intense or less intense, appearing as they do only in the complex links in which they are immanent, it makes no sense to speak of an excess of energy or libido associated with drive (121, 3).

On this point, Lacan observes that in fact it is often the case that the individual with 'criminal tendency' is the one who appears to lack, rather than exhibit, an excess of energy/vitality/libido (121, 4).

Even though it is possible for the perpetrator of misdemeanours and crimes to 'get off' on their acts, this does not imply that such acts are mobilised by an overflowing of instincts (even where such acts suggest the presence of 'perversion') (121, 5). Again, while it is true that those who end up being sent for criminological examination often exhibit signs of perversion, psychoanalytically speaking, each criminal subject's tendency to act can only be understood, one by one, in terms of their neurotic structure, ego formation and/or developmental stagnation, and object fixation as the case may be (121, 6).

In fact, the psychoanalytic concept of the Id is a more concrete notion by which to begin to grasp what has attempted to be explained with the notion of instinct. However, as a concept, it is a difficult one to grasp (121, 7).

It is not to be thought of as the sum total of the individual's innate dispositions (121, 8).

But it might be usefully thought of as what in the subject, insists, or rather persists (as a permanent feature), as repetition automatism (121, 9). In other words, taking into consideration the effects of repression and identification, something else at work in the subject acts in such a way as to indicate its relevance to recidivism (122, 1).

We find this repetition (recidivism) at work in the choices made by people in their marriages, professional lives, and friendships, as well as in their criminal acts (122, 2).[90]

Indeed, there is no guarantee whatsoever that the repetition automatism associated with the Id brings about a satisfaction (in the common sense of the term); far from it, as what seems to be an index of the Id at work in the subject is the repeated failure to satisfy. This suggests a field of enquiry where criminal 'satisfaction' could be examined (122, 3).

However, Lacan recognises the limits of the dialectics he has established here with crime and criminality, since something of the Id is after all ineffable, and irreducible to objectification (122, 4).

Psychoanalysis bears witness to an unspeakable enjoyment (jouissance) which is fantasmatic, produced in accordance with the subject's ambiguous relations with reality and pleasure (122, 5). Reality is fabricated out of narcissistic illusion. Lacan refers to Empedocles' scales of Strife and Love' which are importantly remarked upon by Freud in his paper 'Analysis Terminable and Interminable' (Freud, 1937, 246). Freud re-labels strife and love as Eros and Death drives, making the point that mental events can no longer be thought of as exclusively governed by the desire for pleasure, that it is only by 'concurrent or mutually opposing action of the two primal instincts' that the rich multiplicity of the phenomena of life can be explained (Freud, ibid, p. 243).

As such, in the light of such paradoxes, it makes no sense to try to conceive of crime in any absolute kind of way (122, 6).

Lacan's efforts – here in this paper – were of the order of contributing a more rigorous understanding of crime and of the way that criminals and criminality have become so mundanely and misguidedly objectified. In fact, Lacan offers a more rigorous truth of crime, one that emerges in the subjective discourse of the criminal, and one which owes its rigour to the discoveries of psychoanalysis from its very practice (122, 7).

Acknowledgements

Thanks to Nadezhda Chekurova Almqvist and Christine Gormley for reading and making helpful comments on this work.

Notes

1 Of the 33 'écrits', ten of these were originally presented at various conferences: 'The Mirror Stage as Formative of the *I* Function', delivered at the 16th International Congress of Psychoanalysis, July 1949; 'Aggressiveness in Psychoanalysis' (1948), and 'Criminology' (1950) at the 11th and 13th Conferences for French-speaking Psychoanalysts, respectively; 'Presentation on Psychical Causality' at the Psychiatric conference in Bonneval (1946); 'Presentation on Transference' at the 1951 Congress of 'Romance Language-Speaking Psychoanalysts'; 'The Function and Field of Speech and Language in Psychoanalysis', delivered at the Rome Congress of the Institute of Psychology at the University of Rome in 1953; 'The Direction of the Treatment and the Principles of its Power', at the Royaumont Colloquium, in 1958; ''Remarks on Daniel Lagache's Presentation, originally presented at the Colloquium on the Word 'Structure' in Paris, January 1958; 'The Subversion of the Subject' at the conference on '*La Dialectique*' held at Royaumont, September 1960; 'Position of the Unconscious', at the 1960 Bonneval Colliquium.

2 The *Revue Française de Psychanalyse*, vol. 1, 1951 can be read in full here: http://gallica .bnf.fr/ark:/12148/bpt6k5458970k/f601.item. It is an interesting collection as it has the entire SPP annual proceedings of 1951 including minutes and summaries of SPP meetings. Lacan's discussion piece was also published in Ornicar, 13, 1984 (23–27).

3 According to Roudinesco, Bataille together with Roger Caillois and Michel Leiris started the 'College of Sociology' – a group of writers and philosophers meeting to discuss social and human phenomena in the 'field of myth and the sacred'. Bataille himself was influenced by Nietzsche, Mauss, and Durkheim, and from 1937 until after the war the group remained active, hosting talks and lectures by Bataille and others including Kojeve, Jean Wahl and Raymond Queneau, at which Lacan was present (Roudinesco, 1999, 135–136).

4 Cf. Lacan (1932/1975). *De la psychose paranoïaque dans ses rapports avec la personnalitié.* Paris: Seuil. Dozens of accounts of Lacan's analysis of the Aimée case exist in psychoanalytic literature. The following stand out for their particular relevance to the present paper and are the ones I will draw mainly from here:
  – for historical context and theoretical development, see Roudinesco (1999). Roudinesco in 1999 had access to new material on the case from Marguerite's son Didier Anzieu and from Jean Allouch, which she did not have at the time of writing her *History of Psychoanalysis in France*;
  – for a close reading of Lacan's doctoral thesis with a view to disentangling the reality of Lacan's thought in 1932 from the glosses of retrospection imposed on it by its republication in 1975 (i.e., the delusions he speaks of in 1966), see Cox-Cameron (2000);
  – and for a reading of the case of Aimée within the context of Lacan's other conceptualisations related to Criminology, see Costello (2002).

5 However, Roudinesco charges Lacan with the accusation that 'he was interested in the woman only in order to illustrate his ideas on paranoia and write a theoretical book that would make him the founder of a new school of Freudian discourse' (ibid. 35).

6 According to Cox-Cameron's erudite summary: 'Jaspers explored the phenomenon of psychosis along two axes, that of the development of the personality wherein certain reactions to lived experience can be inscribed as readily understandable, and that of psychic process where something new intervenes, a factor which may be either of organic or of psychic origin, which insinuates itself into the subject's life usually by a series of what he calls primary disturbances. These primary disturbances often manifest themselves by a gradual awareness of irritating noises, unease, impressions of being somehow targeted, presentiments of danger' (Cox-Cameron, 2000, 21).

7   Her persecutors included a former work colleague who was hugely influential upon
     her early life, her older sister who had been a key figure in her growing up years, and
     who had moved in with Aimée and her husband and child and more or less taken
     over Aimée's functions as housewife and mother, and key female figures in the arts
     and theatre world (Huguette Duflos, Sarah Bernhardt, Colette), see Roudinesco (ibid);
     Benvenuto and Kennedy (1986). In addition, see Lacan's remarks and summary of the
     case in his 'Presentation on Psychical Causality' (2006/1946, 138–139).

8   Cox-Cameron remarks that the central relationship of Aimée to her sister within which
     the shadowy doubles of her dead sister and mother resided, was duplicated in the
     intense close friendships which easily turned to hatred, and the succession of admired
     and hated female figures. Lacan found the key to Aimée's psychosis here in this central
     relationship (Cox-Cameron, 2000, 31).

9   In his 'Antecedents' paper, he says that the screen of Aimée's delusion blew down as
     soon as her hand touched '"in a serious act of aggression" one of the images in her
     theatre' (2006/1966, 52). In his 'Presentation on Psychical Causality' he says: 'The effect
     of this act – once she realized the high price she would have to pay for it in prison – was
     the implosion of her beliefs and fantasies involved in her delusion' (2006/1946, 139).

10   'Ce qu'elle 'réalise' encore, c'est qu'elle s'est frappée elle-même, et paradoxalement c'est alors seule-
     ment qu'elle éprouve le soulagement affectif (pleurs) et la chute brusque du délire, qui caractérisent
     la satisfaction de la hantise passionnelle' (Lacan, 1975 [1933], 250).

11   Cf. Lacan. (1933). Motifs du crime paranoïaque: Le crime des soeurs Papin. Le Minotaure 3/4,
     25–28: Roudinesco (ibid. 62);

12   See Roudinesco (ibid, 64). However, as Appignanesi argues, whereas Aimée with her
     ambivalent hatred of her sister had struck out at a displaced version of her ego-ideal
     which she both loved and hated, the Papin sisters with their 'Siamese twinning' didn't
     turn against each other but acted as one in two parts (Appignanesi 2011,. 271). In his
     article on the Papin sisters, Lacan wrote: 'Aimee frappe l'être brillant qu'elle hait justement
     parce qu'elle représente l'idéal qu'elle a de soi. Le besoin d'auto-punition, cet énorme sentiment
     de culpabilité se lit aussi dans les actes des Papin' (Lacan, 1933, 28).

13   Appignanesi, ibid.

14   See Chiesa's (2007) most impressive study of subjectivity in Lacan's theorisations.

15   Essentially these two 'moments' are understood within the development of his thoughts
     as presented in the group of papers beginning with his 'Mirror Stage' theory of 1936
     (Lacan, 2006/1949), his paper 'Beyond the Reality Principle' of 1936, his article on
     'The Family Complexes' in 1938, his 'Presentation on Psychic Causality' of 1946, and
     his paper on 'Aggressiveness in Psychoanalysis' of 1948.

16   In 'The Family Complexes' article, Lacan remarks that 'the connections of paranoia
     with the fraternal complex can be seen in the frequency of the themes of filiation, usur-
     pation and spoliation, just as its narcissistic structure reveals itself in the more paranoid
     themes of intrusion, of influence, of splitting, of the double, and of all the delusional
     transmutations of the body. These connections explain the fact that the family group
     which is reduced to the mother and siblings presents a psychic complex in which reality
     tends to remain imaginary or at most abstract. Clinical experience shows that in fact the
     group composed in this way is very favourable to the development of psychosis and that
     one finds it in the majority of cases of délires a deux' (Lacan, 1938,35).

17   Roudinesco remarks that Lacan's 'sociological' analysis of the individual within the
     family 'offered an astonishing potpourri of ideas about the sacred, antibourgeois nihil-
     ism, and a sense that Western civilaation was deteriorating', all of which was inspired by
     Lacan's association with the 'College of Sociologists' supplemented by interpretations
     of the works of Marcel Mauss and Jakob von Uexkull (Roudinesco, ibid. 143).

18   Roudinesco (op.cit.) and Chiesa (op.cit.) each carry out very thorough summaries of
     the complexes. Chiesa claims that it is possible to impose a Hegelian terminology on

Lacan's complexes, stating that each complex (qua synthesis) allows the unfolding of a particular stage of psychic development (qua thesis) following a crisis (qua antithesis), and producing a new crisis (Chiesa, 2007, 29). Lacan does refer to Hegel in 'The Family Complexes' explicitly in these terms (Lacan, 1938, 12) and refers to the master-slave dialectic (Lacan, 1938, 22). However, Roudinesco notes that Lacan by 1939 only 'knew' Hegel through the commentaries of Kojève, Koyré, and Wahl (ibid. 165).

19   In 'The Family Complexes', his comments on the 'structure of infantile jealousy', and its role in the origins of sociability and consequently of knowledge itself as human knowledge is revealed by investigations that suggest for Lacan that jealousy at its most fundamental does not represent biological rivalry but rather a mental identification (ibid. 25). There are two possible ways out of the 'rivalry': 'Depending on the extent of this adaptation one can admit the beginning at this stage of a recognition of a rival, that is to say of "an other" as object'. However, in this recognition of the rival, there are the possible reactions of parade, seduction, and despotism, and the introduction of a paradox: 'each partner confuses the other's role with his own and identifies with him; but each can sustain the relationship with a quite insignificant degree of participation from the other and so live out the whole situation on his own, as we can see from the sometimes total discordance of their behaviour. All this is to say that the identification specific to social behaviour at this stage is based on a sense of the other that one is bound to misunderstand without a correct conception of its totally imaginary value. In fact jealousy can still manifest itself long after the subject has been weaned and is no longer in a situation of vital competition with his brother. The phenomenon seems therefore to require as a precondition a certain identification with the sibling's state. Moreover, analytic doctrine, by characterising as sadomasochistic the typical libidinal tendency of this stage, certainly underlines that here aggressiveness dominates the affective economy, but it also makes clear that it is always both active and passive, that is, underpinned by an identification with the other who is the object of the violence' (ibid. 27).

20   In his 1936 essay 'Beyond the "Reality Principle"', in the context of arguing about the constitutive function that psychology has *vis a vis* the truth, Lacan writes that science need know nothing about truth (63, 4). Moreover, the search for truth, so-called, in the testimony of the subject, has created a 'moral attitude' that is a condition of the existence of science. But truth, he argues, remains foreign to the order of science: 'science can be proud of its alliances with truth; it can adopt the phenomenon and value of truth as its object; but it cannot in any way identify truth as its own end' (ibid). In his later essay on 'Science and Truth' from 1966, he reiterates his 'problem' with the notion of science as productive of truth, and with the 'human sciences' in particular: 'There is no such thing as a science of man, and this should be understood along the lines of "there's no such thing as an insignificant savings". There is no such thing as a science of man because science's man does not exist, only its subject does. My lifelong repugnance for the appellation "human sciences" is well known; it strikes me as the very call of servitude' (729–730).

21   In his paper on Aggressiveness in Psychoanalysis he had argued that 'only a subject can understand a meaning; conversely every meaning phenomenon implies a subject' (83, 6).

22   In fact, however, as Malinowski points out, suicide is an act which is over-determined. While it is true that it embraces the 'desire of self-punishment', it also satisfies the motives of revenge, rehabilitation, and sentimental grievance (Malinowski, 1985, 95). Again, and as Malinowski remarks, the particular Trobriand Islander who was guilty of breaching the exogamy prohibition took his own life because it was 'the only means of escape' available to him (ibid, 78). In another scenario, he may very well have got away with it and as Malinowski argues, in any case, not have attracted any harsh punishment. It was only when a scandal broke out and everyone turned against the guilty pair and

by ostracism and insults that one or the other could be driven to suicide (ibid, 80). Therefore, notwithstanding his point that the signification of punishment is correlated with beliefs around responsibility, it is however, misleading of Lacan to suggest here that suicide is *the* punishment attached to the crime of exogamy in the Trobriand Islands.

23   The 1578 handbook for inquisitors spelled out the purpose of inquisitorial penalties: *quoniam punitio non refertur primo & per se in correctionem & bonum eius qui punitur, sed in bonum publicum ut alij terreantur, & a malis committendis avocentur.* Translation from the Latin: 'for punishment does not take place primarily and per se for the correction and good of the person punished, but for the public good in order that others may become terrified and weaned away from the evils they would commit'. *Directorium Inquisitorum*, edition of 1578, Book 3, pg. 137, column 1. Online in the Cornell University Collection

24   Commentators from philosophy claim that Gorgias is a reflection on the nature of rhetoric and its connection with democratic politics as well as a reflection on morality and how we should live (Klosko, 1984); a debate about the power of rhetoric and the ethics of power (Johnson, 2011); or a reflection on the relationship between morality and self-interest (Wolff, 2014).

25   Gorgias (c485–c380BC), a citizen of Leontini, a Greek city in Sicily and the most famous teacher of his time in the field of Rhetorics (Johnson, 2011). According to Robert Wolff (2014), the structure of Gorgias may be compared to Book 1 of 'Republic'. In both there are three interlocutors with whom Socrates speaks, and in each case, the first interlocutor is an older man incapable of offering properly challenging arguments to Socrates. The second interlocutor is a younger man, a disciple or a son of the first speaker, and the third guy is the most important opponent, and one who gives Socrates a run for his money. And Gorgias, like many of Plato's dialogues, concludes with a myth about the afterlife. In 'Gorgias', the title character is the first of his three interlocutors and Socrates confronts him with the problem of whether or not he is responsible if one of his students makes unjust use of rhetoric (456, Lamb). First, Gorgias states that the teacher cannot be responsible but is later shamed into admitting that rhetoric can be used unjustly and that he had better look into the idea of educating his students about justice. Polus, the second interlocutor is Gorgias's student from Acragas (another Greek city in Sicily). With Polus, Socrates claims that rhetoric is just a way of flattering the audience, telling them what they wish to hear. Not liking the sound of this, Polus defends his craft, claiming that rhetoricians are the most powerful members of society. Socrates tries to convince Polus that powerful rhetoric is only valuable when used for just ends. In addition, he introduces the idea that justice is always preferable to injustice and that if you've done wrong it is better to be punished as this will make you just and happier in the end. Socrates comes up with the paradoxical conclusions that rhetoric is good for two things: if you are guilty of a wrongdoing you can use rhetoric to convince a court to find you guilty and inflict a punishment upon you, this in turn makes you just and less miserable, if on the other hand your enemy is guilty, you can use rhetoric to convince a court not to convict him since that would have the effect of rendering him less miserable, by the same argument. This discussion paves the way for the entry into the dialogue of the third interlocutor, Callicles, the unscrupulous Athenian who longed for political power in the City and who believes that the *naturally* superior should be given free rein to rule. This discussion finally leads to the conclusion Lacan claims in 105, 1 in the essay.

26   Lacan is applying a Kojevian-inspired Hegelian reading of Plato here given the initial remark about the Master's limits marked by the reality of the Slave incarnated in the 'free man of Athens'.

27   Callicles is the 'Athenian' in the dialogue and certainly makes some claims about superiority as a quality belonging to the better, and the wise, in opposition to 'slaves and other sorts of fellows who are good for nothing' being only superior in physical strength (489c).

28 'And it is fitting that every one under punishment rightly inflicted on him by another should either be made better and profit thereby, or serve as an example to the rest, that others seeing the sufferings he endures may in fear amend themselves. Those who are benefited by the punishment they get from gods and men are they who have committed remediable offences; but still it is through bitter throes of pain that they receive their benefit both here and in the nether world; for in no other way can there be riddance of iniquity. But of those who have done extreme wrong and, as a result of such crimes, have become incurable, of those are the examples made; no longer are they profited at all themselves, since they are incurable, but others are profited who behold them undergoing for their transgressions the greatest, sharpest, and most fearful sufferings evermore, actually hung up as examples there in the infernal dungeon, a spectacle and a lesson to such of the wrongdoers as arrive from time to time' (Socrates, 525c–525d, Lamb).

29 Perhaps this is where the expression 'talking a lot of old cobblers' comes from. Or 'cobblers!' uttered as a refutation in modern English (London) usage.

30 http://robertpaulwolff.blogspot.ie/2012/03/platos-gorgias-mini-tutorial-conclusion .html

31 The term 'Depth Psychology' is attributed to Eugen Bleuler. Coming from the German term *Tiefenpsychologie*, it was originally coined by Bleuler to refer to psychoanalytic approaches to therapy and research that take the unconscious into account (cf. Ellenberger, H. 1970, 562). The term has more recently come to refer to the ongoing development of theories and therapies pioneered by Pierre Janet, William James, Sigmund Freud, and C. G. Jung. Depth psychology explores the relationship between the conscious and the unconscious and includes both psychoanalysis and Jungian psychology.

32 As epitomised by the work of B.F. Skinner at the time of Lacan's writing.

33 In his 1916 paper on 'Some Character Types Met within Psycho-Analytic Work '(S.E., XIV, p. 333), Freud states that guilt derives from the Oedipus complex and is a reaction to 'the two great criminal intentions of killing the father and having sexual relations with the mother'.

34 See S. Freud (1903) 'Totem and taboo' (S.E., XIII, p.158).

35 In 1927, in his short paper on 'Humour', Freud advances the idea that – in 'particular situations' the Superego behaves differently: that through its agency, a humorous attitude is made possible. He admits that it looks like he is developing an ad hoc hypothesis but concludes by saying that there is still much to learn about the nature of the superego (Freud, 1927, 165–166).

36 In fact, there is a fourth who emerges crucially as the plot unfolds.

37 Actually. there has been some considerable debate as to whether and in what way Dostoevsky actually wrote 'God is dead, thus all is permitted'. In 'Dostoevsky Did Say It: A Response to David E. Cortesi', Andrei Volkov (2011) examines some of the lines of argument in this debate. Citing the Pevear and Volokhonsky translation of the text into English, he notes that it is regarded as most consistent with 'a Russian understanding of the formal properties of the Russian text'. Pevear and Volokhonsky render the passage, a speech from Fyodor Karamazov (the father) as follows:

    'And Rakitin doesn't like God, oof, how he doesn't! That's the sore spot in all of them! But they conceal it. They lie. They pretend. "What, are you going to push for that in the department of criticism?" I asked. "Well, they won't let me do it openly", he said, and laughed. "But", I asked, "how will man be after that? Without God and the future life? It means everything is permitted now, one can do anything?"' (Dostoevsky 1990, p. 589) (cf. Andrei I.Volkov. 2011, Internet Infidels, Inc. http://infidels.org/library /modern/andrei_volkov/dostoevsky.html).

38 F. Dostoevsky. (1877). *The Dream of a Ridiculous Man* (Trans. Constance Garnett) http:// www.online-literature.com/dostoevsky/3368/.

39 Cf F. Nietzsche. (1999/1883). *Thus Spake Zarathustra*. (Trans. Thomas Common). US: Dover Thrift Editions. The notion that God is dead is also a theme in F. Nietzsche. (2001) *The Gay Science*. Ed. B. Williams (Trans. J. Nauckhoff), Cambridge: C.U.P. Cambridge Texts in the History of Philosophy.

40 Slavoj Žižek (2006, 94) argues that one way of reading Lacan's claim that 'God is dead and hence nothing is permitted anymore' (what he calls Lacan's 'true formula of materialism') is not that God is dead but rather, God is unconscious. See also Lacan's reiteration of God is dead in his Seminar XVII (Lacan, 2007, 119–120).

41 In his paper 'On my Antecedents' Lacan states that Alexander and Staub's 'self-punishment' concept led him to Freud (52, 8).

42 This is perhaps also an implicit reference to his work on Aimée (a case of self-punishing paranoia).

43 Lacan is referring here to the work of Alexander and Staub in their book *The Criminal, the Judge and the Public: A Psychological Analysis* (1931). William Healy (who Lacan refers to later in the essay, see para 110, 1–3, and fn 31) had come to Berlin in the late 1920s to discuss Alexander and Staub's book on criminology, especially because of their emphasis on the role of the superego in criminality. Advancing the idea that crime was to be understood as a social phenomenon rather than an individual act, and that social dysfunction and criminal behaviour were correlated, and attempting to use psychoanalytic theory to describe criminal behaviours of delinquents, Alexander and Staub's work is considered an important contribution to the social determinism of the time (Alexander, 2015, 76). Although Lacan went on to criticise Alexander's idea of the 'corrective emotional experience', at the same time he recognised in its author 'a man of great talent' (Lacan, 1994, 174). In the preface of their book, Alexander and Staub foreground an understanding of 'judgements of justice' as pinned to the superego: 'we want to understand the criminal in order to be able to judge him correctly, so that our judgement may be just beyond question [...] The sense of justice belongs to the most fundamental factors of human social organisation; any disturbance of the common sense of justice has a destructive effect on society. When the sense of justice is disturbed then that part of the ego which was called by Freud the superego [...] loses its power over the asocial impulses of the individual' (1931, xix). According to her biographer (Bertin, 1982), Marie Bonaparte had a long-time interest in the 'criminal mind' and interviewed Mme Lefebvre who had shot and killed her five-and-a–half-month pregnant daughter-in-law in cold blood. The article in which the work is described appeared in the first issue of the *Revue Française de Psychanalyse* (1927). In her article, Bonaparte interprets Mme Lefebvre's murder of her daughter-in-law as an Oedipal crime: the incestuous desire the child has for the parent is also experienced by the parent for the child, as such, Bonaparte argues, it was 'Jocasta' who killed the rival for her son's attentions (ibid., 161). In addition, she points to what Lacan would later call the 'Intrusion Complex' (Lacan, 1938), arguing that in the pregnant daughter-in-law there was revived all the unconscious rivalry she had felt towards her unborn sister in her mother's pregnant belly (ibid., 163). Moreover, she interprets Lefebvre's testimony – of feeling that in carrying out the crime she was 'doing her duty' – as the 'categorical imperative' of the superego (ibid., 190). This she viewed as constituted from a devout and scrupulous religiosity (ibid., 192). Bonaparte's interest in crime continued with the case of Caryl Chessman in California who had been on death row for a number of years (Bertin, 1982, ibid).

44 According to Gerald Moore (2011, 36), Lévi-Strauss's *Introduction to the Work of Marcel Mauss* in Mauss's *Sociology and Anthropology* had a decisive and immediate impact on Lacan as the essay outlined a theory of the symbolic that would serve as a point of departure for Lacan's reading of Mauss. Moreover, Moore asserts, that this reading was de facto, Lévi-Straussian (ibid., 37). Moore notes that although Lacan claims in his presentation on criminology (this essay) that it is Mauss's formulation that 'the structures of

society are symbolic', that in fact, this was 'scarcely thematised' in Mauss's own work. Rather, though, it was the central theme of Levi-Strauss's 'introduction' to Mauss's work, in turn to be understood less as an introduction to Mauss (for Moore, more of a conclusion), and more of an introduction to Lévi-Strauss. In fact, as Moore points out, it was Lévi-Strauss who claimed: 'like language, the social is an autonomous reality, the same one moreover; symbols are more real than what they symbolise' (from Lévi-Strauss's Introduction to the work of Marcel Mauss, quoted in Moore, ibid, 38).

45　In his 'Presentation on Psychical Causality' (150, 4), Lacan claims that the value of the Oedipus complex is in 'bringing a psychical circle to a close', stemming from the fact that it represents the family situation, 'insofar as the latter, by its institution, marks the intersection of the biological and the social in the cultural'.

46　Cf. Lacan. 'The Family Complexes' (1938, 73).

47　The reference is to the Zuni Indians of the Zuni River Valley in Western New Mexico and Hopi Indians of Eastern Arizona (from AD 700). Although Lacan states that 'by law', responsibility for the care of the infant passes to the father's sister, this isn't strictly speaking borne out in the anthropological literature. It seems rather that a child belongs to his/her mother's clan and is said to be a child of his/her father's clan, having ceremonial relationships with both (Kroeber, 1917, 48, 91). However the child's maternal uncle can be asked to step in to help to reprimand him/her for small misdemeanours, and a 'ceremonial' father can be chosen by the child's father from the household of the father's sisters (Frisbie, 1996). In addition, at marriage, a young man joins the communal economic unit of his mother-in-law's house while maintaining his obligations to his mother's house and that of his sister's. The man continues to have obligations to his sister's household and she in turn is obligated to help her brother and his children in both ceremonial and economic matters (Goldman/Mead, 1937, 321–323).

48　As he had argued in 'The Family Complexes', the degraded form of the Oedipus complex coordinated with the rise of the 'conjugal family' featured an incomplete repression for the mother and a narcissistic bastardisation of the father (Lacan, 1938, 78).

49　The references here are to August Aichhorn's work Verwahrloste Jugend: Die Psychoanalyse in der Fursorgeerziehung from 1925, translated into English as Wayward Youth in 1935 and Kate Friedlander's 1947 book The Psycho-Analytical Approach to Juvenile Delinquency: Theory, Case-Studies, Treatment. Originally a teacher, Aichhorn worked in a child guidance clinic operating a diversion from custody scheme (if his treatment was successful, the young person got a non-custodial sentence) and he also ran an experimental training school for delinquents (Lacan alludes to this work further on in the essay at para 116, 6, and see fn 57). In his book, Aichhorn set out to explore the application of psychoanalysis to pedagogy. He claimed that children only become social beings as their basic drives are civilised by experience. If that process is disturbed, they become 'latent delinquents' whose delinquency will become manifest on provocation; so treatment was intended to deal with children's susceptibility to delinquency (see www.children-webmag.com/ for more information on Aichhorn's work). Freud wrote the foreword to Aichhorn's book, in general framing the work and its author favourably, though it is commonly noted that Freud stated there that psychoanalysis 'wasn't suited to children'. In fact, this is a qualified statement in the context of Freud's differentiation between education and psychoanalysis on the one hand, and his idea of neurosis as being an adult matter on the other. While he states that psychoanalysis can be called in by education as an auxiliary means of dealing with a child, it is not a suitable substitute for education. The possibility of analytic influence rests on quite definite preconditions that Freud sums up under the term 'analytic situation'; it requires the development of certain psychical structures and a particular attitude to the analyst. Where these are lacking – Freud says – as in the case of children, juvenile delinquents, and impulsive criminals something other than analysis must be employed, though something which will be at one with analysis in its purpose (cf. S. Freud, 1925, 274). It is easy to see Aichhorn's influence in Kate Friedlander's understanding of the 'neurotic character'. She foregrounds the asocial or rather, the anti-social character formation in delinquency, claiming that the specific factor in the causation of the anti-social character formation is probably the constant alternation of too much frustration and too much gratification of primitive instinctual instincts (Friedlander, 1947, 117). Lacan makes reference then to Glover's (and Aichhorn's) critique of the concept of the 'neurotic character'. Glover published an article in the *British Journal of Medical Psychology* in 1925 on the neurotic character and devoted the third chapter of his book *On the Early Development of Mind* to a thorough-going critique of it (cf, Glover, 1956/2010, 53–64). Glover concludes that '[n]eurotic character studies are essentially tentative and have no claims to finality@ (ibid, 63).

50 The term *'irrealiser'* is treated differently by commentators on Lacan's use of it. Fink (2006,777) points out that the term doesn't suggest an 'unrealizing' in the sense of undoing the 'reality' of the crime, but rather draws attention to its imaginary and symbolic motives/intentions/components. He provides meanings for the term from the *Tresor de la Langue Francaise*, which include 'to not accomplish'; 'to render unreal by thought or imagination'; 'to lose one's identity or personality by identifying with or projecting oneself into a different world'; or 'to lose one's real character by taking on an enchanting or fanciful form'. Costello (2002,115) remarks that the first translation into English of the essay by Bracher, Grigg, and Samuels renders the term as 'de-essentializes'; but Costello prefers 'de-realises' and understands it (like Fink) as a restoring (of crime) to the symbolic dimension.

51 See B.Alimena (1887) *La Premeditazione in rapporto alla psicologia, al diritto, allo legislazione comparata.*Torino, 1888. Bernardino Alimena had taken the view that the murderer who acts with premeditation is a particularly dangerous criminal because premeditation is 'a sign of an irreducible nature' (in Chamberlain, A.F. Some Recent Italian Psychological Literature, 1900, American Journal of Psychology, 11.Available on JSTOR).

52 See John Ray's English Proverbs 1678 and James Kelly's 1721 Scottish Proverbs ('As good be hanged for an old sheep as a young lamb').

53 Jeremy Bentham was an English utilitarian philosopher and social reformer (1748–1832). His campaign for social and political reform, especially in the area of criminal law had its theoretical basis in his utilitarianism as laid down in his Introduction to the Principles of Morals and Legislation, published in 1789. His principle of utility was to guide action such that it could produce the maximum amount of happiness – defined as pleasure and as an absence of pain. In the criminal register, Bentham's utilitarian rules mandated that an offence should cause the least amount of mischief possible, and in any case, that a 'man' having decided on a course of mischief, should 'do as little mischief as is consistent with the benefit he has in view' (Bentham, 1789: IV, 2;V3).

54 Cesare Lombroso (1835–1909) was an Italian psychiatrist and military medical doctor and later a professor of criminology. He developed the characterological theory of the 'born criminal'.Taking 3000 anthropometric measurements he claimed to have discovered the presence of biological traits in criminals (unusual size/shape of face and jaw, strange eyes, dark skin, long arms, etc.).According to his theory, persons with more than five of these biological traits were born criminals. The born criminal was an atavistic anomaly, reproducing physical and psychical characteristics of remote ancestors, he was a 'savage born into the modern world' (Ellwood, 1912, 721).

55 William Healy's (1915) *The Individual Delinquent* was the result of five years of study and investigation by the Juvenile Psychopathic Institute of Chicago led by Healy. Based on the study of 1000 juvenile delinquents, Healy sought to analyse the causes and conditions that led to anti-social conduct.To Healy is attributed the multi-factorial theory of delinquency; in his research he established a methodology for the complete study of the offender by a variety of specialists, thereby moving away from European criminology's

stress on genetic factors. He stated: 'following the acquirement of several facts from the study of the individual case we see great advantage in the careful grouping of them for the purpose of drawing safe inferences' (Healy, 1915, 5).

56 The Nuremberg trials were conducted between 20 November 1945 and 1 October 1946. Gilbert, a German-speaking military psychologist worked as a military intelligence officer during WWII. In 1945, he was sent to Nuremberg as a translator for the International Military Tribunal for the trials of WWII prisoners. During the trials, he became the confidant of Goring, Pohl, Frank, and others. He participated in the Nuremberg trials as the American military chief psychologist and provided testimony attesting to the sanity of Rudolf Hess. The 'elegant' English Judge was Lord Justice Sir Geoffrey Lawrence. For the transcript of the session of the Nuremberg trial proceedings with Frank's testimony under Judge Lawrence is available at http://avalon.law.yale .edu/imt/04-18-46. See also, Gilbert (1979), *The Psychology of Dictatorship*, and Gilbert (1947/1995) *Nuremberg Diary*.

57 Fink (2006, 778) suggests that Lacan is referring to Melitta Schmideberg's article in Eissler's (1949) 'Searchlights on Delinquency', in which she and Martin Grotjahn (and Aichhorn and Friedlander among others) had chapters. Schmideberg was carrying out successful treatments with arsonists which she writes about in a later paper, also her desire to provide practical applications of theory and clinical research in order to prevent recidivism (1953, 30).

58 Martin Grotjahn's article in Eissler's collection was on the 'Primal Crime and the Unconscious'. Elaborating on this motif in popular culture, he went on in 1966 to publish a book entitled *Beyond Laughter: Humor and the Subconscious*, in which he applied a Freudian reading to the success of crime/detective/murder mystery novels. His basic argument there was that as we all harbour murderous (Oedipal) wishes in the unconscious, the most 'important' murder is therefore the murder of the (opposite sex) parent. Unaware of our (unconscious) impulse to murder this parent, we suffer guilt and ambivalence which is sublimated in our reading of the murder fiction genre. Either we identify with the murderer (father) or with the detective (child) or with the murder victim (mother), cf. A. A. Berger Popular Cultural Genres: Theories and Texts (1992, 88–89).

59 See M. Klein (1921) 'The Development of a Child' (where she theories how the infant protectively splits off an unwanted part of the mother) and M. Klein (1926) 'The Psychological Principles of Early Analysis' (in which she describes the child's oral and anal sadistic attacks on the mother as resulting in a persecutory superego or internal mother imago). See J. Lacan (1949/2006) 'The Mirror Stage as Formative of the I Function'.

60 Lacan continues his discussion of Kant's Categorical Imperative in his seventh seminar *The Ethics of Psychoanalysis* (1959–1960). See also, Neill (2011) *Lacanian Ethics and the Assumption of Subjectivity*.

61 The reference is to Angelo Hesnard's (1949) *L'univers morbid de la faute*. Hesnard was one of the founding members of the société de psychanalystes française in 1926.

62 It seems likely that Lacan is referring here to the First Indochina War (generally known as the Indochina War in France, and as the Anti-French Resistance War in contemporary Vietnam) which began in French Indochina on 19 December 1946 and lasted until 1 August 1954. Fighting between French forces and their Viet Minh opponents in the South dated from September 1945.

63 He uses the term 'probation' here but clearly the term 'probation' can also refer to the period of time between the arrest and trial whereas it seems clear from what follows that Lacan is referring to the criminal's account of his/her crime as confession, as 'testimony': suggesting the route probation from the Latin probation meaning – 'testing'.

64 According to Blanshei (2010, 320), the university arose around mutual aid societies of foreign students called 'nations' for protection against city laws that imposed collective

punishment on foreigners for the crimes and debts of their countrymen. These students then hired scholars from the city to teach them. In time the various 'nations' formed a larger association, or *universitas* (the university). Over time, the university's position grew in the form of collective bargaining with the city, and derived significant revenue from the foreign students who would leave if they were not well treated. The foreign students in Bologna gradually received greater rights and collective punishment was ended.

65   Cf. 'Of the Error of Human Judgments When the Truth is Hidden', from '*The City of God*' in Augustine, *De civitate Dei*, Book 19, Chapter 6:
       What shall I say of torture applied to the accused himself? He is tortured to discover whether he is guilty, so that, though innocent, he suffers a severe punishment for crime that is still doubtful, not because it is proved that he committed it, but because it is not known that he did not commit it. And through this ignorance of the judge, the innocent man suffers... And the judge thinks it not contrary to divine law that innocent witnesses are tortured in cases dealing with the crimes of others... or that the accused are put to the torture and, though innocent, make false confessions regarding themselves, and are punished; or that, though they be not condemned to die, they often die during the torture.

66   This 'turn' is nicely reflected in the treatment of criminal motivation in TV crime drama series. It used to be said of the series 'Colombo' that everyone knew who the murderer was since invariably she/he was the first person Colombo met, and from there it was a case of building knowledge of that character in order to understand their motivations which unravelled in the story alongside the crime trajectory. Some 40 years after Colombo, the rise of the new crime thriller from Scandinavian TV in particular appears to depend for its success on the incomprehensibility of 'motive', which allows the series to effectively defer and displace criminal intentionality from one character to another (e.g., The Bridge, The Killing).

67   According to Candea (2010, 1), Gabriel Tardé's work, now reclaimed from a century of 'near oblivion', has been linked to Foucautian microphysics of power, to Deleuze's philosophy of difference, and most recently to Actor-Network theory. Bruno Latour has referred to him as 'the forgotten father of actor network theory' (ibid).

68   Roger Grenier was a journalist who followed post-war trials which inspired his first essay in 1949 '*le role d'accuse*' where he had argued that the accused party in the courtroom is like the new boy at school; everyone else knows each other and he's the odd man out (cf. Alice Kaplan, The Collaborator: The Trial and Execution of Robert Brassillach, 2000, 269).

69   French Penal Code of 1810: 2nd Book, Chapter 1, On the Persons Punishable, Excusable, or Responsible for Crimes or for Delicts.

70   The Jesuits in Italy were reproached for being responsible for the decline of science and for being guilty by association with Galileo's persecution (Merrill, 2003, xx). However, there is still much debate on the subject (see, for example, Feingold, 2003; Finocchiaro, 2005).

71   According to the analyses of the Polish poet Czeslaw Miłosz (The Captive Mind, 1953), several variations of Ketman existed for different functions (National, Professional, Skeptical, Metaphysical, and Ethical). The phenomenon of Ketman was discovered by Comte Joseph Arthur de Gobineau, regarded by Donski (2008, 140–141) as the founding father of racist anthropology (Gobineau, *Religions et Philosophie dans L'Asie Centrale*, 1865). According to one of the Persians Gobineau encountered on his travels 'not a single true Persian could be found in Asia'.

72   Chinese refusals are rooted in maintaining *Mainzi* and *Lian*, which are oriented towards a person's public image. In Chinese, it is necessary to preserve the interlocutor's face while leaving a way out for the refuser him/herself. Based on reciprocity, each one's *Mianzi* has to be preserved. As such there is an entire classification of refusal strategies in

Chinese custom. In addition, ritual refusals are a strategy for preserving *Mianzi*. In this way, an invitation to stay for dinner or lunch is in actual fact a strategy to ask someone politely to leave or a conventional way to say goodbye! In this way, the only appropriate way to respond to a ritual invitation is to decline it (www.carla.umn.edu/speechacts/refusals/chinese.html). In fact, Lacan refers to Yang, but actually according to Hu (1944) – one of the probable sources to which Lacan had access, the practices of *Mian zi* and *Lian zi* from the words *Mian* and *Lian*, respectively, are used more often. *Mian* refers to face, personal esteem, and reputation, *Lian* refers to respect, dignity, and prestige, while *Mianzi* refers to social status and *Lianzi* to moral character (Hu, Hsien Chin, 1944).

73   See op cit., Lacan, 1938, 14–40.

74   Regnault remarks that Lacan's use of Hegel in order to understand subjectivity begins in 1948 on the subject of aggressivity in psychoanalysis where he says that before Darwin, Hegel provided the ultimate theory of the proper functioning of aggressivity in human ontology. In 1953, in his Rome Discourse, the emphasis is on the structuring moments of Hegelian phenomenology. By the seminar of 1953–1954, Hegel no longer provides for Lacan, the essential law of human becoming, but rather, the law of the Imaginary. However, by the time of writing the 'Position of the Unconscious' paper, Hegel is criticised in favour of Descartes, and Lacan can be seen to have 'given up on the synthesis'. http://londonsociety-nls.org.uk/Publications/002/Regnault-Francois_Hegels-Master-and-Slave-Dialectic.pdf.

75   In this paper, Wallon argues that dialectical materialism is opposed to existentialism and to its essential indeterminism, because, in fact, our mental life is perpetually conditioned by the situations in which it is engaged, be they in accord with its own propensities or contrary to them. But relationships between the organism and the environment are further enriched by the fact that the environment itself is not constant. A change in the environment may result in either the extinction or the transformation of the organisms existing within it. Thus, it becomes the role of different environments, according to their differences, to evoke or bring to the fore different capacities, already potentially present, in a species or in individuals. It is dialectics that has given psychology its stability and its meaning, and which has delivered psychology from the alternatives of elementary materialism or vapid idealism, of crude substantialism or hopeless irrationalism. Through dialectics psychology is able to be at once a natural science and a human science, thus abolishing the division between consciousness and things that spiritualism has sought to impose on the universe. Marxist dialectics has enabled psychology to comprehend the organism and its environment, in constant interaction, as a single, unified whole. And finally, in Marxist dialectics, psychology has a tool for explaining the conflicts out of which the individual must evolve his behaviour and develop his personality (www.marxists.org/archive/wallon/works/1951/ch16.htm).

   Lacan also refers at this point to the idea that Marxists (Dialectical Materialists) are busy looking in the wrong place for signs of Hegel's dialectics at work while not noticing that its use in psychology can be seen to generate laws of human ontology. This may be a reference to the 'discussions' among philosophers about the nature of 'infinity' and how the question is resolved or not from the relative positions of idealism/materialism.

76   Cf. Freud's (1921) paper on 'Identification' in *Group Psychology and the Analysis of the Ego*, and his treatment of the concept as a whole is summarised in Laplanche and Pontalis (1988); Lacan's trajectory of thinking and conceptualising on Identification is summarised by Evans (1996), and his Ninth Seminar (1961-1962) is dedicated to the concept. See also, Lacan's remarks on Identification in his paper 'Beyond the "Reality Principle"' (2006, 71–72), and in his 'Mirror Stage' essay (2006, 76, 79).

77   The phrase was written by Rimbaud in a letter to Georges Izambard (13 May 1871) https://fr.wikisource.org/wiki/Lettre_de_Rimbaud_%C3%A0_Georges_Izambard_-_13_mai_1871.

78   This seems a somewhat weak parallel with the induced experimental neurosis, especially as the concept 'other' is introduced in the back door here! The experiment with
the dog doesn't rely on an unconscious identification with the stimulus or the reward,
in the same way that the aggressive tension arising at the mirror stage and in encounters
with the 'other' does so on the imaginary axis.

79   The reference here is to the Eissler collection of papers *Searchlight on Delinquency* mentioned earlier in the essay, in which Anna Freud and Kate Friedlander had papers (see
110,7;111, 2; fn 35); Freud's paper was entitled 'Certain Types and Stages of Social
Maladjustment'. There, Freud had emphasised the rule of early disturbance of object-
love consequent on absent, neglectful, ambivalent, or unstable mothering, or multiple
impersonal carers. The outcomes of such disturbances in relation to aggression could
lead to manifestations on the spectrum from overemphasised aggressivity to wanton
destructiveness (for an up to date view on how Freud's paper is historically located in
the field of work on 'anti-social tendencies' see Reeves, 2012). The Bowlby reference
is to his paper 'Forty-four Juvenile Thieves: Their Characters and Home Life' (1944)
in which he demonstrated a correlation between separation from or rejection by the
mother in early childhood and that child's later anti-social behaviour (see Issroff et al,
2005,72). Friedlander's important contribution in her Psycho-Analytic Approach to
Juvenile Delinquency again testifies to the strength of the notion agreed up by analysts
of this time that delinquents are those who have been frustrated in their early relationships (1947, 127).

80   Lacan is probably referring to Piaget's 'The Moral Judgement of the Child', which was
published in 1932.

81   On 12 October 1936 during the celebration of the *Dia de la Raza* at the University
of Salamanca, Millán-Astray got involved in a heated argument with Miguel de
Unamuno, the Basque writer and philosopher in the presence of Enrique Pla y
Deniel, the Archbishop of Salamanca, and Carmen Polo Martínez-Valdés, the wife
of Franco, and Millán-Astray himself. According to the British historian Hugh
Thomas in his magnum opus *The Spanish Civil War* (1961), the affair began with an
impassioned speech by the Falangist writer José María Pemán. After this, Professor
Francisco Maldonado decried Catalonia and the Basque Country as 'cancers on the
body of the nation', adding that 'Fascism, the healer of Spain, will know how to
exterminate them, cutting into the live flesh, like a determined surgeon free from
false sentimentalism' (https://en.wikipedia.org/wiki/Jos%C3%A9_Mill%C3%A1n
_Astray).

82   Cf. L. Wittgenstein (1922/2009) *Tractatus Logico-Philosophicus*; I. Kant (1787) *Critique of
Pure Reason*; E. Husserl (1929/1969) *Formal and Transcendental Logic*.

83   Cf. J. Boutonnier (1950).

84   Paolo Zacchia (or Zacchias) is credited with being the one to make significant progress in establishing a systematic study of psychopathology in the seventeenth century.
The modern clinical examination of the patient began with Zacchia's development of
a schema for studying the diversity of symptoms found in mental illness (Vallon and
Genil-Perrin, 1912). The clinical frame of reference developed by Zacchia allowed for
a differentiation of the patient's presentation into the traditional disturbances of overt
behaviour to which he added an assessment of disorders of the major psychological
functions: emotions, perceptions, and memory (Ellenberger, p. 93, 1970). The inclusion
of an analysis of disturbances of mental functions was a major advancement in the clinical examination of the patient.

85   Especially to someone from a different culture (like Sun Yat-Sen, leader of the Chinese
Nationalist Party and 'Father of the Nation' in the Republic of China, whose travels to
America may have influenced his 'Three Principles of the People', his core philosophy
of nationalism, democracy, and livelihood for all).

86   Something of the tone of this comment can be found in his 'Mirror Stage' essay (80, 5) in his concluding comments on neurosis and psychosis, where he suggests that the subject's 'capture by his situation' gives us the most general formulation of madness – the kind found in the asylum as well as the kind that deafens the world 'with its sound and fury'. It is the sufferings of the neurotic and the psychotic that inform psychoanalysis about the passions of the soul, which in turn provides a kind of index of the 'amortization rate' (rate of diminution or decrease) for the 'passions of the city'.

87   As Evans points out, Lacan disagreed with Strachey's translation of *Triebe* into Instinct, claiming that it missed Freud's distinction between Drive and Instinct (Evans, 1996, 46). In his essay 'On Freud's "Triebe" and the Psychoanalyst's Desire!' he states: 'It can never be often enough repeated, given the obstinacy of psychologists who, as a group and per se, are in the service of technocratic exploitation, that the drive – the Freudian drive – has nothing to do with instinct' (2006, 722). See also, Lacan's Eleventh Seminar, *The Four Fundamental Concepts of Psychoanalysis*, for his elaborated treatment of the concept Drive (Lacan,1981).

88   Freud describes the drive as 'a concept on the frontier between the mental and the somatic, as the psychical representative of the stimuli originating from within the organism and reaching the mind, as a measure of the demand made upon the mind for work in consequence of its connection with the body' (1915, 121–122).

89   The Jeannot knife is the French version of the Theseus paradox. The Theseus paradox raises the question of whether an object that has had all of its component parts replaced, is at the end of the day, the same object. It is attributed to Plutarch's Life of Theseus in which Plutarch had asked whether a ship that has had all of its wooden bits restored is, after all, the same ship. The Jeannot knife variation would have had its blade and handle replaced any number of times (https://en.wikipedia.org/wiki/Ship_of_Theseus).

90   This may be a reference to Yousof Karsh. According to the Metropolitan Museum of Art, he is 'one of the greatest portrait photographers of the twentieth century', whose book *Faces of Destiny* was published in 1946.

References

Aichhorn, A. (1935). *Wayward Youth: A Psychoanalytic Study of Delinquent Children Illustrated by Actual Case Histories*. NY: Viking Press.

Alexander, I. V. (2015). *The Life and Times of Franz Alexander: From Budapest to California*. London: Karnac.

Alexander, F., & Staub, H. (1931). *The Criminal, the Judge and the Public: A Psychological Analysis*. New York: Macmillan Co.

Alimena, B. (1887). *La premeditazione in rapport alla psicologia, al diritto, alla legislazione comparata*. Torino: Bocca.

Appignanesi, L. (2011). *All About Love: Anatomy of an Unruly Emotion*. London: Virago.

Bentham, J. (1789). *An Introduction to the Principles and Morals of Legislation*. London: Oxford University Press.

Benvenuto, B., & Kennedy, R. (1986). *The Works of Jacques Lacan: An Introduction*. London: Free Association Books.

Bergen, A. A. (1992). *Popular Cultural Genres: Theories and Texts*. London: Sage.

Bertin, C. (1982). *Marie Bonaparte: A Life*. Newhaven: Yale University Press.

Blanshei, S. R. (2010). *Politics and Justice in Late Medieval Bologna*. Boston: Brill.

Bonaparte, M. (1927). Le cas de Mme.Lefebvre. *Revue Française de Psychanalyse* 1 (1), 193–198.

Bourgeron, J.-P. (2005). Cénac, Michel (1891–1965). *International Dictionary of Psychoanalysis*. http://www.encyclopedia.com/doc/1G2-3435300234.html.

Boutonier, J. (1950). Réflexions sur l'autobiographie d'un criminel. *RFP* XXIII, 182–214.

Bowlby, J. (1944). 44 Juvenile Thieves: Their Characters and Home Life. *International Journal of Psychoanalysis* 25 (19–52), 107–127.

Candea, M. (2010). *The Social after Gabriel Tardé: Debates and Assessments*. London: Routledge (Advances in Sociology).

Chiesa, L. (2007). *Subjectivity and Otherness: A Philosophical Reading of Lacan*. Cambridge, MA and London: MIT Press.

Costello, S. J. (2002). *The Pale Criminal: Psychoanalytic Perspectives*. London and NY: Karnac.

Cox-Cameron, O. (2000). Lacan's Doctoral Thesis: Turbulent Preface or Founding Legend? *Psychoanalytische Perspectieven* 41/42, 17–45.

Donskis, L. (2008). *Power and Imagination: Studies in Politics and Literature*. NY and Washington: Peter Lang.

Dostoyevsky, F. (2003). *The Brothers Karamazov: A Novel in Four Parts and an Epilogue*. Trans. D. McDuff. Harmondsworth: Penguin Classics.

Dostoyevsky, F. (1990). *The Dream of a Ridiculous Man*. Available to read at: http://www.colorado.edu/studentgroups/shortfiction/RidiculousMan.pdf.

Eissler, K. R. (1949). *Searchlights on Delinquency*. New York: International University Press.

Ellenberger, H. (1970). The Discourse of the Unconscious. In *The History and Evolution of Dynamic Psychiatry*. New York: Basic Books.

Ellwood, C. (1912). Lombroso's Theory of Crime. *Journal of Criminal Law and Criminology* 2 (5), Article 6, 716–723.

Evans, D. (1996). *An Introductory Dictionary of Lacanian Psychoanalysis*. London: Routledge.

Feingold, M. (2003). *The New Science and Jesuit Science: Seventeenth Century Perspectives*. Netherlands: Kluwer.

Fink, B. (2006). Notes to "A Theoretical Introduction to the Function of Psychoanalysis in Criminology." In J. Lacan (ed.), *Écrits: The First Complete Edition in English*. Trans. B. Fink. London and New York: Norton & Co., 776–779.

Finocchiaro, M. A. (2005). *Retrying Galileo, 1633–1992*. Berkley, CA and London: University of California Press.

Freud, S. (1896). *The Neuro-Psychoses of Defence*. S.E. III, 43–68.

Freud, S. (1900). *The Interpretation of Dreams*. S.E., IV & V.

Freud, S. (1903). Totem and Taboo. S.E., XIII, 1–163

Freud, S. (1907). *Obsessive Actions and Religious Practices*. S.E., IX, 117–127.

Freud, S. (1915). *Instincts and their Vicissitudes*. S.E., XIV, 109–140.

Freud, S. (1917). *Mourning and Melancholia*. S.E., XIV, 239–258.

Freud, S. (1921). Identification. In *Group Psychology and the Analysis of the Ego*. S.E., XVIII, 105–110.

Freud, S. (1923). *The Ego and the Id*. S.E., IXX, 3–66.

Freud, S. (1923). The Ego and Superego. In *The Ego and the Id*. S.E., IXX, 28–39.

Freud, S. (1925). Preface to Aichhorn's *Wayward Youth*. S.E., IXX, 273–278.

Freud, S. (1927). *The Future of an Illusion*. S.E., XXI, 5–58.

Freud, S. (1928). *Dostoyevsky and Parricide*. S.E., XXI, 175–198.

Freud, S. (1937). *Analysis Terminable and Interminable*. S.E., XXIII, 209–254.

Friedlander, K. (1947). *The Psychoanalytic Approach to Juvenile Delinquency: Theory, Case-Studies, Treatment*. London: RKP

Frisbie, T. (1996). Zuni. *Encyclopaedia of World Cultures*. www.encyclopedia.com/topic/Zuni.aspx.

Gilbert, G. M. (1947/1995). *Nuremberg Diary*. New York: Farra Straus. First Da Capo Press.

Gilbert, G. M. (1979). *The Psychology of Dictatorship: Based on an Examination of the Leaders of Nazi Germany*. Greenwood Press.

Glover, E. (1956/2010). *On the Early Development of Mind*. London: New Brunswick and Transaction Publishers.

Goldman, I., & Mead, M. (1937/1961). *Cooperation and Competition Among Primitive Peoples*. New York: McGraw Hill.

Healy, W. (1915). *The Individual Delinquent: A Text-Book of Diagnosis and Prognosis for All Concerned in Understanding Offenders*. Boston: Little Brown.

Hesnard, M. (1949). *L'univers morbide de la faute*. Paris: PUF.

Hu, Hsien Chin. (1944). The Chinese Concept of Face. *American Anthropologist* 46 (1), 45–64.

Isroff, J., Reeves, C., & Lamptman, B. (2005). *Donald Winnicott and John Bowlby: Personal and Professional Perspectives*. London: Karnac.

Johnson, D. M. (2011). *Socrates and Athens*. Cambridge University Press.

Kain, P. J. (2005). *Hegel and the Other: A Study of the Phenomenology of Spirit*. New York: SUNY.

Kant, I. (1787). *Critique of Pure Reason*. Cambridge Edition of the Works of Immanuel Kant. Trans. and eds. P. Guyer & A. W. Wood. C.U.P.

Keehn, J. D. (1979). *Origins of Madness: Psychopathology in Animal Life*. London: Pergamon Press.

Klein, M. (1921/1988). The Development of a Child. In *Love, Guilt and Reparation and Other Works 1921–1945*. London: Vintage.

Klein, M. (1926). The Psychological Principles of Early Analysis. In *Love, Guilt and Reparation and Other Works 1921–1945*. London: Vintage.

Klosko, G. (1984). The Insufficiency of Reason in Plato's Gorgias. *The Western Political Quarterly* 36(4), (Dec., 1983), 579–595.

Kojéve, A. (1969). *An Introduction to the Reading of Hegel: Lectures on the Phenomenology of Spirit*. London: Basic Books.

Kroeber, A. L. (1991/1948). *Zuni Kin and Clan*. NY: The American Museum of Natural History. Original work published in 1917.

Kutter, P. (2013). *A Guide to Psychoanalysis throughout the World. Volume I: Europe*. Friedrich Frommann Verlag.

Lacan, J. (1932/1975 rpt). *De la psychoses paranoïaque dans ses rapports avec la personnalité*, 2nd ed. Paris: Seuil.

Lacan, J. (1933). Le problème du style et al conception psychiatrique des formes paranoïaques de l'expérience. *Le Minotaure* 1, 68–69.

Lacan, J. (1933). Motifs du crime paranoïaque: Le crime des soeurs Papin. *Le Minotaure* 3/4, 25–28.

Lacan, J. (1936). Beyond the "Reality Principle". In *Écrits: The First Complete Edition in English*. Trans. B. Fink. London and New York: Norton & Co., 2006, 58–74.

Lacan, J. (1938). *La Famille: Les complexes familiaux dans la formation de l'individu*. Trans. C. Gallagher as: *Family Complexes in the Formation of the Individual*. Available to read at www.lacaninireland.com.

Lacan, J. (1948). Aggressiveness in Psychoanalysis. In *Écrits: The First Complete Edition in English*. Trans. B. Fink. London and New York: Norton & Co., 2006, 82–101.

Lacan, J. (1949). The Mirror Stage as Formative of the *I* Function as Revealed in Psychoanalytic Experience. In *Écrits: The First Complete Edition in English*. Trans. B. Fink. London and New York: Norton & Co., 2006, 75–81.

Lacan, J. (1950). A Theoretical Introduction to the Functions of Psychoanalysis in Criminology. In *Écrits: The First Complete Edition in English*. Trans. B. Fink. London and New York: Norton & Co., 2006, 102–122.

Lacan, J. (2006). On My Antecedents. In *Écrits: The First Complete Edition in English*. Trans. B. Fink. London and New York: Norton & Co., 2006, 51–57.

Lacan, J. (1957). The Direction of the Treatment and the Principles of its Power. In *Écrits: The First Complete Edition in English*. Trans. B. Fink. London and New York: Norton & Co., 2006, 489–542.

Lacan, J. (1994). *The Four Fundamental Concepts of Psychoanalysis*. Trans. A. Sheridan. Ed. J.-A. Miller. Harmondsworth: Penguin Books.

Lagache, D. (1993/1948). Contribution to the Psychology of Criminal Behaviour: Psychoanalytic Commentary on an Expert's Report. In E. Holder (trans/ed.), *The Work of Daniel Lagache: Selected Writings 1938–1964*. London: Karnac.

Laplanche, J., & Pontalis, J.-B. (1988). *The Language of Psychoanalysis*. London: Karnac.

Malinowski, B. (1926/1985). *Crime and Custom in Savage Society*. New York: Harcourt, Brace & Co.

Merrill, B. L. (2003). *Athanasius Kircher (1603–1680) Jesuit Scholar*. Connecticut: Martino Publications.

Moore, G. (2011). *Politics of the Gift: Exchanges in Post-Structuralism*. Edinburgh: Edinburgh University Press.

Neill, C. (2011). *Lacanian Ethics and the Assumption of Subjectivity*. London: Palgrave Macmillan.

Nietzche, F. (1883/1999). *Thus Spake Zarathustra*. Trans. T. Common. New York: Dover Thrift Publications.

Nietzche, F. (2001). *The Gay Science*. Cambridge Texts in the History of Philosophy. Ed. B. Williams, Trans. J. Nauckhoff. Cambridge: C.U.P.

Nobus, D. (2000). *Jacques Lacan and the Freudian Practice of Psychoanalysis*. London: Routledge.

Pavlov, I. P. (1927). Conditioned Reflexes: An Investigation of the Physiological Activity of the Cerebral Cortex. Trans. and Ed. G.V. Anrep. London: Oxford University Press.

Plato. *Gorgias*.

Rajali, D. M. (2007). *Torture and Democracy*. Princeton: Princeton University Press.

Regnault, F. (1998). Hegel's Master and Slave Dialectic. London Society of the New Lacanian School. http://londonsociety-nls.org.uk/Publications/002/Regnault-Francois_Hegels-Master-and-Slave-Dialectic.pdf.

Roudinesco, E. (1999). *Jacques Lacan*. Cambridge: Polity Press.

Tardé, G. (2001/1912). *Penal Philosophy*. New Jersey: Little, Brown & Co.

Thomas, H. (1961). *The Spanish Civil War*. London: Eyre & Spottiswoode.

Torrino. (1888). Some Recent Italian Psychological Literature. In A. F. Chamberlain (1900) *American Journal of Psychology*, 11. Available on JSTOR.

Vallon, C. and Genil-Perrin, G. (1912). *Crime et Altruisme*. Lyon: Konig.

Wittel, F. (1949). The Ego of the Adolescent. In K. R. Eissler (ed.), *Searchlights on Delinquency*. New York: International University Press.

Wittgenstein, L. (1922/2009). *Tractatus Logico-Philosophicus*. New York: Cosimo Books.

Wolff, R. (2014). Plato Tutorials. Available at http://robertpaulwolff.blogspot.ie/.

Wolpe, J. (1958). *Psychotherapy by Reciprocal Inhibition*. Stanford University Press.

Zafiropoulos, M. (2010). *Lacan and Lévi-Strauss or The Return to Freud (1951–1957)*. CFAR. London: Karnac.

Žižek, S. (2006). *How to Read Lacan*. London: Granta.

8

PRESENTATION ON PSYCHICAL CAUSALITY

Mattias Desmet

Introduction

'Presentation on Psychical Causality' is a written version of a presentation given in 1946 at the psychiatric conference of Bonneval, France. This conference was organized by Henry Ey, one of France's leading psychiatrists at that time and a former fellow student and friend of Lacan. The audience consisted of about 30 people from the psychiatric world, who were often involved in discussions of themes surrounding the causality of madness, as they continued at Bonneval for several years. Lacan's presentation was the first one to be given at the three-day conference. It was originally published together with all other presentations (and associated discussions), in a volume entitled 'Le problème de la psycho-genèse des névroses et des psychoses' ('The problem of the psychogenesis of neurosis and psychosis,' Ey, 1946). Reading this volume, in particular Ey's introductory text (Ey, 1946, pp. 9–20) and his reply to Lacan's presentation (Ey, 1946, pp. 55–60), is recommended for those interested in knowing more about the intellectual climate in which Lacan gave his presentation.

The question at stake at the conference was quite straightforward: Are the causes of madness biological or psychological in nature? The point of departure for all presentations at the conference was a text in which Ey defined his position with respect to this question (Ey, 1946, pp. 9–20). He maintains in this text that he rejects 'all psychological causality of psychopathology' (Ey, 1946, p. 10) and that the cause of madness is always a 'morbid organical process' (Ey, 1946, p. 20). As we will learn, this statement in the end turns out to be as ambiguous as it seems clear-cut.

Lacan's presentation is composed of three parts. Part one presents a critical scrutiny of Ey's organo-dynamic theory on the causality of madness, leading to a radical rejection of it. In part two, Lacan offers an alternative theory in which he situates the causes of madness on the psychological level. In part three, finally, Lacan discusses the mechanisms at work in psychological causality in a more general sense, that is, not limited to the phenomenon of madness. The theory presented in parts two and three is typical for what is usually called the

DOI: 10.4324/9781003368649-9

imaginary period of his work. As such, it resembles – sometimes quite literally – what was put forward in earlier writings, such as his doctoral thesis and his article on the mirror stage. Nowhere else in his oeuvre, however, does Lacan treat the issue of psychological causality in such a systematic and explicit way. If one reads the text in an open-minded way, one realizes that what is said there remains highly controversial and remains a challenge to all those interested in the question of psychical causality.

Few – maybe even among those who call themselves Lacanian analysts – will follow Lacan where he concludes that there is no correlation between 'the differentiation of the nervous system and the wealth of psychical manifestations' (see part 3, paragraph 83). If psychological experience is not caused by the nervous system, where does it come from? Is it perhaps 'suspended in air,' to use the words of Ey (1946, p. 13)? It's beyond the scope of this paper to go into this question – be it from a philosophical or any other perspective – and even less to formulate an answer. Rather, I open up the gaping hole of the question a bit more by referring to a case study – published in *Science* (Lewin, 1980) under the title 'Is Your Brain Really Necessary?' – on a patient of whom over 95% of the brain tissue was atrophied, while his psychological functioning remained completely intact, to the extent of scoring 126 on an IQ test.

From the beginning until the end of the text, it is clear that Lacan conceives the psychical apparatus in terms of a structured set of *imagos* or *ideal identifications*. These identifications are 'irreducible phenomena' (see part 3, paragraph 64). In no way can they be traced back to any other level, for example, the level of neurobiological functioning. They deserve to be qualified as monads and their status in psychology is comparable to the status of the atom in classical physics (see part 3, paragraph 61). As such, the imagos are to be considered the true and ultimate object of psychology. From 1950 onwards, Lacan radically moved the focal point of psychical life from the imaginary to the symbolic. In *Seminar on The Purloined Letter*, for example, one of his major texts of his symbolic period, Lacan says: 'The teaching of this seminar is designed to maintain that imaginary effects, far from representing the core of analytic experience, give us nothing of any consistency unless they are related to the symbolic chain that binds and orients them' (Lacan, 1966, [2006], p. 6). Later again, Lacan will move from the symbolic to the object *a*, the part of subjective experience that perpetually escapes symbolization and thus remains 'real.'

This doesn't detract from the fact that what Lacan has to tell us about the action and effects of imagos for understanding psychical experience is irreplaceable. While Lacan's theory holds that the imaginary is embedded in a symbolic framework, which in its turn, gravitates around and emanates from a real core, it remains an order of psychical determination that cannot be reduced to either the symbolic or the real. Therefore, Lacan's writings of the imaginary period by no means are rendered redundant by his later work.

'Presentation on psychical causality' is a multi-layered text *par excellence*: Lacan criticizes Ey's theory; Ey's theory elaborates on Huglings Jackson's theory; Jackson reacted against mechanist conceptions of neurological functioning; mechanist theories reacted against dualism, and so on. Before I enter into a paragraph-by-paragraph elucidation of Lacan's presentation, I give a rudimentary overview of these different conceptual layers, focusing particularly on the theories of Ey and Jackson.

The organo-dynamic theories of Jackson and Ey

In the 17th and 18th centuries, the medieval concept of man gave way to Cartesian dualism and, later on, to mechanist conceptions. The basic idea of dualism is well-known: there are two, more or less independent ontological givens: on the one hand, we have phenomena with a certain extension in space, governed by the laws of classical mechanics; on the other hand, we have the level of thinking, governed by moral laws. Mechanism, on the contrary, denies the existence of the plan of thinking, or at least considers it to be no more than an epiphenomenon of the plan of extension. Whatever is usually referred to as soul and spirit, then, is considered a not intended, arbitrary side effect of mechanical interactions between physical, spatially extended particles (e.g., La Mettrie, 1747).

The rise of psychiatry as an academic discipline at the beginning of the 19th century more or less coincides with the rise of mechanist conceptions of psychical life. From then on, madness is increasingly conceived as a problem of the body. It is removed from the sphere of morality, under the firm conviction that ultimately, it can be understood in terms of a mechanical deficit of the brain. In this context, it is interesting to note that founders of psychiatry, such as Pinel and Esquirol, often stressed the importance of 'moral treatment,' but, nevertheless, radically situated the cause of madness at the level of the brain (Ey, 1975, pp. 19–20). Mechanist thinking in psychiatry manifested as the anatomo-pathological paradigm, striving for 'botanical' nomenclatures in which specific psychiatric disorders are linked to specific organic-mechanical deficits in the nervous system. It is clear that the contemporary DSM project is attracted by the same ideal.

Huglings Jackson, from the beginning of his career in the middle of the 19th century, passionately disagreed with the rigid mechanist conceptions in neurology and psychiatry. He disagreed with the idea that the brain was a 'dead,' static mechanic. Inspired by Darwin's theory of evolution, he argued in favor of a dynamic conception of the brain and put forward a conception of an organism in which the force of evolution constantly re-creates and re-integrates the organic structures so as to create a new organism that functions at an ever higher, more adaptive level. Jackson's ideas were new in the field of neurology and psychiatry. Today, if we conceive the different parts of our brain in terms of lower and higher brain structures and in terms of reptile, mammal, and primate brains, then we owe this in a certain respect to Jackson.

In Jackson's view, the evolutionary order of appearance of the different forms of existence – first unanimated matter, then plants, animals, and man – is by no means arbitrary. The evolutionary process proceeds in a specific direction: it creates ever less strictly determined, or ever more free, forms of existence. Unanimated objects – stones, water, air – are more strictly determined and less free than plants. While a stone has no freedom and can only passively undergo its environment, a plant can rotate its flowers toward the sun and close its leaves when the air is too dry. In other words, a plant has a certain capacity to adapt to the surrounding reality in function of its survival. In turn, plants are less free than animals, which, for example, can relocate themselves when they are attacked.

Man, then, is the culmination point of the evolutionary process. In man, evolution created the organic structures – more specifically, the cortex – that gave rise to human consciousness. In line with classical theories on the different psychological faculties, Jackson distinguishes four so-called *higher functions* in consciousness, namely will, memory, reason, and emotion. The Ego coordinates the actions of these higher functions. In its struggle to adapt the organism to the environment, it constantly observes and evaluates reality to decide which action is needed. To execute the required action, the Ego subsequently commands the motoric system (Ey, 1975, p. 97). Human consciousness, or the Ego, is considered the ultimate manifestation of the evolutionary force, and thus, to be completely free and undetermined.

Each specific higher function of the Ego is related to a specific brain region. If these brain regions are damaged (due to a physical, biological, chemical, etc. agent), the corresponding higher function fails, or, in Jackson's discourse, 'dissolves.' In this case, the organism lapses into more primitive modes of functioning associated with more primitive evolutionary phases. What seems a bit paradoxical in Jackson's theory is that the Ego emanates from the structures of the brain, and at the same time is considered to be completely free. Jackson, like Ey, holds that consciousness and the Ego need specific brain structures to manifest, but once they do, they are completely free and not determined by these brain structures.

By means of this theory, Jackson indeed succeeds in avoiding the rigidity of mechanist conceptions on the causes of psychical experience in general and madness in particular. The link between the causal organic deficit and the ensuing symptoms is less direct (Ey, 1975, p. 60). Mechanist theory supposes that all symptoms of madness – negative (everything a madman cannot do that a normal man can do) as well as positive (everything a madman does that a normal man doesn't, e.g., hallucinations, delusions, bizarre behavior) – are strictly determined by specific mechanical defects in the brain. Jackson, on the contrary, holds that only negative symptoms are the direct consequence of mechanical deficits. Positive symptoms, on the other hand, actually have nothing to do with a mechanical deficit. They are determined by the activity of a more primitive, but healthy-functioning brain area that is unleashed by the defect of the higher brain region (e.g., Hughlings Jackson, 1884, in Ey, 1936, p. 1). Compare it to the collapse of the Roman Empire: ceasing the provision of fresh water through the aqueducts is a negative symptom caused by the collapse; the fact that descendants of barbarian tribes re-manifested old rites is a positive symptom. In this respect, the theory of Jackson is more plausible than mechanist theories. It's hard to imagine, after all, that a broken mechanic can strictly determine a phenomenon as complex and well-organized as a delusion.

Ey was directly inspired by Jackson. Ey belonged to the vitalist medical school of Montpellier and as such, he supposed the activity of a creative, vital force in nature. This force is the motor of the ever-creative process of evolution. In most respects, Ey's conception of the evolutionary process and the way it creates new and higher – less determined and more free – organisms is quite similar to Jackson's theory. The most important contribution Ey made to Jackson's theory was probably the introduction of a psychoanalytically inspired personality concept.

Personality – which, to Ey, seems to be more or less synonymous with the Ego – has both an energetic aspect and a historical aspect. In the first place, it is considered an energetic system that constantly distributes the energy available to the organism. This happens in such a way that the organism's chances of survival are maximized. As the personality develops, however, it progressively changes survival strategies. Ey refers to the succession of strategies as 'the psychical trajectory' (Ey, 1946, pp. 12–13) of a personality. The earliest, most primitive adaptive strategies are not lost. They are stored somewhere in the organism and form the deeper layers of personality. Furthermore, the different strategies are not experienced as completely isolated from each other. There is a sense of continuity in the personality since it integrates and connects all the different phases of the adaptive struggle to each other in one global story, associated with global gestalts and images of the organism.

The complete personality organization is inscribed in the brain. As it develops throughout the different phases of the organism's adaptation to reality, it changes the brain. It creates new brain structures from which new, ever more adaptive psychical activity emanates. To Ey, as explained above, psychic activity is dependent on certain brain structures, but it is not determined by them. There is something typically vitalist in Ey's view on determination. Ey says the following about this:

> The world appears to us as a series of hierarchical forms: the world of matter ruled by the laws of physics, the world of life ruled by the laws of biology, and finally, the psychical world which is the object of psychology. Nor is the world of biology reducible to physics, nor is the psychological reducible to the biological. Each of these structures is the necessary but not the sufficient condition for the structure that is superior to it. What thus characterizes the psyche? It is the set of functions that guarantee a personal adaptation to reality. Psychical life

thus introduces in the world a type of causality that is truly different from physical causality and instinctive tendencies. (Ey, 1946, p. 12; author's translation)

In general, Ey distinguishes three major, historical layers in personality (Ey, 1930, pp. 20–21). The first layer consists of what he calls the primitive and elementary instrumental functions a child acquires first, such as motoric habit and language (see also Ey, Ajuriaguerra, & Hécaen, 1947, p. 12). The second layer represents phenomena such as play, dreaming, and fantasy. At the third and highest level of the personality – also called the 'psychical field' – we find the higher functions of an organism (Ey, Ajuriaguerra, & Hécaen, 1947, p. 13). These functions concern all conscious mental activity that evaluates reality and determines which actions have to be undertaken to adapt the organism to the environment, ranging from intentional motoric actions needed to manipulate the environment to the intentional use of discourse to persuade others in the function of social adaptation. At the highest level of personality, man is considered the pure manifestation of the vital force, and as such, completely free.

In line with Jackson's theory, Ey distinguished two major types of pathologies of the brain (Ey, Ajuriaguerra, & Hécaen, 1947, pp. 12–13). First, there are the so-called *local dissolutions*, i.e., dissolutions of the lower, primitive, and instrumental functions of the personality that are hypothesized to be situated in local, specific brain structures. Such dissolutions are supposed to be the object of neurology. Second, there are the *global* or *uniform* dissolutions. These dissolutions affect the higher – or *apical* – functions of the organism, i.e., the functions of the personality that are responsible for the distribution of energy in the function of the adaptation of the organism to the environment. According to Ey, these functions are not located in one specific brain area, and the organic factors that are responsible for the global dissolutions, therefore, are global deteriorations of the brain (Ey, Ajuriaguerra, & Hécaen, 1947, p. 13).

It is important to note in all of this that Ey differentiated between the *cause* of madness and the *determinants* of madness. In line with Jackson's view about the determination of negative and positive symptoms of madness, Ey holds that an organic factor is responsible for the decay of the higher functions (i.e., the negative symptoms of madness), but that the positive symptoms that arise as a consequence of it are determined by the historical, psychical trajectory of the personality. In other words, just like the negative symptoms, the positive symptoms are *caused* by organic decay of the brain but *determined* by the complex life history of the patient.

Also like Jackson, Ey thus holds that the causes of psychopathology are always organic in nature. In his introductory text, Ey (1946, p. 9) clearly formulates two basic statements: (1) the causes of psychopathology are always organic in nature; (2) normal psychical activity, on the other hand, is caused by psychical factors, i.e., it cannot be reduced to the organic. Although Ey more or less claims that these statements are inductively based on 'objective truths' (e.g., Ey, 1946, p. 55), it seems they are rather direct deductive consequences of his axiomatic, vitalist point of departure. As a vitalist, Ey equals psychological activity with the manifestation of the free activity of the vital force. As such, it is limited to conscious, intentional mental acts (see also Rouart, in Ey, 1946, pp. 83–85). Psychopathology, on the contrary, is radically defined as un-free activity, a prison for the soul (Ey, 1946, p. 20). Since psychical activity liberates and psychopathology imprisons, psychical activity cannot cause psychopathology. Consequently, psychopathology must have organic causes.

Where Ey puts forward clinical arguments for the organic causation of madness, they are usually not very convincing. He refers, for example, to the fact that psychotherapeutic treatment of madness always stumbles upon a kernel that resists all understanding. He concludes therefore that this kernel must be organic in nature and that it must be the ultimate cause of the pathology of the patient (Ey, 1946, p. 19). Ey doesn't seem to take into consideration that there might be psychical objects that resist understanding as well (see also Rouart, in Ey, 1946, p. 85). Remarkably, in this light, however, this doesn't keep him from advising psychotherapy to each and everyone who suffers from psychopathology (Ey, 1946, p. 119).

This concise overview of the theories of Jackson and Ey should allow us to begin the paragraph-by-paragraph exegesis of Lacan's presentation. In doing so, we will paraphrase the paragraphs of the original text, thus putting the often obscure conceptual twists and turns in a different light. This means that we won't *explain* the original text or present a thorough conceptual analysis of it. In referring to Lacan's text, we refer both to the page numbers of the original French text (found in the margin in the English translation) and to the paragraph numbers.

'Presentation on psychical causality:' Paragraph-by-paragraph

The short introductory paragraph on top of the first page situates the presentation in the context of the Conference of Bonneval and refers the reader to the small volume (Ey, 1946) in which all presentations made at the conference are published (123).

1: Criticism of an organicist theory of madness: Henry Ey's organo-dynamism

Lacan introduces his presentation by referring to the invitation by Henri Ey. He characterizes his position with respect to the causality of madness as a radical one. What he puts forward in this presentation, indeed, is not a safe, cautious position, holding, for example, that madness is caused by 'a little bit of everything,' for example, a mix of biological, psychological, and sociological causes. On the contrary, he rather radically situates the cause of madness at the psychical level. This brings a twofold position: on the one hand, he must elucidate this radical position, which is never easy, and on the other hand, he must do so in the context of a discussion he didn't contribute to, and to an audience that is not acquainted with his theory. He thus warns the audience: they should not expect to understand everything (123/1).

Lacan tells the public that he avoided speaking in public for several years because of the war and the dominance of the Nazis. He wonders whether this means that he failed to live up to the duty to speak the truth. In other words, was he a coward during the war? He leaves it to the audience to judge whether or not the research he will present may suffer from a potential lack of truthfulness. On first impression, this paragraph seems rather redundant, a little bit of 'spielerei' before getting to the point. However, as we will see in the rest of the presentation, the relationship between the subject and its truth is precisely what, according to Lacan, is at stake in the causality of madness (123/2).

In any case, Lacan says, he doesn't fail to live up to the requirements of truth at the present day, since he takes pleasure in defending it at the conference (123/1–123/3).

Lacan brings a tribute to the work of Ey. At the same time, he expresses his surprise that they now have opposite opinions on the causality of madness, while initially, they rather agreed on it. With the latter, he refers to their student years, when both Ey and he passionately rejected mechanist theories on madness in favor of psychological theories (e.g., Ey, 1946, p. 55) (124/2).

According to Lacan, Ey progressively went in the wrong direction since he published his article in which he proposed to apply the principle of Jackson in psychiatry (Ey, 1936). From then on, the theory of Ey became more and more organicist in nature (124/3).

Ey's organo-dynamism is essentially the same as organicism, which means that in the end, mental problems are held to be strictly determined by the laws of classical physics (124/4).[1]

Although Ey makes organicism more dynamic and enriches it with concepts from gestalt psychology, his theory is nevertheless not fundamentally different from the theory of mechanists *pur sang* like Clérambault. This doesn't mean, however, that he considers the theory of Ey worthless, since he values the theory of Clérambault. The latter also appears later on in this presentation, where he calls Clérambault 'his only master in psychiatry' (see part 2, paragraph 30) (124/5).

Organicism, by definition, situates the cause of psychopathology in the organism. In Cartesian terms, the organism belongs to the extended world, governed by the laws of mechanics. All psychical functions described by Ey – energetic as well as instrumental functions – are conceived in terms of anatomical and organic/chemical processes. Hence Lacan's claim in the previous paragraph that Ey's theory is similar to the mechanist theory of Clérambault (124/6–125/1).[2]

Lacan announces that he will show what the difference is between his thinking about the causes of madness and Ey's (125/2).

He will prove that the theory of Ey doesn't have the characteristics of 'a true idea' (125/3).

Lacan expects that the reader might be surprised that he evokes the notion of 'truth.' This notion is particularly troublesome, especially since the pragmatists claimed that truth only exists in a utilitarian sense: a statement is only true insofar as you can use it for some purpose. However, Lacan states that you can't really understand the phenomenon of madness if you don't see how it relates to the phenomenon of truth. It is precisely because the phenomenon of madness is related to the phenomenon of truth, that madness touches the very being of man. In madness, man manifests a certain meaningful truth that touches the essence of his being (125/4).

Lacan refers to Spinoza to elucidate what he means by a true idea: *A true idea must be in accordance with what is ideated.* Thus, if you construct a theory to understand the experience of madness, the theory must be in accordance with this experience, i.e., the theory must really grasp the experience and reflect its nature (125/5).

Ey's doctrine fails to meet the criteria of a true idea. The further Ey develops his theory, the less it grasps the experience of madness. This implies that it cannot solve the problem it wanted to solve (125/6).

This problem concerns the fact that neurology and psychiatry are *limited.* All medical specialisms are limited, but in the case of psychiatry (and to a lesser extent also neurology), the limitations are particularly problematic because of the special nature of its object, namely madness. Lacan praises Ey at this point for continuing to use the term madness, even if this antique term stinks a bit for those who would like to consider madness as a disease like any other disease. These people would prefer to use a more medical term, and thus include it in the biomedical discourse through which they aspire to explain all human suffering. In other words, they want to reduce all suffering to the same *omnitudo realitatis*, which is a Latin term Kant uses in Chapter 22 of his *Critique of Pure Reason* to indicate a transcendental ideal that determines every aspect of every particular phenomenon (125/7).

Are the insane really comparable to patients suffering from other diseases? Is the only difference that the insane are locked away while other patients are simply hospitalized? Is it thus only a difference in the way they are (socially) treated? Or is there a real, essential (scientific) difference as well (125/8–126/1)?

While Ey started out well and initially seemed to confirm the difference between madness and other diseases, he progressively removed himself from the right track by adopting the theoretical principles of Jackson. The theory of Jackson explicitly aims to equate psychiatric problems with neurological problems. A defect at the level of the brain is considered to be the cause of both types of problems. More specifically, neurological problems would be the consequence of local brain lesions; psychiatric problems would be the consequence of global lesions (see introduction). Empirical examination of this theory by Hécaen, Follin, and Bonnafée[3] (se Ey, Ajuriaguerra, & Hécaen, 1947, pp. 33–80, presentation by Ajuriaguerra and Hécaen at the 1943 conference of Bonneval) doesn't really confirm this idea, however. They present a series of clinical observations disconfirming the hypothesis that neurological problems (e.g., aphasia, functional pain, hallucinosis, agnosia) are caused by local lesions and psychiatric problems (e.g., dementia, hypochondria, hallucinations, delusions) by global lesions (126/2).[4]

Lacan puts forward another empirical observation disconfirming the theory of Ey. He refers to the famous single case study presented by Gelb and Goldstein on a patient who suffered from a global mental and perceptual dysfunctioning as a consequence of a local brain lesion (destruction of both calcarine sulci).[5] This is exactly the opposite of what Ey's theory predicts (126/3).

The symptomatology of this patient was truly global. Over and above the symptoms listed in the previous paragraph, there was also a quite dramatic change in the level of sexual functioning (126/4).

Thus, there is a very clear gap here between the organic lesion, which is *local* in nature (i.e., situated at a very specific place at the back of the head, namely the calcarines in the visual cortex), and the clinical symptomatic picture that is *global* and *apical* in nature (i.e., global loss of the apical, or superior, personality-related functions). This case therefore falsifies Ey's theory – which predicts that the consequence of a local lesion would be the local loss of a *specific* (and not a global) psychological function – in the most straightforward way (126/5).

Furthermore, Ey's theory doesn't allow for a differentiation between the patient of Gelb and Goldstein and a madman. According to Ey, madness equals the decay of the global and apical, personality related functions. This is exactly what this patient suffers from. Nevertheless, it is clear that this patient is *not* a madman. What then, Lacan wonders, is the difference according to Ey? Lacan anticipates Ey's possible answer. Perhaps Ey would say that this man distinguishes himself from a madman because a part of his personality remained intact. Lacan rejects this argument by enlisting a number of observations that conflict with it (126/6–127/1).

Lacan repeats the question: In what respect can Ey distinguish this patient from a fool? If Ey can't answer the question, he will try to do so himself (127/2).

Lacan anticipates another possible answer for Ey. This patient might differ from a madman in that the psychological problems are specific, *noetic* (more or less a synonym of *cognitive*) problems. However, this argument doesn't hold, since a noetic problem, in Ey's terms, refers to a global dissolution (which Ey holds to be typical for madness and not for neurological disorders) (127/3).

Besides the fact that Ey's theory seems to be falsified by clinical observations, it is also internally inconsistent. On the one hand, Ey explicitly states that madness is caused by an organic lesion. On the other hand, some parts of Ey's theory strongly suggest it is the reaction of the personality that is typical for madness.[6] Lacan argues that the more Ey rejects psychological causality, the more he elaborates a theory on 'psychological activity' that is full of contradictions (127/4). This is elaborated further in the following paragraphs, especially in the last paragraph of page 129, which carries over to page 130.

From this paragraph onwards, Lacan criticizes the introductory text of Ey (Ey, 1946, pp. 9–20) paragraph-by-paragraph. First, he criticizes the way in which Ey systematically undermines the arguments in favor of the psychological causality of psychopathology. Ey (1946, pp. 10–12) argues that neither emotional shock, nor the unconscious effects of trauma or pathogenic suggestion prove that psychical causality exists. The latter, in particular, raises eyebrows. Pathogenic suggestion – as demonstrated by Charcot, among others – refers to the induction of hysterical symptoms by means of hypnotic suggestion. As such, it is usually considered a strong argument in favor of psychical causality, even by the most fanatic organicists. Ey, however, suggests (see Ey, 1946, p. 11) that people sensitive to pathogenic suggestion must be organically predisposed to be so since hysterical symptoms cannot be induced by hypnosis in *everybody* (127/5).

Another argument in favor of psychological causality that is dismissed by Ey is the (psychoanalytic) idea that psychopathology is caused by a regression of Ego functioning. According to Ey, however, this doesn't hold, since the regression of the Ego, in the final analysis, is also caused by organic dissolutions (127/6–128/1).

Lacan mocks Ey, saying that it is as easy for him to say that all these examples illustrate 'everything except psychological causality' (Ey, 1946, p. 11) than it is for us to observe that he is not embarrassed to do so without actually giving any arguments at all (128/2).[7]

Lacan questions Ey's (1946, p. 11) claims that all theories that maintain that psychopathology is caused by psychical factors could do so on Cartesian grounds. According to Ey, Descartes considered the psychical level to be completely independent of the body. Hence, scholars inspired by Descartes could not do anything other than suppose that psychological problems have psychological causes, since the independence of body and soul precluded a priori consideration of bodily (organic) causes. On this point, Lacan remarks that Descartes did not consider body and soul to be completely independent at all. For Descartes, all errors at the level of thinking are caused by bodily passions. Thus, the psychical level is directly related to the level of the body. Actually, Lacan remarks, Ey could easily have used this aspect of Descartes' theory *in support* of his own theory, which similarly holds that all troubles at the level of the psyche are caused by the body (the organism) (128/3).

The next paragraph continues the line of reasoning and is written in a very sharp, almost contemptuous tone. Lacan concludes that it is better that Ey doesn't consider his theory in line with Cartesian theory. Ey's psychophysiological parallelism (i.e., the idea that each specific psychological experience is correlated to a specific physiological process in the brain) is closer to the naïve parallelism of Hippolyte Taine than to the sublime parallelism of Spinoza. Moreover, the idea that Ey would claim that his naïve parallelism is similar to

Descartes' lofty conceptions on the parallel existence of the plan of extension and the plan of thinking (i.e., 'the fundamental Cartesian intuition,' see Ey, 1946, p. 11) clearly makes Lacan shiver with aversion. In this case, Lacan holds, we would have to conclude that the influence of Jackson on Ey was even more dramatic than previously thought (128/4).

Lacan continues in the same tone. After having discredited the psychogenetic theories, Ey presents his own dualistic theory, which states that mental disease is an insult and a fetter to freedom and thus cannot be caused by free, psychical activity (128/5).

The dualism of Ey seems to be particularly troublesome since it equates 'freedom' with 'free play.' If there *is* such a thing as freedom for a human being, it has nothing to do with being able to do anything you want (i.e., having free play). Ey's position is also characterized by the use of the word 'deployment.' Psychical life 'deploys' the intrinsic capacities of the organism in a Darwinian sense: it adapts the organism maximally to reality (128/6).

Together with Kurt Goldstein, Ey holds that 'being' is similar to 'integration.' Everything that exists, exists because it integrates. Goldstein was one of the first biologists who argued in favor of a holistic conception of the brain, holding that the functioning of the brain system cannot be reduced to interactions between its physio-chemical parts (Goldstein, 1940, p. 7), but rather only becomes comprehensible from the global Gestalts that determine the organism as a whole and that integrates all its different parts (Goldstein, 1940, p. 401). Ey (e.g., 1946, p. 12) similarly holds that an organism is always an integration of structures, such as physical (e.g., molecular structures of brain cells), biological (e.g., organs), and psychical structures (e.g., the personality). The psychical structure is the superior structure, which integrates all lower structures. It coordinates all actions the organism has to take to adapt (as a whole) to the environment. In this integrated organism, everything has adaptive ends, even the existential problems. It is clear that Lacan doesn't think highly of this attempt of Ey to integrate all these different layers of discourse (physics, biology, psychology, etc.) into one global theory. In the final sentence of this paragraph, he scorns Ey's use of the term 'dialectical hierarchism,' which shows that Ey really doesn't understand Hegel's use of the term 'dialectic' (128/7–129/1).

Although the discourse of Ey is fascinating, it crushes both the truth about the psyche and madness (129/2).

Lacan continues, always in the same, ridiculing tone. What Ey says about psychical activity must make man feel like a visionary prince, who has a perfectly accurate perception of the one and only reality, always in control, deciding in a sovereign way what action to take to adapt to that reality. If you want to believe that this really is the condition of man, you must ignore a lot. It reminds Lacan of the well-known Vaudois proverb: 'Nothing is impossible for men; and that what he can't do, he ignores.' In line with Freud – who claimed that the Ego is not the master in its own house – Lacan holds that the human subject, rather, is fundamentally ex-centric and *out of control*. It is fundamentally subjected to the action of the imagos, a slave of its ideal identifications rather than a visionary prince. In the second half of this paragraph, Lacan refers to three chapters of Ey's introductory text – chapters respectively entitled 'The psychical trajectory' (Ey, 1946, pp. 12–13), 'The psychical field' (Ey, 1947, p. 13), and 'The trajectory in the field' (Ey, 1946, pp. 13–15) – and says that so far, he could agree with Ey, since what he says there about personality is more or less in line with the ideas he himself presented in his doctoral thesis (129/3).

When he continues his reading of Ey's text, however, it becomes increasingly difficult to agree with him. This is particularly evident when he reads that for Ey (1946, p. 14) the spirit in Cartesian dualism is a spirit without existence. Lacan remarks that, on the contrary, for Descartes, it is the spirit (thinking) that gives certainty of existence ('I think therefore I am'). In the same vein, he is a little perturbed when he reads that, for materialism, the spirit is only an epiphenomenon (Ey, 1946, p. 14). There have been materialists who showed more respect for the spirit. In the dialectical materialism of Marx and Engels, for example, the spirit is immanent to matter and is responsible for its movement. Movement is a dialectical process, an alternation between thesis and antithesis, and as such, it is the essence of both matter and mind (129/4).

Lacan continues: according to Ey, true psychical causality is associated with our 'psychical activity,' which is located in the reality of the Ego. In its struggle to adapt the organism to the environment, the Ego must harmonize the conflicting demands of the objects, the other, the body, the unconscious and the conscious subject. Lacan radically refuses this conception. First: the whole idea of the Ego working itself to the bone to reconcile conflicting demands is wrong, he says. The unconscious, for example, doesn't demand anything from us. It puts us asleep and thus makes us accept all kinds of things without us really ever noticing it. Similarly, do we really work ourselves to the bone to meet the demands of others? Lacan rather believes La Rochefoucauld, who stressed time and time again the fundamental self-love[8] (i.e., egoism, 'l'amour propre') of man. Even when man thinks he loves someone else to the extreme, he actually in the first place loves himself (129/5–130/1).

Thus, the whole theory on psychical activity seems like a dream, a kind of naïve wishful thinking. Not the dream of a clinician who is sensitive to all manifestations of the unconscious in the narratives of his patients (130/2).

No, it is rather the wishful thinking of an automaton constructor, i.e., someone who strives to conceive psychical activity as an automatic, organic process. Lacan thus accuses Ey that he became exactly the kind of theorist they used to make fun of when they were students. All theorists who conceive man as a (organic) machine somewhere need a little man – a homunculus – in the machine who is responsible for these aspects of the machine's functioning that can't be explained in mechanical terms (130/3).[9]

Freud's observations revealed that hysterical symptoms – drops in consciousness, hypnoid states, and so on – were manifestations of subjectivity. Through their symptoms, the hysteric women held on to their desires and refused to be the object of any master. Subjectivity is the little man in the machine, it is what always escapes the control of any master. Hysterical women confront the master with the same argument as Polyxena: 'It's better to die than to live as a slave.'[10] No matter how one conceives man – be it from an idealist perspective or from a materialist-organicist perspective – he will always somewhere refuse to strictly obey the theoretical laws you put forward, for example by producing symptoms (psychopathology). This is a completely different view of psychopathology than Ey's, which holds that psychopathology is the consequence of a defect in the organic machine (130/4).

Lacan criticizes another paragraph of Ey's introductory text (pp. 12–13), in particular the belief that psychological activity would always culminate in noble ideals, moral conscience, and lofty 'vital programs.' Sometimes, it culminates in the ideals, moral conscience, and vital programs of a Nazi.[11] Furthermore, Lacan doesn't agree with Ey's vitalist axiom that integration is the ultimate virtue (see also paragraph 31). The ideals of the Nazi also have an integrating effect, in this sense that they orient and harmonize all different aspects of his existence. However, this still doesn't make them noble (130/5–131/1).

After this highly critical and often sneering scrutiny of Ey's theory, Lacan reassures the public – which exists mainly of Ey's pupils – that he doesn't want to belittle them. However, in order to free their thinking about madness from the noose in which it is strangled, he has to put things straight and clear ('reduce the number of terms'). In order to be entirely successful, he should be Socrates himself, or otherwise, just take the analytic position (i.e., 'listen to you in silence'). This is a sideways stab since it means that the discourse of Ey and his students is symptomatic, something that should be analyzed. The discourse of a madman (131/2)?

Lacan reassures the audience again: He likes the authentic, dialectical discussion at Bonneval, in which the pupils actively challenge the discourse of Ey by trying to raise all kinds of counterarguments (e.g., Ey, Ajuriaguerra, & Hécaen, 1947, Ey, 1946). He likes it more than the rigid and dogmatic way ('idolatrous reverence for words') by which analysts pretend to stick to the discourse of Freud. However, he warns that they must be aware that their words (or theoretical conceptions) might evoke unintended associations outside their circles (131/3).

When you talk about the object of the human sciences, you have to be aware that this is much more delicate than talking about the object of other sciences. After all, talking – the process of speech itself – is exactly what human science is about. This echoes what Lacan said in paragraph six of page 125, namely that a true idea must be in accordance with what it ideates. If you talk about speech, you have to take care that the way in which you talk is in accordance with what you want to say about speech (131/4).

If you don't take care of that, what you say will always be misinterpreted. The way in which you say it will lead people astray, away from what you really intend to say (131/5).

241

He gives the example of the vicissitudes of one of his own texts – 'Beyond the reality principle' – which was dramatically misinterpreted by his colleagues. In this text, he actually wanted to define the object of psychology, i.e., define what actually has to be studied in psychology. However, it was interpreted as if it was about the relativity of reality (131/6).

Lacan refers to Georges Politzer, who – for reasons of not wanting to be misinterpreted – decided not to formulate the theory that would probably have made him immortal. Politzer wrote a lot about the object of psychology and psychoanalysis. In aspiring to define the object of psychology and thus establish psychology as a science, Lacan warns that we have to be modest and admit that we do not have the slightest clue at this moment about any general law that explains why our therapeutic actions are effective (131/7–132/1).

At the very moment we start understanding that the imprints of hands that prehistoric man left on the walls of his cave actually enabled him to get a grasp of himself, we realize we actually know less of the matter that constitutes our psyche (of the object of psychology) than they do. What Lacan means is that prehistoric people made prints of their hands in order to be able to identify with the image of their own body. These images, then, are the 'matter' they use to construct their Ego. For them, it was much more difficult to obtain this 'matter' than it is for us (we, for example, have a mirror at our disposal), which made them much more aware of the fundamental importance of it. Lacan thus anticipates what will be presented in the second and third parts of the text, namely the fundamental importance of the imago for psychical experience. The imago is the matter our Ego is made of. This matter, however, is not something rigid and fixed. On the contrary, it is dynamic and alive. Therefore, our theory on this matter should not be rigid either. If our theory does not represent something fixed, but rather represents something alive, such as psychical life, then our theory must not use words in a fixed way either. *A true idea must be in accordance with what it represents.* Unlike Deucalion, who made men out of stones, we should avoid making a theory on psychical life out of rigid words with a fixed meaning (i.e., we should not use our concepts as if they are stones) (132/2).

Rather than aspiring to tell the fixed and final truth about psychical life, it would be enough on that day to be able to define its object. He stressed that it is necessary for psychology to do this: psychology must make explicit what the object it investigates actually is. In the last part of the text, he will conclude that the object of psychology is the imago (132/3).

2: The essential causality of madness

Lacan repeats the question put forward in part 1 (paragraph 14): Why is it of more interest to organize a conference on the cause of madness than on any other kind of pathology? Is a madman more interesting to us than, for example, the case of Gelb and Goldstein referred to earlier on? This case shows that symbolism is fundamentally dependent on visual perception. It was a lesion in the visual cortex that produced the problems at the level of the symbolic activity of the patient. This observation supports the proposition Lacan defends in this presentation (and in his early writings in general): psychical experience is caused and determined by the action of a structured set of visual forms, referred to as imagos, ideal images, or gestalts (132/4).

Again: What other human value is involved in madness compared to the patient of Gelb and Goldstein (132/5)?

Lacan relates an anecdote: when he defended his doctoral thesis, the jury didn't take him seriously when he said that it was important to realize that madness is a phenomenon at the level of thinking. Lacan clearly wanted to situate the object of psychology (madness) in a Cartesian discourse ('I think therefore I am'), but a member of the jury interrupted him and urged him to move on and talk about something more serious (132/6).

Now, 14 years later, he will try to finish what he wanted to say at the defense of his doctorate. In the meantime, not that much has been said that really gives an answer to the question as to what the object of psychology is. At least, he remarks ironically, enlightened minds such as those who interrupted him at the defense of his doctorate might realize by now that Bergson – whose vitalist philosophy was quite popular at that time – will not bring us much further in answering this question (132/5–133/1).

Before taking into consideration the facts about madness, it is good to consider the discourse that constitutes the facts. Every fact, after all, is only a fact because there is a discourse that makes it into a fact. Discourse on madness, as it is used in psychiatry, traces back to Descartes (133/2).

Lacan refers to a sentence in the first pages of the *Meditations*, where Descartes started his quest for certainty and truth by radically doubting everything that can be doubted. As we know, this will lead him to the conclusion that the only thing that is beyond any doubt, and which consequently must be true, is that he doubts (or *thinks*) (133/3).

The sentence referred to by Lacan immediately follows Descartes' introductory ascertainment that you cannot be sure that your body exists. In this sentence, Descartes wonders whether he might be a madman, since madmen sometimes believe they don't have a body. He reassures his readers, however, that he doesn't consider himself a madman, and he moves on without coming back to the issue of madness (133/4).

Lacan says it's a pity that Descartes didn't consider the issue of madness for a longer time, since it could have been of major interest to his quest for certainty (133/5).

Therefore, Lacan invites the reader to reconsider the phenomenon of madness by using Descartes' method. He values this method more than that of Clérambault, the revered professor who used to interrupt his hallucinating patients by saying that what they said was not true. Lacan agrees that this master nevertheless referred to truth, but the way in which he groundlessly claims to know the truth shows that he actually doesn't know more about it than the patient. In other words, the master deludes as much as the patient (133/6).

Rather, Lacan invites his audience to follow Ey, who, in his earliest writings,[12] like Descartes in the sentence quoted above, stressed the importance of *belief* in understanding the phenomenon of madness (133/7).

Lacan underscores the ambiguity of belief. It is at the same time *less* and *more* than knowing. It is less than knowing, since what one knows, one is sure of; what one believes, one isn't sure of. From a different angle, it is also more than knowing. If you *know* someone is innocent, it doesn't say anything about your appreciation of that person. If you *believe* someone is innocent, however, it usually means that you engage toward that person (133/8–134/1).

In making a phenomenological analysis (of madness), one shouldn't hurry too much. If one doesn't wait until one finds the right discourse, one will never obtain a clear picture of the phenomenon of madness ('the figure of the phenomenon of madness' will not appear).[13] Ey jumped to conclusions by moving too quickly from the concept of belief to the concept of error. Ey readily concluded that hallucinations and delusions have to do with perceptual and cognitive error. By drawing this conclusion too fast, however, Ey prevented himself from doing further research and discovering the essence of madness. Once he concluded with the theme of madness, once he thought he understood madness, the phenomenon became fixed, objectified, and generated no further questions (134/2).[14]

Lacan refers to a passage in 'Hallucinations and delusions' in which Ey (1934) holds that there are two possible ways to look at hallucinations. Either one considers them meaningful phenomena that are comprehensible in their relationships to the erroneous thinking and delusions of the patients; or one considers them the meaningless consequence of a neurological problem. It is clear that Ey identifies with the first (therapeutic) approach and that he considers the second useless and potentially harmful (134/3).

A few pages further in the same book (Ey, 1934, p. 168), however, Ey seems to defend the second position where he explains that ultimately, the fundamental error and the delusional beliefs in madness are caused by a cerebral deficit (134/4).

In trying to discover the truth about madness, Ey jumped from the concept of belief to the concept of (organically caused) error. It's at this point that he has taken the wrong path. Even when man strives for truth (like Ey does), he sometimes goes astray (134/5–135/1).

Cognitive error can potentially be caused by a lack of mental power, but belief can't. There are plenty of examples of extremely intelligent people who believed in something that turned out to be wrong. Ey also proves this, since he believed the wrong thing (namely that madness is caused by an organic deficit) at the height of his intellectual labor (135/2).

The notion of belief – as an essential aspect of madness – should not be related to error, but to misrecognition. This is an ambiguous term. It means that someone refuses to recognize something. To be able to *refuse* to recognize something, however, one first has to *recognize* it. More specifically with respect to madness: what appears in the hallucinations and delusions is something that actually belongs to the psychical experience of the madman, but that the madman refuses to recognize as such (135/3).

Lacan continues: Ey confirms that hallucinations are made of contents of the psychical experience ('the dough of the personality') of the patient. However, Ey doesn't wonder why the patient himself is not aware of this. For example, the paranoid subject that feels haunted by its persecutor is unable to see that the persecutor is a product of his mind, i.e., that the intentions ascribed to the persecutor are actually his own intentions. That's exactly why we call someone mad, because he is unable to see that what he is scared of is not something 'real,' but rather one of his own imaginary productions. The real question, however, is: What is it exactly that the madman refuses to recognize about himself (135/4)?

What is more important about hallucinations and delusions than the fact that the madman believes in them, or how he perceives them, is that they have a *meaning* to him. They always address the subject, they talk to him, and when he does not know what they mean, they strike him with perplexity. This perplexity is the strongest proof that the subject *struggles to understand* that the symptoms are experienced as meaningful, significant phenomena (135/5).

At the beginning of part two of this presentation (132/6), Lacan wondered in which respect a madman is different from any other patient. He wondered what specific human value lies in madness that is absent in other (medical) conditions. Now he formulates an answer to this question: madness differs from other conditions because it represents a certain *pathos* and because it *signifies* something. Both aspects more or less reverberate in the statement that madness *means* something to the madman. The fact that it signifies something relates the phenomenon of madness to *language* (135/6).

Lacan rejects a naive nominalist conception of language. Language is not a system of 'signs' that refer to specific aspects of an independently existing 'reality' (135/7–136/1).

By using language, man creates an identity that is actually false. Man constantly uses language to lie, but from time to time, truth breaks through the imaginary veil of our words. The truth that underlies appearance, propped up by language, betrays itself in many ways (136/2).

- On the one hand, the truth manifests in certain *non-intentional expressions*, for example, in a slip of the tongue (as abundantly illustrated by Freud in his *Psychopathology of everyday life*), in the change in emotions we undergo while speaking (these changes at the level of the passions of the soul reveal something about what really matters to us, beyond what we say), or in the narratives that determine our existence (for example, the narratives about our childhood, which make up our mythic history of our existence).

245

- On the other hand, the truth also manifests in an *intentional* way, as the explicit intention to discover what universal structure underlies the particularities of our experience. Applied to the psychoanalytic cure: one of the mainsprings of the psychoanalytic cure is the intention to discover the universal structure that underlies the particularities of the speech produced by free association. At that time, Lacan conceived this universal structure in terms of a structured set of imagos with which we identify. These imagos consequently are our truth; they are what our subjective existence ultimately boils down to (136/2).

This question invoked by language – namely 'what are the universals that underlie the heterogeneity of our experience' – is the question that is central to all philosophy. An experience of truth is always an experience in which something is *revealed* to us about the universals that underlie the manifold meanings that arise from our experience (136/3).

A word is not a sign that refers to a thing. A word is a crossing-point of significations. The word 'knots' has different meanings together. Lacan illustrates how the word 'curtain' ('Rideau') refers to a variety of significations. The last sentence of this paragraph is an important one and typical for this stage of Lacan's thinking. What exactly is meaning? The meaning of a word, in the end, is identical to a certain *image* or *imago*. When we speak, our speech is constantly accompanied by a series of images. These images, however, are not readily accessible. We have to discover them. They have to be unveiled, for example, through a psychoanalytic cure. What we find out then is that there are certain fundamental images – for example, referring to our father, mother, and so on – that are central in our signifying system. These imagos are the basis of our identity (136/4).

Thus, as we speak, we reveal the images that truly drive us and that constitute our attitudes. Our common sense is one of these attitudes. Lacan quotes Descartes then, where he says, in the first part of his *Meditations*, that common sense seems to be the thing that is most evenly distributed on earth, since even people who claim to be short of everything usually feel like they possess a fair share of common sense. That is actually true, says Descartes. Everybody is indeed endowed with reason, but we all use it in different ways. Some use it to make progress on the right path, others on the wrong. Lacan comments ironically that, although common sense is well-distributed, some apparently haven't received enough of it to see, like Descartes, that it is equally distributed (137/1).

Psychology should take as its object of investigation the points in speech where multiple meanings appear, i.e., the parts of discourse that form a knot of significations. These parts of discourse are usually considered *nonsense*. We say a discourse makes sense if it seems to mean one and only one thing. In this case, we say it is clear what someone says: 'This is what he means, and nothing else.' These parts of speech, however, are not interesting to psychology. Psychology should focus on the nonsense, such as the kind of speech people use when they fall in love (i.e., 'the words of passion'). People who are in love talk nonsense. The other means everything, and therefore, the words that are used to express what the other means, read like nonsense (137/2).

Lacan invites us now to consider the significations of madness. The speech of madmen is quite original, with all kinds of Kabbalah-like associations, neologisms, playing with homonyms, and so on (137/3).

It is in the *language* of madness that we can find its essential structures. It is not a coincidence that scholars such as Clérambault and Guiraud – who used a mechanist theory that for the rest is completely false – were exceptionally sensitive to the more mechanical aspects of the madman's speech, namely the gamut of structures running from the so-called postulates of delusions to mental automatism (137/4).

This is why Lacan thinks that, paradoxically, nobody did more to show that the cause of madness is psychical in nature than the mechanists did (137/5).

Lacan calls Clérambault his only master in psychiatric observation and regrets that he left this master too soon to go to the academic world (to write a doctorate) (137/6).

Lacan used Clérambault's method of observation in studying the case he presents in his doctoral thesis (Lacan, 1932). He showed that the psychopathology in his case – for which he coined the term 'self-punishing paranoia' – was psychogenetic in nature (138/1).

He selected this case because of the patient's literary talents and he chose to call her 'Aimée' after the name of the central figure in the patient's novels (138/2).

He presents this case here because he thinks that it illustrates the complete phenomenology of madness (138/3).

Lacan describes a series of imagos that characterize and determine the subjectivity of Aimée. In their interconnectedness, they represent her basic psychical structure. The imagos include (1) an imago of a maleficent female persecutor, characterized by vanity, coldness, and neglect of maternal duties, (2) an imago of purity and devotion, which was the opposite of the maleficent ideal, (3) an imago of a-sexuality, (4) an imago of someone who lives an ordinary existence, and (5) the opposite of the latter imago, a Bovary-like imago of someone who lives a chic, extravagant life. The sister of the patient was a central figure in the de-stabilizing of this structured set of imagos. At a certain moment, she came to take over the household tasks of the patient and took her child away from her because she deemed Aimée unable to take care of it any longer. The sister's interventions on the one hand liberated Aimée from her duties as a mother, but at the same time made her furious, pushing other, aggressive, imagos to the fore. Aimée, however, in no way connected the anger to her sister. She *misrecognized* the fact that it was her sister that made her angry. As a consequence, the aggressive imagos progressively manifested in a series of delusions that culminated in a ferocious passage à l'acte in which she stabbed an actress

247

whom she held to be a danger to her child. After this act – for which she was sentenced and jailed – the delusions disappeared (138/4 – 139/1).

Thus, the psychosis of Aimée is situated within the context of her *personality*. That means: within the context of the psychical characteristics (the set of imagos) that determine her global subjective experience (139/2).

From the beginning, one can see that in the case of Aimée, *misrecognition* plays a role (139/3) (see also 134/3).

Of course, one could simply say, like Descartes does (see 133/4), that madmen *believe* they are someone other than they actually are. This is also what the theory of Jules de Gaultier on Bovarysm[15] says: people have a constant need to believe they are someone other than they are (139/4).

However, thinking that you are someone other than you are cannot be what really distinguishes a madman from a normal person. After all, Lacan says, even the most normal people show traits of Bovarysm. It's the very essence of man to aspire to match certain ideal images that actually refer to someone he is not. Furthermore, even if one believes one is who one actually *is*, one can be mad. For example, a king who believes he is a king is also mad (139/5–140/1).

What citizens expect from a king is that he *plays the role* of king, not that he believes he *is* a king. Even if believing he is king leads to extreme awareness and loyalty to his royal duties, it would still leave the citizens with a feeling that there is something awry with his majesty.

The difference between the two is that the one who plays the role of a king can take a distance from this role, while the one who believes he is a king cannot. Furthermore, the latter is more infatuated (140/2).

Lacan gives two further illustrations of the same issue: a young man from a rich family who believes he 'is really someone' (and is thus mad) and Napoleon who did not believe he was 'Napoleon' (and thus, is not mad). Indeed, Napoleon only created the illusion of thinking he was Napoleon when he related his life to Emmanuel Las Cases, his secretary and biographer at Saint Helena (140/3).

It is exactly this difference between thinking you are someone and knowing you play a role that is at stake in madness. If you think you really are what you identify with, then you have radically misrecognized parts of yourself. The case of Aimée illustrates this. In Aimée, we have two strictly opposite sets of identifications, which we will simply call the malign and the benign identifications. The malign identifications are stirred up by the sister's interventions in Aimée's household, yet they are rejected and projected onto other women. These women are experienced as persecutors that intend to harm her child. This is the level at which the misrecognition has to be situated. Aimée identifies completely with the benign imagos and consequently cannot do anything other than *misrecognize* that the uprising, malign identifications are a part of herself (140/4).

Aimée reacts by 'imposing the law of the heart' to others. This means that she imposes her own goodness onto the world by fiercely fighting the malign identifications as they manifest in reality. What she doesn't realize, however, is that it is her own wickedness she attributes to the world (to others). This is why we call a madman mad. Furthermore, what the madman experiences as his own purity and goodness is nothing other than the virtual mirror image of his own wickedness. What he misrecognizes is that it is because he is so wicked that he needs to be so good. The only way to escape the wickedness as it manifests in reality is by aggressively imposing the law of his heart to reality. In a strange twist of fate, this action, through the punishment it evokes, finally strikes the one it intended to strike: the madman himself (140/5).

Lacan says that the theory he just presented about madness is not new but is already to be found in Hegel. In *The Phenomenology of the Spirit*, Hegel describes how the beautiful soul – which is synonymous with the pure, lofty soul – tries to impose the law of the heart to the evil world (Hegel, 1807, p. 383). In doing so, the beautiful soul misrecognizes that 'It is the heart, however, that is itself the source of derangement and perversion' (Hegel, 1807, p. 226). Thus, Hegel draws attention to the dialectical interdependency, the hidden, sinister complicity, between good and evil. This process is not only typical for madness, we find it in each life. Each life reads like a sequence of identifications with ideal images that temporarily fixate the being of the subject (141/1).

In madness, there is a direct, unmediated impact of the ideal image on the subject. This goes hand in hand with infatuation, since at that moment, the subject has the experience of *being* the ideal image (for example, being a king, being Napoleon). Paradoxically, while being fixed in this image, the subject realizes freedom, since at that moment the subject becomes what it always wanted to be (141/2).

Lacan refers to Hegel in a twofold way. First, he refers to the fact that Hegel considered Napoleon to be the person endowed with 'the world soul,' who would install a new world order – 'a universal and homogeneous state' – according to the ideal of the French Revolution.[16] Second, he mentions that Hegel, in *The Phenomenology of the Spirit*, refers to Karl Moor as an illustration of the fundamental structure of madness (i.e., the beautiful soul that tries to lash out its own evil without realizing it). Karl Moor is the main character in Schiller's novel 'The Rover.' He is a sensitive and heroic young man and a passionate idealist who fights the unfair and corrupt feudal authorities. In the end, however, he kills the woman he is in love with and turns himself in to the law. It's clear that this example shows the same structure as the case of Aimée: an infatuated beautiful soul, aspiring to lash out evil in the world, committing a murderous attack that finally turns out to be auto-punitive (141/3).

Instead of elaborating on the example of Karl Moor, however, Lacan prefers to give a more amusing example. He will show that the dialectical process between the infatuated, beautiful soul and the bad world is also present in Alceste, the main character in Molière's celebrated comedy 'The Misanthrope.' First, however, he wishes to draw the audience's attention to the fact that this comedy play doesn't cease to be a problem for the literary establishment, which seems to fail to understand the play. The reason for their lack of understanding is that if they could arrive at an understanding of it, they would also understand that what Molière ridiculed in this play actually applies to them. In other words, the infatuated literary establishment – just like the madman – reacts to the play by misrecognizing a part of themselves (141/4).

Alceste is the kind of person who identifies with the beautiful soul. He loathes the vulgar and detestable world and radiates pathos of eminence and loftiness. Phillinte is a more moderate character who often tries to calm the fanatic Alceste in his disapproval of all that is mundane and worldly. This is where the literary establishment – who passionately identify with Alceste's 'noble' strivings – gets confused. 'Does Molière really choose the side of Phillinte and disapprove of Alceste's noble struggle against the world? If this is the case, it means that Molière also considers us to be fanatics that have no grounds to feel superior' (141/5).

The problem is that they refuse to see that Molière clearly wants to show that Alceste – with whom these refined intellectuals identify – is actually mad. Why? Because he is unable to see that the decadence he so passionately fights in the world is actually the decadence of his own heart. Thus, if these fine gentlemen would understand what Molière wants to say, they would have to conclude they are mad as well (141/6).

The reason why Alceste is mad is not because he loves Célimène – a woman who betrays him. *En passant*, Lacan ridicules Ey's theory on adaptive psychical activity: loving a woman that betrays you can be explained as not being adapted to reality. No, the reason why he's mad is that he refuses to see through the flirtatious game Célimène plays. This game is typical for the idle rich who have little else to do than indulging in romantic intrigues as a way to pass their time and satisfy their narcissism. He is trapped in this game without seeing it is a game. He thinks he *is* a lover, rather than seeing that he just *plays the role* of a lover in the big romantic comedy orchestrated and directed by Célimène. All this satisfies another narcissism in Alceste, the narcissism of the beautiful soul, who thinks it is too good for the low and vulgar world (141/7–142/1).

It is the latter type of narcissism that distinguishes Alceste from Célimène's many other lovers. Unlike Alceste, they realize they play a flirtatious game. Alceste, on the contrary, believes that his love is sincere and wishes that the other admirers were like him. This is where Alceste would want to impose his 'law of the heart' to the world, the filthy world. He asks nothing less of Célimène's other admirers than that every word they say to her comes straight from the heart (142/2).

Lacan then comments ironically: 'Yes, every word should come from the heart, but when the heart of Alceste speaks, it says quite strange things.' For example, it says he wouldn't love Célimène if he didn't know she loves him. Here Alceste shows he is not as pure as he pretends to be: he only loves Célimène because she loves him! Alceste thus confirms in the most straightforward way La Rochefoucauld's statements about self-love: man always loves himself, even when he seems to love someone else (see part 1, paragraph 35). It is clear that this is radically in contrast with Ey's theory, which equates human psychical activity with noble and lofty ideals, striving to meet the demands of others (142/3) (see also 130/5–131/1).

Lacan then refers to Clérambault's major clinical contribution, namely the identification of the clinical category of the *delusions of passion* (later referred to as *erotomania*). Clérambault would diagnose Alceste as such, rather than taking his love for Célimène seriously (142/4).

Lacan continues: it's true that everybody who falls in love believes that, even if everybody else dropped the love-object, he would continue to love. However, in the case of Alceste, there is something a little bit over the top in this fantasy. To prove his love for Célimène, he longs for her to be in the deepest distress: poor, ugly, and left alone by everybody. In any case, that what Alceste calls love, desires about the same as the most ferocious hate (142/5).

Lacan wonders: if Alceste sincerely wants to prove his love to a girl who is poor and unsuccessful, why then doesn't he love such a girl? The answer is simple: unlike Célimène, such a girl would not be the center of everybody's attention. Consequently, such a girl would not allow him to demonstrate to everybody the purity of his soul. It is this kind of narcissism that is also responsible for the position Alceste migrates to by the end of the play. He leaves society to withdraw somewhere in nature, alone, as a victim of his own purity and of the decadence of society. As a beautiful soul, he believes he is too good to be able to live in society (142/6).

What Alceste does – in his struggle to prove that he is better than everybody else – thus resembles the basic mechanism in the formation of the Ego. The formation of the Ego is always a narcissistic act, and, as such, an auto-aggressive act. In order to become the object of the desire of the other, we identify with something we are not, and we stop being what we are, i.e., we kill ourselves (142/7–143/1). Or, as Lacan (1966, p. 124) puts it elsewhere, 'it might be said that at every instant, man constitutes his world by committing suicide.'

This narcissism is illustrated by Alceste's reaction to Oronte in the play. Oronte is an outspoken man who does his best to come across as multi-talented – for example, by writing poems and composing sonnets – but actually gives us the impression of being an imbecile. He is one of the admirers of Célimène. However, Célimène insults him at a certain moment, and he turns his back on her. His pride clearly appears to be stronger than his love. Earlier on in the play, he writes a sonnet to impress Célimène and he asks Alceste what he thinks of it. Alceste becomes furious and pontificates that his sonnet is a ridiculous attempt to be admired by Célimène, rather than a sincere expression of true love for her. Alceste's fury, however, actually betrays that he identifies with Oronte: the sonnet confronts him with the fact that he too is driven by ridiculous pride than by true love (143/2).

All this makes clear that Ey's theory is fundamentally wrong where it conceives madness as a deficiency in the organism's capacity to adapt to reality.

The act of madness – for example, Alceste's furious reaction to the sonnet of Oronte or Aimée's ferocious attack on the actress – is in no way the consequence of a deficit in the subject's adaptive capacity. Rather, it is a meaningful act that must be situated in the context of a subject's narcissistic dynamics. This is clear in clinical work with patients as well as in the confrontations with madness in a juridical context (143/3).

Lacan refers to Guiraud's explanation of madness, termed the *kakon* and defined as *a problematic sentiment of interior strangeness* (Guiraud, 1931). We can understand this as follows: in trying to be the object of the desire of the other, the subject identifies with an ideal image. The kakon is a part of the subject's drive that doesn't fit the ideal image, or, in other words, that can't be integrated into this image. As such, it is fundamentally incompatible with what one wants to be for the other. Therefore, it is a threat to the narcissism of the subject and it puts the subject at risk of falling from the desire of the other. Delusions and hallucinations are attempts to deal with this kakon, to control it by situating it in the outer world and consequently attacking it there (143/4).[17]

This is exactly what Alceste does. In fighting the vulgarity of the world, he actually targets the part of himself that is incompatible with his beautiful soul. Thus, he finally victimizes only himself by withdrawing from the world and from the other to a place where 'as a man of honor, one is free.'[18] Lacan says that it is good to consider the issue of freedom for a while, since it is not at all trivial that it appears in this context in Molière's play (143/5).

The structure of classical comedy is such that things are not openly conveyed, but masked. Descartes also realized this. He knew that somewhere, life is like a comedy play. We are all actors in a scene and as such, we shouldn't openly reveal everything. At a certain moment, for example, he knew that he was about to become famous, but he preferred to think about this in terms of 'becoming an actor in a worldly scene.' He didn't think about it too seriously and he didn't say it openly. He actually only mentioned it in his unpublished *Secret Note*. This is exactly what the madman is unable to do. He doesn't realize he only plays a role and takes himself 100 percent seriously (143/6) (see also the discussion on pages 139 to 140).

Lacan says he could have chosen more realistic examples to illustrate all of this. He could have illustrated it, for example, by referring to Stalin bringing the people involved in the October Revolution to trial in Moscow in 1936. It's clear that Stalin also wanted to impose the law of his heart onto the world. However, Lacan holds that the imaginary space, which is so clearly revealed in Molière's work, as in all products of the poetic mind, is actually prior to what happens in the real world. It is the imaginary space that is the cause of the real world, and not the other way around. It is therefore more interesting to focus on the imaginary space revealed in the work of poets than on reality (143/7).

Then Lacan goes back to the issue of freedom. It is clear that every time the issue of freedom appears in the play of Molière, Alceste manifests his tendency to become mad in a more intense way. Thus, freedom and madness seem to be directly associated with each other (143/8).

The way in which Lacan describes the relation between freedom and madness in this one paragraph is extremely interesting and needs some explanation. The identifications Lacan refers to in this paragraph are identifications with the ideal image. What he says is that it is precisely those who are most attracted by the ideal imagos that are most prone to madness. Thus, the idealists (i.e., those who strive in a more or less fanatic way to live up to their ideals) are most susceptible to madness. That is a keen observation and therein comes the issue of freedom. Man lives with a certain awareness of how his life could be if he were completely free. In such circumstances, he would fully realize what he considers to be ideal, i.e., his ideal images. Thus, the ideal images we identify with simultaneously define our being – since they are the ultimate determinants of our existence as human beings – and our freedom – since they define how we would be if we were completely free (143/8).

Thus, rather than being the consequence of an organic coincidence, madness is the latent potential (virtuality) that is present in every human being, to close the gap between what one is and one's ideal image. Everybody who decides to close this gap – and thus identify completely with his/her ideal image – enters the realm of madness (144/1).

Far from madness being an insult to freedom, as Ey (Ey, Ajuriaguerra, & Hécaen, 1947, p. 20) claims, madness and freedom go hand in hand. It is precisely to the extent that we aspire for absolute freedom that we are prone to madness. In other words: 'Madness follows freedom as its shadow' (144/2).

The being of man – as it is determined by the same ideal images that are involved in madness – cannot be understood if one doesn't understand that madness is the upper limit of its freedom. If one aspires to be completely free, one becomes mad (144/3).

Lacan introduces a humoristic intermezzo to interrupt the very serious presentation he gives. He refers to what Ey and he wrote on the wall of the hospital ward during their clinical placement: 'Not just anyone who wants to goes mad.' He says that he still agrees with that (144/4).

However, he disagrees with Ey as to what is responsible for one person going mad while the other doesn't. While Ey claims that madness has to do with *limited* mental capacities (an organic mental deficit), it appears to Lacan that some don't go mad because they do not have sufficient mental capacities (or talents) to reach the level of infatuation needed to become mad (144/5).

Lacan claims that madness doesn't have to do with one or another deficit, such as a weak organism (as Ey holds), a deranged imagination, or intrapsychic conflicts that go beyond the strength of the Ego. On the contrary, it is more probable that someone with a very strong organic constitution, a very powerful Ego, and blessed with all the talents of the world will go mad. This indeed shows again the radical difference between the conceptions of Ey and Lacan (144/5).

Lacan's line of reasoning at least explains the observation that so many people with superior characteristics become mad. This observation was problematic for 19th-century psychiatry, which, like Ey, conceived madness in terms of a (organic) deficit, thus, as a consequence of *inferior* characteristics (144/6).

Lacan refers to Homais and Bournisien, two characters in *Madame Bovary*, the novel of Flaubert. Homais and Bournisien are opposite and identical in character. They are both rather stupid, dogmatic, and fanatic. However, they identify with opposite ideologies. Homais is a materialist pharmacist who considers himself a freethinker; Bournisien a spiritual, conservative catholicist. The two are constantly involved in ideological disputes. Homais ridicules Bournisien by referring to saints who appear to be rather mad; Bournisien ridicules Homais by referring to freedom fighters who went mad. If one considers madness a consequence of being too talented rather than a consequence of inferior organic characteristics, the low blows between Homais and Bournisien would have to cease, since it would be no longer an insult to be called mad (144/7).

The work of Pinel – who considered madness a consequence of an organic deficit – might have made us more tolerant of the madness of ordinary people. After Pinel, we just consider them *unlucky* because of their putative organic inferiority (and not, as was supposed before him, possessed by the devil). However, this did not make us more respectful toward the people who are at risk of madness because they are too talented (144/8).[19]

Lacan then shifts back to Homais and Bournisien: they were both stupid, yet only Homais was mad. While Homais cannot take any distance from his ideological convictions, Bournisien would like to agree with Homais on the condition that the latter could be reasonable and recognize the existence of spiritual needs at least (144/9).

Lacan repeats: his theory on madness disarms both Homais and Bournisien, since neither the madness of freedom fighters nor saints can be used anymore as an insult. Thus, we can refer again to Joan of Arc (who was a freedom fighter) and to the apostle Paul (who was a saint) without being afraid that people will think we are mad ourselves. After all, the voices the former heard and the altered state of consciousness that made the latter fall off his horse are due to supreme characteristics rather than to organic inferiority (144/10).

Lacan wonders: now he has shown that Ey's conception of madness is wrong, must he not watch out that, according to his own theory, he should consider himself to be mad? After all, if he is convinced that he knows the truth about madness, he might be like Homais, who was always convinced that he said the right thing! Must he not watch out that he himself, i.e., Lacan, might think he is Napoleon (144/11–145/1)?

Lacan doesn't think so. He thinks he has been cautious not to speak with too much conviction about the nature of madness. Indeed, if you read Lacan, he often talks in approximate terms. He usually avoids using terminology that sounds as if an absolute truth is put forward. This, however, is what the physician does who claims that the madman talks nonsense (see 133/6). How can the physician be so absolutely sure about that? In the end, he is clearly as mad as the madman himself, since they both pretend to be absolutely sure (145/2).

77. In the case of Aimée, for example, Lacan never pretended to know the absolute truth about this woman. He always kept a respectful distance from the truth of this subject. In the end, only the patient herself can say the truth about herself (145/3).

What Lacan said about madness can finally be situated within the context of the antique formula – which is also quoted by Nietzsche – that tells us what we have to become: *become what you are*. In becoming what we inherently are, we become free. However, if we try to be what we are in a premature way – without having emancipated ourselves sufficiently from the suffocating impact of the desire of the other – we go mad. Thus, the madman is someone who claims freedom when he hasn't conquered it at all (145/4).

In the last part, the imago, as a mode of form and action, as an order of determinations, will be discussed (145/5).

3: The psychical effects of the imaginary mode

Lacan starts the last part of his presentation by stating that the history of the subject ultimately equals the history of its ideal identifications. Throughout life, the subject identifies with a series of imagos that are invested with libido. These imagos are clustered in a more or less integrated, structured set that forms the Ego of the subject (145/6).

This conception of the Ego is fundamentally different from theories (like Ey's) that conceive the Ego as the synthesis of the organism's adaptive relations to reality. The latter, moreover, have something paradoxical, since they aspire to describe a *subjective* experience in *objective* terms (145/7).

In Ey's conception, the decay of the psychological experience of the Ego (which is what happens in madness) is equal to a functional dissolution, i.e., the decay of the brain regions associated with the organism's higher functions. Thus, Ey supposes a *parallelism* between psychological functioning and brain functioning; he supposes that the psychological experience of the Ego is perfectly correlated to physiological processes in the brain (145/8).

We can't reproach Ey for succumbing to parallelism. Although his whole oeuvre went in the opposite direction, even Sigmund Freud succumbed to parallelism at certain moments. Moreover, from a tactical point of view, Freud had no other option than supporting parallelism to a certain extent, since not supporting it would have implied academic excommunication at that time (145/9–146/1).

Parallelism manifests in Freud's theory where – just like Ey – he conceives the Ego as a set of mechanisms ('appareils') that adapts an organism to reality (146/2).

In the end, however, this parallelism is an organicist illusion. The notion of *error* in Ey's work shows how this illusion is linked to a realist metapsychology: On the one hand, there is an organism; on the other hand, a reality; the organism has to adapt to reality; therefore, it has to perceive reality in an accurate way; if it errs in perceiving reality, it suffers from madness. Such a theory, however, in no way makes more concrete what the psychological processes are that take place in the Ego that perceives reality (146/3).

Although everybody asks for a theory of the Ego, there is little hope that it will effectively be realized as long as everybody refuses to accept that Freud's theory ('a peerless master') of the Ego is wrong (146/4).

Similarly, both Freud and Ey claim that psychical activity ('lived experience') boils down to reflection and objective assessment of reality in order to adapt to it. However, the oeuvre of Merleau-Ponty convincingly demonstrates that the major part of psychological activity – for example, the process of perception – happens *before* any objective evaluation of reality. To illustrate this, Merleau-Ponty refers to gestalt-psychologists' experiments on so-called visual illusions. These experiments make clear that perception actually arises *before* any conscious mental act. Furthermore, which percept arises is fundamentally dependent on which gestalt (or imagos) is activated by the experimenter before the stimulus is presented. Later on in this presentation, Lacan gives an example of such an experiment (see 157/2). It is only after the perception of the illusion manifests that the process of objectively evaluating what was first perceived can begin. Thus, what is central in perception, and in all other psychical activity, is not objective assessment, but 'the action of the gestalts.'[20] Consequently, the gestalts (imagos) are the real object that should be studied in psychology (146/5).

Thus, Ey's strong, unified (synthetic) Ego, which evaluates reality in order to adapt the organism to it, and is thus always in control, doesn't appear to match the observations of Gestalt psychology. When we study the Ego in our clinical work, where it appears in the context of the broader subjective experience of patients, we see that the Ego is not at all a neatly synthetized or unified instance. On the contrary, it is full of contradictions. Take as an example what Freud says about the *verneinung*. People often deny things that clearly apply to both themselves and others. For example: 'Don't think I am always late because my father used to force me to be in time!' In the *verneinung*, we see an Ego divided between two ideas ('My father is the cause of a present problem' and 'I don't want you to think that this all has to do with my father'), of which, one (the first) is misrecognized. The second idea shows the strong inter-relatedness of the Ego with the other (146/6).

Lacan maintains that what we call our Ego is nothing other than a set of *ideal images*. Freud also uses this term, and this is the part of his theory of the Ego where he finds the right track again. Lacan holds that this ideal image doesn't have a lot to do with the organism (146/7–147/1).

Our psychological understanding of how the Ego comes into being will be better the more we avoid thinking in terms of an instance that integrates all adaptive functions. The Ego has nothing to do with that (147/2).

This is exactly what Lacan demonstrated himself in his phenomenological analysis of the fertile moments of delusions. He preferred not to publish this work, but the title he gave it was nevertheless used. This title – Paranoiac Knowledge – was chosen to provoke, since mainstream psychiatric discourse had conceived paranoia as a *deficit* at the level of knowledge (147/3).

Lacan says that what he calls 'paranoiac knowledge' resembles a certain reaction in childhood that is called *transitivism*. Later on in life, this reaction doesn't disappear completely and re-manifests, for example, in situations of rivalry. This could be said to basically boil down to a manifestation of the Ego's *Urbild*. In a situation of rivalry, the subject will react by manifesting its ideal self in an attempt to overcome the rival (147/4).

The term *transitivism*, coined by Charlotte Bühler, refers to the fact that young children do not distinguish sharply between themselves and other children. For example, if a child observes another child fall, it could cry as though it has fallen itself. In this case, the child is truly captured by the image of the other, in the sense that it reacts as though the perceived image of the other refers to itself (147/5).

Lacan says he will not present the series of examples Bühler gives. He only remarks that transitivism has both a positive (sympathy) and a negative (jealousy) pole. Thus, a kind of primordial ambivalence toward the other is constituted, since he is at the same time loved as the self and hated as a rival in the struggle for the love-object (e.g., the mother). The child actually mirrors the other, i.e., it experiences the other's image as its mirror image. Everything that happens to that image is thus experienced as if it happens to itself (147/6).

Transitivism only manifests if the age difference between two children is smaller than one year (148/1).

An imago only has an impact on the condition that it is recognized as a member of the same species (i.e., on the condition that there is a generic resemblance) (148/2).

Human babies recognize the face of another human being after no more than ten days (148/3).

They immediately start imitating the face of others. Thus, the other immediately has an impact on the infant. By looking at the other and imitating him, it projects its self-experience into the image of the other; it experiences itself as being the image of the other.[21] We can understand this better if we remember that human reality (the *umwelt*) is fundamentally a social reality and if we remember the fundamental intuition of Hegel (148/4).

Hegel held that man's ultimate desire is to have his desire recognized by someone else. That's why it makes a difference for human beings if he has to prepare his own food or if someone else prepares it for him. If someone else prepares it, we feel recognized in our desire for food. We want to exist as a desiring subject for the other, and we only do so if the other sees/recognizes our desire and acts in response to it. According to Hegel, the ultimate goal of the master is to force the slave to recognize his desire: I want a house, and you will respond to this desire by building it for me (148/5).

In the process of trying to gain recognition from the other, the subject identifies with a specific imago. This imago synthetizes what the subject thinks it means to the other: 'This is what I am for the other.' All particular characteristics of this subject are part of this global imago. This imago thus becomes universal in the sense that the subject will manifest it in relation to every other (148/6).

The more a subject identifies with a specific imago, the more it feels it consciously knows who it is. This gives the subject a feeling of liberty, since it feels like it can choose to be who it wants to be. However, this feeling is illusory, since, actually, the subject identifies with this imago *because the other desires so*. Thus, the more it identifies with this imago, the more it lives according to the desire of the other, i.e., the more it becomes a slave of the other (148/7).

In terms of this imago, does it thus install a fundamental relationship between the organism of the subject and the reality it lives in? If it does, we should find signs of such a relationship elsewhere in psychical life as well (148/8).

The practice of psychoanalysis shows that this is indeed the case. The constant repetition of the psychical complex around the imago – which is referred to as the Oedipus complex and which is the basic structure of what is called 'the unconscious' – shows this very clearly (148/9).

The imago is something we are no longer aware of, but at the same time it determines all our bodily 'habits.' It is this unconscious image (imago) of our body that determines how we experience our body. If we identify with the image of a weak other, we will experience our body as weak; if we identify with the image of a physically strong other, we will experience our body as strong. We will, however, remain unaware that it is the image of the other that determines our particular experience of the body (148/10–149/1).

This is why the imago can lead to the strong somatic symptoms of hysteria. At the same time, however, this imago is also responsible for the way in which we construct our reality (149/2).

The identification with the imago of the other leads to ambivalence: on the one hand, the other is liked as an equal; on the other hand, the other is hated as a rival in the struggle for the desire of the love-object (see also paragraph 15). Over and beyond this ambivalence with respect to the rival, there is also a painful dependency on the love-object. Whatever the desire of the love-object is, the infant must try to live up to it. The Oedipal identification with the father – as an authority figure that maintains a law to which the infant, its rivals and the love-object are subjected – offers an endpoint to this restless imaginary world. Different psychoanalytic schools conceive the psychical effects of this Oedipal identification in different ways, but they all seem to agree that this identification radically changes the subjective experience (i.e., the reality) of the subject. Concretely, in imaginary reality, there is no clear difference between persons (recall *transitivism*, where the I and the other are interchangeable). The identification with the father, however, entails that the I and the other(s) start to 'floculate' (i.e., 'flesh out'), i.e., they all start to be experienced as autonomous individuals. This has to do with the fact that the father maintains a law that draws a border between self and other. For example: 'You are not allowed to take the toy of another child'; 'Other children are not allowed to take your toy'; 'You are not allowed to hit someone' and so on (149/3).

Oedipal identification, however, not only changes psychical reality, it also changes the body. After this, children become less sensitive to pain, for example. Thus, the identification raises the child's tolerance for pain, similar to desensitizing medication (149/4).

The Oedipus complex, moreover, plays a central role in the way in which we experience space and time. Even Bertrand Russell – someone with mechanistic inspirations – agrees that our perception is not structured according to space and time (i.e., we have no continuous experience of a dimensional space and a chronological time) if there is not a minimal distinction (or distance) between the self and the environment. As Lacan argued, before the Oedipal identification, there is no clear distinction between the child and its environment (i.e., the other). It is also remarkable that Russell associates this distinction with a feeling of *respect*. Respect is precisely what the identification with the father introduces. The father holds that everybody should respect the other according to the law. In this way, the law introduces a certain boundary and distance between people that should be respected (149/5).

This is also what Lacan tried to show in his doctoral thesis: the so-called elementary phenomena of psychosis are a consequence of a lack of an Oedipal identification, which entails that a clear boundary between the self and the other is not installed (149/6).

In describing these elementary phenomena, Lacan extended Freud's catalog of mechanisms operating in the unconscious. Freud, for example, described symbolism and condensation, two mechanisms of the formation of dreams. Lacan hopes, moreover, that the term 'unconscious' will be replaced by the term 'imaginary mode'[22] (149/7).

During his clinical work with Aimée, it became clear to him that she could not say when or where she first experienced the elementary phenomena of her psychosis (certain psychotic intuitions, convictions, illusions, etc.). In the same way, she couldn't situate her dreams in (symbolic, con-sensual) time and space (149/8–150/1).

In this way, we see that time and space are experienced in a completely different way in imaginary and symbolic (Oedipal) reality (150/2).

Lacan compares the imaginary experience – which he referred to as 'paranoiac knowledge' – with the limbo and with a mirror palace. In a mirror palace, images are multiplied, deformed, and projected into all directions in such a way that it is difficult to get a grasp of 'reality.' This imaginary world fades when the Oedipal identification installs law, order, and a border (150/3).

Lacan doesn't agree with Freud that the Oedipus complex is a universal structure (e.g., *Les Complexes Familiaux*, Lacan, 1938). Only patriarchal societies have an Oedipal structure. Some societies, obviously, are structured in another way (150/4).

It is remarkable that there is already a reality – 'an outside world' – from the very first days after birth. Organic tendencies – such as hunger and thirst – are not the only things that exist. From the beginning we have an experience of objects – or others – that exist outside of us. The borders are not always clear, as the phenomenon of transitivism shows, but we are nevertheless aware that other people exist. How does this experience actually come into being (150/5)?

This is what Lacan's theory of the Mirror Stage is about (150/6) (see accompanying essay in this volume).

Lacan comments briefly on the first presentation he gave on the mirror stage in 1936. He was interrupted by Jones and refused to submit his paper for publication (150/7–151/1).

In this presentation, he wanted to show the interconnectedness of a variety of infantile behaviors during a specific phase of life (151/2).

More specifically, it concerns the remarkable behavior of a child, in the second half of its first year, when it is confronted with its own image in the mirror. In this situation, the child reacts differently than, for example, a chimpanzee. This difference qua reaction has nothing to do with the fact that the child might be more intelligent than the monkey. It is actually the other way around; the monkey is more intelligent at that age. This is apparent, for example, in its superior capacity to handle instruments (151/3).

It is the jubilating, triumphant reaction to the mirror image – something that is completely absent in the chimpanzee and in all other animals – that is really interesting. It shows that the mirror image really captures (the psychical experience of) the infant (151/4).

This is precisely what Lacan had noted during his study of paranoiac knowledge (151/5).

Other researchers – like Lhermitte – also remarked that the image of one's own body has a very specific psychical status (151/6).

This appears from a large number of subjective experiences all of which all have to do with the image of the body. Most important is the relationship of this image to proprioceptive sensations. Aristotle's illusion[23] can serve as an example here (151/7).

Lacan further illustrates the relevance of his theory on the mirror stage by enlisting more examples of phenomena that show how the image of the body is decisive for psychical experience (151/8).

The phenomena typical for the mirror stage are related to the fact that, in terms of the maturation of the nervous system, the human child is born prematurely. During the first six months of life, the nervous system is not sufficiently developed for life outside of the uterus. One of the consequences is a serious lack of motoric coordination. Most animals, for example, are able to walk within the first hours after birth. For humans, this takes about one year (152/1).

This motoric helplessness elevates the need to anticipate what appears in reality by means of gathering visual information. Who is approaching me? Is it my mother? Or is it someone else? The capacity to recognize visual forms of humans is particularly important. Most animals, for example, rely on smell rather than visual information to identify their relatives. This also means that in the construction of the Ego, the child first identifies with visual forms, rather than auditory or olfactory stimuli. It is the relationship to the visual form of itself in the mirror that psychoanalysts call 'narcissism' (152/2).

The narcissistic identification with the visual form of the body is related to suicide, the death instinct, and primary masochism. By identifying with an image of the body, the child is estranged from the direct experience of its body. It becomes something it is not, and thus actually commits a suicidal act. Long before a child thinks of death, this suicidal tendency is thus already present in its subjective experience (152/3).

It was brilliant of Freud to have understood in his observation of children that separation from the caregivers has a liberating effect, for example, in his grandson's fort-da game. In separating from them, the child liberates itself from its dependency on them and from their suffocating desire. It thus escapes their totalitarian power (152/4).

These enacted separations are the first of a long series of refusals to accept the caregivers' gifts. These separating acts are precisely the moments in which the psychical system restructures and develops (152/5).

Development always starts from a primitive Ego that is radically alienated, in this sense that the infant's awareness of itself is strictly determined by the image of the other-caregiver. It mirrors the other's face and body, and its self-awareness is constantly exchanged for awareness in the mold of the other's image. That is what Lacan calls 'the primitive sacrifice,' a suicide at the level of self-awareness (152/6).

This is also what we find in madness (152/7), as was illustrated by the cases of Aimée and Alceste.

This initial dissonance between what one is and the Ego determines all subsequent phases of psychical history. Psychical history is the process in which this dissonance is progressively weakened. As a subject develops, it can reduce the gap between what it is and the ideal images it has identified with, for example throughout a psychoanalytic cure (152/8–153/1).

Every time one has the illusory experience that this opposition disappears – i.e., every time someone wrongly thinks he actually is his Ego or his ideal image – one sees how the narcissistic, suicidal aggression intensifies (153/2).

The fallacious conviction that one matches the ideal image – which is the essence of the phenomenon of madness and which can, strangely enough, be evoked by certain intoxications – only manifests when a subject reaches the age in which it can make reasonable choices (153/3).

The infant's choices for the first identifications are not really *choices*; it can't choose which image of the other it identifies with. In this respect, the choices are innocent, meaning that the child can't be blamed for them. These identifications have the same structure as madness (152/7), but in themselves, they only lead to the kind of madness that all humans share, namely the madness by which man thinks he is man. In other words, in his attempt to be accepted by the community of man (for example, the family), man identifies with the other. In this way, man can think of himself as belonging to the category of mankind (153/4).

In this respect, the characteristics that make us think we are human actually don't have a lot to do with our body. They are something that is added to the body by identifying with the image of the other. Thus, we are more than our body. We are our body as it is experienced through the image of the other. Nevertheless, the only way in which we can know something about what our being is *beyond the alienating impact of the image of the other* is by knowing our body (153/5).

Thus, while Descartes thought that the passions that arise from our body (sex, hunger, thirst, etc.) are the fundamental illusions of man (i.e., what prevent him from seeing the truth), Lacan, on the contrary, holds that it is the narcissistic identification with the image of the other that is our fundamental illusion. This identification means that we can only experience the desires that arise from our flesh in a de-formed way, in the mold of the image of the other (153/6).

When the spirit wants to see the body (and the desires that arise from it), it is always limited in doing so by the basic and undividable unit (i.e., the *monad*) of the imago of the other. The imago of the other is a global entity, a global form or *gestalt* that organizes and determines the way we see ourselves. What the mind sees is always mediated by this gestalt (153/7).

If we could stop thinking about who we are, and even not expect that we are something, we would see that the image we identified with actually doesn't exist. We would realize that our being is not reflected in the mirror. We believe we see our being in the mirror because we need the image that appears there to think about our being. This thinking, however, fundamentally errs in the sense that it substitutes our being for something it is not (153/8).

61. Thus, the imago is the true object of psychology. It is the basic, undividable building block of psychological life (i.e., the *monad*, see paragraph 59). In this respect, the imago is to psychology what the atom (*a-tomos*, un-cuttable, what cannot be cut) is to the physics of Galileo (153/9).

It's clear, however, that we cannot fully understand what the imago is. The imago always presents as self-evident. What we consider to be reality – our lived subjective experience – is already an effect of the activity of the imago. As such, the effects of the imago manifest before we can understand it and therefore, the nature of the imago itself remains obscure (153/10).

The imago is associated with a specific kind of space and time. It is a spatial entity without extension that can't be divided. As such, the imago is a pure idea (without extension) that nevertheless creates an illusory, extended reality. The time of the imago is associated with the interval between the expectation and the release (the manifestation of the imago as a reality). First, we have a period of expectation, and then a period in which what we expect actually appears (153/11).

Lacan then comes to the issue at stake at the conference: Psychological causality, actually, comes down to identification. The true psychological cause is identification. This phenomenon, in itself, is absolute, in the sense that it can't be reduced to any other level, for example, the level of biology. An infant identifies with an imago in order to solve a problematic experience during a certain psychical phase. For instance, the first (imaginary) identifications with the image of the other are necessary to exist as a human for another human. The Oedipal (symbolic) identification is then necessary to escape the paranoid anxiety associated with the imaginary phase. Thus, every identification entails a metamorphosis at the level of the relationship with others (153/12–154/1).

Lacan remarks that people could object here and accuse him of using a circular argument.[24] The argument 'Madness knows a psychological causality because it is caused by a pure, irreducible psychological mechanism (i.e., identification)' indeed is a circular one, since the explanans contains the explanandum. Perhaps he just wanted to construct a metaphysical (i.e., non-materialistic) conception of man, at all costs (154/2)?

To show that this criticism doesn't hold, Lacan will show the effects of imaginary identification in the animal world (154/3).

It is clear that, if Lacan's theory on the imago is to be true, observations of animals should confirm it, especially those that live in groups (i.e., the *gregarious* types). Lacan had said this ten years previously, when he stated that the Freudian discovery of the mechanism of identification can make an important contribution to biology (154/4).

Such contributions to biology have actually been made since 1939, and two examples will be presented (154/5).

First, a paper by Harrisson Matthews published in 1939 in *Proceedings of the Royal Society* (154/6).

One knows that the female pigeon will not ovulate if it is isolated from other members of its species (154/7).

Matthews' observations show that the *sight* of another pigeon – male or female, it doesn't matter – without any other form of sensory stimulation (hearing or smelling) suffices to trigger ovulation (154/8).

If they cannot see each other but they can hear or smell each other, the females do not ovulate. This shows that it is the *visual* image that is decisive.

Upon seeing a *male* pigeon, the female pigeon will ovulate within 12 days; upon seeing a *female* pigeon, ovulation can take approximately two months (154/9).

What is even more remarkable, however, is that, if the researchers put a mirror in the cage of the female pigeon, allowing it to observe its own mirror image, it will also ovulate, yet after 2.5 months (154/10).

In the male pigeon, there is a comparable phenomenon: if they do not visually encounter the female brooding the eggs, there is no secretion of milk in their crop (155/1).

A second interesting paper is one written by Chauvin and published in 1941 in *Annales de la Société entomologique de France* (155/2).

Chauvin studied the *Schistocerca*, a species of grasshopper of which two types exist, a solitary type (living solitarily) and a gregarious type (living in groups). The two types differ with respect to sexual behavior, eating patterns (voracity), motoric behavior, the form of their limbs (morphology), and the colors of their limbs and shields (pigmentation) (155/3).

These colorings are the most visible difference between the two types. Both types go through five developmental stages. The solitary type has the same green color throughout all stages. The gregarious type changes colors, and, for example, has black striations on different parts of the body, in particular, on the hind femur. These are the most visible differences between the two types, but there are many other differences as well, so much, in fact, that one could argue that they differ biologically in every respect (155/4).

Chauvin carried out several experiments showing that *Schistocerca* of both types – gregarious as well as solitary – that are raised in isolation without ever perceiving the characteristic forms of the species always develop into solitary types. When they *do*, however, perceive such forms during the first larval periods, they develop into gregarious types. For example, if you put two larvae of a solitary individual together in a cage, they will evolve into gregarious types. Further experimentation showed that the senses of sight and touch are decisive in this. Furthermore, a larva of a solitary type will evolve into a gregarious type if it is raised in the presence of another larva, but also in the presence of an adult *Schistocerca*. The latter holds even if this other is from another, resembling grasshopper species, such as the locust. However, if the other species are too different, for example, a *Gryllus*, then the larva will develop into a solitary type (155/5).

Chauvin concludes that the factor that decides whether the *Schistocerca* will develop into either a solitary or a gregarious type thus seems to be the *recognition* of a specific form and type of movement during the first larval periods. Being a physiologist, these observations are highly problematic to Chauvin. As a physiologist, he cannot believe in psychological causality. He rather thinks physiology determines recognition (which is a psychological phenomenon), and not the other way around. However, in the case of his *Schistocerca*, it is clear that it is recognition (of a specific form or *gestalt*) that determines physiology (i.e., the different biological characteristics of the solitary and the gregarious types). This clear-cut observation of psychological causality leaves him confused (155/6).

Lacan mentions some other remarkable findings of Chauvin. If two solitary *Schistocerca* couple, the chance that a gregarious type develops from the larva increases based on the time the parents spend together during the coupling (155/7–156/1).

And the other way around holds true as well. If the experimenter prevents two coupling solitary individuals from spending time together, and thus only allows rapid and brief coupling after being put together, the number of gregarious types that develop from the offspring are far lower than is on average in nature (156/2–156/3).[25]

The decisive role played by the imago in this is better illustrated by other findings of Chauvin, but this theme would take us away from the issue of psychological causality of madness (156/4).

Lacan concludes his explanation by saying that – unlike Ey supposes – there is no such thing as a parallelism between the nervous system and psychological experience. For example, some lower animals such as the crab have a very limited nervous system and still demonstrate high intelligence (156/5).[26]

Lacan states that his text should not be interpreted as an ironic challenge (in the sense that when man realizes his ultimate desire, i.e., becoming free, he simultaneously becomes mad). Rather, it should be read as a warning about a major threat to mankind. What we just learned about madness does not allow us to cure it. However, it might open up the possibility of inducing madness. As long as knowledge of madness had the status of a 'metaphysical theory,' people had the liberty to not take it too seriously. Nevertheless, the impact of imagos (for example in the findings of Matthews and Chauvin referred to above) has the status of guaranteed scientific knowledge. Indeed, it is on this basis that scientific techniques can be developed to manipulate the impact of imagos on the human being. The development of scientific techniques that refine the play of images ('the art of the image') according to the laws of the imago can be effective to the extent that people have no way of doubting the truthfulness of the imago. If someone is no longer able to doubt, however, what he considers to be true, he inevitably becomes mad (156/6).

85. Someone who truly understands the way in which imagos govern our construction of reality could radically manipulate the way people construct reality. This could be done in such an effective way that nobody would be able to doubt it. In this way, he could create a series of ideals that are beyond doubt – with the label 'true guarantee' – to which everybody is alienated, and he would have the perfect instrument for mass manipulation. This is precisely the risk that science exposes us to: the belief in a 'guaranteed truth' (156/7).

This is not new of course. In a certain sense, this is what, for example, religion does. It attempts to create a certain ideal image that people will not doubt.

In this way, they also manipulate the way in which people construct reality. However, scientific discourse is far more systematic and compelling (156/8).

The theory presented here clearly shows the resemblance between, on the one hand, the different types of madness and, on the other hand, the scientific techniques (the therapies) developed to cure them. Lacan lists several types of madness – the hysterical claim on the love-object, hypochondriac fixation on the body, and suicidal tendencies in delusions of negation – that testify to the morbid impact of an imago on psychical life. Subsequently, he lists several therapeutic techniques that make a certain imago arise in the psyche of patients: medical explanations that calm the patient (they sedate him, since a name is given to what he suffers from), Charcot's hypnotic induction of epilepsy, and the narcissistic catharsis strived for by some psychoanalysts (156/9–157/1)

Lacan considers it a small miracle that Gestalt psychology was able to predict the following optical illusion. If you make an arrangement of blue-colored sections spin in front of a screen that is half black, half yellow, then the perception of this phenomenon is radically different depending on whether you see the framework that supports the spinning, blue-colored sections or not. Seeing the framework or not activates a different gestalt (or imago) and thus makes a different percept arise (157/2).

Imagine what such a knowledge could do if it was applied, not to the imagos involved in an arbitrary optical phenomenon, but to the fundamental imagos that determine the way in which a subject (a being) relates to the world. It is clear that the example of the optical illusion in the previous paragraph enables us to understand that the culture in which one is born, and which provides a specific mental framework, will determine perception. Thus, different cultures lead to radically different visual perceptions (157/3).

The way in which the imago impacts on our perception is very hard to understand, it is harder to see than the gazelle's footprints on a rock, since it happens before we know it.[27] Nevertheless, one time, we will find out how it exactly works (157/4).

Lacan says that he referred to great philosophers – such as Plato, Descartes, Hegel, and Marx – in an amorous way. He didn't do so to claim that he 'goes beyond them.' It was due to their authentic passion to unveil truth, and such truth is always timeless (157/5).

This kind of truth does not need to be labeled a 'guaranteed truth,' but is always new. It can never be repeated. If it is repeated, it dies, and it stops being true (157/6).

Notes

1   This interpretation of Lacan is debatable. As explained in the introduction, Ey conceived mental problems as *caused* by organic factors, not determined by them.
2   This is similar to what Follin and Bonnafée – two psychiatrists also presenting at the conference (Ey, 1946, pp. 129–163) – stated. They also refer to the mechanist theory of

Clérambault. In a nutshell, this theory states that madness is caused by mental automatisms emanating from neural mechanisms that cannot be influenced by conscious mental acts. From this, Follin and Bonnafée conclude that the difference with the theory of Ey is negligible. While this seems true at first sight – the theory of Ey similarly states that madness emanates from automatic psychic activity emanating from the lower brain centers after organic damage inflicted on the higher brain centers – it seems that Ey has a point when he radically rejects the criticisms of Lacan, Follin, and Bonnafée (e.g., Ey, 1946, pp. 55–60). The alleged similarity indeed doesn't take into account the major difference between the theory of Ey and Clérambault, namely that for Clérambault, mental automatisms were strictly determined by physical laws governing all brain activity, while for Ey, it is clear that automatic activity is *not* strictly determined by such laws. This appears, for example, from the quote in the introduction, stating that the on level is never strictly determined by the biological level it arises from, which in turn is never strictly determined by the physical level.

The second half of this paragraph makes even clearer on what grounds Ey (1946, pp. 55–60) rejects the criticism of Lacan. The quotes presented by Lacan clearly show that in Ey's conception, chemical and anatomical cerebral processes generate/cause a weakening of the energetic processes; this prevents the higher psychic activity from emanating from the weakened brain areas; this, in turn, causes psychopathology. However, as explained in the introduction, this doesn't mean that Ey considers the phenomena of mental disease (i.e., the symptomatology) to be *determined* by the chemical and anatomical cerebral processes that cause it (as mechanists do); he only claims that it is *caused* or *triggered* by these processes.

3   This reference is incorrect. Lacan actually refers to Ajuriaguerra and Hécaen (see Ey, Ajuriaguerra, & Hécaen, 1947, pp. 33–80), who gave a presentation on this issue in 1943 at the previous conference of Bonneval.

4   Ey (1946, pp. 55–60) will say in his response to Lacan's presentation that he was not impressed by the argumentation of his pupils, without presenting counterarguments, however.

5   The validity of this case was later doubted. Decades after the original clinical assessment, the brain of the patient was investigated a second time, and no traces of brain damage were observed (cfr. Bay, Lauenstein, Cibis, 1949). The author wishes to thank Dominiek Hoens for bringing this to his attention.

6   Ey (1946, p. 113 and p. 130) reacts to this criticism by stating that it doesn't concern a theoretical contradiction, but a well-considered theoretical position, namely that madness has a 'double nature,' i.e., that it is *caused* by an organic factor, yet *determined* by personality characteristics. This is also what we explained in the introduction.

7   Fink's (Lacan, 2002, p. 128) English translation of this paragraph doesn't seem to be entirely correct. The words ' qu'à nous de constater qu'une position si aisée ne lui donnera pas d'embarras' are translated as 'as it is for me to note that adopting such a facile position allows him to avoid running any risk.' The right translation is 'as it is for us to note that such a facile position does not embarrass him.' What Lacan means is that it is strange that Ey is not embarrassed by claiming such things in such an 'easy' way. When one reads the text of Ey (1947, pp. 10–12), it is striking indeed to see that Ey makes these claims without actually giving any proper argumentation at all.

8   In Fink's English translation of the *Ecrits* 'amour propre,' this is translated as 'pride.' I think 'self-love' is a more accurate translation.

9   For reasons mentioned in the introduction, Lacan's equating of Ey's theory to a mechanist-reductionist theory on psychical life is at least somewhat short.

10   Polyxena was one of the princesses of Troy who fell in love with Achilles. However, she led him into a trap in which he was killed. In revenge, the son of Achilles killed Polyxena. Before she died, Polyxena said she'd rather die than live as a slave. This also refers to Hegel's master-

slave dialectic, which is central in the second part of the text. The slave is someone who uses the opposite argument: 'It is better to live like a slave than to die.'

11   This shows how fundamentally different Ey's and Lacan's theories on the Ego are. For Ey, the Ego is a manifestation of the supreme and pure Spirit, for Lacan, the Ego is a structure that has the function to deceive and to aggress. Vitalism holds that the Ego is a manifestation of the Spirit, and the Spirit is all noble and all good. For Lacan, the Ego – whether it is based on vile or noble imagos – is always deceptive and aggressive in nature. It is deceptive in that it is always based on an identification with an external image that masks the subject; it is aggressive since it always strives to overcome its rivals, if necessary, by being more noble than they are. This brings us back to the self-love of La Rochefoucauld (see paragraph 35).

12   Lacan refers to a set of articles by Ey compiled in a volume entitled *Hallucinations et Délires* (Ey, 1934).

13   This refers to the metaphor of the double mirror elaborated later in his first seminars (e.g., Lacan, 1953). The figure of the flowers in the vase only appears before the hollow mirror if the eye of the subject is in the right position. This means: if there is a symbolic discourse that orientates the eye of the subject in the right direction.

14   'The comical example' referred to by Lacan in this paragraph probably refers to the 'revered professor' in paragraph nine. Just like his patients, the professor pretended to know the truth, albeit only by saying to the patient that what he said was definitely not true. Thus, in the final analysis, the professor was as delusional as his patients.

15   Jules de Gaultier coined the term *bovarysm* after 'Madame Bovary,' a novel by Flaubert (1857) about a woman who escaped the banality of her life by holding on to an imaginary identity of a rich and successful woman.

16   This new world order would be the beginning of the end of history. In Hegel's conception, history started with a fight that ended with a first master dominating a first slave. In the universal state created by Napoleon, all people would be equal, and thus, the dialectical opposition between master and slave would find its synthesis and would be neutralized (Kojève, 1947, p. 44). This new state, installed by Napoleon, would be comprehensible in terms of his dialectical theory, which he considered to be the absolute knowledge, beyond which nothing substantial is left to know.

17   It is not difficult to see how it is the concept of the kakon that is transformed into the object *a* in Lacan's tenth seminar. The object *a* is defined there as this part of the other that 'is incorporated, but not assimilated' (Lacan, 2004).

18   I prefer this translation over Bruce Fink's translation of this sentence: 'Where I'll be free to have an honest heart' (Fink, 2002, p. 143).

19   Bruce Fink's English translation (2002, p. 144) is questionable at this point: It says 'the madness involved in taking supreme risks,' while it is probably more accurate to translate this as 'the madness associated with risks of supreme nature,' or, in other words, 'the madness of those that are at risk because they have supreme characteristics.'

20   Lacan phrases this: 'the gestalt action,' which is similar to what he says in his later work about the signifier ('The signifier is what represents the subject to another signifier,' Lacan, 1964, p. 207) and jouissance ('Ce qui pense, calcule et juge, c'est la jouissance,' Lacan, 1973, p. 9). It shows that also in his imaginary period, Lacan conceives the subject as fundamentally ex-centric: what acts is not the subject, it is the gestalt.

21   In *Agression in Psychonanalysis* (Lacan, 1966, p. 113), Lacan holds that a process of *einfühling* happens in infants; literally translated, the infant *feels itself in* (the image of) the other.

22   Thus, what Lacan suggests is that, for example, the dream reality, where the unconscious is considered to manifest more freely, is actually the imaginary reality. This means reality as it was before the Oedipal identification.

23   Aristotle's illusion: cross your middle finger and your index finger, close your eyes and touch your nose in such a way that it is between the two fingers. It will feel as if you have two noses.

24   Bruce Fink (2002, p. 154) translates 'pourrait m'opposer qu'il y a une pétition de princ-
      ipe' as 'might object that I am begging the question.' The more literal translation –
      which I think is the one to be preferred – is 'that I am guilty of a circular argument.'
25   This implies that the coupling behaviors in one way or another influence the genetic
      material, or at least, that this behavior in one way or another is registered and impacts
      on the organism that is engendered. In other words, it is a strong plea for Lamarckian
      genetics.
26   This is also what Lacan meant with his remark in paragraph 40 and 41 of part 3: the fact
      that the child recognizes itself in the mirror – i.e., identifies with the gestalt or imago in
      the mirror – has nothing to do with the fact that its nervous system is highly developed.
      After all, the chimpanzee at that age has a much more advanced nervous system and
      it doesn't identify with the imago. Thus, the process of identification – which Lacan
      considers the true mechanism of psychological causality – has nothing to do with the
      nervous system.
27   The reference to the footprints of the gazelle is typical for Lacan in that it is *over-
      determined*. It is used as both a metaphor and as an example: the difficulty implied in
      seeing footprints on a rock is a metaphor for how difficult it is to see how the imago is
      involved in the construction of our reality. At the same time, the fact that some people
      can see the footprints and others can't is an example of the impact culturally transmitted
      imagos have on perception.

References

Bay, E., Lauenstein, O., & Cibis, P. (1949). Ein Beitrag zur Frage der Seelenblindheit – der
      Fall Schn. von Gelb und Goldstein. *Psychiatrie, Neurologie und medizinische Psychologie*, 1,
      73–91.

Chauvin, R. (1941). *Annales de la Société entomologique de France*, 3, 133–272.

Ey, H. (1934). *Hallucinations et délire*. Paris: Alcan.

Ey, H. (1946). *Le problème de la psychogenèse des névroses et des psychoses*. Paris: Bibliothèque
      des introuvables.

Ey, H. (1975). *Des idées de Jackson a un modèle organo-dynamique en psychiatrie*. Paris: Alcan.

Ey, H., Ajuriaguerra, J., & Hécaen, H. (1947). Rapports de la neurologie et de la psychiatrie.
      Paris: Hermann.

Ey, H. (1936). *Des idées de Jackson d un modèle organo-dynamique en psychiatrie*. Toulouse:
      Privat.

Flaubert, G. (1857). *Madame Bovary: Mœurs de province*. Paris: Michel Lévy Frères.

Goldstein, K. (1940). *Human Nature in the Light of Psychopathology*. Cambridge: Harvard
      University Press.

Guirauld, L. (1931). Les meurtres immotivés. *Evolution Psychiatrique*, 4, 25–34.

Hegel, G. W. F. (1807). *The Phenomenology of the Spirit*. New York: Translation published
      by Oxford University Press in 1977.

Hughlings Jackson, J. (1884). On affectations of speech from disease of the brain. *British
      Medical Journal*, 12, 703–707.

Kant, I. (1781). *Kritiek der reinen vernunft*. Riga: Hartknoch.

Kojève, A. (1947). *Introduction à la Lecture de Hegel*. Paris: Éditions Gallimard.

Lacan, J. (1932). *De la psychose paranoïaque dans ses rapports avec la personnalité*. Paris: Seuil.

Lacan, J. (1938). *Les complexes familiaux*. Published in Les Autres Ecrits. Paris: Seuil.

Lacan, J. (1964). *Seminar XI: Les quatre concepts fondamentaux de la psychanalse*. Paris: Seuil.

Lacan, J. (1966). *Ecrits*. Paris: Seuil.

Lacan, J. (1973). ...Ou pire. *Scilicet* 4. Paris: Seuil.

Lacan, J. (2004). *Le Séminaire livre X – L'angoisse*. Paris: Éditions du Seuil.

La Mettrie, J. O. (1747). *L'homme machine*. Leiden: Luzac.

Lewin, R. (1980). Is your brain really necessary? *Science*, 210, 1232–1234.

Matthews, H. (1939). Visual stimulation and ovulation in pigeons. *Proceedings of the Royal Society, Series B*, 126, 557–560.

INDEX

★★Page numbers in **bold** reference tables.
★★Page numbers in *italics* reference figures.

For Product Safety Concerns and Information please contact our EU
representative GPSR@taylorandfrancis.com
Taylor & Francis Verlag GmbH, Kaufingerstraße 24, 80331 München, Germany

www.ingramcontent.com/pod-product-compliance
Lightning Source LLC
Chambersburg PA
CBHW050630280326
41932CB00015B/2596

9 781032 437378